LANGFORD – 'AN OBSCURE ESSEX VILLAGE TRANSFORMED'

LANGFORD – 'AN OBSCURE ESSEX VILLAGE TRANSFORMED'

Irene Allen and Patrick Chaplin

Allen-Chaplin Publishing

First published 2014
By Allen-Chaplin Publishing, Langford, Essex
© Irene Allen and Patrick Chaplin 2014
ISBN 978-0-9928296-0-5

Copies of this book are available from the publisher c/o
www.stgileslangford.co.uk
ireneallen815@gmail.com
patrick.chaplin@btinternet.com
Tel: 01621 855447 or 01621 856040

Printed and bound in Great Britain by
Print on Demand

This book is dedicated to all the people of Langford, past and present who have inspired and made this book possible. But especially to (for Irene) my late husband Tony, my parents Bill and Edith Smee and Jock Agnew; and (for Patrick) my late mother Joyce Chaplin, my father Albert (a true 'Langfordian') and my wife Maureen.

CONTENTS

FOREWORD

I will never forget the moment when, as a sixteen year old schoolboy, I arrived with my parents and my brother in the village of Langford, rounded St. Giles' church, and saw for the first time the beautiful façade of Langford Hall which was to be our new home.

Although boarding school, Cambridge and my legal career in London prevented me from spending as much time as I would have liked at Langford, I was always pleased to return to a place with which my family had had such a strong link for many years.

I was delighted, therefore, when Irene Allen and Patrick Chaplin, the co-authors of this history of Langford, asked me to write a foreword for them. Patrick had begun research back in the 1970s and more recently teamed up with Irene who was working on her history of St. Giles'. Together they have produced a fascinating history, beautifully illustrated and packed with intriguing information. St. Giles' church is rightly well known for being the only remaining village church in Britain with an original western apse, but there is much social as well as architectural history bound up in Langford's beautiful little church.

The authors have ranged widely with chapters on health and education, commerce and trade, the railway, the waterworks, sport and leisure as well as notable former inhabitants of the village. There is a touching account of Langford throughout the two world wars and, for me, a particularly poignant chapter on the sad demise of Langford Grove. As with all histories, some facts will continue to be elusive, but I hope I have persuaded Irene and Patrick that it was unlikely to have been the Byrons who were responsible for the closure of Langford's only ever pub!

This is a true labour of love involving years of painstaking research. It was a sad day for me when my father decided he had to sell Langford Hall and most of the remaining estate in the early 1980s, but this wonderful history which Irene and Patrick have produced, telling the whole thousand year story of Langford for the first time, is something I will always treasure.

Robin, 13th Lord Byron

ACKNOWLEDGEMENTS

There are so many people to thank for their contribution to this work: for the insight into family archives, the interviews with present and former villagers, those who have kindly lent photographs and illustrations to be included in the book, and those whose unfailing encouragement has led to this final product. We would like to take this opportunity to thank the following for their input:

Jock Agnew, Revd. Tom Barnfather, Suzanne Benbow, Dennis Bullard, Lord & Lady Byron, Wally and Paula Cant, Brian Chalk, John and Joy Chalk, Philip & Jean Chalk, Ted Chalk (D'cd), Patricia Chancellor (née Humphrys), Albert Chaplin, Beryl Claydon, Jenny Clemo, Richard Cooper, John and Isabelle Doubleday, Lynda Downes, Jo Edkins, Barbara Evatt, Mr. R. Foster, Monica Green (neé Simpson), Angela Hall (née Parmenter), Peter and Celia Hansell, Shirley Harrington, Ron Harvey (D'cd), Tim Hawkins (D'cd), Madeleine Hinton, Maureen Hyam (née Hollingsworth), Mary Kenyon (née Humphrys), Claire Lille, Peter Lomas, John Low, Eric Major, Peter Manley, Revd. Sandra Manley, Simon Mannering, Margaret Manning, Gerald Matthews, Bert Morris, Stephen Nunn, Tom Packe, Christopher Parkinson, Albert and Mary Parmenter, Harvey Pipe, Roy and Merle Pipe, Revd. Kenneth Robinson, Terry and Christine Rushbrook, Derek Sayer, Ernie and Joyce Scott, Janet Search (née Clanachan), Chris and Caroline Spong, Marilyn Swart, Doris Thorogood, Paul Tritton, Ted and Margaret Watson, Penelope Wilkins, Helena Wojtczak, Keith and Glynis Yuill and the staff at Essex Record Office.

PHOTOGRAPHIC ACKNOWLEDGEMENTS

The authors have, by their best endeavours, traced the owners of the copyright of as many of the photographs included within this text and obtained their permission (with due acknowledgement) to use said images in this work only. However, in some instances the original copyright holders have not, as yet, been identified. If such copyright holders are identified or identify themselves in the future then the authors would be happy to correct the information in any future edition of this book.

The bulk of the images are from the Allen-Chaplin Collection, but we are also grateful to (in alphabetical order):

Jock Agnew – Page 24 – Font
Revd. Stuart Batten – Page 29 – Revd. Geldart
Suzanne Benbow – Page 196 – Frederick Wakelin
Ann Bond – Page 61 – Maurice Green in Witham Road
Lord Robin Byron – Page 199 – Geoffrey Byron; Page 201 – Robin, Robyn and Charlotte Byron
John & Joy Chalk – Page 53 – Brick House; Page 210 – Walter Harry Chalk and his children; Page 245 – The Estate Workshop
Philip Chalk – Page 111 – William Chalk; Page 224 - The Chalk Family
Patricia Chancellor – Page 40 – Captain Humphrys
Chelmer & Blackwater Navigation Company – Page 214 – Plan of waterways
Curator of *The Discovery* – Page 453 – Michael Barne
Lynda Downes – Page 185 – Spencer Thompson in the fields
The Peter Edwards Museum and Library – Page 403 – The 1902 Essex Cricket team
Alec Fraser – Page 36 – Angel with church
Kevin Gribble – Page 395 – War memorial with new plaques

Angela Hall – Page 141 – Langford School Class 1921; Page 242 – Win Parmenter on retirement

Mrs. Harrington – Page 181 – Langford Grove prior to demolition; Pages 373 & 376 – Air Crash at Langford Park

Peter Lomas – Page 193 – Alfred Lomas

Gerald Matthews - Page 29 – Sanctuary; Page 37 - Reredos

Langford Parochial Church Council - Page 14 – Plan of church

G.R. Mortimer – Page 266 – The Railbus

Tom Packe – Page 33 – Elizabeth Packe

Derek Sayer – Pages 320, 321, 322 – Views from the top of the waterworks chimney

Janet Search – Page 66 – The Harvey Family; Page 145 – The School in the 1950s; Page 240 – The Old Post Office; Page 241 – The Post Office; Page 344 – 'Susie Sewing shirts'; Page 350 – Stanley Charles Harvey; 353 – Postcard from Langford

Miranda Seymour – Page 102 – Revd. Frederick Ernest Charles Byron; Page 450 – Revd. Byron

Caroline Spong – Page 459 – Isaac Walter and Sophia Grout and their family

Doris Thorogood – Page 341 – Essex Cycle Regiment

Paul Tritton – Page 198 – Major Tritton

Penelope Wilkin – Page 370 – Home Guard in Maldon

Keith Yuill – Page 156 – White Lodge

and

Reproduced by courtesy of the Essex Record Office

Page 7 - (C/DR 111) Extract from Chapman and André Map of Essex 1777

Pages 20 & 22 - (T/P 196/4) 'Ecclesiae Essexienses' by Henry William King, Antiquary

Page 68 – (I/Mo 182/1/2) Temporary hospital shelters taken by the late F.J. Reynolds

Page 86 – (D/F 8/632) Plan of Langford School by Frederick Chancellor

INTRODUCTION

This book has taken many years to write.

Basic research was begun in the early 1970s when Patrick spent many inclement summer and cold winter lunch hours reading through many dusty tomes in what was then the 'Essex Room' at the library in Duke Street, Chelmsford. Occasional correspondence was entered into and interviews undertaken in order to afford this 20+ year old local government officer a better perspective of the village in which he lived from the age of two until he left Langford in 1973. Pressures of work and other priorities led him away from local history but he retained his manuscripts, photographs and notes and kept a close eye on developments within the village through local newspapers, hoping one day to return to his research. In the late 1980s the Langford and Ulting Parish Council appointed him the Local Historical Recorder for the two villages.

More than thirty years after his research had begun his interest in the history of Langford was reborn with an approach for information from Irene who, as Churchwarden of St. Giles' Church, had decided to undertake her own research into the church itself; never really intending that it should go any further. Irene spoke with Patrick's father, Albert Chaplin, about her proposal and he suggested that she contact Patrick with a view to talking to him about the research path he had previously trodden so as to prevent her from undertaking any unnecessary work.

Patrick and Irene had grown up in the village together during the 1950s and 1960s yet their formative meeting in the year 2007 was the first time they had sat down to talk to each other for any length of time for over three decades. What actually occurred was a kind of 'meeting of the minds'; their combined love of the village leading to their working together on a project that would eventually result in the production of this book. Irene's Guide to St. Giles' Church was published in 2008, and she took over from Patrick as the Local Historical Recorder in 2013. (Other works by the authors which are ongoing are comprehensive studies of the St. Giles' Church and the Waterworks.)

In today's world where money seems to be the only focus, Irene and Patrick have taken time out to produce a book that will never make them money; far from it. Their early discoveries eventually saw the light of day in a three-week exhibition in words and pictures held at the Museum of Power (a former waterworks building) in 2009.

Langford – An Obscure Essex Village Transformed is a labour of love. Thanks to Irene and Patrick the whole story of this small, some might think insignificant, village is told for the first time.

Map of Langford c. 1897

CHAPTER ONE
THE PARISH

There have been settlements in Langford (the village of the long ford) since at least the Middle Bronze Age - some 3,500 years ago. During the late Iron Age, and into the Roman occupation of Britain, there was a significant port within easy walking distance at the junction of the Rivers Chelmer and Blackwater, but throughout time Langford has remained essentially rural and agricultural.

Mentioned in the Domesday Book (1086) as Langheforda the village name has also been spelled in other records as Langefort, Langord (1252), Lankford, Longeford (1306) and Lanckford(e) (in reference to the Hall) (1592). The earliest reference using the present day spelling of 'Langford' appears in 1252.

Lords of the Manor
The parish of Langford is an old one, and the 'Lords of the Manor' equally so. Before the Norman Conquest at the time of Edward the Confessor's reign (1042-1066), the land on

1

which Langford Hall now stands was owned by two Saxon lords, named Gola and Anglemar who were in possession of the estate, but to date no further information has been found about them. By the Domesday survey the manor belonged to Ralph Baignard [Baynard], who is shown as No. 33 in the list of landowners.

Baignard was attendant to King William I, and was rewarded with twenty-five lordships in Essex, including Langford. The church was probably built on the half hide of land recorded as *Ralf's Manor* (half a hide of land was equivalent to 60 acres). His loyalty to the king was not shared by his son Geofrey who, with William Malet, Baron of Eye, joined a conspiracy against Henry I (1100-1135). In 1111 Malet was deprived of his Barony and the Baignard estates were given to the king's steward, Robert Fitzgislebert, from whom the families of Fitzgilbert and Fitzwalter are descended. William Baynard [*sic*], grandson of Ralph, also forfeited his Barony and lands for joining the conspiracy.

In the reign of Henry II (1154-1189) the manor was owned by Geoffrey de Ambli. However, before July 1176 a Charter was co-granted to the Abbey at Clerkenwell by the three daughters of William and Alice Capra (Agnes, Alice and Constance), and their husbands for the souls of their parents. Alice, with one of her nieces, had become a nun at Clerkenwell. In her book *Noblewomen, Aristocracy and Power in the Twelfth-Century Anglo-Norman Realm*, Susan M. Johns notes that Agnes, Alice and Constance 'were the co-heiresses of the manor of Langford, Essex, from which the rent of 30 shillings was granted.'

Afterwards the manor belonged to the Preyers family from Sible Hedingham. By the marriage of Margaret, the daughter and heiress of Sir Thomas Preyers, to Robert de Bourchier (who was the first recorded Patron of St. Giles' Church), it passed into the noble family of de Bourchier. Robert, who was also Lord Chancellor of England from December 1340 to

October 1341, died in 1349 and the estate was settled on his son John, Lord Bourchier and his heirs. (This settlement included a clause whereby by Sir John de Preyers received £40l a year during his lifetime). At the time of his death, Robert de Bourchier,

> held the manor of Langford with the advowson [*the right of the living*] of the church of Oliver de Bohun as of his maner of Norton by the service of four shillings and tuppence a year.

During the Peasants' Revolt of 1381, the Manor of John, Lord Bouchier was attacked, and documents burnt. After his death his son, also named John, held it until his death on 21st May 1400. The estate then passed to his son, Bartholomew, who held 'one moiety [*half*] of this manor of the King by the service of half a knight's fee, and the other moiety of the Lord Fitzwalter by the like service.' Bartholomew's widow Idonea, held it until her death on 12th September, 1410 - 'one half of Henry, Earl of Hereford as the Hona of Mandevill and the other half of the Lord Fitzwalter.' Elizabeth, the only daughter and heir of Bartholomew and Idonea, conveyed it in turn to her two husbands - Sir Henry [*Hugh*] Stafford and Sir Lewis Robesart - but as she died without issue on 1st July 1433, the estate of Langford passed to her kinsman Henry Bourchier, Earl of Eu. Henry was made Earl of Essex on 30th June 1461, and when he died on 4th April 1483, he was succeeded both in estate and title by his grandson, also called Henry. This Henry was captain of Henry VIII's bodyguard, and it was probably on his instructions that Langford Hall was constructed in the 1520s, during the early part of the King's reign, and seems to have begun life as a fortified and moated farmhouse.

The second Henry, Earl of Essex, died on 13th March 1540. He left a daughter, Anne, who made the mistake of marrying William Parr, Marquis of Northampton in 1541 for, shortly afterwards, William forfeited all his estates for espousing the cause of Lady Jane Grey. (Lady Jane Grey (1537-1554) was married, against her wishes, to Lord Guildford Dudley in 1553 as part of a plot to alter the English succession in her favour on the death of Edward VI. Lady Jane was declared Queen of England in 1553, was seized and imprisoned after only nine days, and subsequently beheaded. She was succeeded by Queen Mary.) William was also condemned to die but his sentence was afterwards commuted to forfeiture of only some of his titles and estates. In 1559 he was again created a Marquis and his consolation prize was the granting to him by Queen Mary, of Langford - 'the Manor with others to hold of the Manor of East Greenwich by fealty [*i.e. as tenant*] in free socage [*i.e. rent free*].'

The Smyth(e) family of Cressing Temple were the next owners. Thomas Smyth(e) died in possession of it on 10th March 1563. He had held the manor 'with appertances to the Queen in free socage.' His son, Clement, died on 16th December 1590 and his 30-year old brother Henry inherited the manor. Henry died on 17th April 1612 without issue, and the manor was then inherited by the next brother, Sir John Nevill (also known as Smythe), aged 59 years. He died on 12th March 1631 (referred to, for some unknown reason, as William Smyth) and his brother Sir Thomas Smyth (alias Nevill) inherited the estate when he was well past 70 years of age. At this time reference can be found of a family named

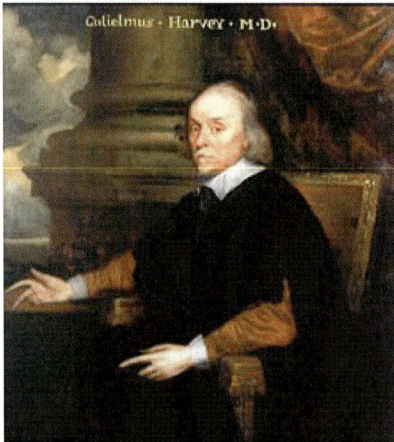

Sammes living at Langford Hall, but whether as tenants or as owners is not clear.

Shortly afterwards the manor was held by Matthew Harvey, sixth son of Thomas Harvey of Folkestone, Kent, and brother of Dr. William Harvey (1578-1657) the highly celebrated physician. William (pictured left) was

4

the first physiologist to understand the heart's function as a pump and the circulation of blood, and it is not unreasonable to think that he may well have been a guest at the hall. On the death of Mathew Harvey the estate was left to his nephew, Sir Elias [Eliab] Harvey of Chigwell, who sold it to Nicholas Wescomb in 1680, who also took over as Patron of the living of Langford. So began the long association of the Wescomb family with the village. Nicholas died in 1696 and his widow, Sarah, who was many years his junior, married a Mr. Bateman and they held the estate until her death in March 1740. The manor was then inherited by the eldest Wescomb son (also called Nicholas), a barrister-at-law of the Inner Temple, who specialised in cases before the Court of Chancery. He died on 16th December 1744 and was succeeded by a third Nicholas Wescomb of Cheverills Green, in Hertfordshire. It was this, third Nicholas Wescomb, who commissioned the building of Langford Grove which was constructed in 1782. He died on 19th August 1808, leaving a widow, Lucy, who died on 9th October 1835.

John Emmerton Wescomb (a kinsman of Nicholas) died intestate at the age of only 56 in 1838, and his estates, which included Langford and Thrumpton in Nottinghamshire, were in chancery for the benefit of his three nieces - the Misses Wescomb. They were the daughters of the Revd. William Wescomb (who was Rector of St. Giles', Langford from 1813 to 1832) and his wife Jane Douglas. The eldest daughter, Lucy Elizabeth Jane Wescomb, married the Hon. George Anson Byron, son of the 7th Lord Byron (and cousin to the poet) on 3rd August 1843, and inherited Thrumpton Hall, in Nottingham.

The Wescombs were 'cash rich but title poor' and their fortune was based on brewing; the Byrons, on the other hand, were an aristocratic dynasty with no money, so were 'title rich but cash poor.' In 1851, the two households were further joined through the marriage of Mary Jane, middle daughter of Revd. William Wescomb, to the Hon. Frederick Anson Byron

5

MA, second son of the 7th Lord. It was through this marriage that the Byron family became Patrons of Langford church, and owners of the village.

The Hon. Frederick Byron was a barrister of Lincoln's Inn, and had a London residence. In addition to Langford Grove, which he also inherited through his wife, he owned a house at Edwinstowe near Ollerton in Nottinghamshire. Frederick died on 4th April 1861 aged only 39. In 1891 his widow, Mary Jane, was the principal landowner and Lady of the Manor. The title of Lord Byron passed to their eldest son George Frederick William on the death of his uncle, George Anson Byron (as he left no heir), but when he also died intestate in 1917, the title passed to his brother Frederick Ernest Charles. Frederick (or Charles as he preferred to be called), had followed in his grandfather's footsteps by taking up Holy Orders. He became Rector of St. Giles' in 1890 - a post he held until 1914 when he became Rector of Thrumpton in Nottinghamshire.) Once he became the 10th Lord Byron, the Langford estates were managed by Strutt and Parker. When Lord Byron died in 1949, the very high post war death duties caused about half the Langford estate to be sold, but there were still nearly 1,000 acres and fifteen or so cottages remaining, but the the 'Lord of the Manor' was no more (although the title is still held by the present Lord Byron).

Descriptions of the village

The Revd. Philip Morant (1700-1770), the eighteenth century historian of Essex, in his work *The History and Antiquities of the County of Essex* (1768), wrote that the parish of Langford 'lies along the side of the River Pant or Blackwater, and the Long Ford here is what occasioned the name. Lang in Saxon is the same as long.'

Thomas Cromwell in his *Excursions in the County of Essex* (1818) observed that the name 'Langford' came from a time when the waters of the Blackwater spread over a much wider area than at present and that the meadow grounds bordering the river had always been extremely fertile.

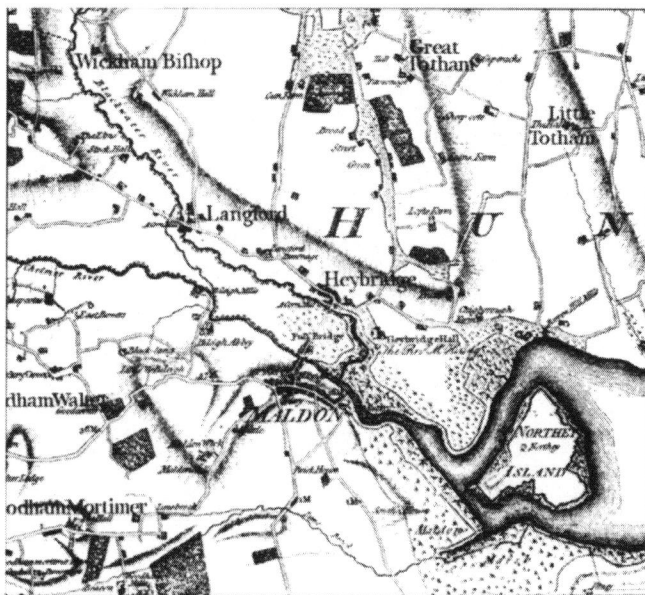

Extract from Chapman and André Map of Essex 1777

So the ford that can be found today to the right of the river bridge as you travel through the village from the church side is much smaller than the original one, and indeed no longer crosses the original River Blackwater at all. In ancient times, water from the mill was separate from the river, and so a long bridge was constructed to enable people to cross. However, the long bridge was a matter of some annoyance to the local people who had to pay for its upkeep for others to use. As it was a cause of constant dispute, it eventually fell into disrepair and was demolished following a high flood in 1820.

In 1837 the whole area of the parish was estimated at 901 acres (4,840 sq. yards) and three roods (a quarter of an acre): including 503 acres and two roods of arable land, 312 acres and one rood of meadow and pastureland, and 54 acres of woodland. Since then the parish area has fluctuated with

7

occasional Government boundary changes. As this book goes to press the Parish Council is seeking to 'claw back' several houses in the village (Mitchell's Cottages, Mitchell's Barn, Langford Place and Langford Old Rectory) which had come under Heybridge Parish following a boundary change in the 1990s.

In 1848 Samuel Lewis, Editor of *A Topographical Dictionary of England* described Langford as:

> A parish, in the union of Maldon, hundred of Thurstable, N. division of Essex, 1½ miles (N. by W.) from Maldon containing 257 inhabitants. This parish, which is bounded on the south by the Chelmer and Blackwater navigation, is about six miles in circumference.

The renowned local historian Edward Arthur Fitch, in his book *Maldon and the River Blackwater* (1905) mentioned that the road to Maldon from Langford church:

> runs eastward over the railway bridge, the path by the side of which leads down to the small flag station, past Langford Rectory into Heybridge, Langford Church being one and a half miles from the Maldon Borough boundary. Rather less than halfway we come to Langford Cross with the sign-post directing to Hatfield, Witham and Maldon. The road running northwards is a very pleasant one, skirting the prettily wooded Langford Park, containing the large and pleasantly situated modern house known as Langford Grove, the residence of the Hon. Mrs. Byron. Past the "Shoulder of Mutton" Inn, the road on the right leads past Captain's Wood into Great Totham.

In 1821 the population of Langford was 251 and in 1831, 273. By 1911 the number had fallen to 205. This drastic reduction was probably due to a certain amount of mechanisation in agriculture which meant fewer agricultural labourers were needed to till the land. In 2011 the population was 194.

On the edge of the heath

In medieval times Langford was on the edge of Tiptree Heath (one of the great heaths of Britain at the time, and anciently part of the Great Forest of Essex which occupied about one half of the county). From an inquisition taken in 1401, Tiptree Heath comprised several thousand acres of common rough and wood-pasture, in which the free-holders and tenants of the parish of Langford (and all the other parishes adjoining the heath - Inworth, Messing, Layer Marney, Great and Little Braxted, Totham, Tollesbury, the Tolleshunts, Wigborough, Maldon, Salcott, Goldhanger and Wickham Bishops) had common grazing rights for their cattle, and 'estovers of the trees and underwood' for repairing their buildings, hedges etc.' (In English law, estovers is wood that a tenant was allowed to take, for life or a period of years, from the land he held, for necessary repairs or fuel.)

In the reign of Henry VIII, 'Common of Pasture' was affirmed by an order in council and the parishes of Wigborough, Goldhanger, Heybridge, Langford, Wickham and part of Kelvedon were added, which regularised an already existing situation. These grazing rights were later reaffirmed by Henry VIII to all parishes, including Langford.

However, grazing rights had some restrictions, and management of the 'common' was carefully defined: pigs had to be ringed, and no goats were allowed from Langford - tantalisingly we are given no reason why. A complex system of byelaws dictated what could and could not be taken from the heath: commoners had the right to cut broom, furze, thorn, and underwood (coppice) for fuel and building repairs, and if there was insufficient, to lop and crop pollards, and to shred unpollarded trees; bark could also be shredded (although the trunk belonged to the landowner!)

9

However, encroachment of this area began in a small way in the medieval period and expanded until the land was enclosed following a succession of 'Enclosure Acts.' Between 1770 and 1867, 8,952 acres of heath, common, green and wasteland was enclosed by Act of Parliament. During this time the greater part of Tiptree Heath vanished and hundreds were dispossessed of their grazing rights. It would appear, though, that the people of Langford rebelled against this injustice. It is recorded that the Lord of the Manor (sadly unspecified), despite the fact that he had already enclosed quite a lot of the common land on his own manor, led the villagers with their flocks and herds to break down the fences on Tiptree Heath, and drive their animals onto it to reassert their rights. Extensive open tracts remained until the early 19th Century when it was finally enclosed under the General Enclosure Act of 1845. (Today Tiptree Heath comprises just 61 acres of common land - it was created as a public common in November 1947, and the site boasts many features including magnificent heathers, two ponds and open spaces.)

The reasons for enclosure have always been contentious, but as Charles Hassell, a leading enclosure commissioner in the late 18th Century, put it:

> At best, they were a waste of valuable land which could be used to feed a rapidly growing population; at worst, they were a major source of social evils, harbouring 'a base encroaching crew' of thieves and idlers whose activities robbed the rest of the local population of their livelihood.

Governance

Governance of Langford had, since time immemorial, been by whim of the Lord of the Manor, and everyday life was ordered by their strictures, but by the late nineteenth century moves were made to make this a more 'democratic' procedure. The first 'Parish Meeting' was held in Langford schoolroom on Tuesday 4th December 1895, and although business-like and practical, it was not wildly exciting. Mr. Travis Nunn was voted into the chair, and the duration of the meeting was almost entirely occupied with the re-adjustment of the rates - all agricultural land having been reduced by two shillings in the pound.

The Parish Meeting took on a more formal role when it became an amalgamated 'Langford and Ulting Parish Council' in 1974. This body has continued to deal with, mainly, uncontentious matters ever since with only planning issues such as the proposal for a mobile phone mast in 2005 (eventually thrown out by the Maldon District Council), and various bids for the building of houses on redundant waterworks land near the Museum of Power in 1996, and in 2012 the proposal to build 147 new houses on the site of the former water treatment plant to the west end of the village, which was turned down in September 2012 by the Council's Planning Committee. An appeal was lodged within months and, fortunately, was rejected on grounds of unsustainability and being out of keeping with the rest of the village.

The Millennium

In 1997 Langford and Ulting Parish Council submitted an application to the Millennium Fund for a project to restore the village ford. This application was successful and work commenced in 1999. Given that this part of the river gave the village its name it was considered fitting that the ford should be the subject of the Millennium Project.

CHAPTER TWO
ST. GILES' CHURCH – 'A GREAT ODDITY'

St. Giles' Church, Langford, is a beautiful listed building (Grade II*) which dominates the centre of the village at the junction of Witham Road and Maldon Road. R. Newcourt, in his *Repertorim Ecclesiasticum Parochiale Londinanse* (two volumes) (1710), stated only that the dedication of this church was unknown because there was a blank where the name of the saint usually appeared. Somehow between 1710 and 1768 it acquired a saint, because Philip Morant in his *The History and Antiquities of Essex* (1768) remarked that the church 'dedicated to St. Giles, is of one place with the chancel, and tyled. In a spire, shingled, are three bells.'

However, as this was all he wrote, it is hardly a detailed description.

St. Giles' Church before restoration

It is difficult to date the original building with any degree of accuracy, for although Roman tiles and bricks were identified in the fabric of the church during work in the 1930s, some experts believe the building is of early Norman construction. However, 'Western works' (i.e. the western apse of St. Giles') is a late Saxon (410-1066) feature and was fashionable throughout northern Europe; they were even sometimes added to existing churches during reconstruction projects.

It is also known that the building was originally shaped like a capsule with two rounded ends and a long middle. Churches of this shape were quite common before the Danish invasion of 1013 but no churches were (supposedly) built in England in this shape after that time, so it is conjectured that St. Giles' was founded in the eleventh century. Strangely enough, though, it is not mentioned in the Domesday Book, so either the building was erected after 1086 or it did not function as a place of religion at that time. It is also conjectured that many churches were not mentioned in the Domesday Book because they were too poor to be taxed, and might at that time have been made of timber and thatch which would earn no revenues.

Arthur Mee, in *The King's England. Essex* (1966) wrote that the church was:

> a building of great interest to lovers of old and rare things. Almost certainly it was here in Saxon England, and until the 19th Century restorer destroyed some of its character it can have changed little in 900 years. This church is almost unique in England in having a western apse, which is believed to be a survival from the first centuries of Christianity, when a separate baptistery was often built at the west end of a church. The apse has three little windows high up, with wide splays inside. Each is about 2 feet high, but only 7 inches wide. One of the original doorways is here, its inner arch also

13

splayed to allow the door to swing. Through a pane of glass in the plaster wall we can see the rough masonry of the Saxon builders. There is a 15th Century font and a double piscine of the 13th Century that has lost its pillar. Marks on the chancel floor indicate the foundation of an eastern apse, so that Langford has made itself famous and unique by saving the west apse and losing the east.

A Unique Building

Other historians and antiquaries have noted the uniqueness of the building. The distinguished Suffolk historian, Norman Scarfe, in an entry on Langford in his book *Essex - A Shell Guide* (1968) noted:

The church of St. Giles is a great oddity: at first sight of 1882, but then one spots a Norman apse at the <u>wrong end</u> of the church! South-west porch leads into it. Next one notices that Langford formerly had an apse at the east end as well: it can be seen in puddingstone at the beginning of its curve in the outside of the S. wall, 34 ft. east of the E. edge of the S. Door. Unique in England and rare in Europe.

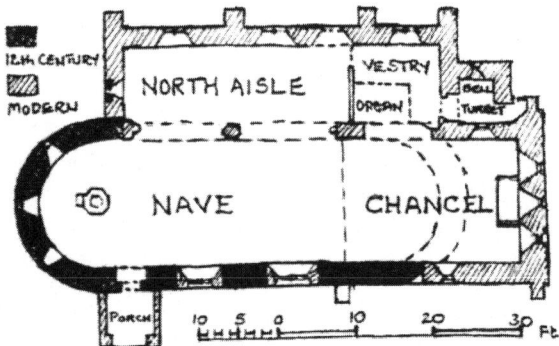

Marcus Crouch in his book, again entitled *Essex* (1969) also pointed out the 'oddness' of the western apse, and mourned the loss of its eastern counterpart. However, he concluded:

14

Even without it Langford church is of unique interest to the collector of village churches; it is also surprisingly satisfying to the eye.

And J. Charles Cox in his book *Essex* (1909) wrote:

The small church (St. Giles) is of supreme interest, as it is the only survival in this country of a western apse, an arrangement at one time fairly common throughout early Christendom.

According to an article on Langford Church by Henry Laver FSA in *Essex Archaeological Transactions* Vol. X, Part 1 (1909):

In the early years of the Christian church in England, soon after the coming of St. Augustine, it would appear that this method of finishing the western end of the nave was not uncommon.

Bettley & Pevsner note:

Langford originally had an E Apse as well. The type is in all probability to be derived from Carolingian and Ottonian Germany, where apses at both ends were quite frequent, though not, it is true, for village churches. Thus, even internationally speaking, Langford was a great exception, and it is much to be regretted that the E apse did not survive the late Middle Ages.

They add, a little sadly,

It is surprising, perhaps, that Browning [*the Architect engaged on the restoration works*] did not reinstate it. As it is, he further disoriented the visitor by adding a bell-turret on the chancel's N. side, replacing a conventional Essex W belfry, as well as the N aisle, vestry and S porch.

The few examples of western apses in Britain were mostly confined to larger foundations dating before the Norman Conquest (such as the cathedral church at Canterbury, believed to be from the seventh or eighth century.) However, none of the major churches built before the conquest were still standing by the end of the eleventh century, and the only church in Britain now with an original western apse is our own St. Giles', Langford. However, despite these statements of uniqueness, very few historians have given much space to descriptions of the church, rather focussing their attentions on the various owners of the manor. This chapter sets out to address this oversight.

The chancel, north aisle and tower walls are of Kentish Ragstone with dressed limestone quoins (a large, dressed corner-stone which forms the external angle at the meeting of two walls) and string courses (a projecting band of masonry running horizontally around the exterior of the church). In the case of St. Giles' it is noticeable in the sanctuary extending into the choir stalls and the walls themselves are two feet nine inches thick. The chancel and nave were built (it is believed) in the eleventh century but sometime in the fourteenth or fifteenth century the eastern apse either collapsed or was pulled down and squared off.

Other information relating to St. Giles' up until its restoration in 1882 is sparse, but there are a couple of very intriguing reports from visitors. A Mr. Sylvanus Urban of Springfield, visited Langford in 1830, and reported:

> The church is low and without any tower, having only a small wooden spire upon the roof. There are some modern windows on the south and east sides. The church withinside is about 18½ yards long by 5 wide. The walls are nearly a yard in thickness; the east side (which is square and not round) is the same…

('Sylvanus Urban' was in fact the pen name of Edward Cave, the Editor of *The Gentleman's Magazine*, which he founded in January 1731. He wrote a great deal about parish churches.) The view of the church he would have seen is pictured on page twelve.

However, in the following thirty years a great change came over the church, for when the antiquary, Henry William King, visited St. Giles' on Wednesday 14th May 1862, he was not loathe to put down his feelings about it sometime later; feelings that are reproduced here in full:

It is a small unpretending Norman structure with later alterations and insertions and one of the five churches in this county with a semicircular apse. [*It is interesting to note that since 1862 when this observation was made, the other four churches with a western apse have been demolished.*] Here the apse is at the west end, but originally, most probably, the east end had also an apsidal termination. There is now no marked division between nave and chancel which are of equal width and the chancel is probably I think an elongation of the original Norman church effected in the 15th century, when I presume the eastern apse was destroyed. Originally like the small church of Little Tey this may have had no distinct chancel. But this part of the structure has undergone great alterations and even partial rebuilding in very recent times. The east window is a most barbarous and disgraceful insertion of wood work of square form. The doorway is a square aperture with a common panelled house door. The utter debasement of this chancel must no doubt be attributed to some former Rector of this valuable benefice, and no subsequent incumbent has had the good taste or church feeling enough to restore it.

Upon the south side of the nave is a square headed 'Perpendicular' window of two cinquefoiled lights with dripstone having horizontal returns, and just within the chancel on the same side is another of uniform size and

17

character. All the windows upon the north side are so effectually built up that there is not even an indication of their previous existence. This fenestral [*i.e. belonging to, or like, a window*] destruction in the Nave however was occasioned by the pride and barbarity of one of the family of Wescomb who, by purchases in the year 1680, became possessed of the estate called Langford Grove and built a mansion there about 98 years ago as I was informed. They were possessed also of the advowson of the church [*the right to present a clergyman to the living of a church*]. The builder of the mansion in the plenitude of his power and the pride of his earthly riches appears to have thought himself too great to worship God in contract with or among his fellow creatures so he opened and destroyed some 12 feet of the north wall of the nave and built for himself and his posterity a great polygonal edifice in the churchyard of brickwork, battlemented, and with a coved roof as high as the church wall a panelled oaken barricade in front opening into the nave. Here elevated several feet higher than the "common herd" with his domestick's put in front and within the church, the Wescomb family with carpeted floor made themselves tolerably snug and comfortable. They <u>did</u> condescend to enter through the church and that is all, but once within their private oratory they were perfectly secluded both from a view of the altar and the vulgar gaze. What may have been their origin I know not, but it may be presumed that they regarded themselves as part of the porcelain clay of creation and not of the "red earth" out of which Adam was formed. In censuring this disgraceful action I am very far from conceding the radical proposition that all men are equal. Beneath this excessive encroachment upon the churchyard lie the mouldering remains of six of the family just now become extinct in name, but two of the daughters of the late Revd. Wm Wescomb, the last of his name, Rector of Langford, wedded each an Hon. Mr.

18

Byron. It appears that a Bishop was found to allow a man to destroy a large part of the wall of the church with its windows for no other reason that can be perceived but to gratify his own pomp and vanity; and it is to be presumed that the parish could offer neither remonstrance nor objection.

Sadly, although King provided two drawings with his report, neither was of the addition to the building that he found so repugnant, but the photograph on the following page shows what the church looked like before restoration.

It seems that at the time of King's visit the western apse was divided off from the nave by panelling with a door in the centre, presumably to provide a small vestry. It was lit by the three very small Norman windows which are still in place although at the time of his visit it appears that the northernmost of the three was blocked. Access to the wooden spire, which rose from the roof at the western end, was by ladders supported by a framework of wood from the basement. It contained three bells. We have no record yet of when these bells were installed, and so far no entrance to the 'basement' has been found, although an exploratory hole is to be drilled through the crypt wall to see if it can be located.

The Church before restoration in 1882

With regard to the fittings of the interior, King noted:

Puls [*Pews*] painted white still exist but they have been reduced to moderate dimensions so that with the exception of the lords of Langford Grove who are still ensconced in their manorial excresceno [*an abnormal, grotesque or offensive outgrowth or projection*] the congregation all face the east. But the altar – I have described several varieties in Essex Churches – rotten and rickety tables, dressing tables with drawers and brass handles, and such like. But this is certainly a novelty - a great square deal box, or rather locker, fixed and painted white with a lifting lid and hinges.

THE HOLY ALTAR !!!

When the clerk opened it I found that it was the receptacle for curtains, cloths, surplice, bible and prayer books, what else I know not, but it was full to the top. An altar on "Sacramental Sundays" and a locker at all times!…

The Bible and Prayer Book, the gift of Mrs. Wescomb in 1841 or 1842 (I forget which) bound in purple morocco are not embossed with the Cross but stamped with the arms of Wescomb impaling Douglas! [*This is where, in heraldry, two coats of arms are combined to denote union, normally for a husband and wife, but also for ecclesiastical use. An impaled shield is bisected 'in pale,' that is by a vertical line.*]

[Regrettably these are no longer in the church, and there is no record of where they are, although perhaps they went to Thrumpton when Lord Byron took up his seat there.]

King continued:

There is but one monumental inscription in the church on a small oval tablet of marble on the south side of the chancel. 'In this vault are deposited the remains of the Revd. William North, Rector of this parish who having faithfully discharged the pastoral office more than 43 years died May 16th 1767, aged 75 years. Also of his affectionate wife Mrs. Mary North who died February 23rd 1777 aged 68 years" [*the present tablet states that it is his sister!*]

In the centre of the chancel a stone marking the entrance to the rectory vault and inscribed "This tomb stone opens to the Rectory vault 1775." The Clerk believes that three Rectors North, Pyke and Phillips are there interred.

Interestingly, there is no sign today of the 'Rectory vault' although this may have been tiled over at the restoration, or lies now under the choir stalls. Sadly the stone denoting the vault is also no longer there, unless it too is under the choir stalls. Revd. North was certainly Rector at Langford, but neither Pyke nor Phillips appear on the list of Rectors, although they may have been curates.

Fixtures and Fittings

Other fittings were mentioned by E.A. Fitch, in his *Maldon and the River Blackwater* (1905) who noted that 'Hatchments for the Westcomb [*sic*] family were in this church before its restoration.' (A hatchment is a diamond-shaped heraldic panel, comprising a shield of arms painted on a wooden panel

Hatchments

or on canvas within a wooden frame). The hatchment was carried in procession to the church where it remained following interment. One can only wonder why they were not put back in the church after restoration, especially as the renovation work was undertaken by the Wescomb's daughter, Mary Jane, but perhaps it was felt that as the Lord of the Manor was now a 'Byron' the Wescomb name should not be prominent. As they were not reinstated, we have to rely on a drawing of them (left) from the visit of Mr. King.

The church was restored in 1881-1882 by Edward Browning, architect of Stamford (1816-1882) and was one of his final undertakings; the work being paid for by the Hon. Mary Jane Byron (née Wescomb), the patron of the living of Langford at that time. The renovations totally changed the character of the original church, as the Chancel was entirely rebuilt and the north aisle (with the crypt beneath), the south porch and the north-east bell turret were renovated; the 'wooden spire' mentioned in Mr. Urban's account had been demolished earlier. Norman-style windows were built into the north and south walls of the chancel, the north side opening into a vestry with the new bell turret at the north angle.

There have been criticisms over the years about the renovations, claiming they destroyed the character of the church, but it was while digging the foundations for the extended chancel that the original foundations of the eastern apsidal end were found, and the restorers marked it out in black tiles on the floor. So now visitors can see the extent of the original church building. They also, very kindly, left on the outside of the church, east of the south window, a recess showing the springing in the wall where the former eastern apse began which gives a truer picture of the size of the original church building, and just how far the chancel was extended. Had the original eastern apse not been lost, St. Giles' would have been a very rare church indeed.

The archaeologist, Dr. Henry Laver, paid a visit to Langford Church during May 1905. He declared that it was a very interesting building, and highlighted the western apse, but he also said:

> It was originally built by the Saxons, part of this work viz: the west end, south door and south wall remaining. The south windows however are quite new. The north windows, which are Tudor, were removed from the south side when the church was restored.

Dr. Laver also declared that the south doorway and arch were particularly interesting. However, in his article on the church in 1909 in *Transactions of the Essex Archaeological Society*, he wrote:

> None of the older work was destroyed at the restoration, with the exception of a rough sepia fresco in outline of, I should think, Saint Christopher. It was a great pity to have destroyed this fresco, which was on the south side, between the windows.

The churchwardens are currently taking advice as to how it can be discovered if the fresco mentioned by Dr. Laver is actually there.

On Saturday 27th July 1907, the Royal Archaeological Association of Great Britain and Ireland, under the presidency of Sir H. Howarth, visited the church. Noting its western apse, their report quoted in the August edition of the parish magazine stated:

To the ordinary mind the conclusion is inevitable that our Church dates from before the Danish invasion (over 1000 years ago) but the speakers of the Association did not seem inclined to put it earlier than late Saxon that is about 900 years ago. Why Langford Church should not have escaped the Danes when so many other Churches did, Copford Church, near Colchester for instance, does not seem quite clear: but people, even Archaeologists do not easily take in an idea which is new to them. Unquestionably however, Langford Church is one of the most interesting Churches in England, although it has passed through so many changes and restorations.

The south doorway dates from c.1100 with plain jambs [*i.e. the closing edges*] and a round arch which splays upward, signifying a very early building. 'Mr. Urban' wrote in the *Gentlemen's Magazine* in 1830 that

> the north and south doors are very plain, with only a chamfered impost moulding. The south door is 7' 10" high by 3' 4" wide and has plain Norman hinges. The north door is 6' 10" by 2' 8"

Unfortunately the original south door disappeared in the extensive renovation work.

The Font is a plain octagonal bowl, stem and base, standing on, it has been suggested, an old mill stone (which is not inconceivable given its shape, and markings, and given the proximity of the Mill to the Church. It is reputedly from the fifteenth century with an oak lid and drain. There is also a stoup in the nave, east of the south doorway, with a two-centred head. (A 'stoup' is a vessel containing holy water generally placed near the entrance of a church, into which worshippers dip their fingers before crossing themselves). The date of the stoup is unknown, although it is certainly from our Catholic past. The sill is modern.

The chancel - the 'priest's' part of the church reserved for clergy, churchwardens and choir - was extended, and now measures 20½ feet long x 16 feet wide and is structurally undivided from the nave. To bring the extension of the chancel in line with the nave, the ceiling was re-worked in wood (barrel-vaulted with moulded ribs), and has been likened to the hull of an upturned boat. The double piscina - the basin near the altar in the southern chancel wall - is thought to be from the thirteenth century. (Piscinae were rare in England until the thirteenth century, after which every church had one.) Piscinae were used by priests for washing the chalice and patens. (A paten is a plate - usually of gold or silver - that is used to hold the wafers during the celebration of Holy Communion.) The water drained into the consecrated ground around the church. However, towards the end of the thirteenth century it became the rule for the priest not to wash his hands in the same drain as the chalice, so double piscinae were built. These are quite rare, and St. Giles' has a very nice, but plain one. This was moved from its previous location when the chancel was extended as it is now outside what was the original eastern apsidal end.

In 1591 Pope Gregory XIV required priests to drink the chalice rinsings instead, to deny potential diversion to any witches! The practice is still followed today, so the piscina is no longer used.

The pulpit, erected at the time of the restoration, is stone

25

lined with wood, and has carved 'morris' bells round the top and a double band of flowers beneath it. The inscription round the font is typically Victorian: "Preach the word be instant in season out of season reprove rebuke exhort with all longsuffering and doctrine" [from 2 Timothy 4:2].

The nave (41' x 16') is the 'people's' part of the church, and has a modern north arcade of two bays, and a seating capacity of about ninety. The north wall of the original building was breached sometime between 1862 and 1881 and a new aisle was added. As this wall had already been breached earlier to accommodate a private pew (which so incensed the Antiquary, Henry King in 1862), it was the only place where the church could effectively be extended without destroying the uniqueness of the western apse. The box pews were removed, and lower, open benches put in their place.

When the north aisle was built, a crypt was installed beneath it, accessible from an external flight of steps and through a wooden door. If the Antiquary, Mr. King, was correct, the site of the external 'excresceno' was above this. The crypt was built to house the mortal remains of the Wescomb/Byron dynasty, and contains the coffins of:

- Nicholas Wescomb – died 19th August 1808, aged 75
- Lucy Wescomb – born 19th February 1745, died 9th October 1835, aged 90
- Anne Standly, sister of Lucy Wescomb, died 10th August 1770
- John William, son of William and Jane Wescomb, died 1st June 1825, aged 8 months on that day
- The Revd. William Wescomb, died 18th May 1832, aged 44
- Jane Wescomb, died 17th May 1868, aged 78
- The Hon. Frederick Byron, died 4th April 1861, aged 39
- Mary Jane Byron, born 1st June 1826, died 1st September 1909, aged 83

There is provision in the crypt for a further eighteen coffins, but once Revd. Byron left Langford to take up his place as Vicar of Thrumpton (and later as the tenth Lord Byron, took up his seat in Thrumpton Hall, Nottinghamshire), there were no more interments. It is interesting to note that had John William Wescomb lived to manhood, the makeup and governance of the village would have been very different indeed.

The bell tower is another curiosity from the restoration works, and the bells (as one expert has remarked), were 'shoehorned' into the space. The bells were hung for ringing full circle and the walls of the belfry and the frame of the oak superstructure were cut away to facilitate this. The bells are hung from timber headstocks in plain bearings in an oak frame. All three swing east to west, the first and second are at high level and the tenor below. The tenor has a chiming hammer. There is a weathervane of a gilded cockerel on the bell tower.

As this book is published, there are moves afoot to refurbish the steeple and gain access to the bells through the tower as at present access can only be gained by climbing on to the roof and walking along the valley. Once this has been undertaken the bells will no longer be able to ring full circle, but will merely chime. The three bell ropes will be replaced by pulleys which will give much less exercise to the ringer on a Sunday morning. (This task is currently undertaken by Churchwarden Irene Allen ringing all three bells simultaneously using both hands and one foot!) The bells were all made by Messrs. John Taylor & Co. of Loughborough cast in 1881:

Tenor - 32.5 inches - 7cwts 1qtr 7lbs (819lbs/372Kg) inscribed 'To the Praise and Glory of the Holy Trinity'
Second - 29 inches - 5cwts 2qtr 0lbs (616lbs/280Kg)
Treble - 26 inches) - 4cwts 0qtr 17lbs (465lbs/211Kg)

These replaced three earlier ones from the old steeple at the western end of the church which were inscribed:

1. 22 inches - 'H P 1707'
2. 24 inches - 'MILES GRAYE MADE ME 1638'
3. 26 inches - + 'Sancte Paule Ora Pro Nobis +' (Saint Paul Pray for us)

The old No. 1 was by Henry Pleasant of Sudbury (taken from "The Church Bells of Essex" in 'Essex Review' No. 9 Vol. III January 1894 p.65). Unfortunately we do not know what happened to the original bells. (With regard to bell No. 2, Miles Graye was a bell founder in Colchester).

When the renovations of 1882 were carried out, an oak-framed partition and door was installed at the eastern end of the North Aisle enclosing the lower portion of the church organ; this formed part of the vestry. This partition is enriched with traceried panels and several beautifully carved little animal heads, which are often overlooked by the casual observer. The space behind the organ, enclosed on the south by the organ itself and a curtain, and on the east by the bell tower, is used as the vestry (and since 2009 has been the home of the 'Heavenly Supplies' community shop).

The sanctuary (pictured on the next page) - the most sacred part of the church - is at the furthest end of the chancel, and houses the altar, where the sacraments are handed out during the service of Holy Communion. During the act of Communion, the Churchwarden draws the bar across between the two communion rails, thereby 'fencing in' the Rector and the server. After the sacraments have been distributed, the bar is drawn back again and the sanctuary becomes 'open' again.

Music

The pipe organ, by C. Martin of Oxford, was made and installed in 1886. It is a magnificent instrument for so small a church, with a beautiful tone; it has two manual and twelve stops in total with a full pedal board. For many years a series of small (and not so small) boys and later, girls, pumped the organ from a small space just inside the vestry door. An electric motor for organ blowing was fitted in 1949, thereby bringing to an end the era of pumping the organ by hand. It was completely overhauled in 1968 by Bishop and Sons Ltd. when a wooden bench seat and glass doors over the keyboard were fitted bringing the organ to the condition that can be seen today.

The choir stalls in front of the organ were designed by Revd. E. Geldart (pictured left) and put in the church in November 1895; the parish magazine noted that it was hoped 'that a way might be found for placing choir seats on the south side of the chancel as well as on the north side.' This was completed in 1898. The choir stalls were erected in the collegiate style, able to seat about 20, and were ready in position on Sunday 20th

November 1898. At the dedication service that evening the sermon was preached by Revd. E. Geldart, Rector of Little Braxted, as their designer. Everyone agreed that they made a great improvement to the appearance of the church and, in a most eloquent sermon preached that night, Revd. Geldart remarked: "Not sound, but love will be their chief benefit. In the first place they are 'first to God,' evidences, on the part of the congregation, of their love to God, and of their desire for His glory, and secondly, they should materially add to the beauty of worship, and to the convenience of the choir." (Although as generations of choristers past and present have voiced, not necessarily to their comfort!)

In September 1899 the beautiful brass lectern was presented to the church in memory of one of its longest serving incumbents - Revd. Charles Verney Shuckburgh. The lectern is in the form of a brass eagle, with the inscription 'In memory of Charles Verney Shuckburgh for 31 years Rector of this Parish. This lectern is presented by his widow Eliza Lucy Shuckburgh.' Revd. Shuckburgh had died in 1874 - some 25 years earlier - and is buried just outside the porch door in an imposing tomb, so it is wonderful to think that his widow felt able to contribute to the 'new-look' church.

Most lecterns are in the shape of an eagle and the Bible rests on its outspread wings. The eagle was thought to be able to look unflinchingly into the heart of the sun, so in the same way, the words from the Bible are supposed to be an unflinching revelation of God. This lectern swivels easily, although as it is extremely heavy it is not so easy to move.

Lighting and Heating

Originally the only lighting for the church was by the windows during the day and candles or oil lamps after dark, and there are various marks in the stonework throughout the church which denote where candle holders and hanging points for lamps were placed; there are also brass candle holders on the pulpit.

In January 1914 lighting within the church was greatly improved with the donation of a beautiful wrought brass hanging candelabra which were given in memory of Lieutenant-Colonel Willington Augustus Shelton, D.S.O. who died at Langford Hall on 14th June 1909 aged 60. (He is buried in the closed churchyard in the North-east corner parallel with the Witham Road.) The gift of the candelabra had been anticipated for some time, the only reason for the delay being, according to the parish magazine of January 1914, 'the utter inability to find any form of lamp or candle holder which would not have been a disfigurement to the church.' The candelabra, which hold twelve candles, were made in Belgium in 1913. Their installation gave great satisfaction as the parish magazine reported in February 1914:

> The brass candelabra were placed in the Chancel, to which it gives a look of great distinction. The little lamp which formerly hung in the Chancel arch was removed to the west end of the church, where it greatly assisted in lighting that end of the church.

Following the death of churchwarden William Chalk in December 1914, his relatives offered to present a handsome brass hanging oil lamp for the chancel arch in his memory, and this was a great addition to the church. William had not only been a much loved and respected churchwarden from 1896 until his death, but also a keen bell ringer.

Candlelight for the church, although romantic, was not always convenient, and posed the ever-present threat of fire - something all churches dread - and with the advent of electricity it was decided to install electric lighting into the church. Bruce Keeble, electrical and wireless engineer, of 31 Market Hill, Maldon was employed to do the work at a cost of £15 9s 10d and completed it in July 1930. Two special electric lights were given by Miss Mary Baker of Langford Lee for lighting the Sanctuary and an electric lamp was also placed in the church porch by the Rector [Revd. E.A.B. Creed].

Village churches are also notoriously difficult to heat, and St. Giles' is no exception. Before the restoration work there was no heating at all, and one can only imagine the discomfort of a long service on a cold winter's day, alleviated only by the 'protection' of the box pews. When these were removed at the restoration the congregation were 'open to the cold,' so a 'Tortoise stove' was installed in a purpose-built boiler house beneath the vestry at the base of the tower. This provided hot air which radiated around the church via channels under the church and then up through grills in the floor. One of the stockmen from Langford Hall farm would come and light the stove at 4.30 on a Sunday morning and the church would be warm by the time the service began at 8 o'clock. Although better than no heating at all, towards the end of its natural life this system began to fail - sometimes dramatically - and smoke and noxious gases were often sent billowing into the congregation.

Electric heating was installed in the church in January 1958. Four radiant heaters were fitted - two each in the east nave and chancel (overhead). In August 1958 two further heaters were installed in the west end of the nave. These were given by Miss Amy Snell of Langford Place (through her executors) in memory of the late Miss Elizabeth Margaret Packe, (pictured right), churchwarden from 1928 to 1956. Two further electric heaters were installed over the north aisle in April 1962 thereby completing the heating plan for the church.

On 27th October 1987 a Faculty (permission from the church authorities) was granted to renew the heating system (which had proved to be inadequate). Purpose-made heaters 550mm in depth and faced with oak veneer were installed in the pews, the prayer desk, pulpit and organ console areas in 1988 (except those in the north aisle which are not used very often.) At the time of writing, investigations are being undertaken to find more efficient ways of heating the church and making best use of the space.

Memorials

In 1896 the magnificent three early English east windows with a cinquefoil in a circle above were installed. They were commissioned by the Hon. Mrs. Byron and her two sisters in memory of their parents, the Revd. William and Mrs. Wescomb. The windows depict the Resurrection, with the words 'Victory. The Lord said I am the Resurrection and the Life', and represent Christ enthroned with (according to the parish magazine of the time) the two 'Maries' on either side, one in each window and St. John above. However, as the 'Maries' have wings, this interpretation is questionable.

The windows were designed by the Revd. E. Geldart, Rector of Little Braxted (who also designed the choir stalls), and at the bottom right hand of the three panels is the symbol of three bees which show that they were made by the Bacon Brothers of London. They were completed in November 1895, but not properly fitted until May the following year. In fact The Hon. Mrs. Byron and her two sisters, Lady Byron and Lady Frederick Fitzroy, stayed at Langford Grove for the first time in nearly 50 years, on the week of 18th May 1896 to attend the unveiling. The parish magazine noted that 'the two latter visited and greatly admired the window which they have lately placed in the church in memory of their father and mother.'

When the brass cross from the altar was stolen in July 1915, a shockwave of disbelief ran through the village. Members of the Baker family, of Mill House, generously offered to replace this with another cross as a memorial gift. The handsome new altar set, comprising a brass jewelled cross, candlesticks, and vases, was dedicated to the service and glory of God on Christmas Morning 1915. The design and workmanship was much admired, and deemed worthy of its exalted position, both for use and ornament. The inscription on the base of the cross describes it as a memorial to the late Edward Lee and Susanna Harvey Baker.

An interesting 'end' to the story is that in August 1924, while the pool below the old wooden bridge over Langford stream was being pumped out preparatory to the building of a new bridge, the stolen jewelled brass cross was discovered. This, after being partially cleaned, was brought by the Foreman and Clerk of the Works to the Rector [Revd. Littlehales] who recognised it at once. The parish magazine of September 1924 noted:

The thief, whoever he was, little realised that the Cross, which he must then have thrown into the pool, would ever be seen again. It will be sent away to be cleaned, and afterwards probably presented to some Church or Mission Room as the Rector and Churchwardens may decide.

Research to date has not discovered where the cross eventually ended up.

Other memorials in the church to generous benefactors took different forms. In the south wall of the nave are two 'modern' windows. The oldest (c. 1916) is thought to be from the studio of the Bacon Brothers and is dedicated 'To the Glory of God and in Affectionate Remembrance of Mary Jane Byron who restored this church.' Mary Jane Byron had died in 1909, and the parish magazine noted the arrival of the window with great satisfaction:

'A new stained glass window was placed in Langford Church in memory of the Honourable Mary Jane Byron by members of her family. The subject depicted is the Meeting of the Risen Saviour with Mary Magdalene. The window-picture is realistic and the figures are pleasing, beautiful colours being introduced into the robes. The window is a beautiful ornament to the little Church, a photo of which is displayed above the main window. A Dedication Service is being arranged at a time when the donors can be present.'

The 'photo' mentioned is a small, yet beautifully detailed picture of the restored church in the hands of an angel in the uppermost part of the window (see next page).

The dedication service took place in 1917.

The second window was funded by the Wynyard family in memory of Churchwarden William Bingham Ashton Wynyard who, for over twenty years, had lived at Langford Rectory (Langford Hall being used at the time as the residence of the incumbent). The subject of the window is 'Jesus Christ Blessing Little Children' - an appropriate subject for someone who was not only a much loved Churchwarden, and Governor at Langford School, but also ran the Sunday school, and helped out on the Choir outings. The inscription is: 'To the Glory of God and in Loving Memory of William Bingham Ashton Wynyard b. 16 Oct. 1863 d. 22 Aug 1915.' The work was entrusted to Mr. Walter Tower, of the firm of C.E. Kempe & Co. (Walter was Charles

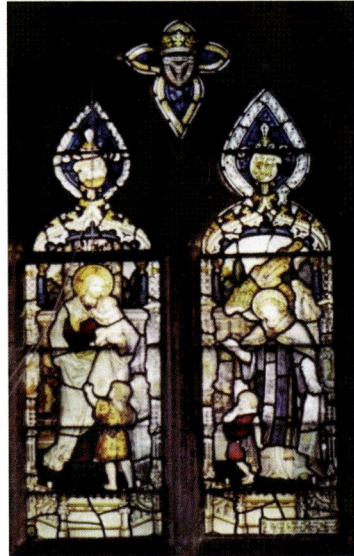

Kempe's cousin and legatee and this is reflected in the 'tower' sign embossed on to the Kempe 'wheatsheaf' emblem in the bottom left hand corner of the glass.)

The window was fitted in October 1918.

In 1917 the seating capacity of the church was increased to 120 at a cost of £3,000, with extra pews being installed. This was perhaps fitting given the renewed interest in church attendance during the Great War. In 1919 a War Memorial was set up, and details of this are given in Chapter Nine.

In 1928 the oak altar was replaced and the very distinctive painted and gilded/carved oak reredos [*an altarpiece or a screen behind an altar*] (below) was made for the sanctuary. The reredos was a gift to the church by Mary Rosalind Baker in memory of her sister, Jeanie Doris Lavender Baker who had been such a devoted member of the congregation.

Plans for the reredos, designed by Gerald Cogswell, were approved in May 1928 and it was dedicated on Saturday 6th October 1928 by the Lord Bishop of Barking. Fortunately the parish magazine printed the whole report of its installation. The official description of the reredos, supplied by Mr. Cogswell, the Architect was fulsome in its praise of the finished article, noting:

> There are very few Mediaeval Reredoses remaining, and none in anything like their original state, and they have been restored at a time when there was very little knowledge of the subject. Since then, Mediaeval illuminated manuscripts and contemporary descriptions have been carefully examined, and this Reredos has been designed with the aid of the more exact knowledge now available. All were elaborately carved, coloured and gilded, as was necessary to give prominence in backing up and setting off the Altar table itself, the most important feature of the Church. This work has been carved in Exeter, by Mr. Herbert Read, of St. Sidwells'

Art Works, in carefully selected oak, it was then treated with coats of 'Gesso,' coloured in Tempera and gilded with 'white' gold, burnished and lacquered by Mr. Marus, of 22 Fitzroy Street, London, who has been trained in the traditional methods. The central feature consists of flying Angels, displaying a wreath, surrounding the Sacred Monogram, and with St. Mary and St. John in nitches at either end, and surmounted with a Cornice with winged Cherubs and an elaborate carved Cresting. The Altar table is framed in with riddle rods, terminated with sconces for candles and silk curtains. The whole of the work has been executed from the full size cartoons of the Architect, Mr. Gerald Cogswell, of 2 Bedford Square, London. The following inscription appears on a band below the centre panel: 'To the Glory of God, and in Loved Memory of Jeanie Doris Lavender Baker, R.I.P., May III MCMXXVII' (May 3rd, 1927).

On Sunday 7th May 1939, the two Churchwardens' staves (or wands), now clipped to the pews (one on either side of the south aisle) were placed in the church. (Churchwardens' staves were originally sharp pointed sticks to prod people and/or dogs, and were known as 'prodders' in the 1600s.) The Rector's Warden's stave with its brass Mitre finial (the decorative top), and the People's Warden's stave with its brass Crown finial, were inscribed 'E. Hedge 1928-38.' One was given by Mrs. Edward Hedge, in memory of her late husband who had been Churchwarden for ten years, and the other presented by Miss Elizabeth Margaret Packe, herself a serving Churchwarden at the time.

The Second World War, as well as the Great War, claimed young men from Langford. One of these was Sergeant Robin Moore, of the Royal Air Force, who had been a member of St. Giles' Choir when a boy. A small statue (pictured right) of St. Giles was given in his memory in 1947 by Miss Katherine Louisa Hunt of Langford Cross, choir mistress at St. Giles' for many years. It now looks out from the wall next to the pulpit, on one of the roof support niches (or what may have

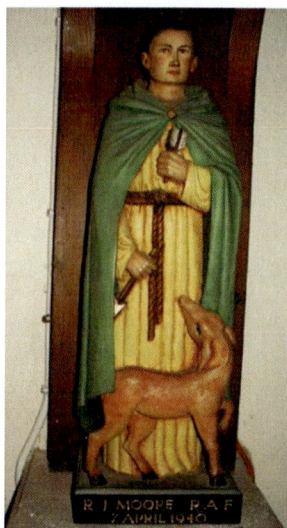

been part of the rood screen). The statue is 21 inches high and bears the inscription 'R.J. Moore RAF 7 April 1940.' Robin's family had expressed a wish that a lasting memorial to him of some kind should be commemorated in St. Giles' where he had worshipped from boyhood. Whether the face of St. Giles resembles that of Robin is not known, but it would be a nice thought. Sadly research to date has uncovered very little about Robin, or the squadron in which he served.

In March 1946, a clock was installed over the porch of St.

Giles' presented by Mrs. Mary Rosalind Pye (neé Baker), of Langford Lee, dedicated to the memory of her late husband, Sydney Graham Pye. The clock is electronically operated and the mechanism, by Gillett and Johnston, is mounted in a compartment at high level in the porch behind the clock face. The original 20" clock bell was also made by Gillett and Johnson c. 1947 but this was stolen during restoration work on the western apse in 2003. A replacement bell was installed which was tuned to 'A' and founded in Whitechapel in the same year as the original.

In 1953 oak panelling behind the altar in the sanctuary was erected in memory of Mary Rosalind Pye - a gift from her executors. The work was carried out by Brian Saunders of Coggeshall, and it was dedicated by Revd. R.V. Seymour in

October 1953, and complemented the reredos which had been installed by Mary in memory of her sister.

A brass plaque was erected in March 1960 on the third pew end of the south wall of the Nave inscribed: 'With thanksgiving to God and in memory of Elizabeth M. Packe, Churchwarden 1928-1956 and of Amy C. Snell.' Miss Packe had been the first, and longest-serving female Churchwarden in St. Giles' Church, and it had seemed fitting to affix the plaque to the pew she and Miss Snell habitually occupied.

In 1965 the Communion Rail was presented by Mrs. Nancy Taylor and family in memory of William and Natalie Wakelin. Natalie was another daughter of Edward Lee and Susanna Baker of Mill House, Langford; a family who gave so much to St. Giles.' The new rail was dedicated by the Rector, Revd. Arthur N. Godsell, on October 18th 1965. The inscription which is carved into it is, on the left hand side of the rail: 'To the Glory of God and in Loving Memory of my Parents,' and on the right hand side: 'William Frederick Wakelin. Nov. 8th 1953 and Natalie Violet Mary Wakelin. Jan. 21st 1963.' This final contribution from the family meant that the sanctuary was full of their incredible gifts to St. Giles.'

A brass plaque was erected in 1969 on the wall of the western apse by the family of the late Capt. C.C. Humphrys, of Wharncliffe, Wickham Bishops (pictured right). It reads: '"For now we see through a glass darkly, but then face to face." In thankfulness for the life of Charles Claude Humphrys, R.N.R., Master Mariner, A dearly loved husband, father and friend. Churchwarden 1950-1967 Died November 3rd 1968 Aged 83

years. Here he worshipped and was sustained.' The design was by Messrs. J. B. Slythe, Funeral Directors. Although his ashes were scattered at sea, there is a memorial to him on his wife's headstone in the cemetery across the road. Claude had been a great churchman and a pillar of the community, always ready to help.

The terracotta statue in the western apse of St. Francis standing with a begging bowl and a bird on his shoulder was donated in 1999 and inscribed 'In loving memory of Barbara Paul Addington-Hall (1915-1998) who saw fun in life and made us all smile.' The 45 inch statue was made by her friend the sculptor Catharni Stern, and stands on a 21 inch cube oak plinth. It was given to St. Giles' by Barbara's husband Robert. Barbara was a member of Langford Parochial Church Council from 1963 to 1980.

In order to encourage the charity of the faithful when they are leaving a church, it is usual for an alms box to be placed near the door, and St. Giles' is no exception. This is in the form of a wall safe and is in memory of Ted and Lucy Chalk – Ted having been Churchwarden from 1956 to 1982 (and then made Churchwarden Emeritus until his death.) The safe was put into the wall by the south door (eastern side) in April 1991 with a brass plaque added above inscribed 'In memory of Walter Edward Chalk also Lucy Rose Chalk, faithful servants of this Church.'

Such visible memorials are discouraged these days by Church authorities, as being somewhat ostentatious and more to glorify the giver than the church, but they stand as a testimony to those who have gone before, and enable a means of providing for church needs 'in kind' that might otherwise not have been possible.

Expansion of the Graveyard

As with any church, there comes a time when its graveyard can take no more burials and, in 1923, the subject of an extension of the burial ground was discussed. Captain Matthew Ffinch, of Langford Meads and Mr. Arthur Edward May of Langford Cross (both Churchwardens at the time) proposed that the Patron, The Revd. Lord Byron, should be approached about providing a piece of ground for increased burial accommodation. Lord Byron was amenable to the idea, but it took almost three years for the ground finally to be made available to the church. At a meeting held on 5th April 1926 it was reported that Lord Byron had given his consent for the handing over of a piece of ground for extension of the churchyard, and it was decided to proceed with the conveyancing as soon as possible.

The land in question (directly over the road from the front of the church) was to be half an acre, and the Churchwardens met with Lord Byron's agent on Friday 27th March 1928 to decide finally where the site should be. An application for a grant from the Diocesan Board of Finance towards the cost of fencing the new graveyard was made in May 1928, and in February 1929 Lord Byron consented to hand over the site. The Deed of Conveyance of the site was signed by the Rector and Churchwardens on behalf of the Parish on 31st July 1929.

The land then had to be fenced, levelled and planted. At a well-attended Church meeting held on Monday 7th October 1929, Mr. Claydon's estimate of £103 2s 0d for fencing, path making and levelling the graveyard, was accepted, and work began. The Bishop of Chelmsford agreed to officially open the new site on Saturday 23rd November. The parish magazine reported:

> Although heavy rain fell both before and after, the actual ceremony was happily conducted in the brilliant sunshine of the Autumnal afternoon. A fairly numerous congregation was present. For the out-door service, the Bishop, headed by the Churchwardens, was accompanied by the Rural Dean and the Rector and choir and congregation followed him in procession

42

round the New Churchyard, chanting or reciting the appointed Psalms. In the centre of the ground the Petition was presented by Mr. E. Hedge (Churchwarden), after which the Bishop made and signed the declaration of consecration. The procession then entered the Church and after the special lesson and prayers, the Bishop gave an instructive and impressive address on 'Life and Death.'

The first burial in the new graveyard was that of William Thomas Bonner aged 64, of Fords Farm, on 30th January 1930, and the burial ground around the church was officially closed on 18th March 1937 except for a few specified interments where provision had been made for a double burial. The cost of repairs and upkeep of the churchyard was then transferred to the Rural District Council, although control of the area remained in the hands of the Rector. In 1974 responsibility for the upkeep of the closed churchyard was handed over to the newly formed Parish Council, and they arranged for the grass to be kept mown on a regular basis and any necessary repairs carried out to the gates and fencing. Responsibility for the new graveyard is still with the Parochial Church Council.

Loss of Independence

St. Giles' had been an independent living since its foundation, but during the incumbency of Revd. Ernest Augustus Butson Creed moves were made to join Langford to Heybridge – a proposition not universally welcomed by either parish. This thorny topic had been discussed and argued about for over a decade, but despite vociferous objections, and protestations from the church authorities that it was not already a 'done deal,' the parishes of Langford and Heybridge were eventually united on 23rd January 1948. Today St. Giles' Church is still part of the United Benefice of Heybridge with Langford, which comprises of the three churches of St. Andrew's, Heybridge, St. Giles', Langford, and St. George's, Heybridge Basin. Whatever objections there were in the past were overcome, but for many years this union was viewed with suspicion when it was certainly a case of 'them' and 'us.' Even today each of the three churches is fiercely independent and retains its own unique character.

Church Choir

There has been a choir at St. Giles' certainly since at least 1886 and it has always been noted for its excellent singing. To encourage its (then all male) members, the choir was rewarded with an annual outing which, over the years, went to some very interesting places – sadly no complete list is available.

1894 - Tower of London
1895 – London sights
1896 – Indian Exhibition at Earls Court
1897 – Westminster Hall & Abbey
1898 – St. Paul's Cathedral
1900 – Woolwich & The Arsenal
1901 – Madame Tussaud's
1902 – Crystal Palace
1903 – Albert Memorial & South Kensington Museum
1904 – Tower of London
1905 – Windsor Castle
1906 – Zoological Gardens, Regents Park
1907 – Crystal Palace
1911 – Royal Mint & Tower of London
1912 – British Museum & National Gallery
1913 – Zoological Gardens
1914 – Outing foregone for the war effort!
1915 – Southend-on-Sea
1924 – Wembley Exhibition
1929 – Mersea Island
1932 – Langford Cross

Both men and boys would travel to the sites together, but in the afternoon the boys would return home with the Rector or one of the Churchwardens, and the men would stay on for dinner and an evening entertainment.

The choir 'uniform' for both men and boys (and later, girls) was maroon cassocks (the long under-coat) and white surplices to go over them. They hung on pegs in the vestry where the choir robed before the service.

St. Giles' has always been fortunate in having a 'resident' organist, and when Mr. E. Gowers, who had been organist at St. Giles' for many years, died in 1914, his place was taken by Mr. Raultone. In May 1914 the parish magazine reported:

> Our organist, Mr. Raultone, was taken ill on Sunday 26th at the evening service, during the singing of the second hymn, when the organ abruptly ceased. He was evidently suffering from a sharp attack of influenza and was quite unable to resume his place at the organ. We may add that the choir behaved splendidly and continued the singing as though nothing had happened.

In November 1927 the Choir was in decline. Miss Katherine Hunt, of Langford Cross, took it over in January 1928 to try and revive it but with little success, and the choir disbanded. However, Miss Hunt refused to give up, for in the parish magazine it was noted:

> The suggestion to set up a choir again in St. Giles' was put by K.L. Hunt in November 1929. On May 14th 1930, the choir were invited to join in the District Choirs' Festival at Coggeshall Parish Church.

It seems that there was difficulty in obtaining basses in the 1930s because many men from the village worked eight-hour shifts at the new Waterworks and therefore could not attend services and practices regularly.

On Thursday 13th October 1932 the choir were entertained at Langford Cross by Miss Hunt and Miss Boothe, who jointly ran the Langford Cross Children's Home. Miss Hunt resigned as Choirmistress in April 1933 and the role was taken on by Mrs. Tritton of Langford Hall, and later in that year her husband, Major Claude Tritton, took over. In February 1937 new cassocks were made for the boys by Miss F. Ward (cutter out), Mrs. Ford, Miss Ford, Mrs. Hedge, Mrs. Chaplin, Mrs. Roper, Mrs. Snow, Mrs. Kemp, Mrs. Pye, Miss Galliphant, Miss Hull and Mrs. Eyre doing the sewing. The parish magazine noted that the cost of material was 'c. £5.' In August 1942 John Chalk, Michael Chalk, Martin Doubleday and Leonard Stubbings were admitted as choristers to Langford choir.

In 1944 Revd. Creed thanked the choir generally and especially the men, usually three or four at the services Sunday by Sunday. He felt that Langford choir compared well to many another parishes of a far larger population. He thanked Miss Hunt for her kindly assistance with the choir and Mrs. Wakelin as organist of long standing. He regretted that since the war began he had been unable to have the usual supper for the choir and church workers, but hoped to reinstate it in the not too distant future.

In 1954 Mrs. Florence Davis (shortly to move into The Homestead, in Maldon Road) took over as organist at St. Giles' and worked hard to establish a new choir. This time it was not confined to men and boys, but girls were encouraged to join. Ten years later one of the co-authors of this book, Irene Allen (or Smee as she was then) was one of their members until she joined the WRNS in 1969.

Florence Davis died in 1979, and the choir quietly disbanded. In 1991 it was revived by Gerald Matthews (Churchwarden at the time) in a new format. The members were called 'The St. Giles' Singers' and no longer had to robe or sit in the choir stalls – they merely went up to the chancel steps to perform anthems and introits [*a psalm or hymn sung before a service*] as required and then returned to their pews.

Part of Langford Choir. Florence Davis is on the far right.
Harold Harvey and Eric Major are left and centre back row

On several occasions, when the singers rose to sing they entirely depleted the congregation, so it was as well that they returned to their seats. Irene also joined them, and is now (at the time of writing) the entire Alto section.

It is interesting to note that when setting up the community shop in the Vestry in 2009, graffiti from several generations of choirboys was found, both on the panelling and where the cassocks and robes were hung. There was even some (mainly from the Chalk family) very high up on the organ housing, so there must have been some enterprising boys in the choir determined to leave their mark!

Sunday School

A Sunday school was run in St. Giles' Church for many years. However, owing to the fluctuating number of children in the village over time, the fortunes of the Sunday school have waxed and waned, and at the present time (2013) there is no Sunday school in operation. But, at one time it was a thriving institution; indeed, in the late nineteenth century it was clearly either compulsory to attend or there were a prodigiously high number of children in the village for the Sunday school numbers were very large.

From 1894 onwards the annual Sunday school treat was held at Langford Grove, where races and games took place, and the children and their parents partook of a splendid tea. Prizes for attendance and achievement were also awarded. The late Ronald Harvey (formerly of The Post Office, Langford) said that when he was a boy, the Sunday school ended at 10.30 and then the children went to Church. Sunday school was held in the School and was run by Miss Jeanie Baker, of Mill House. Church attendance was compulsory, and if you didn't attend someone would come round to find out why you weren't there! But it wasn't all bad as the Sunday school and the Choir both had their own outings.

The Sunday school ran through both world wars with a variety of leaders until the mid-1950s. It re-started in September 1966, and it was around this time that one of the co-authors' sister (Sheila Smee) ran the school; always insisting that Irene went along, come what might! When Sheila left the village the Sunday school was taken over by Mrs. Eveline Pipe (Churchwarden).

Other Church Organisations

Over the years St. Giles' Church made many attempts to provide for the spiritual and social life of villagers, and set up clubs and organisations to serve this perceived need. Some were longer lasting than others, but all served their purpose at the time.

Men's Club

A Men's Club was founded, and opened on Monday October 1st 1894. The Parish magazine noted that it would 'be open for the winter months' and hoped it would be well patronised. However, it had to be closed in November 1896 due to the loss of many of its members who had either left the parish or migrated too far to be able to use it. The club was finally closed due to lack of members in 1898, but was re-established in November 1901 and proved a great success; sadly no record is available of when it closed again. Many years later another Men's Club was established in the former school building which flourished into the 1970s.

Mothers' Meetings

For the ladies, the Hon. Miss Alice Byron, sister of the [then] Rector, set up her 'Mothers' Meetings' in 1894. These, like the meetings for the men, were held during the winter months, running from 1894 to 1914, and when the new Rector arrived (Revd. Littlehales) his wife ran them from then on, but so far no date of their cessation has been found.

Scouts, Guides and Cubs

A troop of Boy Scouts was formed in early 1912 by Michael Barne of Langford Place. Barne was Scout Master and Stanley Harvey, of the Post Office, was Patrol Master. The troop proved very useful during the Great War but was disbanded shortly after when Mr. Barne left the village. It was reinstated in 1921 and the position of Scout Master was taken on by Miss Joyce Littlehales, daughter of the then Rector.

When Revd. Littlehales left Langford and moved to Allensmore in Herefordshire in 1930, Joyce Littlehales relinquished the post of Scout Master, and was replaced by Gilbert Parker, who had been Patrol Leader for some time. In 1931 the new Rector, Revd. Creed, was asked to act as Chaplain to the 1st Langford St. Giles' Troop. With the success of the Scout troop, and the amount of small boys in the area who were too young to join, a cub pack was formed. Five boys were duly invested as Cub Scouts on 6th November 1931 by the District Commissioner, and Mrs. Parker was appointed as 'Lady Cub Master.' Sadly both troops had disbanded by 1938.

A pack of Girl Guides was established in February 1922 in the Waring Room, Heybridge (opposite St. Andrew's Church), and girls from Langford were invited to join. It is unclear how long the Girl Guides continued but the next reference to it appears in the August 1932 parish magazine when it was announced that 'A pack of Girl Guides was formed under the guidance of Miss Cunningham of Langford Cross in July 1932' but there is no indication in researches to date just how long this pack lasted.

Mothers' Union
A branch of the Mothers' Union was formed in Langford in February 1916 when twelve new members were enrolled, and three old members of other branches were present, and later transferred to the Langford branch. This organisation continued until the 1940s when it joined with Heybridge. The Heybridge and Langford W.I. was disbanded in November 2008, and then amalgamated with Freshwater W.I. in February 2009, to become Heybridge W.I. This is still in existence.

Girls' Club
Mrs. Jones, the Headmistress of Langford school, started a club in 1919 for girls above school age, whom she invited to her house. The November 1919 parish magazine noted that on 22nd October, Miss F. Ward, a teacher at the school:

> very kindly commenced dressmaking with the members. Six girls cut out and commenced to make a blouse. It is proposed to hold the meeting every Wednesday evening from 6.30 to 8.45, and to have a Social once a month, also a competition once a month (last Wednesday in month). The girls pay one penny a week. Two invitations have already been given for the Social Evenings, by Mrs. Littlehales, our President, and by Mrs. Grout of Stock Hall. Hon. Sec. R.M. Jones.

Unfortunately it is not known when the Girls' Club folded.

Lay Helpers' Union

The annual meeting of the Lay Helpers' Union was held in Heybridge on Wednesday June 24th 1914; the Rector (the Hon. and Revd. F.E.C. Byron) and several members from Langford were present. Sadly to date there is no further information on this organisation.

Like many churches, especially in rural areas, St. Giles' played a pivotal role within the community, not only from a religious and pastoral point of view, but also in caring for its inhabitants by way of the provision of any number of organisations to improve the well-being of its immediate and broader communities. Sadly, closeness of association to the church within all communities both rural and urban has lessened over the years as more commercial services and providers outstrip the popularity of church-going, and people look more to Government than their local communities for help and support.

However, St. Giles' Church, Langford, retains an active and very proactive small group of supporters. Weekly attendance levels for Sunday services may seem low, but often exceeds 5% of the population of the village. Through 'The Friends of St. Giles,' established in 2005, the beautiful church and its activities stay in focus, and indeed St. Giles' plays host to any number of special fund-raising events including talks and musical extravaganzas. A church Open Day is held every year when (weather permitting) the crypt is open for guided inspection by the public.

As a Grade II* listed building the future of the 'great oddity,' the unique church of St. Giles' *as a building* is secured, but without the efforts of the small number of loyal supporters its future as a facility for the community could well have been allowed to disappear.

Due to a number of thefts over the years the church is not open all day but it can be accessed during the times that the community shop is open (currently 1000-1200 every day) or otherwise by arrangement with the Churchwardens, whose details can be found on the notice boards, in the church porch or on our website www.stgileslangford.org.uk.

CHAPTER THREE
THE HEALTH OF THE PARISH

Before the arrival of the National Health Service on 5th July 1948, there was little help available to those who succumbed to sickness, even though in the nineteenth century, some believed that access to health care should be part and parcel of a civilised society. Debilitating childhood diseases - most now thankfully a thing of the past - were rife in years gone by, and Langford has seen its share of these. This chapter provides a brief glimpse into the health of the parish.

In her Will dated 8th November 1680 (proved on 25th January 1681), Sarah Hall, widow of Langford, gave 'My customary cottage in Langford called Foster's Garden to the parish of Langford for the use of the poor of the parish.' 'Foster's Garden' was where Brick House now stands in Hatfield Road.

Brick House in the 1930s

A conveyance made on 2nd July 1878 from the Guardians 'and others' of the Maldon Union (Langford Parish) to the Hon. Mrs. Mary Jane Byron passed on to the latter a piece of land and three tenements in the parish formerly used as poorhouses for the sum of £60. The transfer of this land and property to the Hon. Mrs. Byron does not mean that after that there were no poor people living in the village; far from it. It is assumed that the poor of Langford, whose fate was finally to repair to the poorhouse, would be accommodated at the nearest establishment of that kind in Spital Road, Maldon.

One of the first records to be found relating to serious illness appears in 1876, which was the year when whooping cough struck in the village, and school attendance suffered accordingly. In 1878 scarlet fever raged through the village and the school was shut down while the disease burned itself out. Records remain silent for another two decades with regard to any other outbreaks but this may have been due to the fact that Langford, being a rural community, was unaffected by illnesses that may have been touching other areas.

Generally, despite the Infectious Diseases Notification Act of 1889, diseases were not being reported quickly enough for the authorities to keep them under control. Dr. John C. Thresh – the Medical Officer of Health for Essex – noted in his *'Summary of the Reports of the District Medical Officers of Health in the Administrative County of Essex for the year 1891'* that diphtheria was prevalent in Heybridge and, understandably, there was concern that it might spread to Langford. The Medical Officer's Report for 1894 also noted:

> The landing of a cargo of London manure is believed to have been the cause of one fatal case of diphtheria. The effluvium from the filth is justly described as 'horrible.' No cases of infectious disease were removed since there is no hospital, but the patients were isolated as far as possible in their own homes, and at the termination of the cases the houses were disinfected, cleaned etc.

Indeed, there was no permanent isolation hospital, but Dr. Thresh noted:

When referring to isolation hospitals at least three areas – Chelmsford (Urban), Chelmsford (Rural), and Maldon (Rural) – possess hospital tents which can be fixed up and be ready for receiving patients within 12 hours of commencing their erection. These, however, are of comparatively little use save for localised outbreaks of smallpox, and for this purpose they are probably more suitable than permanent structures, as they can be fixed near the locality in which the outbreak has occurred, and sufficiently far from any human habitation to reduce the risk of the contagion being carried by the atmosphere, to a minimum.

In 1894 influenza was widely prevalent in the parish, and even struck at adults. Mrs. Grout of Stock Hall, Mrs. Jiggins (Senior) of Luards (off Ulting Lane), Mrs. Smith ([Langford] Hall Cottages), Mrs. G. Everett (Hatfield Road) and Mrs. T. Ward of Maldon Road were all seriously ill, but recovered.

July of that year was a particularly sad month for Langford as it endured an alarming outbreak of smallpox. It was discovered too late, that Joseph Moss, who had died the previous month, had been suffering, not from blood poisoning as had been first imagined, but from a very virulent form of suppressed smallpox (where the pustles do not fully develop), although it was never discovered how (or from whom) he had caught it. Very sadly, nearly all those who had seen or come in contact with Joseph also contracted the disease, and had to be removed immediately to the 'temporary hospital' – which comprised of the two cottages in Langford Park (now one house [pictured above] known as 'Ravens') – kindly lent by the

Hon. Mrs. Byron. Those in the hospital were Edward and Mrs. Hedge, and their daughter Alice (of Luards, Ulting Lane), H. Woodley (Woodham Walter), Emma Moss, Mrs. Woodley, and Mrs. Little (of Hatfield Road). Sadly the case of Mrs. Woodley proved fatal, and she died on Tuesday 3rd July 1894 after only a few days' illness. All the other cases recovered. The parish magazine noted sombrely:

> It is seldom that so sad a sight meets the eye in Langford, as the funeral of Mrs. Woodley, which owing to the terrible nature of the complaint of which she died, took place on Wednesday, only a few hours after her death, in the presence of none but those who were naturally obliged to be present. The Ambulance Car carried the coffin to the grave, where the whole service was conducted, but many testified their sorrow by their presence outside the churchyard, from which they were however excluded. The deceased, who lived at Woodham Walter, was a daughter of James Moss and was 37 years of age.

Although Mrs. Woodley lived in Woodham Walter, she regularly visited her father in Langford and was well known within the community.

One consequence of smallpox being prevalent in the neighbourhood was that nearly everyone in Langford was vaccinated, and on a certain Monday, some seventeen Langford men were to be found wandering about the village unable to work, 'with bad arms and sad faces.' Some were even unable to do this and had to keep to their beds, but happily all recovered, and everyone agreed that vaccination, although inconvenient and painful, was 'better than smallpox.' Once the threat was past, the temporary 'Infectious Hospital' was broken up (in August 1894) and all the convalescents returned to their homes. However, it was a miracle that more people did not die considering the danger to which they were exposed.

Later in the year (1894) parishioners were disturbed to learn that the Rector (the Hon. Frederick Ernest Charles Byron) had been taken ill on Sunday 11th November with a sharp attack of influenza. The attack, which came on suddenly, became so acute that before the service had actually started he was forced to retire into the vestry in a fainting condition, and the service had to be abandoned. To show the extraordinary nature and rapidity of this complaint, the parish magazine stated that 'the patient's temperature rose immediately to 103 degrees. The Rector wishes to express in our columns his great gratitude to all those who so kindly gave their help and who conveyed him home.' It appears that the Revd. Byron was prone to attacks of influenza and over the years this became a matter of great concern to the parish.

The New Year brought little relief, as there were very serious cases of illness in the parish during January 1895. So serious were they that prayers were offered in church for Thomas Smee of Hatfield Road for two Sundays, his life at the time being in great danger, but thankfully he recovered. Mrs Henry Everitt of Ulting Lane was still very seriously ill, but Eliza Mott of Langford Park Cottages was out of danger and recovering. No record has yet been found showing what these villagers were suffering from although, as we shall see below, scarletina, diphtheria and typhoid fever were rife in the Maldon area at this time. However, Mrs. Moss of Hatfield Road was recovering from a severe attack of bronchitis. The Hon. Mrs. Eyre (Aunt of the Rector), who was staying at Langford Grove, had also been very ill but 'improving.' Mr. Shadrack Smith (of 'The Cottage near the Church'), who had been the Rectors' warden for the last year, was also seriously ill. Of course not everyone in the village who was in bed was ill. Arthur Everitt of Hatfield Road broke his leg while skating (the winter having been severe enough to allow skating on the river) and was laid up for some weeks.

Dr. Thresh reported on eighty-eight cases of scarletina, diphtheria and typhoid fever in the Maldon Rural District area. His report included a statement that an outbreak of smallpox had occurred at Langford in July, and that thirteen cases had been reported. The outbreak formed the subject of a Special Report where he highlighted the case of Joseph Moss, noting:

An aged man died from unrecognised smallpox and nine persons who visited him when he was ill were subsequently taken ill. The woman who performed the last offices to the dead and the two undertakers who placed him in his coffin were afterwards attacked by the disease. Two cottages in Langford Park were again utilised for Hospital purposes as well as the Hospital Tent.

In his report Dr. Thresh (pictured left) made the following observation which, although not directly relevant to Langford, gives a clear indication of how diseases were spread throughout the district at the time:

In certain parts of the County there are many persons belonging to the sect of 'Peculiar People' who, having no faith in medicine, never call in a medical attendant. As they are unable to diagnose disease and cannot be proved to know the nature of the illness from which any member of such a family may be suffering, necessary precautions are not taken, the cases escape notification, and we are powerless since no penalty attaches to non-notification unless the responsible person can be proved to know what disease the patient is suffering from…In the Maldon district there are many 'Peculiars' and every year some instance is recorded in which disease has spread on account of their neglect.

In 1897 Revd. Byron gave the parish more cause for concern. He was taken suddenly ill on Friday 9th July with a sharp attack of fever brought on probably by a chill, which confined him to his bed for nearly a week. Unfortunately the clergyman who was expected from London to take over his duties, failed to put in an appearance, and consequently there was no service at the parish church, it being impossible to find anybody else to take over at such short notice. The parish magazine recorded that despite the Rector being prone to illness this was the first time he had been unable to attend service during his tenure. The services on the two following Sundays were taken by the Revd. Davis, late curate of Fulham.

Mrs. (probably Eliza) Mott who had suffered a serious bout of bronchitis in June 1895 was seriously ill once more and was moved to the London Hospital on 7th August, 1897 where she would receive 'every attention and assistance, which careful nursing and the best results of science can give.' At the end of August Mrs Mott returned from the London Hospital 'much benefited.'

November 1897 was another trying month for many in Langford, visited as they were by severe attacks of influenza. Almost every member of The Grove, residents and staff was attacked by it. The Hon. Mrs. Byron had a very severe attack, and for some three weeks had been in great danger, but she improved. Mrs. Chalk (although we are not told which one) and John Etherton (of the Cottage by the Church) suffered further by a complication of pleurisy. Three funerals - a large number for such a small parish - took place during that month. They were those of Mary Frost (4th November) aged 65, Emma Smee (14th November) aged 69 (of Hatfield Road) and 83-year-old William Rudrum (of the Post Office) on 25th November.

In 1897 Maldon Rural District reported twenty-six cases and one death from scarlet fever. There was also another outbreak in Langford in October 1899. All the cases except one (Langford resident Annie Bell, of Maldon Road who was very dangerously ill) were mild. (It is interesting to note that 1899 was the first year in which 'cancer' was mentioned as a disease prevalent in the district.)

Living Conditions

The living conditions of the working classes were very much a cause for concern, and in that same year Dr. Thresh reported that the condition of the cottage property in certain portions of the district had been the subject of much consideration. He stated that in the purely rural parishes where labourers earned from 11s to 14s a week:

> Cottage owners cannot expect any reasonable return upon the outlay required for cottages built to meet the requirements of our bye-laws.

The result was that as the old wooden and lath-and-plaster structures became beyond repair, the tenants would either have to leave the district or continue to live in houses unfit for habitation. It is unclear how much of this statement refers to Langford (if at all) but it is suggested that this reflects the general conditions under which many agricultural workers would have lived in the village.

The house pictured on the previous page, formerly in Witham Road, Langford, is typical of this. It looks picturesque here (taken from the churchyard), but conditions became very bad and the building was demolished. ('Boswells' now stands in its place).

Part of the same house is shown (left) with a very young Maurice Green in the roadside gateway. The site now has two large detached houses with a spacious parking area in front, and the barn has been converted into a third house – 'Willow Barn.'

Reports from the Rural Sanitary Authority in Maldon highlighted housing problems, and these were reported in local newspapers. The *Essex Chronicle* of 12th January 1894 noted:

Overcrowding was reported at the house of Jacob Hull, at Langford, where the wife, husband and 11 children occupied two bedrooms; also at the house of George Willsmore, Holloway Road, Langford, where the husband, wife and nine children lived. Both these Langford houses were said to belong to the Hon. Mrs. Byron, and to be in a very bad state. It was ordered that notices be served upon the owner to put them right.

In 1900 Dr. Thresh reported on public sewerage and refuse collection stating:

Privy cesspits are chiefly in use, but these are being replaced as far as possible by pail closets. Public scavengers [*forerunners of today's 'bin men'*] are employed in the more populous parishes such as Heybridge, Tollesbury and Southminster; elsewhere the refuse is usually thrown into a hole dug in the garden. The hole is often close to the cottage, and frequently receives liquid slops.

In this modern age of electric light, instant (fresh) running water, central heating and wall-to-wall carpeting as standard it is hard to imagine the real nature of conditions under which the villagers of Langford had to live. Water was often taken straight from ditches with all the consequent health problems that that caused, like vomiting and diarrhoea, skin rashes and even developmental problems if drunk for a long period of time, and there were very few wells about. It would be nearly a quarter of a century before water could be drunk straight from the tap, and in the meantime, other health hazards plagued the village.

In early 1900 Mrs. Prior of The Orchard [*Orchard Cottages*], Langford, died aged 68 from bronchitis following an attack of influenza. She had lived in the parish for some thirty years and was buried in the churchyard on Tuesday 16th January. Of course not only the old suffered; Edith Alice Steward, infant daughter of Mr. & Mrs. Steward of Hatfield Road also died from influenza the following day. With so much illness about, it was clear that some way of isolating those with contagious diseases was necessary other than just utilising local houses. The Isolation Hospitals Act 1901, sought to give the County Councils more effective power, notably in enabling them to contribute to the cost of such hospitals. A proposal of the Sanitary Committee that contributions should be on the basis of £20 a bed was quickly whittled down to £5.

Up to 1914 there was improvement, particularly in the urban areas, but the County Council's contributions, apart from 1903-1904 (£2,978) were never much in excess of £2,000 annually and in some years considerably less. In 1901 Dr. Thresh reported that 'Maldon (Urban and Rural) possess properly equipped tent hospitals' although one wonders how tents would have been able to stop the spread of disease. However, the Heybridge Hospital tent was used in July 1901 for a sudden outbreak of typhoid fever.

The general health of Langford was poor in 1902 with diphtheria and influenza being the biggest culprits, and those at Langford Grove were quarantined because of scarlet fever. The school had to be closed for a short time in January 1902 owing to an outbreak of measles, and the Health Report for that year which, although again not directly referring to Langford, gave a worrying description of an outbreak of smallpox:

> The disease was introduced by a tramp into a socialistic community at Purleigh residing in a large barn. None of the inmates would submit to vaccination and eight of them contracted the disease and one died. There was no extension of the disease amongst the people living in the neighbourhood, most of whom submitted to re-vaccination.

Tramps (and itinerant workers) were familiar visitors to most villages and Langford was not immune from such threats. This example also indicates how easily disease could be spread from village to village. Therefore, it is no wonder that health officials were worried about such cases for they had risen from eighteen in 1900, to 227 in 1901 and a staggering 1,335 in 1902.

In December 1902 good news came in the form of the opening (at last) of a permanent Isolation Hospital in Heybridge which would also serve the people of Langford. Discussions about this hospital had begun in 1892 when the Port Sanitary Authority opened negotiations for a farm house at Heybridge which they intended converting. The site was finally obtained in 1896 for joint urban and rural use, and it was proposed to build two – one north and one south of the River Blackwater.

The Hospital, provided by the Maldon Joint Hospital Board, which was clearly leading from the front in terms of controlling the spread of disease locally, consisted of three blocks on a site of three acres on Broad Street Green Road, Great Totham. The hospital was brick-built and replaced the tented isolation hospital which had been set up along Colchester Road. The new hospital could:

> Accommodate 10 patients suffering from two diseases at the same time, an ample administrative block, an ambulance and steam disinfector. Disinfection of bedding and clothing is carried out here at the expense of the Borough. Rooms are disinfected by formalin spray.

It also included a substantial house for the Matron. Water was obtained from a bore hole in the Thanet sands and was pumped by a Robinson hot air engine to storage tanks. The sewage was pumped on to an irrigation plot. The total cost was £5,000 and the result was 'a most complete little hospital.'

There was a good deal of serious illness in the village again in 1903, and this time influenza was much in evidence, although, thankfully, not to the extent to which it had visited some other parishes at the time. There were two outbreaks of scarlet fever in May 1903 - one at Stock Hall and the other at Bevis Hall - and parents were requested not to let their children go to infected houses until a clean bill of health was given. Scarlet fever again broke out at Bevis Hall later in the year. The patient, young Harry Willingale, was doing well, but it meant a great deal of worry and anxiety to his family for some time. Fortunately, Harry recovered completely and no new cases appeared.

Annie Bell, of Maldon Road, had diphtheria in October 1904, but her condition began to improve. It was not contracted in Langford, but 'brought from Maldon'! In fact concern had been steadily growing again about the number of tramps and travellers that frequented the lanes. Dr. Thresh reported in 1904 that tent and van dwellers on Totham and Tiptree Heaths had given rise to many complaints. The bye-laws were frequently disregarded and legal proceedings against 'these nomads' were apt to be ineffective. Thresh added that 'It is hoped, however, that strict supervision by the Sanitary Inspector will lead to a decrease in their number.' It was known that gypsies travelled from the Heath to Langford for work, and their state of health was always a concern to villagers.

One serious case of illness reported in the February 1906 issue of the parish magazine was that of Mr. Chapman at Station House. Mr. Chapman, the husband of the station mistress, was struck down suddenly, and slowly became weaker. Most unfortunately, at the same time, he became totally blind.

With the National Health Service still many years away, it was common practice in villages at this time, including Langford, for pregnant women to have their babies at home. The Midwives Act of 1902 had been passed chiefly to ensure the provision of a 'better class of midwife.' By the end of 1905 there were 194 women registered as practising midwifery in the county. However, Dr. Thresh warned that 'many of these are poor, ignorant women with no idea of what sepsis [*blood poisoning*] means, nor of the importance of cleanliness.'

Mr. Howlett, living near the Church, was seriously ill with typhoid fever in October 1906. Fortunately this was the only case in Langford at the time, but there were two very serious cases in Heybridge and all three were traced to the eating of clams taken from the River Blackwater below Heybridge. The parish magazine cautioned:

> We cannot too strongly impress on our readers the danger of eating any shellfish taken from a river polluted with sewage. Nine cases out of ten are

traceable to this cause, so much so that oysters are regarded with the gravest suspicion by the general public, and the market for them has been immensely reduced in consequence. Cooking of them of course makes the danger much less, but even then the amount of boiling required in order to destroy the typhoid germs is so great that it cannot be said to make them absolutely free from risk.

The editor of the magazine also reported that Mr. Harvey, of the Post Office, who had been ill with pleurisy, was much better. Mr. Ernest Goodey, of Orchard Cottages, was, however, still confined to his bed with the same complaint, intensified by influenza. Evelyn Hull, of the Park Cottages, was reported as 'getting on well,' but it was very doubtful whether she would be well enough to return to school that winter. Mr. Howlett had by now recovered sufficiently so that he was able to come downstairs, though still too weak to make it up again without assistance and Mr. Goodey was reported as able 'to get out of doors for a short time.'

The Harvey family outside the Post Office
(l-r Harold, May, Minnie and Cecil)

In January 1909 another outbreak of scarlet fever was discovered in Langford. It began at the Post Office and, with the exception of a few doubtful cases, it ended there. Four occupants of the Post Office, which had been temporarily closed, namely Mrs. Harvey, and her children, Frank, Beatrice and Harold had to be removed to the Isolation Hospital at Heybridge. Then an epidemic 'of sore throats of a severe character, accompanied by illness more or less marked and, curiously enough, occurring just about the time of infection,' caused very considerable alarm; so much so that for a day or two the school had to be closed owing to the fall in the number of children attending. The parish magazine warned:

> It may not be amiss here to warn parents of the extreme necessity of care in cases of mysterious illness, especially at the appearance of any kind of rash. A rash is almost invariably the sign of a contagious disease; and although the child itself may be hardly ill at all, it at once becomes a centre of grave danger to others. Scarlet fever is not, as some people seem to think, a childish complaint, but a most dangerous disease; and the germs are so powerful that they may be hidden for an incredible time and yet retain all their deadliness. Therefore parents should be especially careful on the appearance of a rash, to call in the opinion of a doctor, as he alone is able to decide what the malady is.

Fortunately the parish library was not open at the time of the outbreak; books being known as a potential source of infection, although the reason for its closure was due to a reduction in the number of users. However, it was hoped that 'if the facility dropped for a year, readers might come to it fresh again another winter.'

At a parish meeting held in the school on the evening of Friday 27th March 1908, complaints as to the conduct of the authorities in not taking two (unnamed) diphtheria cases from

Langford into the Isolation Hospital were forwarded to the authorities. But by March 1909 all fear of scarlet fever had passed away for the time being, and those who were the original victims, although still in the Isolation Hospital, were reported to be doing well.

In October 1912, twenty-seven out of forty-three children were absent from Langford school through measles; owing to the very severe outbreak, the school had to be closed for a fortnight, re-opening in November.

There were three cases of diphtheria in Langford in August 1912. They all occurred in one family, the name of which was not recorded in the parish magazine. The three were removed to the Isolation Hospital at Heybridge for treatment where they all made a full recovery. The following year parents were again warned of a very serious outbreak of scarlet fever in Maldon. This situation continued into 1914 and it was noted in the Essex Medical Officer for Health's records that the hospital was seriously overcrowded during the year, and that some wooden shelters had to be erected for temporary use.

The temporary wooden shelters set up at the Heybridge Isolation Hospital (the chimneys of Woodfield Cottages can be seen in the background)

Then there appears to be a period of relative calm in terms of the contracting of serious illness. However, owing to an outbreak of measles among the children of the village in April 1920, the school was again closed for two weeks by order of the Medical Officer.

From 1924 to 1926 the cost to keep one case in the hospital was £52.8s.0d and to treat that case was £48.3s.5d. In 1929 this had fallen to £4.9s.8d and £22.0s.1d respectively. In 1935 the Maldon Isolation Hospital still had ten beds in operation and cited the cost of keeping a patient for a week as £5.6s.4d and the cost of treatment per case at £11.17s.9d.

Mental Illness
One of the most misunderstood health problems in the nineteenth century, and indeed remains so today, is that of mental illness. Under the Lunacy Act of 1890, 'pauper lunatics' thought to be in the 'wrong' parish (i.e. not the one in which they were born) were to be returned to their home town. One case in point was that of William Partridge who was born in Langford in 1861.

In 1898 a notice was sent to the 'Guardians of the Poor of the Maldon Union' from Bishops Stortford stating, in very legalistic terms, that on 18th August 1898, William Partridge, a 'Pauper Lunatic,' was found in the Parish of Bishop Stortford and, after examination, was removed to their asylum. The notice claimed that as he was not 'legally settled in the Bishop Stortford Union [Workhouse]' and came from Maldon, they should be paying for him. The claim was that William was the son of James and Mary Partridge (both deceased) and was born at Langford in the Maldon Poor Law Union area on 18th April 1861. The notice claimed that William had lived with his father at the Downs, North Street and other addresses in Maldon up until January 1883 which, they said was sufficient 'to render him settled in the Parish of St. Peter, Maldon in the Maldon Poor Law Union in accordance with the provisions of 39 and 40 Vict. cap 61 sec

34. That the said Pauper Lunatic has not gained a subsequent settlement or status of irremovability.'

At this time William was about 37 years old, and Bishop Stortford Union sought to claim from Maldon Union the sum of £3.11s.1d for his examination, and £6.16s.7d to the Treasurer of Bishop Stortford Union for his upkeep for a year, making a total of £10.7s.8d. They also noted:

> AND ALSO to pay to the Treasurer of the said Asylum [Bishop Stortford] the reasonable expenses of the future maintenance of the said Lunatic in the said Asylum so long as he shall remain confined in such Asylum.

Regrettably we are not told what finally happened to William. There is a note on the order which was examined at the Essex Record Office [ERO D/DCf B479] which bears the legend 'Removed by Mr. Baldwin 13/1/99.' Whether or not William was returned to the area of his birth appears lost to history, and he is certainly not recorded as being buried in the parish.

Parish Nurse

The Parish Nurse held an important role in terms of the health and welfare of any village community. During this period she was a vital link between the nursing profession, the medical profession and the church. She visited people in their homes and would refer the more serious cases to the local doctors. Clearly, in a comparatively isolated village such as Langford, she was a vital asset to the community. In September 1896 the parish magazine noted:

> Those who were nursed by the Parish Nurse learned that some working men in Witham have been from house to house and have collected over £8 for the nurse fund quite of their own accord to show their appreciation of this institution which they say has reached the working man's home.

The amount collected in Langford Church, on Accession Day, 1897 for the Cottage Nurse's Institute, was £7.7s.2d. The parish magazine stated:

> When it is considered that this sum is exclusive of the donation sent straight to the fund, I think all must agree that Langford has given only another evidence of the great liberality which it always shows on occasions of a special offertory.

Negotiations were afoot in November 1906 for Langford to join Heybridge in the use of their Parish Nurse. It was proposed that Langford should have the benefits of the Nurse's visits at the rate of 4d. a visit or 7/- for three weeks. The visit would last one hour. This, of course, 'would not interfere with the present nursing arrangements under the superintendence of Miss A. Luard.' (With a name such as this it is assumed that this lady was in some way related to the Luards of Luards Farm off Ulting Lane some of whose remains are buried in Langford Churchyard. However, research has yet to reveal if this was indeed the case.)

The collections in St. Giles' Church on 1st September 1917 were given to the Heybridge and District Nursing Association. The association also benefited to the amount of £4.10s.0d from the proceeds of a concert which took place on Tuesday 11th February 1919 in the schoolroom. The parish magazine of March 1919 reported:

> An attractive programme included Plantation Songs by the Misses Hunt and Messrs. Skipwith and Wilberforce. Songs by Miss D. Hunt, M. Willmott, R. Crowe, the Revd. C. G. Littlehales [Rector], and Messrs. Skipwith and Dowse. Recitations by Miss E. Luard, and an amusing Duologue by Miss E. Luard and Mr. J. D. Wilkinson. All the performers did excellently and evoked very hearty applause. The room was quite full, and a most enjoyable two hours passed without a dull moment.

Clearly the relationship between the Parish Nurse and the people of the village was a close one as indicated by the following extract from the December 1925 issue of the parish magazine:

> Though we feel sure that our members will regret the departure of Nurse Roberts whom they had got to know so well, we are certain they will welcome her successor, Nurse Parry, who has taken her place and comes to us with good credentials. She is residing in the Crescent Road, Heybridge. As a parting present in recognition of her good services, Nurse Roberts expended the money subscribed on an Ebony Dressing Table, Set of Brushes etc. which we thought subscribers would be interested to know.

The nursing association continued throughout the inter-war years, and a Garden Fete at Langford Hall on 18th July 1936 raised money for the Heybridge and Langford Nursing Association and also for the Langford Parish Magazine Fund. An orchestra from Langford Grove School played under the leadership of Mrs. Curtis, and was greatly appreciated.

In late 1952 and early 1953 the village suffered from the consequences of the cold and snow. Both children and adults suffered from influenza and chicken-pox. The times of services had had to be re-adjusted for Christmas 1952. The reason for this was that Revd. A.S. Bousfield, who was standing in for the Rector at the time (Revd. B.A. Whitford), was himself taken ill.

Accidents

Over and above serious illness that plagued the village during the latter part of the nineteenth and two decades into the twentieth century there is evidence of some non-medical trauma in the form of what is commonly described as 'accidents.'

Some have looked back with nostalgia to the 'rural idyll' of days gone by but, then as now, accidents occurred, and in the late nineteenth/early twentieth centuries there was no welfare state to help them. An accident, therefore, could ruin lives and bring destitution to a family especially if it stopped the breadwinner being able to work.

For example, on 4th August 1847 Mr. Wilson, aged 24, the 'junior son' of Mr. Wilson of Langford Grove, who was formerly the Danish Consul, died as a consequence of his carriage being overturned. Then, on the night of Monday 18th March 1895 a very serious and alarming accident occurred to Henry Ager, at Langford Grove. The parish magazine provided villagers with the details:

> Mr. Ager lived in a bothy by the stable yard and kitchen garden, and before retiring to bed on the night in question, sat by his kitchen fire reading by the light of a paraffin lamp. Whilst so engaged he fell asleep and his paper or papers apparently slipped from his knees into the fire, setting alight to his clothes. Fortunately, having woken up, he was unable to open his front door, and so ran into his bedroom, and having rolled himself in his rug extinguished the flames. He then proceeded to call the coachman, who lived close by, and who, having aroused Mr. Brown the butler, and others from the Grove, drove off to fetch Dr. Scott from Maldon.

> In the meanwhile, Mr. Ager was well dressed with salad oil by those attending him, and on the arrival of Dr. Scott had his burns, which extended over his legs, back, hands, neck and face, thoroughly bandaged. A trained nurse from the Diocesan Nursing Institute arrived early next morning to attend to the case. Mr. Ager was in great danger for two days owing to the severe shock, his pulse being from 140 to 150, but is now in a fair way towards convalescence.

The *Essex Newsman* of 23rd March 1895 gave further details:

Harry Ager, aged 20, working for the Hon. Mrs. Byron, sustained very serious injury due to the upsetting of a paraffin lamp…The Butler, Mr. Brown, hearing his screams, rushed to the hut with the coachman. They did all they could for the poor lad, dressing the burns with salad oil, and sent for Dr. Scott, who arrived in haste. It was found that the sufferer was terribly burned about the lower part of the body, legs, hands, arms and neck. Everything possible was done for his relief, but he now lies in a very critical condition. Mrs. and the Hon. and Revd. F.E.C. Byron have been exceedingly kind. A trained nurse is in attendance.

Harry's wounds were much deeper than was at first supposed, and he had to be inoculated with skin, kindly given to him by friends. ('Inoculation by skin' is a treatment whereby skin cells, usually from other parts of the patients' body, are injected in order to regenerate growth in the affected areas). However, in Harry's case it would appear that the skin was obtained from donor friends, doubtless due to the fact that his own was so badly burned.

Doctors feared that it would be quite a year before Harry would be able to go to work again. He was still in the Chelmsford Infirmary in July, but was considerably better, although as yet unable to walk or stand. However, he was taken in a reclining chair to a garden party given by the Bishop of Colchester in July, and greatly enjoyed it. Harry was able to leave hospital and return home in October 1895 but it was some time before he completely recovered.

On Monday 3rd February, 1896, a shocking accident occurred to a carter named William Doe, who was walking beside his wagon on the Station Bridge at Langford when the one o'clock train passed under the bridge and frightened the horses. They galloped down the hill and knocked William over, the wheels of the wagon passing over him and breaking both his thighs. Fortunately, Frederick Chalk was going over the bridge at the time on his bicycle and hastened to find Dr. Scott, from Maldon, who set the poor man's legs on the bridge, where he lay for about an hour in great agony. He was taken by Mr. A. Barber to his home at the World's End, Hatfield Peverel, and was attended there by Dr. Gimson who stated that Doe was the most cheerful and uncomplaining patient, although it would be many weeks before he would be able to use his legs again.

Another incident, which could have been fatal, occurred at Langford Grove on Thursday 20th February 1896. The Hon. Mrs. Byron, who was suffering from influenza, woke up about 8 o'clock in the morning to find her room full of smoke, and a chair near the fireplace with her clothes on it was blazing furiously. The parish magazine recorded:

> Her cries awoke her maid [Laura Bruce] who, with great presence of mind, threw a heavy garment upon the blazing mass and extinguished it, before it had time to ignite the room which otherwise it must in a few moments have done. No cause for the outbreak can be assigned, except that a piece of burning wood must have fallen out of the fire, which had been lit about half an hour previously.

In May 1896 'an accident was occasioned to Mr. Coker, who had a very narrow escape when his neck was momentarily dislocated by a blow from a young horse.' Fortunately Mr. Lomas, of Langford Hall, was present at the time, and was able to put it back promptly! This was no mean feat.

A very serious accident occurred on Tuesday 27th October 1896 to Mrs. Grout of Stock Hall Farm, and her daughter Ella, who, with Mrs. Grout's youngest child, were driving down Market Hill, Maldon, when the carriage ran upon the houghs [the thighs] of the pony, which immediately bolted, overturning the carriage violently on to the ground. Mrs. Grout, 'who was taken up insensible,' was badly cut about the face, as was also her daughter and the child. Thankfully all three were reported as doing as well as could be expected, although the two former were 'likely to be confined to their beds for some time.'

But it was not only horses that caused accidents. Health and Safety legislation was non-existent in the nineteenth century, and modern factories could be places of great danger. For example, Herbert Algar, a 'Standard 1' child at Langford school had his finger cut off by an oil-cake machine. In August 1897 Langfordian Willie Ward met with an unfortunate accident at the Heybridge Iron Works, losing the top of his left hand little finger through it being caught in a cog wheel.

On Monday 17th July 1899 'a most serious accident' occurred to Mr. Bentall (of Maldon), between Langford Church and the railway station. Mr. Bentall, who was driving a spirited 5-year old, was met by three motor cars at which his horse took fright, overturned and smashed the cart, and threw Mr. Bentall violently to the ground.

He was quickly conveyed to Mr. Barber's at Langford Post Office, and Drs. Facey and Brown being summoned, was found 'to be suffering from such severe concussion of the brain that for some days he lay in a most critical condition.' The parish magazine reported that Mrs. Bentall was quickly on the spot, and everything that could possibly be done was done.

> Miss Bailey proved a most efficient nurse until two trained ones could be procured. The occupants of the second motor car, which caused the accident, did their best to 'repair the mischief they had done' and procured a nurse, whose services, however, were not required.

Another terrible accident occurred on Saturday 11th August 1900 at Mitchell's Farm. A little boy named Arthur Dowsett, who was on a visit to his grandparents, Mr. & Mrs. Storey of Mitchell's, was accidentally shot by 'the going off of a gun'

76

which was being used by Fred Bell for scaring birds off the radish seeds. Death was instantaneous, the charge entering the poor boy's head. The funeral took place at Burnham, which was the boy's home. The parish magazine noted that 'Great sympathy is felt, both for the Storeys and also for the Bells.'

The *Essex Newsman* of 18th August 1900 reported on the same incident:

On Monday evening Mr. John Harrison, Coroner, held an inquest at the Half Moon Inn, Heybridge, touching the death of the five-year old son of Philip Dowsett, mariner, of Heybridge, who was accidentally shot on Saturday. Mr. J. C. Harrington was foreman of the jury.

Mary Taylor, wife of a labourer, living at Langford, stated that at 5.40 p.m. on Saturday, when in her house, she heard a youth named Bell call out that he had shot the little boy, Arthur Philip Dowsett. She went out into the field, and there saw the poor boy lying on his back, with a large wound in the top of his head, from which the blood was flowing freely. He appeared to be quite dead, and she carried him into his grandmother's house.

P.C. Tilbrook stated that he found the boy lying upon a couch in his grandmother's house, Mitchell's Farm. He was quite dead before six o'clock. In the boy's pockets were 16 empty cartridge cases.

Frederick Bell, aged 15 years, employed by Mr. Wakelin, farmer, of Langford Hall, stated that on Saturday he was employed scaring birds from a radish seed field at Mitchell's Farm, for which purpose his master supplied a gun and cartridges. Deceased accompanied him, and at about half past five he was standing close to the witness, who had the gun on his left arm. Upon turning suddenly round the gun hit deceased on the head and exploded. Seeing that the boy was hurt very much, witness ran for assistance.

John Storey, shepherd, stated that his grandson, the deceased, had been staying with him. Dr. Allen, of Langford, said the boy had a large wound in the front of the head, which penetrated the brain. The skull was broken and part of the brain was protruding. The boy's cap was burnt where the charge had passed through. The cause of death was injury to the skull and laceration of the brain.

The jury returned a verdict of 'accidental death,' and found that the blame attached to no-one.

Yet another serious accident occurred one Monday in October 1904 opposite Langford Mill, when Nellie Lucking, from The Orchard [*Orchard Cottages*] 'who was hanging onto the back of a timber wagon,' became entangled in one of its wheels and had one leg so terribly mangled that it had to be amputated at once below the knee, Drs. Ewens and Bawtree being in attendance. Mr. Hollingdale, of Mill House, who was fortunately on the spot, rendered invaluable 'first aid' assistance and also 'did the greatest good by helping with the little one after the accident, finally going off to hasten medical assistance.'

The child was then removed to her home at The Orchard in Mr. W. Chalk's cart, and here the operation was successfully performed, Mrs. Grout and Mr. Chalk giving great assistance. Nurse Ager, of the Parish Nursing Institute, was later sent by Miss Luard. 'This' the editor of the parish magazine suggested, 'should be a warning to Langford children, who are far too fond of clinging to the backs of carts and carriages, and even of that most dangerous engine which usually pays Langford two visits a day to the public peril.' What this 'most dangerous engine' was, sadly, was not given.

A gloom was cast over the whole parish by the sad accident which occurred close to the Railway Bridge on Friday 17th September 1926, and resulted in the death of Frank Stewart, aged 40, a labourer at the Southend Waterworks. Owing to a ground fog he was knocked down by a motor cyclist (who was also injured), and his skull was fractured, causing death. He was buried on Wednesday 22nd September in Langford Churchyard, the last offices being performed by the Rector, Revd. Littlehales, in the presence of a few sympathetic parishioners.

On 21st March 1929, Willie Bonner, of Fords Farm, Langford, aged eighteen, died. He had run into a lorry on his motorbike on 9th March and was so seriously injured that he was taken, unconscious, to Chelmsford Hospital, but he died twelve days later without regaining consciousness. He was a member of the Church Choir, one of the organ blowers, and a member of the Boy Scout Troop in Langford. He was described in the parish magazine as 'a lad with a splendid physique, strong, silent and industrious.'

The *Chelmsford Chronicle* of 29th March 1929 reported the incident under the headline 'LANGFORD LAD'S DEATH – CRASH INTO LORRY'

> At the Chelmsford hospital on Saturday, Mr. Coroner C.E. Lewis, sitting with a jury, held an inquest on William Charles Bonner...Wm Thomas Bonner, father, gave evidence of identification. His son, he said, had been riding a motor cycle for not quite a month.

William Challis, of Mitchell's Farm, Langford, stated that at 12.30 p.m. that day Willie Bonner had stopped outside his house (facing Heybridge) and spoke to him, sitting astride his machine with the engine running. After their chat, Willie said he was going home and, putting his motor cycle into gear, went to turn round in the road and was hit by a lorry coming from Langford. William said that neither he nor Willie had seen the lorry as they had their backs to it, but he believed the lorry was going very slowly.

The lorry driver, Herbert Gibson, of the Square, Heybridge, who was employed by Messrs. May and Butcher, of Heybridge, said that there were seven workmen in the lorry at the time. He had seen Willie on his motor cycle by the side of the road, and had sounded his hooter. Willie had pulled right across the road in front of him, and there had been nothing he could do, so hit the motor cycle broadside on. He had gone to the boy's aid, but found him seriously injured. A doctor and the police were sent for immediately. Herbert said: "I didn't have a million to one chance to avoid the motor cycle. I never expected him to move from the side of the road, but he suddenly came right across in front of me."

When the police arrived, they found the motor cycle wedged under the engine of the lorry, and Willie was lying by the roadside seriously injured. The Heybridge Isolation Hospital ambulance arrived, and took Willie to Chelmsford Hospital, where he was unconscious on arrival, and bleeding profusely from his left ear. His right ankle was fractured. He remained unconscious until his death on 21st March, due to a fracture of the base of the skull, and laceration of the brain.

The jury at the coroner's court returned a verdict of accidental death, and exonerated the lorry driver from any blame. They expressed sympathy with the father of the deceased.

Whilst death was commonplace in Langford as in any other village it was not uncommon for the decease of more important villagers to be recorded in the parish magazine even though they may have died of natural causes.

Mr. Henry Wallis, aged 78, a retired Blacksmith, who lived in Hatfield Road, Langford, died quite suddenly from heart failure while going to the well for water. Mr. Charles Cornelius Dorking, also from Hatfield Road, who was with him at the time, rushed for help, but the deceased had expired before he could be carried to his home. He was laid to rest in the churchyard on Saturday 17th July 1911 beside his wife who had also died quite suddenly, from a heart attack, only eleven months before.

Drownings

As a village with so much water flowing through it, Langford has, regrettably, suffered many deaths through drowning, especially of young children.

On 9th June 1880, a little boy, Harry Gaywood, aged five, drowned shortly after leaving school. His classmates followed him to the grave when he was buried three days later.

The parish magazine of August 1895 noted

> Mr. Wynyard [*who lived at the Rectory, taught the Sunday School and was later to become Churchwarden*] is willing to give swimming lessons to any of the male inhabitants of Langford, should any be anxious to learn. In a village like Langford, through which two rivers (the Chelmer and the Blackwater) run peculiar facilities are offered for bathing and swimming.

Despite this offer, on Friday 6th September that year James Dorking who, with another little boy, was fishing in the river close to Langford Mill, lost his balance and fell into the water. The parish magazine recorded that when help arrived it was too late, and 'all efforts to restore animation were unsuccessful.' The sad news was carried to his parents who were expecting him home from school. The funeral took place at Langford Church on Monday, 9th September and was attended (among others) by the children of Langford School.

James Dorking would have been 11 years old on the day following the accident.

There was another drowning, this time of Robert Cranmer whilst bathing in the Blackwater at Beeleigh in June 1896. His body was discovered by a lad named Thomas Easter, who communicated the fact to Robert's brothers, and the news was broken to his widowed mother. His funeral took place at Langford on 18th June the Revd. H. Eyre, Vicar of Great Totham, officiating in the absence of the Rector. The parish magazine noted:

> This was the second death by drowning during the last year and it would perhaps not be out of place to remind our readers that Mr. Wynyard will give swimming lessons to any men and boys who care to learn.

At first sight it might seem strange that only males were invited to be taught to swim, but of course in those days it would perhaps not have been 'seemly' for Mr. Wynyard to teach women or girls. Sadly we do not know how many men or boys too up the offer. Ironically, Mr. Wynyard himself was to suffer death by drowning on 22nd August 1915 whilst on holiday in Scotland. Strangely enough, although his death certificate states that he 'drowned,' on the reverse it notes that his death was not due to an accident, but to 'suicide.'

The arrival of the National Health Service

Our survey of the health of the village has been well informed by the reports published in the parish magazines since the 1890s but as the quality of life generally improved such reports became fewer in number. Major diseases were being successfully combated by the introduction of vaccinations and improvements in water supply. Parents generally became better educated on matters such as cleanliness in the home and personal hygiene. As a result of this combination of factors, reports of serious outbreaks of life-threatening illnesses in the village abated.

The National Health Service changed things for the better from 1948, and since then no major illnesses have occurred in Langford and, mercifully, there was nothing for either the parish magazine or the local newspapers to report on the health of the village.

CHAPTER FOUR
EDUCATION

Before Queen Victoria came to the throne the education of the under-classes was of little importance to those in high authority, indeed some saw educating the masses as a sure road to anarchy. But it was during Victoria's reign that major changes were introduced to do just that. In rural communities, such as Langford, children working the land or helping at home was seen as the priority and, as we shall see, this remained so even when 'proper schooling' came to the village; right up until the closure of the school in 1922.

Fortunately the Langford School Log Book for the period 1875 to 1902 has survived. Research into this valuable resource, and detail after that period gleaned from parish magazines, has enabled the authors to paint a very clear picture of the trials and tribulations and occasional pleasures afforded by the educational process. A number of school mistresses and one school master tried (some might argue in vain) to interest Langford's youngsters in the three 'r's in the schoolroom in preference to pea-, potato- and acorn-picking, or simple truancy. One difficulty encountered has been tracing where some of the children actually lived, a task made more complex by the fact that some of the families were itinerant travellers, only present in the village for the pea-picking and harvest seasons.

When the London Diocesan Board of Education report was published in October 1839, in answer to the question 'What schools for the Education of the Poor?' the Revd. Charles Matthew, Rector of Langford, confirmed that there was only one school in the village. This school was exclusively for girls (boys attended the school in Maldon), twenty-four were enrolled, and it boasted an average attendance of twenty. The management of the school was by the School Mistress, (unfortunately unnamed), the children being taught in a room at her house. The school was under the occasional inspection of Mrs. Wescomb of Langford Grove (the Lady of the Manor) and the Revd. Matthew.

The school had been established for some twenty years prior to this. As regards the level of educational provision in the village, Revd. Matthew stated, 'I think the means are equal to the wants.' He was probably right. Langford's prime industry was farming, and nineteenth century England was only then beginning to alter its views and consider the possibility of 'education for all.' Although the subjects taught are unknown it can be assumed that as a girls' school, the subjects would be around home economics and possibly preparation for a life in service.

The Elementary Education Act 1870 created School Boards which were given the power to create new schools and pay the fees of the poorest children. The managers of such 'Board Schools' could insist on the attendance of all children between the ages of five and thirteen. However, in certain quarters, knowledge, especially amongst the working classes, was still deemed a dangerous thing. It was not until thirty-five years after the Diocesan Board report in 1874 that the National School at Langford – a mixed school catering for all ages – was built on land belonging to the Byron family. On 20th September 1875 Miss Eliza Gimson Jones undertook the duties of Schoolmistress at the school, and by then a new Rector, the Revd. Frederick Thomas Tayler, was in post.

The New School

Langford School was purpose-built to accommodate forty children with a house for the Schoolmistress forming an integral part of the building; an adjoining door allowing her access from her front room directly into the classroom. The plans for the new school (shown on the next page) had been drawn up by Frederick Chancellor in 1874, and was a beautiful building, positioned a few hundred yards from the church in the centre of the village. However, Miss Jones found her pupils somewhat lacking, for on 24th September 1875 she wrote in the School Log Book:

> Admitted 53 children into the school this week. Eight could read and write their own names and add a few figures together; two could work Standard III, the remainder were entirely ignorant of writing or arithmetic.

Miss Jones clearly had a task on her hands but what could she expect from children of a small, mainly lower class, seasonal community the majority of which had never been subjected to education before? In addition the school, built only the previous year to accommodate forty pupils was now, in theory, more than twenty-five per cent over-subscribed.

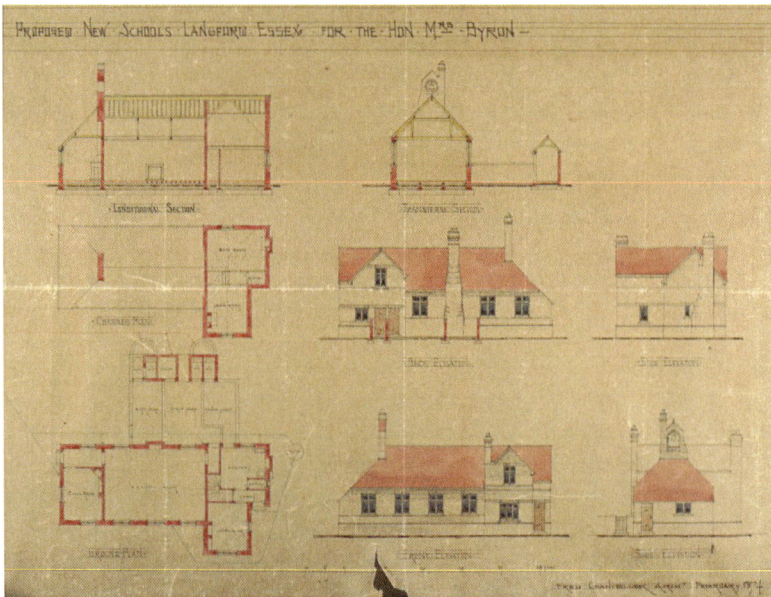

The Plans for the new school by Frederick Chancellor

On 1st October Miss Jones' frustration with her class was already showing as she recorded that she had 'classed the children this week and reduced them to order.' The Revd. F.T. Tayler, as he would do for years to come, had given the

Religious Instruction. Another child was added to the register the following week, and Miss Jones noted that the Rector had given the elder classes Religious Instruction whilst she had taken the infants. In due course the pattern was that Revd. Tayler usually arrived two days a week to give Religious Instruction to the children. On 15th October she noted the registering of another child. However, the average attendance was down to forty-seven 'on account of potato gathering and picking acorns,' an indication that the children's lives did not, as yet, revolve around education but continued to be influenced by the demands of the seasons. So the School Log Book recorded each change of schoolchild; one added here, one removed there as patterns of life changed.

On 22nd October 1875 Miss Jones recorded that two children had 'removed' from the village and one had been admitted. This bought the total on the register to fifty-six. She also noted 'Very great improvement in the writing and arithmetic.' Also on that date Miss Jones commented in the log simply, 'Weather wet.' The weather clearly stayed wet for by 12th November the average was only 39 being 'less than usual owing to the floods.' In addition a family with three children had left the village.

There was a strange entry in the Log Book for 26th November 1875: Miss Jones noted, seemingly with some irritation, that 'The Honourable Mrs. Byron sent for all the maps from the school and will not allow Geography to be taught here.' The Hon. Mrs. Byron was the daughter of Mrs. Wescomb and who, on her mother's demise, had become the Lady of the Manor. Perhaps the order to remove the maps was designed to keep the lower orders in their place by not allowing them to look or think beyond their own local boundary, or maybe the Hon. Mrs. Byron genuinely believed that Geography was, in itself, a 'frivolous' subject. However, this can only be speculation as no explanation of her action appears in the log book.

Whilst during the summer the school could be aired by opening windows, heating the school in winter seems to have been a perpetual and somewhat serious cause for concern. On 3rd December 1875 Miss Jones noted in her log that she 'had not any coal on Tuesday so did not open the School.' However, in the afternoon 'Mr. Wood sent some to go on with.' It is assumed that the person who came to Miss Jones' aid was John Wood, the tenant farmer at Langford Hall just down the road. The following week school attendance was down to just thirty owing to the deep snow in the village, children being unable or, as can be surmised, their parents being unwilling to send them to school in such conditions.

By Christmas Eve 1875, and just before the school broke up for one week's Christmas holiday, Miss Jones was feeling rather optimistic:

> This is the beginning of another quarter. I found that many of the second class had improved so much as to be more than equal to the first so I have raised one boy and four girls from the second to the first class.

In 1875 Lord Sandon's Elementary Education Act became law requiring that all children must be in school until they reached the age of ten. This placed a duty on parents to ensure that their children received elementary instruction in reading, writing and arithmetic; created school attendance committees, which could compel attendance, for districts where there were no school boards; and the Poor Law Guardians were given permission to help with the payment of school fees. However, this appears not to have been well received in Langford and, in fact, largely ignored.

The New Year began with more heavy snowfalls which reduced the average attendance to thirty-seven, but this did not prevent Revd. Tayler giving Religious Instruction to the upper classes (the older children) of the school. On 21st January 1876 Miss Jones highlighted the problems the atrocious weather and the school itself were posing for the pupils. She wrote in the log book:

> Small attendance this week owing in great measure to the fearful state of the school ground, which the children have to cross to get into the school. It is a grass field, has never had any gravel on it, consequently on the breaking up of the frosts and in rainy weather the water stands in pools so that their poor little feet are saturated. Then the school room has been so full of smoke, (*possibly due to burning damp wood or poor ventilation*) we could not see for the first hour, having doors and windows open gave the children and myself cold; the parents have chosen rather to keep them at home especially the infants. I consider the infants as the root and foundation of a good school, and when they are neglected it is labour in vain to attempt a sound education either religious or secular. The Revd. F.T. Tayler gave Religious Instruction to the elder classes. Mrs. Tayler paid a visit to the school this morning. I ought to have 65 children but have only 49 at present.

One wonders where all these children came from when the population of the village at that time was only 234. Rural communities were renowned for having large families but given that Ulting had its own school, as did Wickham Bishops, if there were indeed 65 children from within the village and its immediate and accessible surrounds then this figure represents 27.8%; over one quarter of the population of Langford.

By February 1876 things appeared to be looking up, Miss Jones recording 'great improvement in second and third classes in writing and arithmetic' and an average of 39. She added that 'on Tuesday the Rector gave Standard II a lesson on notation (*the representation of numbers or quantities by symbols*), and that on the Monday she had admitted a little boy Charles Henry Perkins which increased the number on her books to sixty.

The School from Maldon Road c. 1920

As the school was only ever built to accommodate forty pupils, the figure of sixty was, in theory, fifty per cent over capacity. However, at this time, and for the life of the school the 'average' always tended to be below that original specification.

On 18th February Miss Jones noted that wet weather and illness had reduced the average to thirty-three. On 25th February the school log reveals the first record of examinations as Miss Jones put the first and second standards through a strict examination and found that they had made great progress in arithmetic, notation and writing although 'spelling is still indifferent.'

March came and the class continued to improve under Miss Jones' tutelage. The first of the month being Ash Wednesday she gave the children a holiday and noted in the log that 'I now have my first, second and third standards in good order and feel sure if they were examined this month they would all take three passes each except two; but the Inspector is not coming until April I am told.' Did she fear then that the children might forget all they had learned by the end of the month?

Spelling seemed always to have been a bugbear with Miss Jones as she noted on 10th March 'a great improvement in all things except spelling.' She added 'their dialect hinders them considerably 'bag,' 'rag,' 'hen,' they call 'baig,' 'raig' and 'hin' so spell them accordingly to their sound. Also 'could,' 'would' and 'should' they call 'cold,' 'wold' and 'shold'...' This is the first and last time the School Log Book makes any mention of the children's dialect as a hindrance to their education.

On the 17th March 1876 Miss Jones wrote, doubtless with some self-satisfaction:

> This school has now been open six months. Considering the total ignorance in which I found these children, and how I have taught them step by step keeping them to the work after hours, it is wonderful to see how they have progressed, especially the infants.

She continued in a very ironic tone

> But more wonderful still to see how very little the elder children know, after all the trouble and anxiety bestowed upon them.

On 28th April twenty-three children were examined by Her Majesty's Inspector in order that Miss Jones might gain a Certificate. By 12th May the report of the School Examination Board had been received. It noted that the school 'is well conducted and the instruction is very creditable.' Encouraged by such a positive report Miss Jones took the opportunity of requesting items for the school presumably to enable her to carry on her good work and make even more positive progress. These included a clock, some maps (even though these had previously been removed on the orders of the Hon. Mrs. Byron), some infants' pictures, book cupboards, a desk stool and some more books. At this time Miss Jones noted that several children were away ill with whooping cough.

After such praise for her pupils' progress it is a surprise to find, on 26th May a note of genuine irritation creeping into Miss Jones' log book:

> Small attendance this week. People send their children shopping to a village about ten minutes' walk from here [*Heybridge or Wickham Bishops perhaps?*] and although the days are long they take the whole of the morning; nothing I can say will induce them to let the children go out of school hours.

This is clearly another indication that, despite the school rules, it was the parents who retained control of their children and not, in this case, the school ma'am.

On 2nd June 1876 the school broke up for the Whitsuntide holiday. On 16th June Miss Jones recorded that many children were still at home 'not recovered from their coughs' or, and this reinforces the point made above, because 'their heads are carried away with the idea of pea-picking.' Nothing it seemed would induce the children to come to school instead, not even the loud ringing of the school handbell (pictured left). The following week was no better; the situation clearly beginning to affect her health as she wrote 'Had very few children as the pea picking has commenced. Was obliged to close the school for a week as I have a severe attack of neuralgia in the head.'

During most of the remainder of July this frustrating position remained the same, successive weekly reports stating:

July 7th – Average 30 this week. I did not expect to have any.

July 14th – Average 29 children still away at pea picking.

July 21st – Average the same the children still away in the fields.

But on 28th July Miss Jones noted, presumably with some relief, that 'most of the children returned to school this week' and perhaps not surprisingly the attendance was good. Having bemoaned the fact of having very few children attending school over the previous three weeks, Miss Jones then had no choice when she wrote in her log book on 4th August, 'I have broken up the school for five weeks for the 'Harvest holidays.'

Although 'Harvest holidays' were never officially sanctioned, it was generally accepted that a good number of school children would be absent at this time as they were involved in helping with harvesting the crops. The school re-opened on Monday 11th September 1876, but although the harvest was gathered in Miss Jones still had cause for complaint. She recorded a small attendance at school 'owing to a Fair being held two days this week at Maldon.'

Most of the children were sent to it by their parents. One poor boy had his leg terribly shot, so he had to keep away from school for some time. The school year ends today, and it has been opened one year.

The new school year did not start very well. Miss Jones' entry in the School Log Book for 22nd September reported that the average attendance at the beginning of the new school year was 'small' with 'many people leaving the village.' The reason for this apparent migration from Langford at this time is not known but it may have been due to itinerant workers, here for the harvest, leaving the village.

By and large Miss Jones had had a fairly successful first year at Langford School but by 29th September her notes reflect continued frustration. Clearly she was finding it hard to cope as is indicated by that day's log book entry which read, 'I have neither work, books or paper in the school and cannot tell what I ought to do.' Having recorded that, Miss Jones added that the school had been full every day even to the extent that extra staff, in the form of a Miss Mary Hardwick, had paid a visit to the school to take a class of dictation and arithmetic, although there was no indication where Miss Hardwick came from, or who appointed her.

Miss Jones' frustration manifested itself again during the month of October in four terse entries:

October 6th - The children have taken a great deal of holiday this week. Four children have left the village…

October 13th – I have scarcely anything in the school to use; no paper, no books, no work and do not know when I shall get any. Weather wet, average small.

October 20th – The new people have not sent their children to school yet. Madam has sent four tons of coal.

October 27th – I have neither paper, ink, work nor reading books in the school. I have written to Madam repeatedly to ask for a supply but without success. It is a farce to keep the school open.

However, despite this desperate and, as she said, farcical situation, Langford School would remain open for more than forty-five years.

November 1876 saw some improvement in Miss Jones' lot, for she wrote on 3rd November 'I have had Madam's permission to spend 30/- in school books.' But attendances remained very poor, Miss Jones reporting in that same log that 'One weakly boy eight years old has been employed scaring rooks, others stayed from school to see a funeral – any excuse is enough for a parent to keep their children away from school.' In addition Miss Jones noted that she had caned a boy [*unnamed*] severely 'for using vile language in school.'

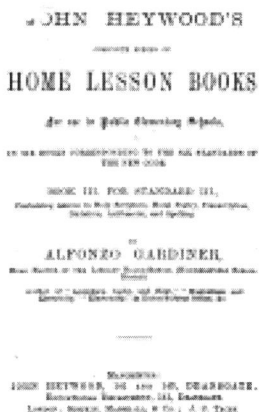

A week later on the 10th November, it seemed that Miss Jones had found part of a solution. She wrote, 'I have introduced "Heyward's Home Lessons" into the school and find them a great help; the children take to them well.' However, there were still frustrations. While on 17th November she stated that 'The girls in standard III are improving in arithmetic and reading' she also recorded that a family which had been in the village for six or seven weeks had still not sent their children to school. Apparently at the end of her tether, Miss Jones wrote 'let them play in the road in a lamentable state of ignorance and dirt.'

As if this was not enough Miss Jones recorded her views of another outrage in the log on 24th November:

> I found 19 bibles all torn in the same place and I could only find one girl Ellen Algar who had torn the margin off one, none of the others would confess to having done the mischief. As the bibles were used in the Sunday school I asked Miss Payne who conducts it to speak to the strange children (that is those who do not attend the Day School) she laughed and made light of it and I gave great offence to the Revd. Mr. Tayler who instead of upholding me in any righteous indignation expressed himself as very displeased with me for speaking about them.

It was hardly the reaction Miss Jones expected, and from then on her working relationship with Revd. Tayler seemed to go downhill.

December seemed no easier for Miss Jones with many issues and concerns demanding her attention:

December 1st – Owing to wet weather the attendance was small - boys out rook scaring

December 8th – Weather wet. Admitted a girl (over 13) into the school. She can read and write but knows nothing of arithmetic. Martha Marber is the girl's name.

December 16th – Mr. Beadel [*the Farm Bailiff at Langford Hall*] paid a visit to the school today and kindly promised some gravel for the playground and a guard for the classroom fire.

But as the year approached its end, Miss Jones reflected on the trials and tribulations of trying to implement the Elementary Education Act in Langford. On 22nd December she wrote:

Yesterday all the elder children took the morning to receive a sixpence which is always given on that day. I fear Lord Sandon's Act will be of little use in a place like this, pea picking takes six weeks, harvest six more and now when other schools are full the boys here are taken to scare crows. Today I close the school for the Xmas holidays.

The year 1877 broke with Miss Jones determined to improve the school numbers. On 19th January she recorded 'a small attendance this week' with only forty-four pupils on the books to begin the New Year. She noted: 'There are ten children who do not come to school and the Guardians tell me they have no power at present to compel them. Two families left the village and single men have taken their place.' She also, perhaps as a reaction to the way Revd.

Tayler had responded to her about the Bible-tearing incident, was determined to stipulate when Religious Instruction was taught at the school. Her record for 26th January included the entry 'Tuesday I altered the figures of my time table, to give the 'Religious Instruction' the first hour from 9 to 9.50 the last hour being so very inconvenient.' Whether she had consulted Revd. Tayler is unclear. By 2nd February Miss Jones was back on her favourite hobby horse, her frustration about the amount of holidays taken by the children and the lack of any control she or the school board had over them. She wrote:

> 2nd February – the people here pay no more respect to the "Elementary Education Act" than they did to the Children's "Agricultural Act." Fred Chapman [*of Holloway Road*] has been rook scaring the last week, this makes the second time, what with 'pea picking', 'harvest' and 'rook scaring' they can scarcely make up their number of attendances. Alice Tring stays at home for weeks, her age is seven and upon inquiry I find she assists her mother in washing and mending while she does not even know her letters.

The rest of February seems to have cheered her up because on the 9th she wrote 'a greater average this week – the third class have made great improvement in writing.' Encouraging signs but would it last? A week later on 16th February, Miss Jones recorded, rather smugly, 'I have a much larger attendance now the hour is altered for Religious Instruction... The Revd. Tayler called on Tuesday and wished to have the Religious Instruction at 11.10 but I could not do so as the hour for it is 9-9.50.' How the good Revd. Tayler reacted to that is not recorded!

In that same log entry Miss Jones recorded:

> So many children from a distance come just as I had closed the registers so lost their attendance mark. I admitted a boy over seven who cannot tell his letters. A

Mrs. Goodey took her children from school because I corrected Ada – she had long wished for an excuse to keep them at home – the eldest girl is at service and can neither read nor write.

Keeping track of attendances and constantly amending the registers must have taken up a good deal of Miss Jones' time. As mentioned above Mrs. Goodey found a way to remove her children from Langford School but one entry in the log dated 9th March indicates that the ingenuity of the local population knew no bounds:

A woman who has not yet sent her child to school sent to say if I would give her a pair of boots she would send her. I sent a good pair thinking she would have no excuse; the child did not come, so upon inquiry I found the woman had determined to wear them herself and says the girl cannot come now till she has a new hat. Her name is Ager.

Later Elizabeth Ager was admitted into the school but Miss Jones wrote 'She is in her eleventh year and cannot read a syllable. Two boys from Standard III are rook scaring,' later noting 'the average is small so many children leaving the village and rook scaring. Herbert Algar [of *Maldon Road*], Standard I has had his finger cut off by an oil-cake machine.' (*The machine was used to press kinds of oil seeds to get the edible oil, such as rapeseeds.*) [See also accidents on page 72]

On 16th March Miss Jones recorded some success with Mrs. Goodey:

After great persuasion Mrs. Goody [*sic*] has been induced to send her children here again to their own school. They were like the 'November Bee,' after wandering around their own hive the best they walked farther and paid more money.

Miss Jones had also ordered some copies of the Elementary Education Act and distributed them among the parents. One wonders what impression the receipt of such a document would have had on the poorer parents and whether or not they themselves were interested or indeed were able to read and understand it. It might be assumed that Miss Jones was selective as regards which parents received a copy of the Act. Whatever the case, this action was no doubt well intentioned and aimed at ensuring parents sent their children to school as required by law. However, this seemed to antagonise the Revd. Tayler still further, for on 12th April Miss Jones recorded:

> Mr. Tayler called at the school and made a great disturbance saying it is not necessary for me to teach the code as it is a private school, but I think it my duty to obey my employer and adhere strictly to the code. Mr. Tayler has been to the parents to tell them not to pay their fees unless I show them my authority for receiving them. He has three times threatened to deprive me of my Certificate. If a man who has no authority whatever over the school as me, can do such a thing, the sooner it is taken away the better; it was hardly gained though it be and it will be easily lost.

On 13th April Miss Jones again found herself undermined but this time by the Hon. Mrs. Byron:

> Madam expressed a wish that her tenant should present her with a 'Clock' for the school. They have consulted together and have decided that a clock is not necessary.

It is not surprising that Miss Jones was irritated by the lack of consultation. In May the previous year she had applied for items of equipment, including a clock.

It was clear that her disagreement with the Revd. Tayler had undermined her authority in the school as her entry on 27th April noted: 'The children take so many holidays the parents

99

say this is a private school and therefore subject to no laws.' The entries in the School Log Book for May 1877 did not improve:

> May 4th – Attendance small. I fear I shall have very few for the examination. Many of the elder girls leaving and going on visits.

> May 11th – The people are determined to break every rule of the school and the children are so disobedient backed up by their parents and their pastor who has told them that this is a private school, which means they can do as they did before this school was built, one boy who had been away 6 weeks brought 2d to pay for that time, another who owed 8d brought 2d.

Unfortunately we do not know what the fees were at that time, or which families refused to pay. The rest of May and early June brought no relief for Miss Jones. She gave Whitsuntide week for a holiday during which she received a parcel of copybooks and paper from the National Society. She noted that the National Society 'must have an extraordinary idea of a village school. They have sent 12 kinds of copybook four of each kind' and to add to her woes: 'the elder girls are leaving school on visits - some to London one to Cambridge - to avoid being at school until they are 13.'

Clearly Miss Jones was becoming highly stressed with no support from parents or the Revd. Tayler. These increasing frustrations of running a rural village school became all too clear in June:

> June 1st – The school year ends today most of the third standard boys have come back from rook scaring, but alas their sums are scared out of their heads and they are so idle one cannot get them to work with all the spirit they had before they went. Fred Wood has not returned although it wants but a week to the examination.

June 4th - This begins the school year. Only 33 to present for examination which takes place on Monday. Many never come to school at all and those who do come take a holiday whenever they choose. Nothing but direct compulsion will ever get the children to school here. Elizabeth Ager [*of Maldon Road*] is a specimen of what the other children were when I opened this school, over ten does not know her letters and goes out to nurse for 1/- per week, and stays from school whenever she likes.

The introduction of another Elementary Education Act (Mundella's Act) in 1880 extended the provisions of Sandon's 1876 Act regarding compulsory school attendance for children aged five to ten years. This may well have pleased Miss Jones, and indeed stressful entries in the log book lessened.

But in 1882 Miss Jones at last moved on to pastures new, no doubt relieved to be free of both the school and the Revd. Mr. Tayler. She was replaced by another Eliza – Miss Eliza Hobby. Whether or not Miss Hobby and the Revd. Tayler saw eye to eye is not recorded but in any event she did not have to tolerate him for long, as he also left in 1882, being replaced by the Revd. Charles Leigh.

Next to nothing is known about Miss Hobby's tenure of Langford School, except that at some time in 1886 she left, and her place was taken by Mrs. Sara Rebecca Paggi. Again, very little is known about this School Mistress except her name and the fact that she worked at the School from 1886 to 1890. After her Miss Louisa Pounds took over. Miss Pounds was born in Kintbury, Berkshire in October 1860, the youngest of six children, and had taught previously in the National School in Stoke St. Gregory, Somerset. The Revd. Charles Leigh left the village in 1890 after eight years as Rector to be replaced by the son of the Hon. Mrs. Byron – Revd. Frederick Ernest Charles Byron.

From 1891 the Hon. Mrs. Byron began a tradition that was to last for many years when, on 4th January she gave a Christmas tree for the children attending Langford Day School, and this was to become the highlight of the school year for many children. In that same year, a further

Elementary Education Act made grants available to all schools to enable them to cease charging for basic elementary education, thereby removing any necessity to keep children from school for financial reasons. On 1st May 1891 Revd. Byron (pictured left) paid his first visit to the school.

In June 1891 attendance was low due to many of the children having gone pea picking. The school was therefore closed for four weeks to enable all the children to help with the harvest. But even in August many children were still away working in the fields, and in September another holiday of a further two weeks was given for gleaning. (In nineteenth-century England gleaning - collecting the grain left in fields by the reapers - was a legal right for cottagers. In a small village the sexton (the person who looked after the church) would often ring the church bell at eight o'clock in the morning and again at seven in the evening to tell the gleaners when to begin and end work.)

For many families in Langford, work on the land was more important than schooling, and in days when life was very much a hand-to-mouth existence, children were essential to provide sufficient food for the household – besides, educating them would merely take them out of their allotted station in life. There was also the belief that girls did not need to be educated as they would become wives and mothers and so not benefit from formal education. It is hard to believe, but even in the twenty-first century there are societies that still believe this.

Absenteeism was still rife in the classroom, but it appears that unlike Revd. Tayler, Revd. Byron made a point of visiting the offending families, and the rate of missing children dropped dramatically under his tenure. It would be most interesting to know what he said to the families, but given that he was a kindly man, it was perhaps more his charm than anything else that won them round.

On 18th September 1891 Miss Pounds noted:

> The Rector gave a scripture lesson three days this week. On and after today the school fee for each child to pay will be one penny, the Rector will pay one penny for each boy.

Revd. Byron also gave the children a Sunday school feast at the Rectory; and his sister, the Hon. Miss Alice Byron gave prizes to the best scholars and also for good attendance, although whether this was for the school in general or the Sunday school in particular is not clear.

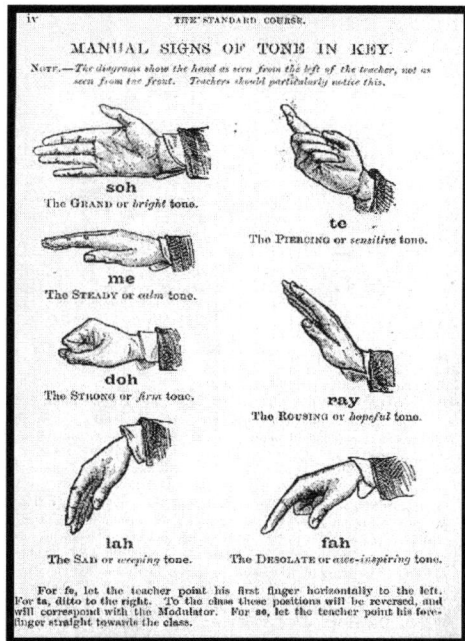

Miss Pounds noted in her logbook in October 1891 that she had begun teaching the children to sing by the new Tonic Sol-fa Method [Doh-Re-Me-Fah-So-La-Te-Doh].

In 1892 the attendance was much better, so whatever Revd. Byron said to the parents clearly worked; however, February saw very heavy snow followed by flooding which affected the numbers able to reach the school. The extended harvesting of various crops throughout the year also made continuous education for the children a chaotic affair, and many boys made it their own rule to take Fridays off! However, Her Majesty's Inspector called on 5th September and his report was very encouraging:

> The behaviour of the scholars is very satisfactory, and the instruction has, upon the whole, been given with very fair success. The arithmetic of the elder scholars will need attention, but the needlework of the girls is good. Some pictures are needed for the walls of the schoolroom, and the infants desks should be altered and made more suitable for very young children.

The new school year for 1893 broke with several children absent with measles. The year was also significant in that the Elementary Education (School Attendance) Act raised the school leaving age to eleven years.

In February 1893 the Hon. Alice Byron sent some wool to make balls for the infants to be used in teaching counting, and the following month she and her brother brought India rubber balls. In July the Hon. Mrs. Eyre (the Rector's aunt) called at the school house and brought some needlework and promised a prize for the best made garment. It is interesting to note that the Rector came to read to the children while the girls did their sewing and the boys drew pictures – an altogether much gentler, yet more 'hands-on' approach to his role.

The Inspector's report for 1893 noted:

> The order is good and the elementary attainments of the elder scholars are satisfactory. A firmer style of handwriting would be an improvement and the younger

104

infants might be better founded. The infants should be comfortably seated, and for their use some larger pictures of animals should be provided. Some books and maps are also needed. A short fence at the back would effectually separate the offices. The boy's yard is in an untidy state.

The School in the 1890s with (it is thought) Miss Pounds

Langford School was essentially a Christian establishment, and in June 1894 the children 'passed exceedingly well in the religious examination.' The report (for religious studies) given by the Diocesan Inspector, the Revd. W.J. Packe, was 'excellent for Bible work and very good for the rest of the work, behaviour etc.' (It is interesting to note that Revd. W.J. Packe, who was vicar of Feering at the time, was also the father of Elizabeth Margaret Packe, who would become Churchwarden of St. Giles', Langford from 1928 to 1956.) The more general Government Inspection was held the following week.

In January 1894 the children assembled at 4 o'clock for tea and Christmas tree. The Rector and his sister gave away the prizes on behalf of the Hon. Mrs. Byron. Every child received a present. The Hon. Miss Byron also presented two handsome work boxes to Fanny Chalk of Church Cottages and Ellen Everitt of Hatfield Road for good needlework from the Hon. Mrs. Eyre. Miss Pound reported James and Amelia Dorking to the Attendance Officer as they had been absent without leave for some time.

But May brought a great amount of influenza to the village, and Miss Pound herself contracted it. Despite that, however, the Diocesan Inspection was good that year:

> Notwithstanding the disorganisation caused by the illness of the teacher, the school has passed a very fair examination and the discipline is satisfactory. Good progress has been made in arithmetic and the recitation is very creditable. Spelling is not so accurate as usual. A small gate is needed in the passage between the offices. Some maps are required for teaching geography.

On 13th February 1895 the school children subscribed 2/- towards a funeral wreath for the Hon. Mrs. Eyre who had died the week before. Miss Pounds paid the remainder. Two days later the Hon. Mrs. Byron sent a very kind note to the children thanking them for the beautiful wreath to commemorate her sister's passing. Miss Pound received a note from her the following week asking the names of subscribers to the wreath, and on 22nd February she presented each subscriber with a new pair of out-door boots.

The children were again examined on Monday 27th May 1895 in religious subjects by Revd. Canon Snell, who was both Rector of Wickham Bishops and the Diocesan Inspector (and, incidentally, father to Miss Amy Catherine Snell who would do so much for Langford church in later years). He declared himself satisfied with the answers given by the children, especially the infants. The parish magazine of July 1895 noted that the report of H.M. Inspector (Mr. Hitchens) advised that the infants should have work with a greater element of play in it, such as is commonly described as 'kindergarten' and accordingly this was carried out. The next issue of the parish magazine remarked, somewhat smugly perhaps:

> It is a comfort to know that whilst so many other Schoolrooms are continually meeting with censure and requirements, Langford Schools fulfil every requisite in this respect.

Langford was clearly ahead of the field as far as modern educational methods were concerned, perhaps due in part to the touch of paternalism in its execution. In November 1895 Miss Pounds noted:

> The Hon. Mrs. Byron gave me permission today to get the apparatus to teach the children drawing as the Revd. & Hon. F.C.E. [sic] Byron is ill with influenza.

Sadly, we are not told what the 'drawing apparatus' was.

In August 1895 the report of Her Majesty's Inspector advised:

> The children have passed a satisfactory examination in elementary work. Some class subject should be taught to interest them, and to draw out their intelligence. The infants should have object lessons and occupations, and lessons are too long. Low infants seats and desks would be useful, and some cheerful pictures would brighten up the school. Some new reading books are wanted.

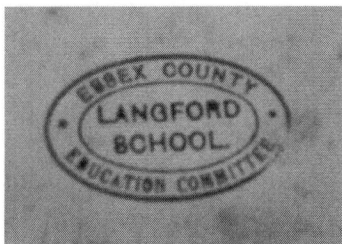

New reading books were duly obtained and stamped with the official school stamp (left). Revd. Byron signed the report with the note "My Lords will be glad to know that the suggestions of H.M. Inspector will be adopted," and later The Hon. Mrs. Byron sent word to say the infants might have the Kindergarten lessons and games suggested by H.M. Inspector. On 6th September 1895 Miss Pounds wrote in the log:

> I am very sorry to say that James Dorking was fishing after school on Friday afternoon about 5 o'clock and fell into the river and was drowned. Charles Everitt 6 years of age was with him, but was so alarmed he did not tell anyone soon enough to save the poor boy.

On Friday 3rd January 1896 a treat was given to all the children attending the Langford Day School, and at 4.30 between thirty and forty children sat down to a substantial tea in the Club Room, after which they went to the School where a large Christmas Tree, 'prettily decorated and well lighted' attracted much admiration. Each child had a present and a cracker over which the parish magazine enthused 'much heroism was shown and no injuries reported.' The following year the parish magazine reported that the tree given by Lady Byron was a large one, again 'well lighted' with candles and this time laden with presents, each child receiving one. The report continued:

> It was amusing to watch the delighted faces of the children as they marched round the fruitful tree. The entertainment was preceded by a Tea given in the Club Room and each child received an orange before going home.

It is sad to think that today the concept of a Christmas tree being 'well lighted with candles' with children marching around in close proximity to it would be condemned under Health and Safety regulations. The party for the children and presentation of a Christmas tree at the beginning of each year remained an annual event until January 1923, several months after Langford School was closed for good.

In June 1896 Miss Pounds was taken very ill and a Miss Emily Burke took over her duties temporarily. Sadly Miss Pounds had to retire due to ill health, and another teacher was sought, but in the meantime Miss Burke filled the gap. (Miss Pounds went on to teach at schools in Kent and Oxford. Her ill health clearly improved, as she died in Oxford aged eighty).

In October 1896 an interesting note appeared in the log book:

> Fred Bell I find has been throwing coal about the school yard after school hours; he also several times has used bad language in the playground, so I think for a time he had better not mix with the other children during playtime. Average for the week 24.6 School open this school year 149 times. Harry Manning aged 11 who has lately come to this school is also not allowed out to play for the same reason as the boy named above. Bad language and a really bad example.

December 1896 brought an outbreak of whooping cough to the village and many children were off school as a result. This situation continued into 1897, and Miss Burke herself, and the Rector, became seriously ill and could not attend the school for some time.

The parish magazine for January 1898 noted:

> Miss Burke, who is leaving Langford School, and is about to devote her time to reading for her certificate, will be succeeded by Mr. William Chalk. All good wishes to Miss Burke, but it is the first time that Langford School has been under the direction of a master.

William Chalk noted in February 1898:

> The Hon. Alice Byron called this afternoon and has promised to send some needlework for the elder girls to do. The Revd. M. Williams [*who took over from Revd.*

Byron while he was abroad for his health] and Mr. Lomas [*of Langford Hall*] came in today and spoke to all the elder boys about their conduct lately out of school hours. William Green suspended till I hear from Revd. M. Williams again and the Hon. & Revd. F.C. Byron.

The following month William wrote:

I have received a circular from the Education Department with regard to the prevalent practice of stone throwing by boys. I have cautioned them to give up such a dangerous practice.

The School children in 1898 –
William Chalk, schoolmaster back row right

It seems that the boys were not the only ones to give trouble to the new Master. Ethel Valentine of Kings Farm, Hatfield Peverel, was removed from the School as her parents did not wish her to comply with the rules, and Millie Dorking, of Hatfield Road, flatly refused to do what she was told. Mr. Chalk therefore sent her home until he had seen her parents about her.

The government report for the school examination, which took place in June 1898 stated that the school was improving under its first School Master, and that the children showed fairly good results in elementary work. 'So far,' the report said, 'this is satisfactory but the children themselves must do their best, or no amount of good teaching will do them good.' The school then closed for three weeks' holiday – no doubt to get over the shock!

In March 1899 William Chalk (pictured left) successfully passed the examination for the Queen's Scholarship. He taught at Langford for four years, later becoming one of the School Managers. During his time the school was re-designated a 'Public Elementary School.' (Relatives of William Chalk still live in the village).

There were few incidents of note occurring for the next few years; the pattern of school life seemingly settling down to a routine even though this routine was pursued against the 'habitual irregularity of the children,' and the vagaries of the weather. In January 1902 the School had to be closed for a short time owing to an outbreak of measles.

In March 1902 Mr. Chalk noted:

> A Holiday given this afternoon to allow children to attend the Operetta "Daisy Bell" at Maldon. The Rector kindly gave all children a ticket. H.M. Inspector suggests that next year Geography be taken by Standard I to VII altogether, England in detail and as much general knowledge of the world as possible.

Whether or not this happened is not clear, but was certainly contrary to the earlier instructions of the Hon. Mrs. Byron who would not allow Geography to be taught. Lectures were also given to the older scholars by Mr. Barnett (of the Band of Hope Union) on "Alcohol and the Human Body."

111

The logbook noted that the children 'were very interested in his lecture.'

The School was closed again on Friday 7th June 1902 for seven weeks' pea picking and the 'Coronation Holidays' for Edward VII. It was on that date that William Chalk, took leave of his pupils. The parish magazine reported:

> The Rector [*Revd. Byron*], who spoke for the children, wished Mr. Chalk every happiness in his new work at Colchester and led them in three hearty cheers. Mr. Chalk responding stated how well the children had behaved with him and hoped they would do equally well in the future.

Miss Ellen E. Mould, the new Schoolmistress, hoped to be in Langford and to open the school on the first Tuesday in August. She took up residence at the School and on 6th August 1902 it opened under her control. A month later, she noted the problems with absenteeism:

> The Dorkings attend School very badly – seems to be the rule for Ethel to absent herself from School on four half days in each week. Miss Chalk [*The Monitress*] sent a message at 9 o'clock this morning that she would not be able to come to school as she was expecting visitors.

By the end of September her patience was clearly waning:

> Miss Chalk absent from school this morning. I have this morning cancelled the attendance of Victor Dorking [*of Hatfield Road*], who left the school yard at playtime (without permission) and went to Maldon with his Mother, who was passing at that time…Several children are leaving the village this week – being the time of year when the farmers exchange their workers. Ethel Ketley [*of Hatfield Road*], has left (Standard V)…I cannot continue the work in Exercise books as I am

quite without ink. I find that the children have come accustomed to add the figure when "borrowing" in a subtraction sum, even in St. IV and I have great difficulty in abolishing the practice. In many exercise books the original figure cannot be distinguished.

On 6th October she wrote:

> Charles Lucking threw a stone in the school yard this afternoon and had the misfortune to hit a little girl, hurting her nose. I sent her home – she saw the Rector and informed him of what had occurred and he came in school and caned Lucking.

Yet despite this, the Rector allowed a conjuring performance in the school one afternoon after school hours.

Miss Mould did not stay long, however, for she left at the end of December to undertake a post with her brother near Leeds. This was a terrible blow as the school average under her short tutelage had been steadily increasing over the previous few months until it reached forty-four. Her departure also coincided with that of Miss Chalk, the Monitress, who resigned her post to take up duties at Witham National School the following week. However, Miss Chalk's younger sister, Emily, took up the position of Monitress.

Strangely the 1902 Christmas holiday did not begin until 6th January 1903 in order that no time might be lost in the change of Mistress. Miss Fanny Chalk, sister of Emily, a pupil teacher, also left the School on 1st December in order to take up her new duties at All Saints School, Witham. The Hon. Mrs. Byron gave the annual Christmas treat to the School children on Tuesday 30th December, and the school was then closed for a fortnight's holiday.

Mrs. Emily Campion, a relief teacher, took charge of the school for a fortnight on re-opening until Miss Bexon, the new Mistress, arrived. However, only a few days before her expected arrival, Miss Bexon wrote to say that she was prevented from coming, but giving no further details. This naturally caused very great inconvenience, but it was hoped to be put right as the Rector was in communication with two or three other candidates. Meanwhile, Mrs. Campion consented to remain in charge.

The new mistress, Miss Rebecca Moreton, took up her appointment at Langford School in February 1903. Before her arrival Mr. Watkins, the Government Inspector, had paid a surprise visit to the school on Wednesday 21st January and complained of the attendance of the children. This did not go unnoticed by the new incumbent as, according to the parish magazine, Miss Moreton had also noted that the punctuality of the children 'left much to be desired.'

On May Day she noted:

> Seven children brought pretty gardens for themselves and the governess in honour of May Day. Admitted four new children. Four others coming Monday. The Revd. & Hon. F.C. Byron M.A. visited the school and kindly released me in order to take the Religious Instruction and so am very glad.

During 1903 Managers were appointed to oversee the running of the school. Four were appointed by the Hon. Mrs. Byron: Mrs. Lee Baker, Langford Mill; Mr. Frederick Wakelin, Langford Hall; Mr. William B.A. Wynyard, Langford Parsonage, and The Revd. & Hon. F.E.C. Byron, Langford Grove, and one by the parish: Mr. Edward Baker, The Limes, Maldon (and of Langford Mill), and one by the Essex County Council: Mr. Walter Chalk. For such a small school this was some body of people.

On 27th May Mrs. Moreton was given three months' formal notice to give up the office of Mistress and to leave schoolhouse, although no reason for this can be found in the records. She left on 9th June. On 27th July Laura A. Chalk, another of William Chalk's sisters, began her duties as Temporary Mistress, and so continued the Chalk's educational 'dynasty.' Miss Alice Harriet Calver, 'Certified Mistress' (!) began work as the new Head in September 1903.

At a meeting of the managers held in the Schoolroom on 16th November business included the election of a correspondent. Revd. Byron was proposed by Mrs. E. Baker, seconded by Mr. F. Wakelin, and unanimously elected. Mr. Walter Chalk was selected by the Essex County Council, and nominated by them as their representative Manager of Langford School. The managers discussed the Agreement with Miss Calver, the new School Mistress. It was read over and agreed that enquiries be made about inserting a clause as to salary. Little did the managers know that Miss Calver would become the longest serving School Mistress at Langford, teaching there for twelve years.

On 9th December Miss Calver observed:

> I have this week examined all children in Standards. Spelling is very weak indeed throughout. I have discontinued taking the Geography of Europe as I found it too difficult for III & IV standards who would not be able to read a Europe geographical reader. Have started the British Isles.

The School closed in July for the pea-picking holidays and re-opened on 2nd August 1904. During the holidays a few alterations required by the Education Department were made. These included a new cloakroom, which would be used by the boys who would enter at what was formerly the girls' entrance.

The School Inspector's report published in October 1905 was better than in previous years:

> The children are in good order, and the teaching is fairly effective. Some of the upper boys answer with

considerable thoughtfulness. The infants appear to be taught satisfactorily on the whole. Reading should receive extra attention.

The Schoolchildren in 1905 – Miss Alice Calver, headmistress second row down first on left

On 31st January 1906 the School was renamed with an Official name and new number: "Langford Church of England School" No. 221.

On 21st February it was noted that:

> Willie Potter left the playground this morning and went home because he was not allowed to remain in school during the interval. His brother Albert did the same thing a month ago because he quarrelled with his companions. Their attendances were cancelled. They were both admitted last December and during this short time they have been very troublesome.

A meeting was held in the Schoolroom at Langford, on the evening of 28th May 1906 to consider the Education Bill which was then before Parliament. The *Chelmsford Chronicle* of 1st June reported:

The parents of children attending school were present in large majority, and numerous other persons, if not quite the whole adult population of Langford. Proceedings, which at the commencement were declared to be non-political, were opened with prayers. The meeting was then addressed by the Rector, the Revd. and Hon. F.C. Byron, and by the Revd. F.T. Gardner, Rector of Goldhanger, who held the meeting for an hour while he explained and examined the Bill and its objects.

The following motions were then proposed: (1) by Mr. Grout, of Stock Hall, seconded by Mr. Walter Chalk: That children be taught during school hours that religion which their parents may wish them to be taught. (2) Proposed by Mr. G. Howlett, and seconded by Mr. Cook: That children be taught by teachers who believe in what they teach. Both these motions were carried unanimously.

The pea-picking holidays in 1906 began on 21st June. On 26th August Kate Bell of Maldon Road was engaged as Monitress, and allowed to teach two and a half days a week while the resident Pupil Teacher was undertaking a course, and on 3rd September she was taken on full time. Lectures were also given by Mr. Barnett on hygiene – his topics covering 'water' and 'the skin and its uses.'

It would appear that truancy from school continued to be a problem in the early twentieth century, as in 1906 Charles Potter, a labourer at Mitchell's Farm, was summoned for neglecting to send his son to school. Mr. Baldwin, the attendance officer, said that every effort had been made to induce the parents to send the child to school, but they had allowed him to go to work. The Clerk of the Court advised Mr. Potter: "You had better inform the person who is employing him that severe penalties are inflicted on anyone employing a child under age." The case was adjourned for a month. The problem was that in a poor agricultural area, every family needed the extra money and, before the introduction of compulsory education, it had always been the custom to send children to work as soon as they were able. [In today's world we are horrified to learn that this still goes on in developing countries].

On 8th April, Emily Chalk, having finished a course of instruction at Chelmsford resumed her duties in the school after an absence of eight months, although many pupils were absent due to an outbreak of measles.

On 19th June Victor Dorking, W. Everitt and H. Howlett left the school, having passed the examination for the Labour Certificate held at Maldon on 3rd June. This certificate was needed to show that a child's school work was of a reasonable standard, and ensured that the workforce was competent at reading, maths and general knowledge, and guaranteed all children a basic level of education. Unfortunately it meant that pressure was put on bright children from poorer families to leave school as soon as possible and earn a wage. The certificate came into use under the 'Employment of Children Act 1903' and stipulated that no child under the age of fourteen should be employed in any occupation before six o'clock in the morning or after eight o'clock in the evening, or for more than nine and a half hours a day, or on a Sunday. These regulations outlawed many of the bad practices relating to the employment of children, but were very difficult to enforce, particularly in remote farming villages, or areas with a high proportion of migrant labourers.

Interestingly, in times of high unemployment governments have often encouraged pupils to continue their education beyond the minimum age as it can improve their prospects of a better job, and helps keep the unemployment figures lower. In 1914 the school leaving age was thirteen, this rose to fourteen in 1918, fifteen in 1944 and sixteen in 1972. These changes were often strongly opposed at the time – by employers and parents, and also by pupils themselves.

The school was closed for Empire Day on 24th May 1907 which was held as a holiday by the children. The first celebration of Empire Day had taken place on 24th May 1902 - the late Queen Victoria's birthday. Although not officially recognised as an annual event until 1916, many schools across the British Empire were celebrating it long before then. However, although there is no actual record of Langford School having celebrated Empire Day before 1907, we are in no doubt that the day would have somehow been marked in Langford.

Typical 'Empire Day' celebrations

The purpose of the day was to 'remind children that they formed part of the British Empire, and that they might think with others in lands across the sea, what it meant to be sons and daughters of such a glorious Empire; that the strength of the Empire depended upon them, and they must never forget it.' An Empire Movement was formed, with its goal in the words of its Irish founder Lord Meath, "to promote the systematic training of children in all virtues which conduce to the creation of good citizens." Those virtues were also clearly spelled out by the watchwords of the Empire Movement "Responsibility, Sympathy, Duty, and Self-sacrifice."

Each Empire Day, millions of school children from all walks of life would salute the union flag and sing patriotic songs, ending with the National Anthem. But perhaps the best part for them was that they were let off school early!

The Diocesan Examinations of 1907 were held by the Revd. Percy Luard, the Bishop's Inspector, on Wednesday 9th October, when he reported:

> Numbers present 29, Old Testament, good. New Testament, very fair, Catechism, fair. Repetition – Scripture, very fair, Catechism, very fair, Hymns, Collection, good. General Report. The religious teaching in this very small school has to be given under very difficult conditions infants and elder children being taught in one class. On the whole the work was as good as can be expected. Nearly all the children are very young; their answering was bright and fairly accurate in the Bible subjects, but rather weaker in the Catechism. The singing is good. Discipline and tone quite satisfactory.

Not exactly a ringing endorsement, but not a bad report overall, and you would be hard-pressed today to find **any** child who could pass this test. Being a 'Diocesan' examination the report would not have covered any mainstream subjects such as arithmetic, writing or notation. What little is known about the children's progress in these subjects is often only revealed in the school log book.

At the Managers' Meeting, held on Monday 18th November 1907, the three members present were Messrs. W.B.A. Wynyard, Walter Chalk and the Revd. & Hon. F.E.C. Byron (Correspondent). Members noted that Miss Emily Chalk had left the School. Miss Katie Bell also left Langford School at Christmas 1907 and Miss Hetty Ford of Red Lodge took her place as Monitress, a post she held until April 1909 when she was succeeded by Eveline Hull of Holloway Road.

Also at this meeting a decision was taken to close Ulting School and distribute the children between the parishes of Langford, Hatfield Peverel and Woodham Walter. A strong movement was also being made in the towns to refuse to accept children in future from country parishes into their schools. One can only wonder whether this was because rural children were so backward when it came to education, or whether the towns feared losing valuable revenues by having to take 'country' children. This is the first indication in the records examined thus far that the managers of Langford School had any authority over Ulting School. Until this point in 1907 none of the Langford School records referred to Ulting (which had been established in 1865.) How and when the managers at Langford were delegated the power in such matters is unknown.

In February 1908, three infants named Harvey (of the Post Office) were ordered to keep away from school for a time because a sister was suffering from diphtheria. The sister attended Maldon School. In fact from February to May several children were absent with colds, 'bad eyes,' or 'sickness.'

On 25th May the children had a holiday to keep Empire Day.

> They assembled in School at 11 o'clock and the Rector gave them a short address. They sang 'Britannia, the Pride of the Ocean' and the National Anthem. Each child saluted the flag as it passed out. The Hon. Alice Byron and Miss Amy Wynyard [sister of the Parish Churchwarden] were also present.

In 1908 the school broke up for a six weeks 'pea-picking and fruiting holiday.' The parish magazine dated July 1908 noted that 'peas about Langford were not so plentiful' as they had been the previous year and that the strangers normally engaged in picking were conspicuous by their absence.

121

In July 1909 parents of children were requested to see that their offspring returned to school punctually on the day of opening. It was of the greatest importance that this should be done otherwise the school average was lowered. Notice had been received from the County Authorities that no children were to be admitted to any Elementary School in the County before they had reached the age of four and a half, and the age might well be further altered to five years old. However, Harold Harvey, of the Post Office (aged five), was absent due to scarlet fever. By the end of the month a large number of children were absent.

> Sixteen children absent today suffering from influenza, colds and sore throats. One or two are afraid to come, owing to the serious outbreak of Scarlet Fever at the Post Office. Four cases have gone from there to the Isolation Hospital. A doctor from Chelmsford examined a few in school and found one little girl named Dolly Cottis – 4 years old in the peeling stage and advised that she should keep away for a time; also her brother.

On 26th February the first Medical Inspection of school children took place in the schoolroom.

March brought deep snow and a declining number of children as they were unable to reach the school. On 17th March, Dr. Thresh, Medical Officer of Health, visited the school owing to a fresh case of scarlet fever occurring at the Post Office. The two little girls affected were again excluded from school. News reached the school on 25th March that Beatrice Harvey, who had been ill since Christmas, died that morning aged 11½.

In April Miss Calver herself was ill with bronchitis, and Eveline Hull took over as Monitress.

During the Christmas holidays of 1909 a new stove was fitted in the classroom as the old one had not been heating the room well enough, so January 1910 saw better conditions in the school. Despite this, however, an outbreak of influenza at the end of January decimated the school attendance record – Eveline Hull, the Monitress – was absent for over a month with the condition.

In April Louisa Gentry became Monitress, and Revd. Byron returned to Langford after a period of four months in Italy for his health as he, too, was prone to attacks of influenza. On 20th May the school was closed for the day as a mark of respect for the funeral of King Edward VII. The school was closed again in June for the pea picking season, and in September two days' absence was given to pick blackberries.

In April 1911 the newly appointed 'Supplementary Teacher' (unnamed) attended All Saints Infants' School, Maldon one morning to receive a course of special training with infants, Miss Gentry being transferred temporarily for reasons unknown. By the 5th the attendance was very poor owing to rough weather and snow storms – only nineteen present in the morning and twenty eight in the afternoon.

In August the temperatures rose, and the girls were given a spelling lesson rather than sewing due to the intense heat (presumably to avoid marks on the fabric) – the thermometer registered over 81° Fahrenheit.

A School manager's meeting was held on Saturday 25th November 1911 for the signing of Form IX (the school returns), which was an 'annual terror' to managers. The agreement between the managers and Miss Louisa Gentry on her appointment as assistant teacher was also signed. The subject was then brought before the meeting of the extremely dirty state of some of the children and it was resolved to take 'energetic measures.'

In February 1912 the school was furnished with fourteen new dual desks and two new chairs; two new easels and two black boards were also supplied. In April Mr. A.F. Butler H.M. Inspector of Schools met the Rector at the school to decide upon the best place to add a new window to the schoolroom. In July the schoolroom, class room and lobbies were coloured and painted inside during the summer holidays. The offices were also lime washed.

In October an outbreak of measles kept several children away from school. This outbreak became very severe, and the School had to be closed for a fortnight.

Miss Calver and the managers had cause for celebration in December 1913 when Langford School won the shield for the last quarter's attendance for the district. Given the horrendous problems experienced by all of Miss Calver's predecessors the award for best attendance record must have seemed like a miracle. Indeed, this was a great triumph and managers and staff hoped that the school would be able to retain it. The shield was of beaten bronze and represented 'three scimitars' (actually the three Seaxes of the County Council's shield), one above the other, and beneath an inscription that the shield had been awarded by the County Council. The shield was held for one quarter, when it passed on to the next school holding the highest average for attendance in the district.

On 20th July 1914 Mr. A.F. Butler, His Majesty's new Inspector of Schools visited to see if the improvements to the lighting of the schoolroom had been completed satisfactorily. On 29th October the school was examined in religious knowledge by Revd. Plumptre, and the children had a holiday in the afternoon. Revd. Byron also resigned the living of Langford on this day after being Rector for nearly twenty-four years. Miss Calver noted:

> He is now Rector of Thrumpton – Derby [*actually this was Nottinghamshire*]. His successor is the Revd. Charles G. Littlehales who was inducted on Saturday afternoon (31st October 1914) by the Bishop of Barking.

On 3rd November 1914 the members of the Committee (Messrs. Wynyard, Hollingdale, Chalk, and The Revd. &

Hon. Byron) signed bills and Form IX. Revd. Byron also resigned as Correspondent as he was shortly to be moving to Nottinghamshire. Revd. Byron was replaced as Correspondent by Revd. Littlehales at the meeting on 7th January 1915. Mumps and severe colds swept through the village and affected the numbers of children attending school.

It is strange to note, that there is hardly a mention of the Great War in any of the school logs or the Minutes of the Managers' meetings examined during this research. It seems almost heartless that such a momentous event in world history should go unrecorded, despite the fact that so many young men from the village had gone to war; many of them brothers of those attending the school, and especially as nearly all the children would have had close relatives fighting at the front. During this period of conflict school life went on, the surviving School Managers' Minute Books for Langford School continuing to make fascinating reading.

On 19th March Miss Calver reported:

> We had a difficulty in getting fire to light this morning owing to so much wind in the chimney which blew the flame and smoke into the room; as it was quite a winter's day it was not very pleasant. Fire was got to burn by 11 a.m. by sending for carpenters' shavings. The temperature in the morning was 45 degrees, and in the afternoon 48 degrees.

It was reported on 30th April 1915 that Arthur Everitt of Ulting Lane had been absent from school for a whole year! The Managers decided to refer the matter to the Council doctor, a Dr. Sinclair, insisting that he be asked 'to either certify the boy as fit to attend school or if not, to authorise removal of the boy's name from the register.' It might be conjectured that this was done out of sympathy for the boy, but that is unlikely as the Minute Book confirmed that 'his continued absence was detrimental to the average attendance record.' They could no doubt see that coveted shield, for which they had worked so hard, being lost to them through this one boy. These tokens were of vital importance to the school, and such success reflected on both the staff and the Managers. On 4th May Revd. Littlehales wrote to Dr. Sinclair and asked him to either pronounce Arthur medically unfit or compel him to attend school.

On 9th May 1915, Miss Calver informed the Managers that she had 'contracted a chill' and would be too unwell to open school on Monday. A further blow to the village was the sudden death on 22nd August of the Parish Churchwarden and school manager Mr. William Wynyard whilst holidaying in Scotland. William had been Churchwarden for seven years and contributed to every facet of village life, and was 'an interested and active school manager,' the Langford Board of Management recording that they had 'suffered a great loss.' The interesting thing about this sudden death was that William drowned – the one person responsible for teaching others in the village to swim. Later it transpired that he had committed suicide. There has been much speculation about the reasons for this, although to date it has not been possible to find the correct one.

The chill that affected Miss Calver was never ever truly shaken off and, although she returned to teach during the summer, by the time autumn had set in, she was again forced to take to her sick bed. On 21st November 1915 it was reported that Miss Calver had been confined to bed with 'threatened pneumonia,' and that her doctor had forbidden her to enter the school for at least a week. By the time Revd. Littlehales visited her the threat had become a reality. He reported that he had 'learned that she is suffering from an attack of pneumonia and will be unable to leave her bed for several days and unable to resume her duties for several weeks.' The diagnosis was confirmed days later and the managers made an appeal to the County Secretary, Mr. Nicholas, for a supply teacher to fill the gap until Miss Calver was well enough to go back to work. By order of the managers the school was closed for a week or until a temporary teacher could be found.

This resulted in an offer from Mrs. B.J. Fraser of Salcott-cum-Virley, who offered to take over at once if required. Another letter was received from Mr. Bright, Clerk to the District Sub Committee, who also offered to help find a supply teacher. On 25th November 1915 the Management Committee wrote to Mrs. Fraser conditionally offering her the post. Revd. Littlehales noted that on 27th November he had received a letter from Mrs. Fraser offering to come and take up the duties of the School in place of Miss Calver, 'who lies between life and death' and that on the following day he wrote to Mrs. Fraser 'asking her to come without fail on Monday' adding that he had 'expected her on Saturday.' Revd. Littlehales noted that Miss Calver seemed 'slightly better.'

On 29th November Mrs. Emilia B.J. Fraser, a trained Certificated Mistress, arrived about midday and took up her quarters with Mrs. J. Crow at the Mill House. Revd. Littlehales called upon her about 3.00 p.m. He recorded, 'I took her into the school and handed her the keys of the table, drawer and cupboard, and arranged with her that the school would be open at 9 a.m. on Tuesday.' He stated further that 'Miss Calver's condition has further improved, but she is still not out of danger.' Mrs. Fraser commenced duties at 9 a.m. when Revd. Littlehales introduced her to the children. She took temporary charge of the School from that day. On 2nd December 1915, Revd. Littlehales asked Miss Calver's brother to procure a doctor's certificate.

The autumn also brought another report on truant Arthur Everitt. Now recorded as being absent for 'two years due to ill-health,' the Managers requested the Attendance Officer, Mr. Wedlock, to strike him from the register. However, the County Education Secretary stated that this was not possible without a medical certificate, and none was forthcoming, so the school Managers had to wait until the boy had reached the school leaving age of fourteen before they could 'strike him off.'

At a meeting of the School Managers on 3rd December, it was noted that Arthur Everitt had undergone a medical examination but that no certificate of exemption had been received. However, the very next day, 4th December, a notice was received that Everitt had been medically examined by Dr. Marjorie Dalby, and a Certificate of Exemption had finally been issued. Therefore Arthur Everitt's name could *at last* be struck from the school register.

Whilst the school managers must have been jubilant about the deletion of Everitt from the school books, Miss Calver's condition deteriorated. Two days later medical certificates were received for her, but despite all efforts to save her, she died in the School House at 3 p.m. on Wednesday 15th December. The parish magazine dated January 1916 carried her obituary:

> With great sorrow and regret we have to record the death of Miss Alice H. Calver, for over 12 years Head Mistress of Langford Church School. Miss Calver developed double pneumonia at the end of November, and though, at one stage in her severe illness, it was thought she would recover, she never rallied sufficiently to confirm this hope, but passed away on the afternoon of December 15th. Miss Calver was a devoted and conscientious School Teacher, and had obtained a strong hold over the children under her charge by her firm kindness and capable tuition. She always obtained good reports, and she will be missed greatly by Managers and Pupils. The funeral took place on Monday December 20th, in the presence of her few relatives, the school teachers and children, and other friends, she was laid to rest at the West-end of the Churchyard. Among other floral tributes of esteem and

respect, was a beautiful wreath subscribed for by the Teacher and Scholars of Langford School.

Unfortunately we do not know where in the churchyard Miss Calver is buried; she has no headstone, and there is no record of exactly where she lies, other than it is at the 'west end.'

The post of Headmistress was advertised in the *Church Times* on 1st January 1916 at a fee of 3s 6d, and at the end of the month (23rd) the post was again advertised in the *Church Times* at a fee of 3s. Applications were received from Mrs. Ballable of Brading, Isle of Wight, Mrs. Larkin, from Wicken, near Newport, Essex, Miss Adela H. Smeeton from Edmonton, Mrs. Williams of Ealing, and Mrs. Trainer of Nottingham.

On 4th February 1916 a reply was received from Mrs. Williams stating that she was forty-two years old, married and a communicant. At a School Manager's meeting on 7th February members decided to offer the position to Mrs. Williams subject to a satisfactory interview and, if she was found undesirable, then the post should be offered to Miss Smeeton at a commencing salary of £70.

Revd. Littlehales wrote to Mrs. Williams on 7th February requesting her to come before Saturday 12th February for interview. However, all did not go well with this visit, for on 12th February Mrs. Williams arrived to pay a visit of inspection and, having been met at Maldon Station, was taken to the school and school house where she 'expressed herself strongly at the dirt and sordid state of the school house,' and decided to withhold her decision until she had consulted with her husband. This somewhat ignominious start culminated on 18th February when Revd. Littlehales received '[an] impertinent letter from Mrs. Williams declining the offer of Headmistress.' Therefore, on 19th February Revd. Littlehales wrote to Miss Smeeton inviting her for an interview, but she replied that she had already accepted another post. The

129

position was re-advertised in *Teachers World* at a further cost of 4s 9d.

This resulted in an application from Mrs. Rose Margaret Jones of 4 Crediton Road, Willesden, London. She visited Langford on 4th March and Revd. Littlehales reported, 'I met her unexpectedly in the village and showed her over the School House. She created a favourable impression. I promised to place her application before the Managers.' Mrs. Jones was duly appointed at a salary of £75 per annum on 9th March 1916. Rent of the house was put at £8 per annum; Lord Byron having consented to reduce the rent 'until the salary had risen to reasonable proportion.' On 15th March the Managers informed Maldon District Sub-Committee that the supply teacher Mrs. Fraser was 'quite satisfactory.' In addition a Mr. William Chandler was asked to undertake the necessary repairs to School House.

On 31st March a letter was received from the Supplementary Teacher, Miss Gentry, resigning with effect from 1st May 1916, so this post was also advertised. Miss Ethel Mary Patten from Chelmsford Road, Purleigh was offered the post – she would cycle to work daily – at a salary of £30. Miss Patten said she would be at the school promptly at 8.45 on 1st May 1916. Mrs. Jones wrote on 22nd April to say she would be arriving and requested fires to be lit in all the rooms of the school house. Mrs. Bell, the school cleaner and caretaker who lived in Maldon Road, was instructed to do this.

The school opened on 1st May 1916 when Revd. Littlehales introduced Mrs. Jones and Miss Patten to the children. News was received that the Education Committee would not sanction £30 salary for Miss Patten, but would allow £24 in consideration of her cycling six miles each way. Revd. Littlehales showed the letter to Mrs. Jones and asked her to explain this to Miss Patten who, not unnaturally, showed great disappointment at the news, but said she would speak to her parents and would probably stay on. However, it was felt that if she declined to stay a recommendation should be made to the Secretary of the Education Committee for the £30 to be sanctioned. As it happened Miss Patten's parents were not willing for her to stay unless her salary was increased (they were looking for £26). Mrs. Jones said that she was pleased with her work and earnestness and Revd. Littlehales said he would recommend an increase in her salary. However, the Essex County Council board would not sanction this, but in the end Miss Patten agreed to stay on at the reduced rate.

At long last, notification was received from Chelmsford that the school clock had been overhauled and was now in perfect working order, and had been despatched to Maldon Station ready for collection. Later there were to be complaints that despite being sent for repair the School clock 'does not go.'

On 6th October Mrs. Jones noted:

> Revd. Littlehales visited the school this morning and he brought the news of the schools having won the attendance shield with an average of 95.8%

This must have given great satisfaction. On 10th October the Diocesan Inspection was held again, conducted by Revd. J.B. Plumptre, and a holiday was given to the children in the afternoon. His report graded the school with Marks of Merit for High Standard (very fair) and for infants (good). However, the report noted that with staff changes it was hardly fair to give the 'customary report' so Revd. Plumptre recorded:

> A short syllabus of work was offered for inspection which no doubt had been conscientiously taught, but the majority of the children were backward in answering though a few answered well. The infant class was well in hand and the little ones answered fairly well.

There was celebration later in the year when Langford School once again gained possession of the Maldon District

Attendance Shield (held at the time by North Fambridge School) for the highest average attendance in the District (95.8%) for the summer quarter ending 30th September. Mrs. Jones and her team were obviously proving very effective as they retained the shield again for the autumn quarter ending 31st December 1916. The School had held the Shield for six months and, as the children were attending splendidly, it was believed that only illness or accident would pull down their average low enough for them to lose it. It was greatly hoped that the Shield would be on the School walls for a long time to come.

In January 1917 Mrs. Jones was confined to her bed with influenza and the school was closed after prayers. This must have given the managers a few anxious moments with memories of Miss Calver still fresh in their minds – indeed they had just received notification of Miss Calver's next of kin.

On 13th June Mrs. Jones wrote to the managers for advice as to the action she should take in the event of a daylight air raid warning being given. The Managers present at the meeting that same day were of the opinion that only in the case of the near presence of enemy aircraft should the children be kept in the school buildings instead of being sent home after school hours. Mrs. Jones was given discretionary power of action in this matter. (It was also noted at this meeting that the school clock was 'quite useless' and it was suggested that a new clock be applied for.)

Having thought they had a clean register and a good chance of successfully retaining the Shield for good attendance, Sydney Challis came along to spoil the record. After being caned for 'disorderly conduct' on 16th March 1917, neither the Schoolmistress nor the school managers saw hide nor hair of him again. Six months later the Managers reported that Sydney's mother had applied for a Labour Exemption Certificate for the boy, but this was refused due to his poor attendance at school. The Managers took into account the fact that for four weeks Sydney had been suffering from pleurisy and begged the District Sub-Committee to reconsider.

On 12th September 1917 Mr. George Howlett of Bevis Hall, Langford was granted a permit to employ the boy from 1st November but, to the chagrin of the School Managers, his name had to be kept on the school register! Thereafter all hopes of keeping the prized Attendance Shield were dashed. Despite young master Challis's absence, the number of children attending the school in 1917 was forty-nine.

Presumably under pressure from the school managers, Sydney Challis' mother again applied for a Labour Exemption Certificate for her son, but this was refused on the grounds that in one year he had failed to make the required number of attendances. However, as he had been off for four weeks in that year with pleurisy, the District Sub-Committee felt that this ought to be taken into consideration. The boy had been away from school since 16th March 1917 and they pressed the District Council for a certificate as they considered him to be 'more beneficially employed on the land.'

Under the 1918 Education Act attendance at school became obligatory for all children up to the age of fourteen. The Act was conceived by Herbert Fisher (1865-1940), the Liberal MP, and included the introduction of medical inspections in school – the era of the 'Nit Nurse' had begun!

On 28th March the School closed at noon for the Easter holidays. Miss Patten asked for the half day to be with her brother who was going to the front the next day.

Although celebrating Empire Day was an annual event, the first to be recorded as cancelled due to bad weather was 24th May 1918. The weather was 'wet and stormy' so the event was postponed to the following Monday. On that day at 4 p.m. the children mustered in the school yard in the presence of a fair number of parents, and sang all together the following little prayer:

Sailor, Sailor on the deep,
Guarding me while I'm asleep,
Don't forget! The children pray
For your safety every day.

Soldier, who dost fight and die,
That no danger may come nigh:
Here another army stands,
The little army of joined hands.

Flying man, high up in air,
Thank you for your watchful care,
Shielding me: remember too,
That my little prayer shields you.

Prayers were then said for the King, his Sailors and Soldiers, by the Rector, who also addressed the children on the subject of 'Patriotism,' applying this duty to home and school life, as well as on behalf of their King and Country. Songs and recitations by the school children, young and old followed – the best of which was the Chorus on the 'Union Jack,' in which each group of children displayed the Cross of St. George, St. Patrick, St. Andrew and St. David, with the various emblems of the Empire's Dominions.

The meeting of the School Managers due to be held on 6th July was postponed to 23rd July to allow Mrs. Jones to attend her daughter's wedding. An interesting account of the proceedings was given in the parish magazine:

On August 22nd 1918, Langford Church was the scene of the wedding of Miss Winifred Edith Jones, daughter of Mr. & Mrs. Alfred Jones, of the School House, Langford, to Mr. Frederick Albert Card Linsell, of the R.A.F., just home from the front. A large number of friends were present at the ceremony.

The service, which was choral, was conducted by the Rector. The bride was given away by her father. Mr. J. Ellison, of Chelmsford, acted as 'Best Man,' and Miss Jones (in the costume of a landworker), was the only 'Bridesmaid.' Afterwards there was a gathering of relatives and friends in the Schoolroom, where the Breakfast was served, and the usual toasts were drunk. The happy pair left about 4.30 (not in an aeroplane, to the disappointment of some), for Danbury, where the Honeymoon was spent.

On 29th August the nurse visited the school and examined every child. She found Harry Everett 'verminous' and Victoria Dorking of Elm Cottages, Ulting, 'slightly so.' Mrs. Jones noted "These children have been warned." Victoria was to die in 1920 aged 8 although research to date has not discovered the reason for her early demise.

In September the children were given a half holiday to gather blackberries for the Government. During The Great War, children in England were given time off school to collect blackberries for the production of juice that was sent to soldiers to help maintain their health. Some of the juice was also used to make a dye. It is remarkable to record the amount of blackberries picked during September, and shows how many 'bramble bushes' were growing in the village at the time:

9th September – 25 lbs
11th September - 24½ lbs
13th September - 35½ lbs
16th September - 43½ lbs
18th September – 68 lbs
20th September - 72½ lbs
23rd September - 50 lbs

25th September - 83½ lbs
26th September – 43 lbs
27th September - 43 lbs

This went on into October, but the later amounts are not recorded.

The school shut for a week from 30th September for potato gathering.

On 19th October 1918 Mrs. Jones reported that half the children were away with influenza and wondered whether she should close the school, but it was decided that a decision would be taken after the weekend. However, on the following day Mrs. Jones was called up to London to her daughter, and reported that she would be unable to return in time to open the School on the Monday, so the children were assembled and, after prayers they were dismissed to their homes. As Mrs. Jones noted that she would not be back until the Wednesday it was decided to close the school for the week.

The following week only nineteen children were present as the doctors had forbidden those still convalescing to return until 4th November. The Secretary of the Education Committee was contacted for permission to close the school for another week, and this permission was granted, but the school was requested to provide a certificate of the number of children present on Monday 21st October.

With the ending of the war it would be assumed that some mention would be made in the school log, but there is nothing recorded at all.

1919 opened with torrential rain which caused widespread flooding and prevented many children from going to school for some time. Whilst the school was closed the hall was used for a rummage sale on 1st December, a Prisoners of War concert on 11th February 1919 and a Day School Children's Entertainment for the Waifs and Strays Society on 19th April.

There had also been so much pressure on a local supplier of coke and coal that on 7th December 1918 the Clerk wrote to Mr. Nicholas saying that 'Houghton has been most dilatory in executing the order for coke and coal' and requesting him to 'stir him up.' Things got so desperate that on 12th December Revd. Littlehales noted:

> Mrs. Jones reports that she has no coal with which to light the stove. I sent her down ½ cwt to go on with from my own stock. On 13th February 1919 a half ton of coal was delivered by Rult and Gutteridge by order of the Secretary. A quarter ton of coal and a quarter ton of coke was delivered by Houghton.

In March 1919 Mrs. Jones was again in bed with influenza for one week, so this was designated as a holiday for the school.

At a meeting of the Managers on 13th September it was agreed that Miss Patten was doing 'excellent work' and that Mrs. Jones was 'carrying on the school in a satisfactory and painstaking manner.' The Chairman suggested that an extra week should be granted in accordance with the King's Command to celebrate the restoration of Peace, and it was agreed that the school should close on 19th September and re-open again on 6th October.

Revd. Luard sent in the report of his visit to the School on 23rd September, noting that twenty-six children had been in the school at the time.

> Great pains are taken in religious training in both the rooms of this very small school and there is a very nice tone. The difficulty of teaching all ages in the same class is very great, and considering the conditions the result is very satisfactory. The children are evidently most interested in their lessons.

At a meeting of the Managers on 6th May it was noted that the outbreak of measles had caused an absence of seventeen out of the twenty-seven children, but that by closing the school the disease had been stamped out and a good attendance had been recorded when the school reopened on 3rd May.

Mrs. Jones advised the Managers on 16th September that Miss Patten had applied for a post at Mundon School. This was much closer to home, and she found the long journey to and from Langford very trying, and asked to be released as soon as possible. It was suggested that she should stay until after the Diocesan Inspection on 15th October. On the same day a letter was received from the Clerk of the District Sub-Committee concerning Miss Patten, and enclosing an application form from Miss Emily Maude Smith, of Maldon Road, Kelvedon. The following day Revd. Littlehales wrote to Miss Smith with particulars of the school, and was astonished that on the same day she paid a visit to the village and gave a very favourable impression. Revd. Littlehales reported that 'although she was older than I expected (39), she said she would send a written application as soon as she had considered everything.'

The formal application and testimonials were received the next day, saying that the least salary acceptable to her would be £77. Revd. Littlehales consulted the District Sub-Committee who responded that £70 would be payable with £5 increments to £100, so he wrote to Miss Smith saying that consideration would be given at the Managers' meeting on 2nd October. The Clerk of the meeting thought that her experience – she was trained to teach kindergarten – would justify the extra £7, but at the meeting Mr. Chalk expressed an opinion that the salary seemed large in view of the small numbers in the school. It would bring the total teaching bill to £300 a year for about twenty children and he thought that under the circumstances an assistant had better be dispensed with. The other Managers felt that it would not be in the best interests of the school to do away with an assistant and thought it unlikely that Mrs. Jones would agree to carry on the school alone. At the vote it was carried 2-1 that Miss Smith's application be agreed at a salary of £77. The Managers appointed Miss Smith to take the place of Miss Patten.

However, at the same time it was agreed that the attention of 'the higher authorities' be called to the small numbers in the school which made them hesitate to recommend this expensive assistant (the only applicant). However, the Managers felt they were only acting within their rights. An informal discussion followed in which it was stated that a good way to reduce the very high cost of the Education Rate would be to re-establish contributions by the parents towards the education of their children, as many of them could well afford to pay a small sum weekly. If the School Managers did report the very low number of children attending the school, then perhaps they did not think through the possible outcomes of their action, as within two years the school would be closed.

At the August 1920 meeting of the School Managers it was reported that a circular had been received from the National Society requesting that there be no handing over of buildings or closing down of the school without consulting the Society. Little notice seems to have been taken of this as the matter was not even on the agenda of the subsequent meeting. Again this would seem to indicate that the Managers had no idea that, already, the fate of this little village school was sealed.

So the report of the last Empire Day celebrations at the school was rather sombre:

In the morning we went through a short programme of song and recitations. Both Captain Ffinch [*a new School Manager and Churchwarden from Langford Meads*] and the Rector spoke to the children on citizenship etc.

Closed after saluting the flag and singing "God Save the King." Half holiday in the afternoon.

Celebrations at the school

As with all Church of England Schools, the County Board of Education was responsible for maintaining and provisioning the premises by way of grants. For example, the annual contribution for 1906 was £56. 0s 0d and by 1915 it was £83.13s. 8d. Local authorities had to consider very carefully whether or not to continue to support certain schools if their attendance levels fell sharply. Therefore, on 6th June 1921 the Elementary Education School Management Committee was asked to consider a recommendation that the County Committee cease to maintain Langford Church of England School.

The case was made on the basis that the number on the books had gradually decreased from forty-nine in July 1917 to only twenty in 1921. The case was further made that the majority of the children lived not more than a mile away from either Heybridge Council School or the Wickham Bishops Church of England School, and that all resided within 2¼ miles of one of those alternative schools, both of which had ample accommodation for the children. The approximate distances

140

from the homes of the children who attended Langford School to the nearest alternative Elementary School were:

	To Heybridge County School	To Wickham Bishops C.E. School
1 mile or less	11	3
1-1¼ miles	-	-
1¼-1½ miles	-	-
1½-1¾ miles	1	-
1¾-2 miles	4	-
2-2¼ miles	1	-

Total children 20

The schoolchildren in 1921 –
Ivy Parmenter first child in the back row on the left

To the Committee it was an open and shut case, and it was agreed to close Langford School and inform the Managers accordingly. The July 1921 issue of the parish magazine reported as follows:

A lot of talk was bandied about the parish relating to the school. Hints were given of the intention of the District Sub-Committee at Maldon, to recommend the closing of the school, owing, simply and solely, to the small number of children attending. The Managers had represented to the Essex Education Authority that they considered economy was to be aimed at in this and all districts in administering the Education Act.

The new scale of salaries, recommended by the Burnham Report had more than doubled the cost of maintenance of the schools, and Langford School was one of the small schools which had been marked down for closure with a view to exercising such economy.

While regretting the loss of the Langford Church School, as part of the corporate life of the parish, the Managers considered that they would be wrong to resist or place any difficulties in the way of the authorities, but had not yet taken steps or made any recommendations either way. In any case, should a definite decision to closure be arrived at, the consent of the Board of Education would have to be obtained, and at least three months would have to elapse before the order to close would take effect.

Meanwhile, Mrs. Jones and her assistant Miss Smith, were offered sincere regret that force of circumstances might oblige their departure from our midst and thanks were given to them both for their excellent services rendered to the School.

By the autumn of 1921 the decision had been reached and was communicated formally to the people of Langford through the medium of the parish magazine dated November 1921. It reported:

It is with great regret that we have to announce the closure of the School. A communication has been received from the Board of Education in London, sanctioning the closing of the School, owing to the small number of children attending. This was followed by a letter from the Essex Education Committee stating that the date of closure will be January 31st 1922. This is final. There is nothing to be done, but 'carry on' till then and say 'good bye' to the School.

It is regrettable that children have been deserting the school, so numbers have dwindled still further, making very 'cold cheer' for those that are left. Mrs. Jones is carrying on the School alone, (as Miss Smith left on September 30th to take up a post at Messing), and we sympathise with her at the state of things that must inevitably break up her home in Langford. We accord her our best thanks for her work in School among the children, and also for her activities in the Parish to further its social welfare. The Tennis Club, Girls' Club, Whist Drives and Entertainments, have benefited by her good-natured and unselfish energy and the Parish generally, and School in particular, will miss her when the time comes for her to leave.

The Revd. E.P. Luard paid his last visit of Inspection on 30th September 1921. The parish magazine quoted from that report in its November issue:

In spite of the handicap of diminished numbers, we have been able to report favourably on the work done during the past year. The last Diocesan Inspection of this dwindling School was made on September 30th when the children showed great interest in their religious lessons, and there was evidence of the care and thought given to the work of the Teachers. I regret the inevitable circumstances which compel the closing of the School which has for many years done valuable service in the teaching of religion on sound Church lines. Certificates awarded to: Willie French, Willie Challis and Lucy Cooper.

The fact that the School was closing had been made known to Lord Byron, and a letter was received from him expressing his regret that 'the circumstances' had necessitated this action. However, in reply to a request by the Rector, he kindly gave permission for the former schoolroom to be used as a Church Room for Parish meetings and entertainments. The parish magazine stated:

> We are most grateful to his Lordship for this permission and thank him warmly, as this will supply a long felt want, with a minimum of expenditure for fitting and furnishing the same. The School is dead. Long live the Parish Room.

Despite the imminent closure of Langford School the annual treat for the children still took place. On Wednesday, 28th December 1921 the members of the Day School enjoyed 'an excellent tea, after which a Bran Tub, which was filled with presents for each child, kindly provided by Lord Byron, proved a great attraction.' After the distribution of the presents, games into which the children 'entered heartily' were played until 6.30 p.m. Finally three cheers were given for Lord Byron and Mrs. Jones and with a parting gift of a bun and an orange, the children dispersed to their homes.

Langford School closed for good on 31st January 1922. Mrs. Jones was appointed to have charge of the Infant Department of the Church School at Bradwell-on-Sea and the Revd. Littlehales received the following letter from her when she had settled in to her new position:

> I was delighted with my testimonial from the people of Langford. Will you kindly let them know through the medium of the magazine, what great pleasure it has given me, and that I intend to have the list of subscribers mounted and framed – not that I shall need anything to remind me of Langford – as I have so many very happy associations to look back upon in connection with my life in the dear little village.

Her parting gift from the School Managers and the children took the form of 'a small, though handsome, silver inkstand.'

So it seemed that the village had lost its only seat of learning. This was certainly the case in terms of a Council or Church school (although of course Sunday school classes continued to be held at St. Giles') but in terms of *private* education the story (albeit brief) was just about to begin. Within 18 months, Mrs. Elizabeth Curtis had opened the exclusive 'Langford Grove School for Girls.' This elite teaching establishment was to remain at the Grove until the late 1930s.

Once the school was officially closed in 1922, the building was duly handed over to the community for use as a village/church hall, and for the next seventy-two years it was used for numerous purposes including Parochial Church Council meetings, elections, the Langford Men's Club, rummage and jumble sales, private and village parties, concerts, whist drives, wedding receptions, Jubilee celebrations and all manner of events you would normally expect to see in a building at the heart of the community.

The school as the Village Hall in the 1980s

But as time moved on, demands of the community changed and no less the demands on a hall fast outliving its usefulness. With the advent of television and other outside attractions, the village hall was used less and less for community activities, and the fact that there were no toilet

145

facilities except for the 'outside privies' which had long fallen into disrepair, questions were asked about the viability of the hall. Discussions took place about whether it was sensible to plough more and more resources into a leased building which was failing, or look for an alternative site. In the end it was decided to write to Lord Byron, who owned the hall and the surrounding land, to say that they wished to surrender the lease.

This had always been the expectation of those in the community involved with the hall. Subsequently over ten years of planning and hard work by a small number of dedicated and enthusiastic local people led to the establishment of a new Langford and Ulting Village Hall born out of a former cowshed in Hatfield Road, on land opposite the Maldon Golf Course road. This building had been bought from the Essex Water Company, and when the conversion was complete, it was highly praised, being described as 'one of the most attractive parish halls in the area.' It won Inkpen Downie Architecture & Design Ltd the Maldon and District Conservation and Design Award in 1996 for their conversion of this Victorian cowshed.

Officially opened on 5th November 1993 by District Councillor Mrs. Patricia Hermann, followed by a celebratory barbecue and fireworks display, the hall has gone from strength to strength, being regularly utilised by groups both within and without the parishes of Langford and Ulting, and at the time of writing it houses the Little Acorns Nursery School during the day.

The opening of the new hall was met with the same excitement and enthusiasm by the villagers in 1993 as the former hall had been when Lord Byron granted the first lease on the old school back in 1922. The building was sold to a private owner in late 1994 and was later converted into a private house called, not unsurprisingly, 'The Old School.'

The only remnant of 'education' that survives in the village are occasional lectures and an annual and well-established series of WEA (Workers' Educational Association) classes and lectures, usually held in the new village hall. There is also an annual Art Show which is very popular, showcasing the work of local artists and subjects.

CHAPTER FIVE
LANGFORD GROVE

As was noted earlier, it was the third Nicholas Wescomb who commissioned the building of Langford Grove, the construction of which was completed in 1782. The new building looked out over Langford Park which at the time was thickly wooded.

Langford Grove as a School in the 1930s

The architect of Langford Grove was John Johnson (1731-1814). Johnson was surveyor for the County of Essex and was to contribute much to the architectural landscape of the county, his other works including Terling Place (1772-1780), Bradwell Lodge (1781-1786), Hatfield Place (Hatfield Peverel) (1791-1795), the New School House, Felsted (1800) and the Shire Hall in Chelmsford (1790-1792). In addition, Johnson designed the White Bridge, near Moulsham Street in Chelmsford (1787) (near the former Caters building) and restored the cathedral church of St. Mary the Virgin, St. Peter and St. Cedd (1801-1803).

Langford Grove has been described as one of the best mid-Georgian houses in Essex. Indeed, Nikolaus Pevsner, in his work 'The Buildings of Essex' (1954) described 'The Grove,' as it was familiarly known, as:

> a very handsome building of white brick. Five bays and two-and-a-half storeys, with a splendid tripartite doorway entrance decorated with Coade stone [*an artificial, cast material made throughout the late 18th and early 19th centuries which, although man-made, looked very much like worked natural stone*] exactly like those of Bedford Square in London. Single-storeyed connecting passages and then three bay, pedimented outer pavilions. On the garden side the centre is a tripartite window, a Venetian window above it, and a three-bay pediment.

Unfortunately, anyone reading Pevsner's work who then travelled to Langford to view The Grove would have been disappointed as the main body of the building had been demolished in 1952. According to Duffield William Coller in *The People's History of Essex* (1861), the house stood in 'gardens with sloping lawns, sheets of water and a finely wooded park of some 120 acres.' A carved mask of 'Janus', an ancient Roman deity,

Langford Grove, The Gallery.

was featured on the keystone of the arch over the main doorway. (Janus was an ancient Roman divinity who guarded the gate or the door; because one goes out to begin an action. Janus became the god of beginnings and the god

149

of the first month (January). He is traditionally depicted with two faces, the second one at the back of the head.)

Langford Grove, The Old Case.

Inside the building there was a main staircase with a wrought-iron handrail and a curving screen of marbled columns on the upper landing. Burke and Savill (*Country Houses of East Anglia*, 1981) noted that the décor was completed with dainty painted ovals in the spandrels of the entrance hall.

Being justly proud of his new home Nicholas Wescomb lost little time in commissioning the artist and draughtsman, Thomas Sandby (1721-1798) from Nottingham, to paint landscapes of the house. Two different paintings (featured on the next page) are known to exist in private collections, but there may have been more.

On 9th August 1808, Nicholas Wescomb died intestate and The Grove passed to his widow Lucy, who lived there until her own death on 9th October 1835. It then passed to Lucy's widowed daughter-in-law, Mrs. Jane Wescomb, wife of the late Revd. William Wescomb, who had been Rector of St. Giles' Church, Langford, from 1813 to 1832.

The next occupants, who took a lease of The Grove from Jane Wescomb at £300 per annum, were John James Strutt, the second Lord Rayleigh and his seventeen-year old bride, Clara Elizabeth la Touch Vicars. In the autumn of 1844, Clara's brother, Captain Hedley Shafto Johnstone Vicars, who was serving in the 97th Regiment (later the Second

150

Battalion, the Royal West Kent Regiment) returned home to take leave of his family at Langford Grove before sailing to Corfu. Captain Vicars never returned to Langford receiving fatal wounds as he led his regiment into battle at Sebastopol in March 1855.

The Grove and the Water Gardens [Thomas Sandby]

The second painting by Sandby showing the Grove from the park

151

On 2nd May 1845, Lord and Lady Rayleigh and their family moved from The Grove to Terling Place which had not been lived in for five years. According to Charles Strutt, '[t]o the accompaniment of ringing bells and booming cannon [*the family*] received an enthusiastic welcome from the villagers.'

In 1851 Jane Wescomb's daughter, Mary Jane, married the Hon. Frederick Byron and they occupied The Grove as their 'seat' in Langford, although while Frederick lived, most of their time was spent in their London house. So by 1859, Major John Wardlaw had taken a lease of the premises. According to Walford's *County Families of the United Kingdom* (1865) Major Wardlaw was born in 1826 and educated at Winchester and the Royal Military Academy. He entered the Army in India in 1845, serving in the Sutlej Campaign at the battles of Moodkee and Ferozeshah and was severely wounded. He was retired in 1851 and, by 1869, was Deputy Lieutenant for Essex, and one of Her Majesty's Royal Body Guard of Scottish Archers and Exon [*one of the four officers*] of the Royal Body Guard of Yeoman of the Infantry Militia.

Langford Grove, Library

The Hon. Frederick Byron, who was the brother of George Anson Byron, the 8th Lord Byron, died on 4th April 1861, at 42 Eaton Grove, London, and was interred in the crypt under the north aisle in St. Giles' Church, Langford. On his death, his widow, the Hon. Mrs. Mary Jane Byron returned to The Grove.

In 1866 Captain William Swabey, hero of the Penninsula Wars, and regarded by some as the 'Father of the Royal Horse Artillery' is recorded as occupying The Grove. It is presumed that he took a lease of part of the building, but no details of him or the length of his occupancy of The Grove have yet been discovered. As he died on 6th February 1872 and is buried in St. Mary's Church, Langley, Berkshire, his tenancy was certainly not a long one.

Jane Wescomb died on 17th May 1868, and although we do not know where she was living at the time of her death, we do know that she, too, was interred in the crypt in Langford church when her daughter, the Hon. Mary Jane Byron and her grandson, Frederick Ernest Charles, lived at The Grove. In 1890 Frederick was appointed Rector of Langford, and by 1902 his sister, Miss Margaret Alice Byron, also lived there. From then on The Grove was used for Sunday school treats (see Chapter 2) and WI meetings. On 1st September 1909 Mary Jane Byron died and the ownership of The Grove passed to her son Frederick Ernest Charles, the Rector of St. Giles' Church, Langford.

He lived there until 1914 when he took up the post of Vicar of All Saints, Thrumpton, Nottinghamshire. In 1917 his brother George, the 9th Lord Byron, died without issue, and Frederick inherited the title of Lord Byron on his death.

In 1917 the *Kelly's Directory for Essex* listed Herbert William Wrangham Wilberforce as living at The Grove.

The Water Garden with the folly at the end

He was the great-grandson of William Wilberforce (1759-1833), the politician who, in 1807, had promoted a Bill in Parliament for the abolition of slavery. Herbert was born on 8th February 1864. *Burkes* (1938) lists him as Sir Herbert (he was knighted in 1931), B.A., LLB Cambs, J.P. Middx., Deputy Chairman of County of London Sessions, Chairman and past President of the All-England Lawn Tennis Club. He was also a stipendiary magistrate.

On 19th July 1919, courtesy of Mr. and Mrs. Wilberforce, the whole parish was entertained in the grounds of Langford Grove where, according to the August parish magazine: 'a thoroughly enjoyable afternoon was spent' by all who were able to attend.

An excellent tea was served to the children at 4.15, followed half-an-hour later by 'a sumptuous repast to the adults in the large Barn adjoining the stables.'

Langford Grove, In the Garden

At the conclusion of the meal, the Rector [*Revd. Charles Gough Littlehales*] proposed the health of His Majesty the King, and the National Anthem was sung. The rest of the afternoon was occupied by a full programme of sports 'energetically carried through by the Committee, some of the events causing great amusement to the less energetic of the visitors.' The Wilberforce family left Langford Grove in April 1923, and the March parish magazine noted:

> For nearly eight years they lived in the village and proved themselves in every way to be keenly interested in all parish doings, and the friends of all. For seven years Mr. Wilberforce ably filled the office of Churchwarden, and by his personal example and wise

counsels was of the greatest assistance in all church matters. Mrs. Wilberforce too, and her two daughters were active in all good works and devoted much time and energy to the social welfare of the village. Their familiar figures will be greatly missed in future, and we certainly feel that they, as a family, will be hard to replace, and it is with the greatest reluctance that we wish them all goodbye.

White Lodge in 1900 (The gentleman with the gun is reputed to be Sir Claude Champion de Crespigny).

Langford Grove boasted two 'Lodges' which guarded the entrances to the estate – East (White) Lodge, and West (Red) Lodge. White Lodge protected the Maypole Road entrance, and Red Lodge the Langford Road entrance. From the White Lodge entrance (shown above) the 'finely wooded park' is clearly visible – sadly no more.

The Red Lodge was so called because it was made of red bricks. Although the two lodges were similar in shape, they were made of completely different materials.

Both lodges are still in use, although they no longer 'guard' The Grove. Both lodges are also now much altered from their original state.

Red Lodge in the 1950s

In 1923 Mrs. Cecil (Elizabeth) Curtis took over the lease of the Grove and set up the Langford Grove School for Girls.

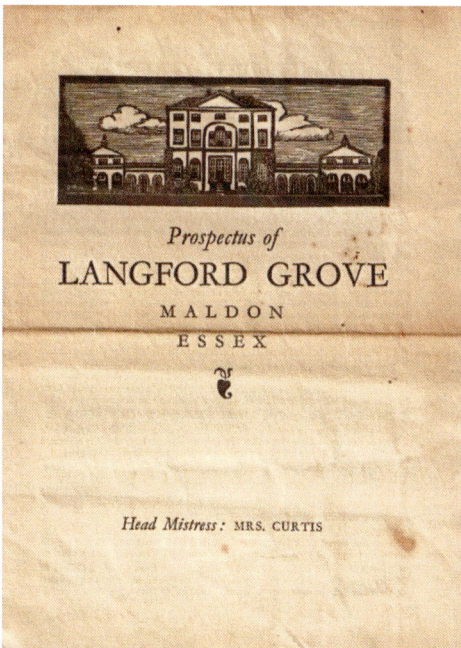

This school was for young ladies up to the age of 18 – an exclusive private boarding school attracting the daughters of wealthy parents, especially those from the continent, mainly France, Belgium and Germany. This large and imposing house with its extensive grounds was an ideal location for such an exclusive school. Until recently very little was known about The Grove's life as a school, but a copy of the prospectus helps illuminate this period of the house's history:

LANGFORD GROVE is a beautiful old house with Adams decorations. It is forty-five miles by road from London, and stands on gravel soil in a large park, with private grounds of thirty acres. The position is a very healthy one with wide stretches of country on all sides and bracing sea-air. It is two miles from Maldon, and within easy reach of sea bathing. There is accommodation for sixty girls. All the rooms are large and airy; the house is fitted with electric light and has central heating on the ground floor. The drainage is certified. There are large playing-fields and tennis-courts. Tennis and rounders are played in summer, and lacrosse in winter. The rainfall is one of the lowest, but water is laid on from Wickham Bishops.

- The chief aims of the School are to train girls to a sense of their future responsibilities, to give them the care and individual attention which it is impossible for larger schools to provide, and to combine the freedom and happiness of home-life with the discipline essential in a school.

- A broad education is given. The girls are taught to make full use of their reasoning powers, and each one is encouraged to develop her particular talents. There is a highly qualified staff which includes resident French and German mistresses. Visiting teachers come from London each week for Drawing, Music, Elocution, Dancing, and Fencing. The divisions for Modern Languages, Mathematics, and Classics are arranged apart from the forms for English subjects, thus ensuring correct grading according to the standard of each child. Debates upon topics of general interest are held from time to time.

- No work is done before breakfast or after supper, apart from an occasional practice.

- Particular care is given to the health of the girls. Great attention is paid to physical development and rhythmical movement, and as much time as possible is spent out of doors. Diet is considered carefully, and includes a great deal of fresh fruit, stoneground wholemeal bread, Grade A milk, and home-grown vegetables.

- The religious teaching of the School is according to the Church of England.

- The girls may go out once a month with their parents on Sunday for the whole day or at midday on Saturday which is a half-holiday. It is particularly requested that visitors should not come on other days except in unusual circumstances.

- In the upper forms the girls are prepared for Public Examination and for the Universities.

- Frequent concerts and lectures are held at the school, and the girls are some-times taken up to London for Exhibitions and performances of unusual interest, according to their parents' wishes.

- During the Summer Term a great many of the lessons are held out of doors, and picnics and expeditions are arranged. The school has a bathing hut on the estuary. Many of the girls sleep out of doors, on camp-beds, during the hot weather.

- There is a school orchestra, coached by a Professor from the Royal College of Music. The girls practice together during the week-end, and spend a good deal of their free time in dramatic work and in drawing in the studio.

The prospectus also outlined the fees:

SCHOOL FEES (*Per Term*)
* **RESIDENCE AND GENERAL EDUCATION:**
  For girls entering the school under thirteen years of age,
  FIFTY GUINEAS.
  For girls entering the school under fifteen years of age
  SIXTY GUINEAS.
  For girls entering the school at fifteen years of age and
  over
  SIXTY-FIVE GUINEAS.

  This includes the usual English subjects, French, Latin, German, Mathematics, Science, Class Singing, Drawing and Painting, Needlework, Drill, Voice Production, Stationery, Swedish Drill, Folk-Dancing, and Aural Training, Handwork for the juniors is also included in these fees. Those who take carpentry share the cost of materials.

  A charge of 7s 6d. a Term is made for Games.

  Medical Attendance, £1. 1s. 0d. Inclusive fees can be quoted for those who live abroad. A few Scholarships

160

are available. Sisters are accepted at slightly reduced terms when at school together.

- **EXTRA SUBJECTS.** *Fees (per Term)*

PIANO   from £5 13s 6d to £5 5 0
VIOLIN AND 'CELLO (Flute, Harp, Piccolo, &c.)
   (according to teacher)
DANCING   £2   5   0
ITALIAN, SPANISH   £2   2   0
RIDING (per lesson)   £0 10   6
FENCING   £2   2   0
ELOCUTION (private lessons)   £3 15   6

The Staff includes an experienced Matron, but in cases of illness, infections or otherwise, requiring a special Nurse her fee will be charged. A health certificate signed by the parent or guardian must be brought by each girl at the beginning of Term.

- Fees to be paid in advance at the beginning of each Term. A full Term's notice or payment of a Term's fees is required before the removal of a pupil. Any change in extra subjects must be made before the end of the preceding Term.
- No deduction is made for temporary absence.
- The School year is divided into three Terms, beginning about the last week in September, the middle of January, and the first week of May.
- Girls living at a distance from London can be met and escorted across London to and from Liverpool Street.
- Entire charge can be taken of those whose parents live abroad, and holidays arranged for them in England, France or Germany.
- Telephone number: Wickham Bishops 2.

A great list was given on the back of the prospectus of those to whom reference might be sought for the school including parents of past and present pupils, high ranking military personnel, members of the Peerage, and Bishops of the Church of England – a very impressive array.

Outdoor studies (weather permitting) were encouraged

But the school was, in many ways, less of an academic establishment, rather one with leanings towards the 'Bloomsbury set.' Angelica Garnett (neé Bell, the niece of Virginia Woolf) was at Langford Grove School from 1928 to Christmas 1935. In her autobiography *Deceived With Kindness – A Bloomsbury Childhood*, she wrote that her mother, Vanessa Bell, who had very liberal views about education, had rejected the thought of sending her to Cheltenham, Bedales or Roedean, and had enquired of her friends for a school 'as little resembling one as possible.' Angelica wrote:

> She finally chose Langford Grove, near Malden [*sic*] in Essex, which was run by an Irishwoman of character and charm, called Mrs Curtis, or Curty for short.

Vanessa, it seemed, believed her daughter would become an artist, like herself, and so persuaded Mrs. Curtis to let her drop any subject she cared to, with the result that she dropped games, and learned only music and the arts, history, French and English.

Angelica noted that after she had been at Langford for two or three years, Mrs. Curtis had fallen in love with Vanessa and Bloomsbury, becoming one of the first enthusiasts, and consequently Angelica, 'pursued by the reputation of her family' actually learned very little. She wrote:

> I could do no wrong and became the spoiled darling of the school, taking part in nearly all expeditions, concerts, theatricals and so forth at the expense of lessons. Enormously enjoyable, I can't say that it was entirely uninstructive. It was indeed an extraordinary school where one was dragged out of bed late at night to take part in a play by W.B. Yeats; where often, instead of going to church, one was prized out of the brown crocodile of waiting girls to go on a picnic with Curty or to spend the day with her son Dunstan on his yacht.

Favouritism indeed, but it appeared that Mrs Curtis also had a stricter side to her:

> Our venial sins were punished at intervals by Curty who gave us large chunks of 'Lycidas' or a piece of music to learn by heart – and yet we went in fear of her, dreading

163

her corrections, lightly handled though they were. The authority of the other teachers paled beside hers, and though no one ever said they went for nothing, none counted beside Curty. But she, presumably often bored by us, would disappear from view: we never saw her either go or return, but we knew from the general atmosphere that the mainspring of our lives was missing.

But not everyone at the school managed (or wished) to drop games from their curriculum, and the school had a thriving Lacrosse team.

Unfortunately we have no names of the girls or year the photo was taken

Angelica also described some of the other teachers at the school during her time there, noting:

Scientific subjects, never having been taught, were not in question, but excellence at maths or geography now went unnoticed compared with an inclination for drawing or the piano.

Other teachers at the time were Miss Baggs, the Deputy Headmistress, ('yellow and scraggy...with greasy hair wound into two plaits on either side of her head') who taught geography and mathematics; the artist and sculptor David Wynn began teaching one day a week at the school.

The Dining Room c. 1930s

The main Art Mistress was Mrs. H. Durrell, who propagated the child art movement in a similar way to Marion Richardson who, in 1915, published a drawing syllabus which was similar to the standard Board of Education drawing programme, but within a year she had begun to encourage her pupils to produce work with little instruction. She developed her own child-centred methods for teaching art which encouraged self expression and allowed the pupils to evaluate their own work. Other influential figures on teaching at the school included Herbert Read, Frances Hodgkins, Duncan Grant and Vanessa Bell herself. Miss Fischer Prout taught drawing and painting, the latter often to be seen:

> veiled like a muslim lady, wandering along the garden path or installed at her easel in the evening, her brush dipped in cadmium, painting by electric light, which was her speciality.

The sculptress, Gertrude Hermes, sent her daughter to Langford Grove School as well. In her book *The Sculpture of*

Gertrude Hermes published in 2011 [by Lund Humphries in association with The Henry Moore Foundation in Hertfordshire], Jane Hill wrote:

> The children went to boarding schools and Hermes was assisted with the fees (some £50 a term). Judith went to Langford Grove, near Maldon in Essex, a permissive, completely unusual girls school, run by a characterful Irish Woman, Mrs. Curtis. Duncan Grant and Vanessa Bell sent their daughter Angelica there (in 1928) as did the Crittals, J.B. Priestley and the Penrose family. Herbert Read and Frances Hodgkins visited at the invitation of the art mistress, Mrs. H. Durrell (neé Lazenby), who propagated the Child Art Movement based on pioneer Marion Richardson's child-centred methods for teaching art.

A Class Room - Langford Grove.

The school often gave exhibitions of their paintings, including one on 18th March 1938 in Witham Public Hall and many of the Langford Grove paintings are now held by the Julia Ramos (Langford Grove School) Collection. This contains forty-three paintings and drawings by pupils of Langford Grove School between the ages of nine and seventeen. It includes views of Langford Grove and other

166

locations, and the paintings were collected and donated by a former pupil at the school, and can be viewed at the Birmingham City University Art and Design Archives, Margaret Street, Birmingham.

An exhibition of children's art from the school was held at the Zwemmer Gallery in London in 1938, which Raymond Mortimer in *The Listener* described as 'Really ravishing paintings that one would love to own,' and T.W. Earp in the *Daily Telegraph* said it was '...the most exciting display of contemporary art at present on view.' Some of the paintings in the collection were also exhibited in the 1946 British Council Exhibition of British Children's Paintings. The creator of the collection, Julia Ramos (neé Rushbury) attended Langford Grove School as a child for a period from 1938.

Those who were gifted at music were sent to have piano lessons with Mrs. Smyth, 'a plump little lady in black satin and a noted teacher of children.' The violin was taught by 'a German Fräulein' who was very gifted and inspired her pupils, although she used to swear at her pupils in German when they went wrong!

Elizabeth Curtis was also a friend of Martin Shaw during the 1930s. Martin Shaw was a composer, educator, arranger and campaigner for the English Revival, and a great friend of the composer Ralph Vaughan Williams. He was a champion of folk music, and encouraged the school's curriculum which emphasised the creative arts: painting and drawing, dancing (eurythmics), and physical exercise.

Although Langford Grove was actually in the country, its proximity to London caused the school to be evacuated to Dorset, once in 1938 and again in 1939, when Shaw's daughter Mary Elizabeth attended it briefly.

Other influential and perhaps more well-known figures gave their time and expertise to Langford Grove School. In an article for *The Spectator* on 7th January 2007, Andrew Geddes recounted the relationship between his mother Margie and the poet John Betjeman, when he noted:

> He invited her to lunch at the Café Royal as a thank-you for arranging a lecture with Mrs. Curtis at Langford Grove School. 'You saved me financially,' he told her. 'I was down and out.' Mrs. Curtis told her later that he had spent most of his time on the roof looking at the leads and endlessly going to the loo on account of his nerves.

The school boasted an excellent orchestra, and many weekends were spent with Mrs. Curtis and her guests singing or playing chamber music. Angelica Garnett recalled:

> Thanks to her [*Mrs. Curtis*] we heard wonderful musicians: the Léner Quartet came to play to us more than once together with Albert Sammons, Emmanuel Feuerbach and a lovely Finnish singer called Lillequist, who looked like a seal in softest black; even, I believe, the Busch Quartet. All came to perform for us at Curty's enterprising invitation.

The school also entered the Instrumental Competitions organised by the Essex Musical Association which were held at The Corn Exchange in Chelmsford in May 1938 taking first and second places. However, in March 1939 Langford Grove pupils again entered the Instrumental Competitions, and although they were very good, they were often just beaten by the girls of King Edward VI Grammar School in Chelmsford.

In August 1925, the Wickham Bishops and Langford Parish Magazine recorded that, 'By the kind invitation of Mrs. Curtis, many of our people attended the excellent performance of *The Taming of the Shrew*, which was given by the girls of Langford Grove School, on Thursday afternoon on July 22nd.' The report continued:

The play was presented on the Front Lawn of the Grove, which was an appropriate stage. The audience was grouped under the Great Cedar tree and listened with wrapt [sic] attention to the performers as they unfolded the plot scene by scene. The acting reflected great credit on their coach and brought forth rounds of applause. Some pretty dances were introduced between some of the scenes which were very well done, and the brilliancy of the dresses of every shade and colour added a charm which it would be hard to surpass.

The Hall, Langford Grove.

That all enjoyed the play we are perfectly sure, and we accord our hearty thanks to Mrs. Curtis for her kind thought in inviting us to witness it, and also for conveying the older people to and fro in her car.

Katie Harvey (wife of Ron Harvey) was an Assistant Cook and later a housekeeper at Langford Grove. She said that Mrs. Curtis, (whom she described as 'a beautiful woman'), rented Langford Grove from Lord Byron (who owned the Langford Estate).

Langford Grove.

At the time Katie worked there Mrs. Curtis did not have a husband, but she did have a son, who lived in London, but came down to Langford for holidays. Mrs. Curtis had a studio built on to The Grove for her son with a flat above. When he came to Langford for holidays he and his friends stayed in the flat. No-one else was allowed to use the flat, except him. 'The Studio' was used by the girls for dance and art, and emphasis on this part of the curriculum increased after Mrs. Curtis was introduced to the 'Bloomsbury Set.' Angelica Garnett recalled:

> On expeditions to London I was nearly always of the party – indeed on several occasions Curty swept Vanessa [*her mother*] into her train and invaded her studio with groups of shy and giggling girls.

Such was the thrall that the Bloomsbury Set had upon the Headmistress of Langford Grove School.

The renowned British Artist Gwen Raverat (1885-1957) also taught for a while at Langford Grove School. Her biographer, Frances Spalding, wrote in her book *Gwen Raverat: Friends, Family and Affections,* that Gwen:

170

obtained a job teaching art one day a week at Langford Grove, a girls school run on somewhat idiosyncratic lines by a Mrs. Curtis, and at the same time continued to work as an artist and wood-engraver

Langford Grove.

But it was not only static art that appealed to Mrs. Curtis. 'Always beforehand with the world' she not only took her charges to see artists at work, but also took them to see *avant-garde* groups of actors from abroad, and encouraged her 'girls' to take an interest in the theatre.

When the Second World War broke out in September 1939, Mrs. Curtis closed the school, and the 'Dr. Barnardos' organisation took over The Grove. The parish magazine of October 1939 reported:

Langford Grove, used to the schoolgirl's stride across its threshold for the past 15 years, will, for the duration of the war, resound to the patter of younger feet. Dr. Barnardo's have taken over The Grove for evacuation purposes. They have moved 30 delicate toddlers under five and 14 babies under a year old from the danger zone at Barkingside to this quiet country mansion. Accompanying the younger children

171

are 27 older girls, who are completing their training for domestic service by helping with the housework and the care of the children. The Barnardo party, in charge of nurses and other helpers, were brought to The Grove in two London Transport buses.

Langford Grove, The Water Garden.

It was a sad sight to see them leave their Village Home, but their new quarters are rich in compensations. The children are all benefiting by the country air and the older girls are greatly appreciating the beauty of nature around them. All are happy in their new environment. One older girl, unconscious of the horrors of modern warfare, was heard to say she hoped the war would never cease, she was so happy in her new home!

But barely a year later, in June 1940, the parish magazine reported:

[The] Dr. Barnardos Home that had been stationed at Langford Grove had to leave on account of war conditions. They are greatly missed, always so ready and willing to help in any way that was of advantage to Church and parish, not forgetting their choir of girls. The Rector received a letter from the Governors

172

thanking him and the parish generally for the welcome extended to them during their stay in Langford.

It would appear that some of these children went to 'Five Corners,' a large house in Wickham Bishops as there was a Dr. Barnardo's Home there from 1940-1945. Presumably Langford Grove, being a much larger building, was deemed more suitable for the army than 'Five Corners'. Whatever the reason, it was a disastrous one for this beautiful building, and the Army's occupation heralded the first phase of the death of Langford Grove.

Little is known about the army's occupation of The Grove during the war years except that the headquarters of the supply column of the 15th Scottish Infantry Division was based there from late 1940 to early 1941, when it moved on to Hadleigh in Suffolk.

Having originally been formed in 1914 as the senior New Army Division and drawn from the second hundred thousand men raised by Lord Kitchener, the 15th (Scottish) Division had ceased to exist in the inter-war period and was only revived in the spring of 1939 as the duplicate Territorial Army Division of the 52nd (Lowland) Division. During the

Second World War the story of the 15th (Scottish) Division is marked by extensive training, charismatic commanders, excellent staff work, a first class fighting record and the unique honour of leading the final river crossing in Germany.

The Division trained in the United Kingdom in the early years of the war. Their Divisional uniform flash was an adaptation of the First World War flash but instead of a Scotch wedge they wore the lion rampant inside the letter 'O,' the fifteenth letter of the alphabet.

Mr. R. Forster was part of the 15th Scottish Infantry Division and remembers his time in Langford stating:

> The Headquarters of the Supply column was stationed at Langford Grove. This I regret was only for a short period prior to moving on to Hadleigh in Suffolk. The Division following the retreat of our troops from France returned to the defence of Scotland and remained there until the build up for the invasion in 1944. Landing on the Normandy beaches they fought in the Battle of Caen and following the break through carried on up to Nijmegen in Holland where everything was halted for the winter, eventually in the following spring finishing up in Germany.
>
> All my memories are pleasant because I had my wife staying with Mr. and Mrs. Chalk [*Ted and Lucy, of Brick House*]. I can well remember the walk down the estate into Langford village and the friendliness of all the people in the village, but especially our good friends Mr. and Mrs. Chalk.

Another couple said they owed their marriage to the Army's occupation of the Grove. Jack Gould, from Somerset, who was stationed there, met his future wife Violet Poney at a dance at Great Totham Village Hall in 1943.

174

On 10th April 1946 the Division was finally disbanded. Its battle casualties in killed, wounded and missing in twelve months of fighting amounted to 11,772. During the Division's time in Langford, locals recall the presence of wooden and inflatable tanks designed to fool enemy aircraft. Germany's 'Lord Haw-Haw' in his infamous propaganda broadcasts is supposed to have mentioned Langford Grove on at least two separate occasions. Local people also recall the day that a Heinkel was shot down and fell on the edge of Langford Park. The date was 24th August 1940 and contemporary records show that the military was quickly on the scene. [Readers interested in the Heinkel crash should consult local historian Stephen Nunn.]

Later in the war The Grove was turned into a convalescence hospital, and Janet Search (then a young Janet Clanachan), from Langford remembers men from The Grove coming into the village in blue suits, white shirts and with a red tie to signify that they were convalescents from the war.

The parish magazine of January 1945 noted:

> On Christmas morning at the early celebration we were glad to see the Sister and nurses from Langford Grove.

But no war lasts for ever. With the cessation of hostilities in 1945 a 'live committee' was set up to raise funds to provide a 'Welcome Home' to all Langford people who were serving with H.M. Forces. Strangely the condition was that only people who had lived in the parish 'for at least six months before the outbreak of war' qualified; thus discounting the troops then still currently billeted at Langford Grove.

175

After the war Mrs. Curtis wanted to re-open her girls' school but found the building beyond repair as a result of the army's occupation as these rather sad photographs show. Many wonderful old mansions had to be demolished as a result of being commandeered and occupied by the Army. It is sad to recall that buildings that had served their country should have been so ill-used. What on earth did they do to make them so uninhabitable?

The Byron family still owned the property and indeed, in a letter to the authors, Mrs. Barbara Evatt, niece-in-law of the 10th Lord Byron, said: "He had such happy memories of Langford, where he was Rector from 1891-1914 he had plans and hopes of restoring the Grove and moving back there.

Unfortunately illness and old age prevented this, and he died at the age of 88 in 1949."

But it was not only old age and illness that stopped the work – he also found the building in such a ruinous state that the cost of repair and renovation had become prohibitive. In the end he decided to sell The Grove and much of the surrounding land to Lt. Colonel Claude Granville Lancaster M.P., owner of Kelmarsh Hall in Northamptonshire.

Unbeknown to Lord Byron at the time, this decision would lead to the more or less total destruction of Langford Grove and the loss of yet another great house in Essex. These days, when 'restoration' projects are being undertaken to save threatened buildings throughout the country, it is very much to be regretted that Langford Grove, which had dominated the skyline in Langford for so many years, could not be saved.

Claude Granville Lancaster (1899 – 1977), known as 'Jubie,' (pictured left) was a British Army officer, Company Director and Conservative Party politician. His mother was Cecily Champion de Crespigny, eldest daughter of Sir Claude Champion de Crespigny, 4th Baronet.

He was educated at Eton College and the Royal Military College at Sandhurst. He served in the First World War as a Captain in the Royal Horse Guards and was Colonel of the Sherwood Foresters from 1939 to 1943. He was also a Chairman of B. A. Collieries Ltd until 1946, and Chairman and Managing Director of the Bestwood Company Ltd. In November 1938, he was elected as the Member of Parliament for Fylde in Lancashire, and he remained in Parliament until he retired in 1970, always sitting on the backbenches. In 1948 he married Nancy, a notable interior decorator and gardener. She was born Nancy Keene Perkins and had previously been married to Henry Field (he died) and

Ronald Tree (they divorced in 1947). Nancy and Claude divorced in 1953.

In 1953 Guy Lister of the firm of Strutt & Parker gave instructions to Gurton Brothers of Coggeshall to demolish The Grove, but to leave one of the outer pavilions remaining. This was to be used as a shooting lodge. Randolph Churchill used to visit Colonel Lancaster at Langford Grove where, according to local residents, there were 'Fast women, and slow horses.' Colonel Lancaster's butler, called Charles, used to arrive early before a party was held to prepare things for the guests. If it was to be a shooting party, local beaters were employed and they were paid thirty shillings for working the Saturday. During such shoots Gun Farm (formerly the 'Shoulder of Mutton' Inn) was used to provide meals for the party. The shooting parties came down on a Friday night, shot all day Saturday until 4.00 p.m. then were away on Sunday; Colonel Lancaster was only really ever in Langford at weekends. He came down to Langford by train and was picked up at the station.

The Langford Grove estate housed the 'Champion Apples' orchard, and a motor house was built that pumped water from the water gardens to irrigate the trees, and in 1959 the lake was dug out to provide much more water for irrigation. The area in front of the 'stage' that the school girls used (see pages 170 and 172) was lost to this as the lake was widened and deepened. The orchards were very beautiful and had vineyard tractors working between the rows. Ron Partridge, from Silver End, ran the orchards, which were next to the main house. The Coach House was in front of the walled garden.

Being related to the de Crespigny family, Col. Lancaster also had access to the de Crespigny estate which had thirty houses in Great Totham, including Keepers' Cottage, Warren Cottage and Gun Farm (which housed two of his employees – Ron Partridge and the Gamekeeper), and further cottages. One of the estate workers (unfortunately not named) was despatched to St. Peter's Church, Great Totham, and St. Andrew's Church, Hatfield Peverel, where some of the family are buried, with the task of keeping the graves and headstones clean and tidy.

The two estates employed a lot of local people –Fred Harding was in charge of forestry, along with his father George, Sam Herod, and a man named Maurice (whose surname is regrettably not known at this stage). Laurie Allen ran the chicken houses (which were at Totham Lodge), housing some 60,000 birds. They were kept till they were eleven weeks old when they were sent to Buxton. Basil Flegg ran the market garden end, John Clark was the 'agricultural man' and, as stated, Ron Partridge ran the Orchard which, as shown right, won several cups from 1960-1967.

Colonel Lancaster also kept Charolais cattle – solid white cows from central France (supposedly the first continental breed to be imported into Great Britain) – and Gordon Rugg from Scotland came to look after them. Once the Colonel died, the cattle were sold off and Gordon returned home.

Local legend (regrettably unsubstantiated) has it that Colonel Lancaster bulldozed the building himself after an argument with his sister Cicely (who was his heir). However, the truth is that, for whatever reason, almost the entire building was demolished on Lancaster's orders, motive(s) unknown.

During the demolition work Colonel Lancaster occupied the 'homestead' a converted farmhouse in the grounds of The Grove. Gurton Brothers carried away the rubble and villagers recalled marbled pillars being removed on the backs of lorries. According to local sources, one fireplace and the bookcases from the library were removed from The Grove and installed in Bradwell Lodge – perhaps a fitting resting place bearing in mind that John Johnson was responsible for designing this building as well as Langford Grove. It is also reported that one of the former corrugated classrooms was purchased by the owner of a café in Mill Road, Maldon. It is known that the bricks of this magnificent eighteenth-century building were used to construct a pair of twentieth-century semi-detached houses in Coggeshall, numbers 8 and 10 Kelvedon Road, and that the classroom (foreground of page 148) was removed and rebuilt as a private residence at the corner of Acacia Drive and Granger Avenue, Maldon.

A year later news of the demolition had still not reached the publishers of Pevsner's *Buildings of Essex* which continued to describe the building as it had been in its heyday. However, the note was added that, 'at the time of writing' the building was derelict. In fact, by the time Pevsner's revised edition had been published, the building had already been demolished.

In 1968 Norman Scarfe, in *Essex: A Shell Guide* made scant mention of The Grove, but managed to sum up his feelings in one short, sharp sentence which read 'one of John Johnson's urbane Essex houses, 1782, that alas our age demolished c. 1953.'

Colonel Lancaster remained the owner of The Grove until his death on 25th July 1977, when his sister, Cicely Valencia Lancaster inherited the estate, but she quickly sold it on. Lancaster's Will, announced in *The Times* of 5th June 1978, showed that he left £2,807,920 net. One obituary detailed his esteemed war service and his contribution to the coal and mining industry, pausing to remind readers that he was also a member of the Select Committee on Nationalised Industries and was Chairman of the inquiry into the activities of the Bank of England, set up in 1969. All very laudable, but very sadly, the people of Langford will only ever remember him as being the man responsible for destroying Langford Grove.

The classical bookcases and columns rescued from Langford Grove *in situ* in Bradwell Lodge

In 1981-82 the Langford Grove estate was split up and sold in lots, local farmers buying up parts of it – Home Farm bought the chicken houses, and the orchards were grubbed up.

The Grove prior to demolition

The remaining pavilion of Langford Grove was bought by Walter Cant, who lives there to this day (2013).

Phoenix from the Ashes?

In late 1988 Mr. Cant was approached by the local historian Stephen Nunn and Patrick Chaplin and asked whether they could undertake a 'dig' at The Grove to reveal the cellars of the building. He was eager to both approve and assist, and at the end of November digging began – the fourth member of the team being Barry 'The Mole' Carpenter. Mr. Cant also revealed his plans to rebuild the Grove, not to its previous grandiose size, but something just a little more modest.

The remaining outer pavilion with the excavated cellars.

However, in 1991 plans to restore Langford Grove to its original eighteenth-century style as a ninety-nine bedroom country hotel and sporting estate were put to Maldon District Council, but were opposed by '57 residents in the Langford area.' Langford and Ulting Parish Council had supported the project, believing it would bring new jobs to the area, but the proposal was rejected as being 'over the top'

An artist's impression of the proposed development

So the chance to restore Langford Grove to its former glory was lost.

CHAPTER SIX
COMMERCE AND TRADE

For hundreds of years Langford was an agricultural community where the main industry was farming, primarily the growing of wheat for the production of flour.

However, at the beginning of the nineteenth century the first signs of developing commerce emerged, a pub, the village shop, the blacksmith; all natural developments within villages up and down the country. In this chapter we look at the diversity of commerce in and around Langford.

Agriculture

Langford has always been an agricultural area with the estates of the local landowners providing work for the populace.

The whole area of the parish in 1837 was estimated at 901 acres (4,840 sq. yds) and three roods (a quarter of an acre): 503 acres and two roods were arable, 312 acres and one rood were meadow and pastureland, and the remaining 54 acres were woodland. The value in imperial Bushels (a British measure of capacity equal to 8 gallons (36.4 litres) used for corn, fruit, liquids etc,) and decimal parts of an Imperial Bushel of wheat, barley and oats at the time was:

Price per bushel		Bushels & Decimal parts
Shillings	Pence	
Wheat 7	¼	265.40060
Barley 3	11½	470.73685
Oats 2	9	677.57576

By 1848 Langford parish contained 1,076 acres, one rood and three perches of fertile land. (Due to the fact that, according to the *Oxford English Dictionary*, roods and perches varied locally it is impossible to translate those measures exactly. 1,076 acres is equal to 435.45 hectares.)

Spencer Thompson (of Black Cottages) in the fields

The land is fertile, free-draining (due to the high level of gravel) and grows many crops. But not every farm thrived of course, and many were sold off on the demise of their owners. The *Chelmsford Chronicle* of 1st March 1833 reported:

TO BE SOLD BY AUCTION BY BAKER & SON
On Tuesday, March 12th 1833, upon the Premises in Langford, Essex, by Direction of the Executors of John Luard, Esq., late of Maldon, in Essex, deceased. The valuable live and dead farming stock, upon Rickards Farm, in Langford; comprising 2 valuable cart horses and a 3-years-old cart colt; six very handsome polled cows with their calves, and down calving; two fat calves; two sows and pigs, two shoats, [*a shoat is a piglet that has been weaned*] a goat, two wagons, two tumbrils, three ploughs, two sets of harrows, stretch rollers, a light van, with pole and shafts, plough and cart harness, barn utensils, ladders, two stack frames on stone piers, a 60-gallon brewing copper, brewing tubs and utensils, beer casks, and various effects. A stack of grass hay, about 5 acres of turnips and cabbages, and

185

the straw arising from a stack of oats to be foddered on the premises.

All very valuable items, and shows the stock of a typical farm of the day. The make-up of Langford's agricultural input was of small farms under the control of one landlord. The names of farms, once familiar to villagers, are now merely names on old maps. Turners Farm was situated in the field between Stock Hall Farm and the road to the left of Orchard Cottages. Luards Farm in Ulting Lane was originally called Hawks Farm, and there were buildings (possibly barns) adjoining Bridge Cottages. Many other small farms have long disappeared; many because they were too small to survive, but some due to the vagaries of the weather – May 1872 was the wettest on record, and destroyed many crops. But it was Langford Hall Farm that provided the most in the way of employment and output.

Langford Hall in 2009

Langford Hall had not been built to any specific architectural rules, but had evolved over the years according to requirement, with three front rooms behind the Queen Anne façade – both upstairs and downstairs – and then a corridor parallel to the road with kitchen and other rooms downstairs and further bedrooms above. It had a large moated garden (part of which is still in existence) that ran down to the River Blackwater.

The need for agricultural workers was great in Langford, and up to the twentieth century was the greatest employer of manpower in the village. Housing had to be found for such workers, and in 1873 proposals were put forward by John Sampson Piggot (who was running Langford Mill at the time) for a series of workers' cottages designed by the architect Frederick Chancellor. Unfortunately Piggot was declared bankrupt before these plans could be put into operation which is a great pity as they would have enhanced the area. .

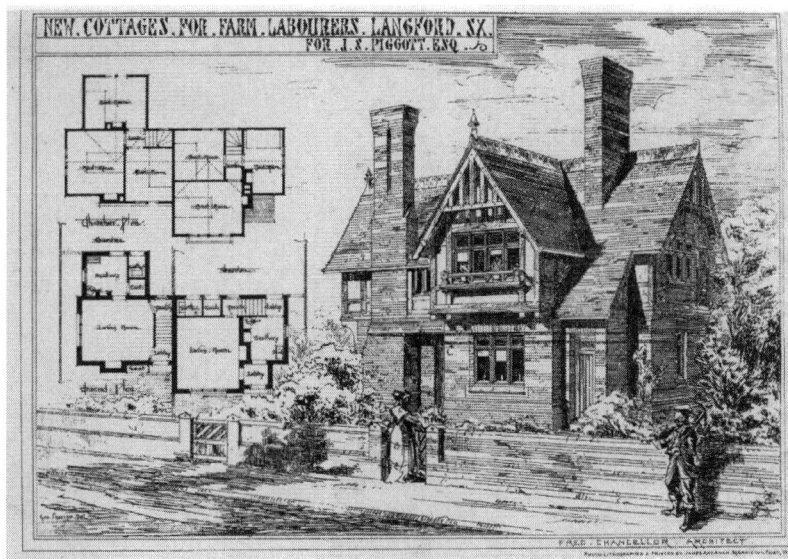

When John Wood, farmer, of Langford Hall, decided to leave the village, the *Chelmsford Chronicle* of 16th September 1887 noted:

LANGFORD HALL FARM
To let, from Michaelmas next, a superior occupation, including excellent residence, suitable agricultural buildings, four cottages, and 496 acres of land, of which 294 are grass, for many years in the occupation of Mr. John Wood and his family. The farm will be let as a

whole or subdivided. For particulars apply to Messrs. Beadel and Co., 97 Gresham Street, London EC.

Langford was in the news again when the *Essex Newsman* of 12th September 1891 reported on a new and innovative invention from Langford Hall:

A new automatic reverter for reaping and mowing machines has been invented by Mr. John C. Moore of Langford Hall. The apparatus consists of splints attached to two straps revolving on pulleys like an elevator, with wooden tines six inches long fixed to the splints so close that there is about one every superficial foot on the revolving part, which travels about one fifth faster than the machine. These tines lift and revert corn or grass into the proper position for the knife to cut it with ease to both horses and machine, and completely clear it off the ground. Hitherto such machines have only been capable of manipulating standing crops; but this invention, which can be attached to any mower or reaper, will cut beautifully any crop whether standing or badly laid.

Harvesting in Langford (whether or not by the new invention is unclear!)

Clearly, Langford was at the forefront of agricultural advance, and this invention was invaluable for crops flattened by rain or wind. The village also provided timber from the Langford Grove Estate, as shown by the following extract from the *Chelmsford Chronicle* of 18th March 1892:

> Messrs. Abrey and Gardner are favoured with instructions to sell by auction, on Wednesday and Thursday, March 30th and 31st 1892, at ten for eleven o'clock, the extensive fall of 170 Elm, Ash and Willow trees, together with a few winter-felled Oak, Poplar, Chestnut, Pear and Beech, with the topwood arising therefrom, as now lying most convenient for carriage near the high road, and the Chelmer and Blackwater Canal, and within a short distance of the G.E. Railway. The timber is well grown, and of great length, elm up to four loads, willow four loads, and ash two loads.

> The company are requested to meet the Auctioneers on Wednesday at Beavis Hall, upon the Hatfield Road, and on Thursday at the top park gate, Langford. A brake will meet the 10.40 train at Maldon each day for the convenience of purchasers.

> Further particulars and catalogues may be obtained of Perry, Estate Carpenter, Great Totham; or of the Auctioneers, Witham, Essex.

Alfred Lomas was the tenant at Langford Hall at the time, and he remained there from 1891 to 1899. Alfred was born in Islington in 1857 and from 1881 to 1884 attended the Agricultural College at Cirencester, where he won several prizes for his work.

At Langford Hall he was noted for his flock of thoroughbred sheep, many of which were prize-winning animals, but he was plagued with local sheep-worrying dogs, as was reported in the *Chelmsford Chronicle* of 11th August 1893:

THE

Essex Cleveland Bay Stud Farm.

THIS IS THE LARGEST STUD OF PURE-BRED "CLEVELAND BAYS" in the South of England, and has been established regardless of expense by the most careful selection and mating of the best mares that could be obtained to produce style and action; many are prize winners at The Royal, Great Yorkshire and Essex Agricultural Shows.

That celebrated Sire, **"Sultan, 667,"** the Champion Cleveland Bay of the world, has been extensively used.

The highest authorities agree that the Cleveland Bay Mare, having such a combination of Power, Bone, and Size, with Activity, Quality, Beauty, and Uniformity of Colour, forms a basis crossed with the Thoroughbred or Hackney, that produces the finest carriage horse that is known.

Inspection of Stud by appointment with—

Mr. ALFRED LOMAS,

LANGFORD HALL, MALDON.

Mr. Lomas has had his sheep worried for the last few days by a spaniel dog. He reported the matter to Supt. Halsey, with the result that the owners of the dog had the animal shot on Wednesday.

But perhaps Alfred Lomas was best known for setting up the famous 'Essex Cleveland Bay Stud.' As its name suggests, the Cleveland Bay emanates from the Cleveland area of North East England. Without doubt it is Britain's oldest breed of horse.

Alfred took a first prize with his mare 'Nellie Farren' at the Essex County Show which was held at Colchester the week of 11th June 1894. The mare was named after the famous English actress and singer (1848-1904), best known for her roles as the 'principal boy' in musical burlesques at the *Gaiety Theatre* at the time. Alfred also took a second prize with his pen of lambs.

The parish magazine of July 1894 noted: 'Langford did most creditably and praise is due not only to Mr. Lomas, but also to G. Coker, and F. Willsmore.' Alfred also entered 'Nellie Farren' at the Royal Agricultural Show, held at Cambridge, where she won 4th prize and, according to the parish magazine 'her foal was also much admired.' The following year Alfred took 1st prize at the Essex County Show with 'Nellie Farren' and for his ewe lambs. He was also showing at the 'Royal' at Darlington. But it was not only County Shows that were impressed with his stock. The parish magazine for November 1896 reported:

On Thursday October 15th, 1896, Major-General Sir Henry Ewart, KCB, Equerry to Her Majesty Queen Victoria, viewed Mr. Lomas' Cleveland Bay stud at Langford Hall, with a view to possible purchase for Her Majesty's stables. Although Mr. Lomas has not at the present moment any animal suitable for this purpose, Sir H. Ewart expressed himself much pleased with what he saw.

The *Chelmsford Chronicle* dated 16th October 1896 reported:

The Cleveland Bay is believed to be the original and indigenous horse of England, obtaining its name from Cleveland, in Yorkshire, which since the time of the Romans may be regarded as its mother country. Mr. Lomas – a very affable gentleman – possesses about 50 of these horses, carefully selected from the best blood, and of considerable value. Some eight of these were exhibited on the present occasion. Nellie Farren, the best mare on the farm, holds an unbeaten certificate as a hunter brood mare in Essex. Her owner has refused an offer of 500 guineas for her. She has dropped seven foals, all of which have been good. Five of these are on the farm now. Her prizes comprise a silver cup at Romford in 1893; 1st, Essex Show, Colchester, and reserve championship; highly commended at the Royal Show, Cambridge, in 1894; two firsts at Southend, in 1895; and – with a foal - £10 reward from the Hunters' Improvement Society, when unable to take the society's gold medal owing to the rules. All her prizes have been won as a hunter brood mare, out of her class as a

Cleveland, which speaks much in her favour. Ellen Terry, one of her stock, is a fine mare of four years. Next to her comes the three-year-old Queen of Beauty, a magnificent hunter-like Cleveland, who is the foal referred to above as having with her mother won the silver cup, and who was highly commended at Darlington last year, although suffering from an accident. Pride of the Village, a very large mare, standing about 17 hands high, and well proportioned, was purchased two years ago from the Duke of Hamilton. A typical Cleveland, muscular, and full of quality, is King Frederick the Great, the promising stallion of the stud. He is one of the five foals of Nellie Farren. For his sire 11,000 guineas was refused by Mr. Burdett Coutts. At the Yorkshire Show – considered the best in England for this class of horse – King Frederick secured first prize in the bay yearling stallion class, and the reserve for the championship for the best Cleveland bay stallion. The two-year-old King is a well-made horse with a "list," the sure sign of pure blood. Other animals shown included Queen, Drayman, and King of York. Sir Henry Ewart expressed himself much pleased with what he had seen.

The *Chelmsford Chronicle* of 18th February 1898 reported:

Mr. Alfred Lomas, M.R.A.C., of Langford Hall, Maldon, has been appointed by Mr. H.E.M. Davies, as his resident agent for the Herringswell and Cavenham estates. Mr. Lomas is a well-known authority upon forestry, is the owner of one of the largest studs of Cleveland Bays in England, and keeps a select flock of pedigree Suffolk sheep.

In April 1898, Alfred (pictured next page) married Ellen Denne, and the parish magazine noted:

Mr. Lomas has returned with Mrs. Lomas to Langford Hall, after their honeymoon, which was spent partly in visiting friends and partly in Paris.

But later in the year the couple decided to leave Langford Hall, and sell their stock. The *Chelmsford Chronicle* of 9th September gave advance warning of the items to be sold off which included:

37 Cleveland Bays
3 Farm Horses
13 Shorthorn Cows,
3 Shorthorn Bulls
61 Grazing Steers & Heifers
61 Black-faced Suffolk Sheep
60 Head of Swine
60 Head Silver-Grey Dorkings

And all the agricultural carriages, machinery, implements and harness. Sexton, Grimwade and Beck in conjunction with Mr. Ernest Prentice, are instructed by Mr. A. Lomas, who is leaving Essex, and retiring from farming, to sell by auction, on Wednesday 21st September 1898, the entire Live and dead farming stock. Sale to commence at eleven a.m. prompt, with the dead stock, cows, grazing stock, sheep, swine and poultry. An adjournment for luncheon at Two p.m. Sale of Cleveland Bays will commence at 2.45. Catalogues with pedigrees and descriptions may be obtained of the auctioneers, Colchester, Kings Lynn and Ipswich.

The celebrated flock of sheep belonging to Mr. Alfred Lomas, who is leaving Langford Hall shortly, was sold by Messrs. Bond and Son in conjunction with Mr.

Ernest Prentice, at their special Ipswich sale, on August 8th 1898. The top prices obtained per head for shearlings [*one- year old sheep from which one crop of wool has been taken*] was £12; two shear £5 15s; three shear £4 5s; ewe lambs £5; ram lambs £21. The total for 220 sheep was nearly £1,000."

The parish magazine also noted the prices:

Mr. Lomas, of Langford Hall, had a large sale of his stock, implements and horse on Wednesday September 21st [*1898*]. The sale was fairly well attended, large sums were realised for some of the horses, 'Frederick the Great' fetching £525, and 'Nelly [*sic*] Farren' £450. The whole sale of horses realised £2337. Mr. Wakelin, the new tenant at the Hall, will take up his residence early in October.

The *Chelmsford Chronicle* of 23rd September 1898 gave a very detailed description of the sale under the heading: 'Stock sale at Langford Hall – Thirty-five Cleveland Bays realise 2,377 guineas.'

In consequence of the impending departure from the county of Mr. A. Lomas, his famous stud of 35 Cleveland Bays, together with other farming stock, was submitted to public competition, without reserve, at Langford Hall, near Maldon, on Wednesday. This sale was conducted by Messrs. Sexton, Grimwade and Beck, in conjunction with Mr. Ernest Prentice, and it attracted a fairly good attendance of agriculturists, dealers, and others. A luncheon was served in a tent on the ground by Messrs. Wright and Son, of Colchester. Mr. Burdett Coutts, M.P., had promised to preside, but was unable to be present. In his absence the chair was occupied by Mr. Lomas, who was supported, among others, by the Hon. C.H. Strutt, M.P. for the division; Sir Claude Champion de Crespigny, Bart., Capt. Townsend, and Capt. White. At half-past two o'clock the horses came under the hammer. Mr. H. Grimwade, who occupied the rostrum, referred to the excellence of the animals, and observed that it was 20 years since an entire stud of Clevelands was offered to the public. The reason of the present sale was that Mr. Lomas had accepted the agency of the Herringswell and Cavenham estates, near Newmarket. The bidding was then commenced, a total of 2,377 guineas being realised.

The full list of the animals and equipment sold in this auction, and their final prices, is given in Appendix 2. It is hard, perhaps, for us to understand how he could bear to part with Nellie Farren after all the prizes she had won for him, but of course this was a commercial venture and as such sentimentality had no place, especially as he was about to move into a completely new sphere of work.

Frederick Wakelin and his family were the next residents at the Hall, although their time of occupation was somewhat fraught. Although he believed himself to be a 'farmer' in reality he preferred to go on grand tours with his friend Montague Hussey, staying in large country houses, it became all too clear that his lifestyle was leading to financial difficulties for his family.

Langford Hall from the Witham Road c. 1890

Frederick had married Fanny Bloxhall, of Maldon, in 1878 and moved to a house on Goldhanger Road, Heybridge, where they had two sons, William and Joseph. When Frederick's mother died, the family moved into Follyfaunts House in Goldhanger, but in 1880 tragedy struck when Joseph was killed in a gun accident. Five more children were born at Follyfaunts, then the family moved to Little Totham Hall, and then to Lofts Farmhouse before their move to Langford Hall.

Frederick Wakelin (pictured left) died in August 1906, of dropsy. ('Dropsy' was an old term for the swelling of soft tissues due to the accumulation of excess water.) His Will shows an estate amounting to £2,180 12s 1d, but after debts had been paid, the family was left in quite a bad financial state. The parish magazine described him as: 'a well-known and genial yeoman, who has occupied Langford Hall for about ten years. He recently celebrated his 51st birthday, and leaves a widow, four sons and four daughters.' It went on to note that Frederick had been a member of the Maldon Rural District Council, where his 'plain outspokenness was very characteristic and much appreciated.'

A sale, which was very well attended, was held on Monday 23rd September 1907 at Langford Hall. A large number of cattle, cows, horses, sheep, implements etc. were disposed of. '…This does not mean that there will be any change at the Hall, as Mrs. Wakelin and her family are still continuing at the farm.' Nevertheless, it must materially have made life very difficult for the family, as his widow, Fanny, had to find a way to support her family and to pay the debts left by her husband, together with the rent for the Hall to Lord Byron. In the end she sought advice from her friend Sir Claude

Champion de Crespigny, who advised her to take in paying guests to meet her financial obligations, and this she did. It was a successful operation, and Fanny managed to keep her head above water until 1915 when the family moved to Barrow Marsh Farm in Heybridge.

During the Wakelin family's difficulties, Messrs. Strutt & Parker became involved in Langford Hall Farm and ran it for Lord Byron. The parish magazine of July 1913 noted:

> Messrs. Strutt & Parker held their great sale of Dutch Cows at Langford Hall, on Tuesday 24th June, 1913. The show ground was in the meadow behind the Hall, between the farm buildings and the River Blackwater, where a grand stand, auction ring etc. were erected. A great many buyers arrived by road and by rail. The chief prices realised were: Black and white cow, Lavenham Auntie – 57 guineas; Black and white cow, Lavenham May – 50 guineas, Lavenham Kate – 40 guineas. Sixty-four lots realised the grand total of £1761.7.6.

In 1915 the Hall was used as a Rectory, and was occupied by the Revd. Charles Gough Littlehales until he left the village in 1931. According to the late Ron Harvey, who had spent most of his life in Langford, after the Littlehales family left the Hall it was occupied for about six months 'by some French people.'

In about 1930, Langford Hall passed into use as the bailiff's house. The occupant at this time was a George Cook, who had the supervision of 65 men – a number which suggests that the farm must still have had much the same acreage as it had done during the tenure of the Wood family.

In 1932 it was occupied by the Churhwarden, Major Claude Henry Tritton, OBE (1935-1950), and his wife. Claude was the fourth son of nine children born to the banker Joseph Herbert and Lucy Jane Tritton of Lyons Hall, Great Leighs. He was educated at Winchester, and in 1901 was Secretary of

197

an Electrical Engineering Company. Claude (pictured right) married Evelyn Mary Strutt (daughter of Edward Strutt of Terling Place) in 1906. He then went out to Kenya to begin a new life in Nairobi, where his first son was born. He tried various occupations without success, and later found his niche as a 'Big Game Guide' and lion hunter. He came back to the UK for World War I, and joined the RASC which at that time was transferring from horse to mechanised transport, although he spent most of his time in a rather unglamorous job in charge of an ammunition depot near Rouen. Whilst there he caught the flu that was endemic at that time, and nearly died from that rather than any military activity. He was awarded the O.B.E. in 1918.

After the war he worked for a time in Piccadilly at Roland Wards, a sort of Safari organisation. This eventually failed, and he bought an antique shop in Winchester, around 1930. Business however was fairly slow and he spent most of his time fishing on the River Wye, near Hereford. He packed in the antique shop in about 1936, and returned to Essex, renting Langford Hall from the Byrons. During World War II Claude ran the Langford contingent of the Maldon Home Guard, and was Chief Warden, based at Maldon Police Station.

The Trittons left Langford Hall in 1949 as it was required for Lady Anna Byron, widow of the Revd. Frederick Ernest Charles Byron, 10th Lord Byron (who died on 6th June 1949), when Thrumpton Hall was sold to George Seymour, nephew of Lady Byron, to clear family debts. Claude and his wife moved to London and lived in a flat at Lowndes Square, near Knightsbridge. He spent some while in a convent nursing home in Braintree towards the end of his life, and died on 8th February 1959. He is buried with the Tritton family at the Church of St. Mary, Great Leighs.

The electoral registers for 1963 show Langford Hall still in the occupation of Lady Anna, who was herself the daughter of an aristocratic clergyman, the Reverend Lord Charles Fitzroy. In her day the telephone number at Langford Hall was *Maldon 83.*

When Lady Anna died on 14th April 1966, Langford Hall became the home of Lt. Colonel (Richard) Geoffrey Gordon Byron (1899-1989) (pictured right) afterwards the 12th Lord Byron, who lived there with his second wife, Dorigen (d. 1985) and their children Richard and Robert. He had inherited Langford Hall under the will of Lord Byron.

The son of a Colonel in the King's Royal Rifle Corps (who won the DSO in the South African War), Geoffrey was born on 3rd November, 1899, and educated at Eton and Sandhurst. He joined the 4th Royal Irish Dragoon Guards a fortnight after the end of the Great War and subsequently he served with the Army of Occupation in Cologne. In 1922 the 4th was amalgamated with the 7th (the Princess Royal's) Dragoon Guards to form the 4th/7th Royal Dragoon Guards. After service in Ireland, the regiment was posted to India and stationed in Secunderabad. In the same year Geoffrey was appointed ADC to the Governor of Bombay, Sir George Lloyd. On his return to Britain in the 1930s he became adjutant of the Duke of Lancaster's Own Yeomanry in Manchester.

In 1937 he was appointed military secretary to the Governor-General of New Zealand, Lord Galway, and during this time he developed a deep affection for the country.

On 10th May, 1940, when Germany launched its invasion, Geoffrey was billeted with the Vicar of Verd, a small French village. (An amusing story connected to this is that when the regiment moved up to confront the invaders, Geoffrey left his wireless and his bicycle with the Vicar. Four years later, when he was commanding the regiment in the north-west Europe campaign, he found himself in the vicinity of Verd and so visited the Vicar. His wireless was returned to him, but he found his bicycle had been commandeered by the Germans!)

In 1942 he took command of the 4th/7th and displayed exceptional skill in training for a new and untested type of warfare, and it is believed that few could have achieved as much as he did. Later, when the regiment was in action, it was noted that Geoffrey never lost his equanimity under the most intense pressure and in the most hazardous situations. He was in command of the 4th/7th when they landed on Gold Beach in the first wave of the assault on Normandy on D-Day, 6th June, 1944. Equipped with amphibious Sherman tanks, the regiment had the complicated task of comingashore in the centre of the landing area, where the sea was very rough and he tide and he tide and he tide high enough to conceal the lethal underwater obstacles which the Germans had (very thoughtfully) provided. Geoffrey dispayed courage and composure which became legendary, and for which he was awarded the DSO. He continued to command the regiment in its advance through northern France, displaying the same indifference to personal danger and unwavering attention to the efficieny and well-being of his men. Geoffrey was a tall, lean, aristocratic figure, and although extremely modest and shy, he had great charm and had the welfare of others at heart, particularly when commanding troops.

In September, 1944, he returned to England where he was engaged in training, and he retired in 1948. Soon afterwards he inherited the Langford estate from Lady Byron, and succeeded his kinsman, the 11th Lord Byron, who had been a grazier in Western Australia in 1983. At that stage there were still about 450 acres and quite a few cottages, including those lived in by the Hanner brothers who were the tenant farmers. Red Lodge, White Lodge and other cottages were sold off during Geoffrey's time. His first marriage to Margaret Steuart, was dissolved in 1945; his second wife, the former Dorigen Esdaile died in 1985, and his eldest son, Richard, was killed in an air crash in 1985 aged 37, and is buried at

Timbuctoo. His younger son Robin (pictured right with his wife Robyn and daughter Caroline outside Langford Hall) is now the 13th Lord Byron. (Geoffrey died on 15th June 1989.)

In 1983 the Langford Hall Estate was acquired from Lord Byron by Edward and Margaret Watson, who run it as Watson Farms, and live in the Hall to this day. They are active members of the church and the community.

The Weather

The weather played a major role in both village and agricultural life. Today a major concern is global warming, but Langford's weather over the last couple of centuries has been varied, and sometimes violent, and the agricultural life (and livelihoods) of the villagers has been very much affected by it. The *Chelmsford Chronicle* of 29th June 1883 reported:

> During the storm on Monday six sheep and a lamb, part of a flock belonging to Mr. John Wood, of Langford, took refuge under a tree, and a flash of lightning barked

the tree and killed the seven animals. The only apparent mark was a slight singeing of the lamb's wool.

A further example of the vagaries of the weather appeared in the first-ever issue of the *Wickham Bishops and Langford Parish Magazine* that was published in 1894. It recorded that the hay harvest had begun on 24th June with 'a very valuable yield' being expected. However, pea-picking had also started 'although great damage has been done to the crops by the severe frost at the end of May.'

But the *Essex Standard* of 5th May 1894 declared: 'Best and cheapest manure is native guano' – a statement substantiated by Walter Smee, of Langford, who said he used it for wheat on very poor land. Results: 'Very satisfactory; quite satisfied.'

The parish magazine reported that the hay crops of 1894 were exceptionally fine, it being 'wonderful that a great deal of hay had been got in [in July] without a drop of rain.' However, barely had these words been written before Langford was visited in the beginning of August by a storm of extraordinary violence. The rainfall, which lasted an hour and a half, amounted to no less than 1¾ inches (4.5cm) which flooded the village. The great promise of plenty was marred by the continuous rain, and in places the corn speared badly. Fine drying weather was needed for completing harvest operations, but another storm in September 1894 caused further havoc.

Later, in November 1894, an astonishing amount of rain fell and the Blackwater and Chelmer valleys were under water but, miraculously, Langford escaped this deluge and no serious damage was done. That autumn was also remarkable for the entire absence of frost, the lowest temperature recorded being about six degrees.

However, over the New Year 1894/95 there was a marked change in the weather. The peculiarly mild winter suddenly turned into one of intense cold; the water became coated with ice and snow also fell. This continued through January, and the intense cold had a detrimental effect on the labouring classes because the ground was so hard that farmers could find little for their men to do on the land. However, February 1895 saw a change from the intense cold to milder weather; this clearly improved as the year progressed, as the parish magazine for August 1895 noted that 'the continuous rain of one weekend in July did an immense amount of good to crops of all sorts, having been the first continuous rain since April, and therefore badly needed.' In that year harvesting in the village began at the end of July.

Tuesday 24th September 1895 was registered in London as being the hottest day of what was a gloriously warm summer. The heat of September was the highest ever recorded for that month in any year. October 1895 was more than usually varied: the heat (of extraordinary intensity for the season) was followed by cold of equal severity, when the thermometer went as low as 23 degrees Farenheit (or 9 degrees of frost). There was still a great deal of rain expected, as the fall for the year had been comparatively small. The trees still presented an extraordinary appearance, according to the November parish magazine 'being for the most part in full summer foliage, due no doubt to the extraordinary heat of September.' This was to lead to problems later in the year as the parish magazine reported that the absence of berries from the holly in December 1895 'made it difficult to give as bright an appearance to the Christmas decorations in church as usual.'

But among the reports of bad (or good) weather, the *Essex Newsman* of 7th November 1896 also reported:

The Essex Technical Instruction Committee have selected the following to receive a course of instruction in horticulture at the Laboratory, Duke Street, Chelmsford: H.W. Ager, Langford; H. Miller,

Heybridge [*There were 14 others from the east London area.*]

This was quite an achievement and an upward step for Harry Ager, although he later threw it in and joined the Church Army. Perhaps his change in choice of career was less fraught than farming, for in 1896 Essex was visited by drought. Springs and shallow wells failed during the summer and in many rural areas water supplies were deficient. But February 1897 was very different as was reported in the parish magazine the next month:

> The heavy rains following upon a heavy fall of snow caused the worst flood that had visited Langford for 10 years, and one of the worst floods ever remembered. The water rose at an incredible pace, and completely cut off the two halves of the village from each other, one or two of the inhabitants of the upper end who had gone into Maldon to shop were unable to return to their homes, the raised footways being submerged to some depth. Thousands of acres along the rivers Chelmer and Blackwater being under water, all this great stream had necessarily to pass through Langford. The river above the Mill overflowed its banks, the water pouring across the meadows in front of Langford Hall, placing the Church and the Mill on an island, tearing up the road, and even entering the club room. Little or no damage was however fortunately done beyond that done to the roadway.

In June 1897 a terrific storm, probably one of the most terrible that had ever visited England, hit Langford. However, miraculously, Langford was spared any serious injury from the storm, which devastated 100 square miles of Essex from West to East, leaving a track of ruin behind it. Langford's toll was the death of one sheep by lightning, and the washing up of a few loads of gravel. The main storm divided into two parts, one going off towards Braxted and the other following

Danbury Hill, thereby leaving Langford in the centre comparatively unharmed. The Langford collection towards the fund to help those who suffered so severely in the 'Essex Tornado' as it became known, amounted to £7.6s. – a very generous sum for so small a village.

Then the snow of early 1900 was succeeded by a rapid thaw which produced a great flood at Langford, the water, on Sunday 18th March being higher than it had been for several years.

A surplus of water was also the main problem three years later, when very heavy rain fell during the first two weeks of June, resulting in the most serious summer flood that had occurred for many years. But the parish magazine reported, more optimistically, that the rain 'did great good.' However, owing to the lateness of the year and the very unsettled weather, the harvest dragged on and by August it had still not been gathered in. The parish magazine remained hopeful stating 'In Essex at least there is more hope than in the North where the crops are, to a large extent, still green and the outlook is very gloomy'; 1903 turned out to be the wettest on record for Langford so far.

There is little information to hand about 1904 and 1905, but March 1906 was very cold indeed, and one of the heaviest snow storms on record occurred during Christmas week. But by the New Year 1906/07 a rapid thaw set in which was followed by yet another serious flood. Fortunately for the village, things improved through the year and the harvest of 1907 was completed during September, the weather having been 'magnificent.' As far as the landowners and people of Langford were concerned it had been a quite exceptional year, as the crop yield had been extremely good and prices had considerably hardened, the parish magazine recording 'White wheat is, at the present time, averaging 40/- per quarter and red wheat 34/- per quarter.' ['Red wheat' was seen as a 'wheat, able to tolerate wetter conditions, but 'white wheat' gave a higher yield of flour.]

Essential to the success of the harvest were the children, and this is first recorded in the parish magazine in its issue dated July 1908 when mention was made of the school breaking up for a six week pea-picking and fruiting holiday. It also recorded that peas were not so plentiful this season and that the 'strangers' (itinerant agricultural workers) normally engaged in pea-picking were conspicuous by their absence.

The weather in June 1911 was ideal except for a few lapses into winter conditions. There was a great promise of fruit, and most crops, with the exception of the hay crop, looked remarkably well. A magnificent rain, lasting fourteen hours, on Sunday 14th June had an excellent effect. July 1911 was probably one of the warmest and driest summers recorded. The thermometer on one day reached 92 degrees Fahrenheit in the shade. The rainfall was practically nil and consequently the harvest ripened extraordinarily early and, at the end of July, harvesting was already in full swing. Whilst many villages and farms in the area were suffering severely from the lack of water due to drought conditions, Langford was unusually lucky and did not suffer.

Reference was made earlier to strangers who arrived every year in the village for the pea-picking. They lived how and where they could whilst in the village, their 'homes' often being the hedges and ditches but this was clearly unhealthy and moves were made to provide suitable accommodation for them. In 1912 a 'pea-pickers camp' under the Peapickers'

Mission was established. This was an organised camp set up at the western end of the village at 'The Elms' by permission of Silas Greenslade, the owner, under the charge of a party of gentlemen from the University of Cambridge, assisted by ladies of the parish who volunteered to help in the work. Bell tents were erected on site for pea-pickers to sleep in. The parish magazine noted: 'The blessing which this admirable organisation gives to unfortunate homeless pickers is beyond words, and it is also in many ways a great advantage to the resident neighbourhood. Cast off clothes were received in the mission tent for the pickers.' Not only did the 'Peapicker's Mission' afford shelter to these seasonal workers, but it also ensured that the 'pickers' were kept in one place and under supervision.

In 1914, the weather again took a turn for the worse. The parish magazine of April that year reported:

> Not for 30 years has Langford been visited by such floods as occurred during March, and for March they were probably unique. On one day the water at the White Bridge over the River Blackwater rose well over the foot-bridge which was provided in case of floods. On the Chelmer the floods were equally severe. For a neighbourhood which bears the record for being the driest in England, this isn't bad for the month of March – the month of dust! Perhaps in consequence of this unwonted wet, there has been a very marked outbreak of influenza in the parish.

It is surprising that very little has been recorded about the effect of the Great War on the agriculture of Langford. As so many of its young men went off to fight (twenty-nine in total), the task of working the fields would have fallen to old men and boys and perhaps women too.

In September 1917 the parish magazine recorded:

The harvest progresses slowly but steadily, but has been interrupted by unsettled weather and extra time has been needed to clear the fields of corn. It was feared that the rainy fortnight at the beginning of September had damaged what would otherwise have been a fine example of grain. It is proposed to hold the Harvest thanksgiving service on Thursday September 20th and the following Sunday.

The year 1918 seems to have had its problems too as, owing to unfavourable weather, the harvest operations were so delayed that the Harvest Thanksgiving Service, originally fixed for 22nd September was postponed until Wednesday 2nd October. Autumn was setting in as the parish magazine recorded:

In spite of a dark night a splendid congregation assembled and joined heartily in the bright service, and testified their thankfulness for an unusually bountiful harvest, which the whole nation will reap an inestimable benefit in this time of difficulty of transport and world shortage.

With the end of the war and the return of Langford's servicemen, agricultural practices picked up and the harvest operations in 1919 were carried on almost uninterrupted in wonderful weather 'the blazing sun producing a fine quality grain.'

The 1919 Harvest Thanksgiving Service was held on Thursday 18th September. The church was fairly full, but the parish magazine regretted that 'so few of the men who are so closely connected with the harvest, join in this service in God's house.' The collections on the day and the Sunday following amounted to £6.10s.5d which was sent to the Chelmsford and Colchester Hospitals.

Three years later the 'blazing sun' caused problems. In June 1922, because of another long drought, prayers were offered up in church for rain, and it seemed that they were heard, for a break in the drought occurred. The parish magazine welcomed 'some splendid showers' which 'had beneficial effects on the field and garden crops' but added gloomily that 'the ground is so dry that nothing but several hours of heavy rain will have a lasting effect.'

The drought continued into the following year for:

> owing to the intense heat and prolonged drought, Harvest operations were terminated early the corn harvest having been got up in splendid conditions.

Between 1922 and 1933 there were no further reports of any devastating droughts or deluges but there was another dry period in 1933 which led to flowers not being so plentiful.

However, farmers were being charged drainage rates at this time, and several summonses for non-payment of this rate were made, one of whom was Walter Harry Chalk. The general complaint was that the work done had not been of any particular value to the owners concerned, and the charges should have been spread over a wider area. The *Chelmsford Chronicle* of 3rd August 1928 reported:

> In the case of Mr. W.H. Chalk of Langford, the sum due was £13 9s. 8d. – Mr. Chalk said he objected to pay one portion of the rate because his land was assessed 50 percent higher than his neighbours. The work done was unnecessary, and did no good whatever. The flood in January he asserted proved that the work was absolutely futile. The Chairman: Do you suggest you want something more done? Mr. Chalk: No. I think the Board should be abolished altogether. The Chairman said he would like to point out to the ratepayers that the Board were anxious to clear up the whole of the arrears of the rate. This had to be done before Michaelmas. It was their duty to do it and their intention to carry it out. The Board were only public servants, trying to carry

out their duty. Mr. Chalk: I think this drainage rate is one of the worst impositions that any body of men has been allowed to take place on the unfortunate ratepayers.

Mr. W.F. Wakelin, Heybridge [*formerly of Langford Hall*], whose rate amounted to £8. 7. 11. said his land was flooded nearly the whole of last winter. It was not reasonable to have to pay a drainage rate when land was flooded for weeks on end, so much so that a boat could be rowed across it.

Mr J. Parish, vice-Chairman, pointed out that last autumn and winter were particularly wet, and low-lying land was flooded to a greater extent than for the past 25 years. Mr. Wakelin said he supposed he would have to pay.

Throughout these droughts and deluges the farmers and villagers coped and continued to produce wheat, barley, oats and peas, etc. and so it remains today although of course modern farming methods, equipment and pesticides have reduced to practically nothing the number of 'hands' and 'strangers' required to bring in the crops.

Walter Harry Chalk (c. 1908) with his children Norman, Walter Edward, and Ellen Mary

Back in the early days as the wheat was being gathered in, much of it was processed at the Mill. But it wasn't only arable crops that were of interest in Langford. The *Chelmsford Chronicle* of 30th July 1937, reported on a 'Prolific Cow':

> Lavenham Chancery 3rd, a 12-year old British Friesian cow owned by Messrs. Strutt and Parker, and housed at Langford Hall Farm, has in 365 days given 3,008 gallons of milk. For the second year in succession this prolific cow has given over 3,000 gallons. She holds the record of having given 73 tons of milk by the time she was 11½ years old. Last year she was the highest yielder in Essex.

Langford Mill

According to the Domesday Book (1086) there was 'one mill' recorded at Langford and no evidence has yet been found by the authors to suggest that it has ever been sited anywhere else other than its present location – a few yards to the west of the church of St. Giles'.

Langford Mill worked with the aid of the River Blackwater, but its affairs were also inextricably linked with those of the River Chelmer, not only industrially and geographically but also socially. At Langford the spirit of mercantile enterprise was grasped with both hands, for while most of the Chelmer mills waited for the construction of the canal to prompt their development, Nicholas Wescomb, owner of Langford Mill, anticipated it.

Various mills would have occupied the site for the previous seven centuries but in 1776 comes evidence of new build. According to a diary entry that year by John Crozier, a Maldon Miller, 'Mr. Parmenter came to Lan[g]ford mill in Essex, pull'd it down and new built it under a lease from Nicholas Westcombe, Esq' In the same diary in March 1782 Crozier records a later operator of the mill and gives an insight of the local amusements and the nature of the miller at that time:

> Mr. Dean of Langford Mill came to ask my father how he did; about 4 o'clock they sat down to a game of all fours; [*also known as High-Low-Jack or Seven Up, 'All Fours' is an English tavern trick-taking card game that was popular as a gambling game until the end of the 19th century*] they kept at it till 2 in the morning; retir'd and the next morning began again after breakfast; played all day Friday and till night. Next day played till 12 o'clock; then betook themselves to Maldon market after a very social set to. I recite this only as a novelty with my father, who never did any such thing in the course of his life, being a man of very opposite cast.

Clearly, on this occasion at least Mr. Dean was a bad influence on John Crozier's father.

During the years up to 1782 Nicholas Wescomb was not only planning and seeing to fruition the construction of Langford Grove on the nearby Langford Park, but he was also developing long-term plans for his Mill. Wescomb anticipated the economic advantages of having the most efficient access by water to London's markets. But for as many years as a mill had stood on the site it was fed by and worked on the River Blackwater, and there was no effective navigable direct link from Langford Mill to where freshwater met the salt water at Beeleigh. Wescomb knew that the Chelmer and Blackwater Navigation Canal was planned, so he arranged for a survey to be undertaken of the Blackwater from his Mill to the Chelmer below Beeleigh to see if the navigable link could be achieved. The plan eventually emerged as the construction of a 'Cut' which began in November 1792 and was undertaken by Samuel Wright, Millwright of Ipswich; the land through which the Cut was to run having been purchased by Wescomb. The Cut generally followed the course of what was then the River Blackwater which met the Chelmer at Beeleigh and thence to Maldon and the sea. (The port of Maldon, less than two miles away by water, was the chief outlet for corn on its way to London.)

Langford Cut was completed by early 1793 as far as the intended lock through which boats were to be lowered into the River Chelmer. The Chelmer and Blackwater Navigation Company (CBNC) found itself confronted with a new channel dug across the path of their projected canal, and two feet higher than their own. They solved this problem by paying Wescomb to dig his ditch two feet deeper. Today the upper part of the cut (on which a disused lime kiln stood within living memory) still has a trickle of water in it, but is now no longer used.

Meanwhile, the Chelmer Navigation was being built and in November 1793 excavations began on Wescomb's land. Wescomb knew about the CBNC's proposals and asked the company to direct their engineer 'to carry the canal across mine without putting me to any inconvenience.'

The CBNC had two choices – either it could cross the Cut with an aqueduct, or permit Wescomb's canal to cut down into the Navigation.

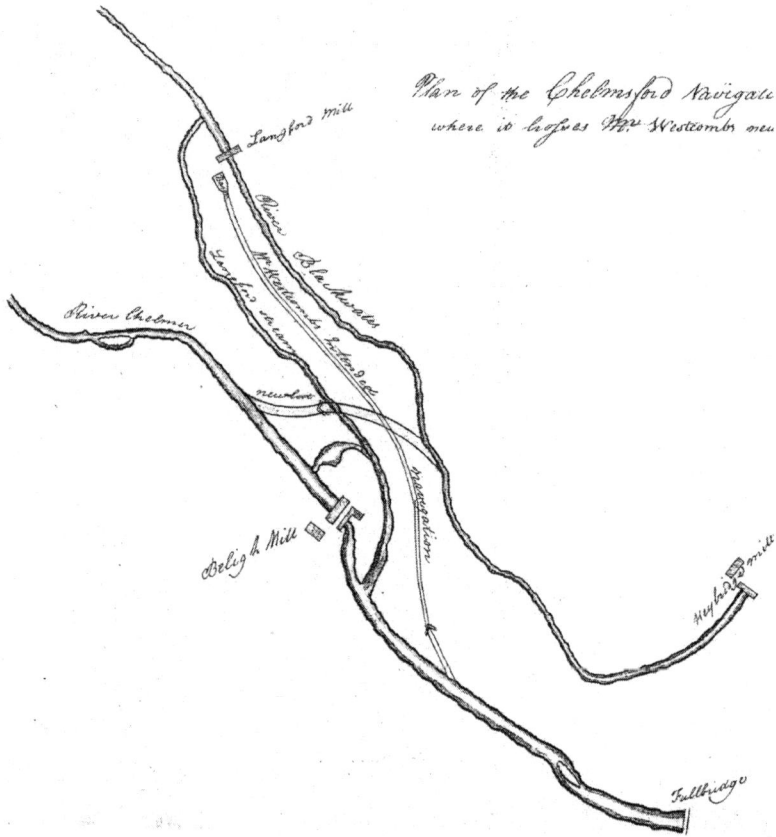

Plan of the Chelmsford Navigati
where it crosses Mr. Westcombs meu

River Chelmer

Langford mill

River Blackwater

newcut

Beligh Mill

Heybridge mill

Fullbridge

As there was little difference in the actual levels of the two waterways the latter alternative seemed the most appropriate; the only problem being that a section of the Langford Cut to the south of where it was to be dissected by the canal, would become redundant (in fact this redundant south section of the Cut has, in modern times, created a formidable hazard for members of the Maldon Golf Club!)

Peter Came in his thesis *A History of the Chelmer & Blackwater Navigation Company 1793-1914* (1971) takes up the story:

> Even if Langford Cut became an integral part of the Chelmer and Blackwater system its water level would

214

have to be lowered by two feet thus making it too shallow for the passage of barges. The Committee was actually in favour of Wescomb lowering the bed of his cut to the same as that of the Chelmer and Blackwater thus obviating stop gates. (Samuel Wright gave an estimate of £274. 3s.1d. for making the depth of Langford Cut 1 ft. 9ins and wider in proportion so that the water would be the same level as that of the Chelmer and Blackwater). The main bone of contention centred around the fact that the Chelmer and Blackwater would impede the passage of boats and towing paths on the Langford Cut and on no account was Nicholas Wescomb prepared to part with the soil of his canal. Meanwhile the Committee were told by Nicholas Wescomb that they 'might proceed with [the] line set out as they had agreed to make compensation.'

On 14th March 1795 Wescomb wrote to the Committee complaining bitterly that the construction works were exceeding the limits agreed and that the Chelmer and Blackwater lock was being built:

> in the very exceptionable spot against which I have so often remonstrated. A lock in this place will be very injurious to my Mill, and be destructive to my canal by subjecting it to Flood and will prevent my making the lock pland [sic] and estimated before the Chelmer Navigation was thought on.

However, the CBNC replied by letter dated 1st April stating that the construction of the lock was being undertaken 'in the spot proposed...and considerably within the 100 yards allowed for deviation.'

The Mill wharf at Langford was not completed until at least 1796 as, on 18th July of that year, Wescomb wrote to R. Tindal of the CBNC stating that the coping stones for the wharf construction had arrived, and asked permission for water to be let down to enable him to finish the job. This was done, and the wharf was finally ready for use by the end of the year.

The old wharf and Granary building (opposite the Mill) – drawing by
H.M. Paterson, 1930

The Chelmer and Blackwater Navigation Canal was opened in 1797 but still no formal agreement had been signed between the company and Wescomb. The latter listed complaints in a letter to R. Tindal dated 23rd August 1797 which were over and above his main gripe which related to the impeding of the passage of boats, vessels and towpaths on the Cut.

His complaints comprised:

(a) He wanted returned to him all the waste corners and angles that the Company did not require for the building of their canal;

(b) His land was being flooded because Beeleigh Weir (the overfall) was too high, and

(c) He was still requiring a means of letting the water down in the Cut.

216

Finally on 29th August 1807 it was all settled. The Chelmer and Blackwater Navigation Company was given permission to dig and deepen the passage of their canal across the Cut, a distance of 180 feet. This was to facilitate the construction of a tow path on the bank of the Chelmer canal and build a 'stank' (a temporary watertight dam) across the Cut before the junction to be used for a towing path until a bridge had been constructed. It was also agreed that a bridge be built across the Cut 'to be used as a towing path whenever Nicholas Wescombe [sic] or his heirs and assigns undertake to reuse the Langford Cut and make it navigable into the River Chelmer.' No records of the building of this particular bridge appear to exist. The probable reason why the bridge was never constructed may have been that the Langford Cut has never been shown to have been navigable any further south of the point where it crossed the Chelmer Navigation.

The entrance to 'Mr. Wescomb's Cut' today

In the early part of the nineteenth century author Arthur Young was visiting a Mr. Dunkins at Beeleigh Mill and during that time he was shown round Langford Mill by Dunkins' partner, Mr. Jonathan Stammers. Young, in his book *General View of Agriculture in Essex* (1807), provides invaluable details of Langford Mill at that time. He wrote that Stammers:

was so obliged to show me his mill and a very fine one it is: has ten pairs of stones, working six or four. One water wheel, twenty two feetfour inches diameter, and nineteen feet wide; fall of water ten feet and a half. The whole work so smooth that the noise is little. He has a navigation, and a wharf, at the mill; coals iron, &c. delivered.

Stammers is last recorded as being at Langford Mill in 1811.

In 1812 the Piggot family lived at Mill House, and held the lease of Langford Mill, remaining in control of it until about 1870. John Piggot & Son were large scale mid-Essex commodity dealers, owning, by 1840, not only the Mill at Langford but also one at Little Baddow and a wharf in Springfield, near Chelmsford. Piggot's commodities included guano (manure), rape, corn, linseed cake, coal and timber. Not wishing to stop there, the Piggots were also farmers and owned premises in Maldon High Street.

In 1863 an assessment of the level of business at Langford Mill was undertaken and it was estimated that during that year 8,318 sacks of flour had been sent by water to Heybridge for shipment to London using the 'flour and corn granarie at the head of the wharf near the mill' despite the railway station at Langford being only some 800 yards down the road. In addition, 581 sacks of flour and 1,994 quarters of wheat were landed at the Mill from Heybridge Basin and 3,050 tons of coal was transported from the Basin to Langford.

However, water transport was now being rapidly replaced by a more modern and faster form of transport (the railway). This would have one short-term advantage to Piggot who was able to negotiate a reduction in the canal toll down from 1½d per ton per mile to 1d per ton per mile due to Eastern County Railways making him an offer at a lower rate. But it would not be long before canal traffic dropped off and gave way to the railway.

By 1870 Frank Trew Cantrell occupied Langford Mill which he leased from the Hon. Mrs. F. Byron (neé Wescomb), and by then the mill's water power had been replaced by steam. The number of mill stones had not been increased which might suggest that the output of the mill was static. At this time Cantrell also ran the Paper Mill at Little Baddow. However, according to John Booker in *Essex and the Industrial Revolution* (1974), the Mill became silent in 1872 and the steam engine was used merely to turn the machinery to keep it in order. It restarted in 1874 with water power only. Although no one knew it at that time, Langford Mill was a mere five years away from destruction.

The mill before it was destroyed by fire in 1879

The present brick mill in Langford replaced the 1776 weather-boarded building which burnt down in 1879. A report of this event was featured in the *Chelmsford Chronicle* dated 28th March 1879. Because of its historical significance (and the fact that it illustrates the lively and imaginative descriptive skills of the journalist involved) the article is quoted in full. It read:

On Tuesday night, March 25th, Langford Mill, the property of Lady Byron, and worked by Mr. F. T. Cantrell, was entirely destroyed by fire. The mill was situated at the distance of about a mile from Maldon, on a cutting from the Chelmer Navigation, was five storeys in height, and worked ten pair of stones, the motive powers being steam and water. Adjoining the mill proper was a large warehouse, containing a quantity of beans etc. and in the yard there were some outbuildings used for the purposes of a coach house and a piggery. On the opposite - the east - side, at a distance of about four yards, was Mr. Cantrell's residence. The mill was composed principally of wood, the brick walls reaching to a height of only about six feet, but the engine room and the warehouse contained more brickwork.

Mr. Cantrell left the buildings, as he thought, safe at 7.15 p.m. on Tuesday when they were locked up for the night, but at half past eight a boy observed the mill to be on fire at the end nearest the house. He instantly acquainted Mr. Cantrell with the alarming fact, and a glance at the premises verifying the boy's tale, a messenger was dispatched to Maldon to give information to the officers of the fire engine stationed there. Before he could arrive, however, the flames had made such progress, despite the efforts of a number of people who speedily collected at the spot, that the borough engine was almost ready to start, one of the firemen having observed the flames and immediately gathered the brigade together. With such expedition were the preparations for action made that in half an hour's time from the discovery of the fire by the fireman the engine was on the scene, the engine connected with the Equitable Fire Office arriving almost at the same time.

The borough engine was placed a little below the mill, the hose being carried through a shed at the side nearest the house. The men who were under the direction of the superintendent and deputy superintendent Mr. G. P. May and Mr. J. W. Hawkes then proceeded to play on the house with two jets to prevent its catching fire and pouring another stream on the Mill. Being so near the Mill, the house stood in imminent danger, and it was solely owing to the efforts of the firemen and the prevalence of a contrary wind that the conflagration did not extend to it.

It was evident from the first that the mill itself could not be saved, and the men with the Equitable office engine, under the direction of Mr. May, after a short ineffectual endeavour to extinguish the flames, attempted to sever the connection between the mill and the warehouse and if possible preserve the latter. Working with a will, they succeeded so far that the fire only reached the roof of the warehouse the whole of which however was soon in flames. Water was thrown on to the building from the engine and the danger in the neighbourhood of the house having been considerably lessened, some of the brigade men assisted at this point, directing water on the flames from the yard in the rear.

By this time the fire had attained such dimensions that it could be plainly discerned from Chelmsford, while at Maldon the streets were lighter than on the brightest moonlight night, and, standing on the hill, it was possible to read a book by the glare. A large crowd numbering nearly 2,000 were attracted from Maldon and the neighbourhood and some few of these rendered efficient help to the firemen, Mr. John Wood of Langford Hall, and Mr. A. Self, of Maldon being prominent. In anticipation of the spread of the fire to the coach house and piggery, the animals were removed to a safer spot.

At ten o'clock all that remained of the mill was a heap of smoking ruins, and two hours later the fire had been almost entirely extinguished, but the engine from the Equitable Office remained in position during the night and the next day to prevent a further outbreak. The only damage sustained by the engine-room and the warehouse was the partial destruction of the roofs, but the beans contained in the warehouse were somewhat damaged. There were quantities of corn and flour in the mill, the whole of which were destroyed, the total damage being roughly estimated at about £3,500. Mr. Cantrell is fully insured in the Manchester Fire Office. The engine used by the fire brigade was a new one, and the officers expressed themselves as thoroughly satisfied with its working.

The Brigade, it may be mentioned, displayed the effect that their training has had upon them in the systematic way in which they did their work; and the indefatigable efforts of the men with the Equitable Office engine also merit high praise. Supt. May, Sergt. Matthews, and several constables lent their assistance in subduing the flames.

The insurance company must have settled the claim very quickly because the mill was rebuilt that same year to plans drawn up by Frederick Chancellor; this time of red brick and comprising five floors. This is the building which still stands today. Ian Linton in his *The Book of Maldon* (1984) describes the new mill as having two external wheels, the larger wheel being on the west side in the pit with the engine and boiler houses behind it, the second wheel being on the east side. Sadly it was built too late to enjoy continuing prosperity. By 1882, the mill was silent.

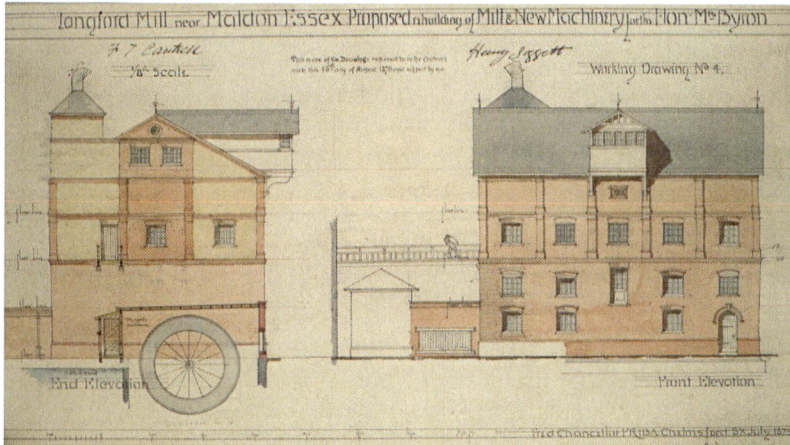

The plans for the new Mill by Chancellor

According to Hervey Benham in his book *Some Essex Water Mills* (1976) the closure was due to economic reasons:

> Sometimes shut down completely for periods, they tried to keep its engines in reserve, but things were so tight that the miller, Edward [Lee] Baker, kept going to the insurance office in the 1880's to pay a five shilling premium when he saw a chance to use steam for a month. When Langford Mill was 'silent', or laid up, a few years before it was burnt down in 1876, the policy allowed for the use of the engine only to keep the machinery in order.

An indicator of these random (or as Benham calls them 'hiccuping') periods of activity can be found in John Booker's work *Essex and the Industrial Revolution* (1974). Booker records that in November 1882 the Mill reopened with water power alone and in 1884, 1885, 1887, 1890 and 1892 and at odd times until 1902 'steam power was allowed for only brief and specified periods by the Insurance Company.'

According to the Record of Insurance Policies (1881-1887) held by the Essex Record Office, in 1882 The Hon. Mrs. Byron arranged the insurance of the mill. It covered 'for building of an engine and boiler house situate adjoining a corn mill in occupation of Cantrell, known as Langford Mill including granary, meal room and stables adjoining.'

Cantrell's occupation of the Mill extended after the fire but not for much longer. By 1886 *Kelly's Directory* was listing Thomas Baker as the occupant, although it was, of course, Edward Lee Baker. Baker and his family resided next door in the Mill House. Thirteen years later *Kelly's Directory* of 1899 records Baker's widow as running the Mill. However, shortly after her husband's death, which occurred on 3rd August 1889, Mrs. Baker had Langford Meads built at the eastern edge of the village. She and her daughters Jeanie, Mary and Lily moved out of Mill House and into their new home in 1905. (Langford Meads (on land between Langford Road and Crescent Road) was demolished at the end of the twentieth century to make way for a number of new homes.)

William Chalk (centre back) and his family

For a few years afterwards the Byron family controlled the running of the mill themselves. William Chalk was employed to manage the mill on a day-to-day basis. William had been

224

in the milling trade all his life, having come from the Great Baddow paper mill after it too had burnt down. William had originally come to Langford around 1879-80. During his time Langford Mill produced stone-ground flour. Recognising the importance of such a natural product the parish magazine reported in December 1907:

> It is hoped that shortly a few loaves baked from the flour at Langford Mill will be offered for sale. The bread will be made, therefore, of English wheat, stone ground, and will be quite free from adulteration. If possible the bread will be sold rather below the current price. A notice (should this be carried into effect) will be placed in Mr. Parmenter's shop window, at which place the bread would be sold.

One major problem that William Chalk experienced in terms of production was that during the daytime there was not enough water coming down the River Blackwater to turn the water wheel. This was due to a mill further upstream (probably Mathews' but possibly T. B. Dixon's of Wickham Bishops) taking the water during the day. Thus it was not possible to work Langford Mill during the day so William had no choice but to work it during the night when the other mill(s) had closed down for the day.

During an interview in the early 1970s a Langford resident, the late Ted Chalk, spoke of going in the evening to watch William (his grandfather) dress the stones. Ted recalled:

> They were great big circular stones with ribs in them, and when they got a bit shallow they didn't grind the corn properly, so someone had to sit and chip at the stone and chip the ribs a little deeper. Naturally, everyone had to wear glasses to do this task as tiny fragments of stone would fly about."

An example of early Health and Safety regulations? Probably just plain common sense.

The re-built mill in 1879

In 1914 control of the day-to-day running of the Mill passed, on the death of William Chalk, to a man named Sexton. Up to the outbreak of The Great War it was estimated that the mill was sending two loads of flour per week to Nevilles Bakery in London via Maldon Station. However, Sexton apparently had more than a talent for milling. After some problems with the accounts he left the village without saying goodbye.

In 1917 Abraham Springett was described in *Kelly's Directory* as 'Mill foreman to Revd. Hon. F. E. C. Byron, M.A.' The mill stopped production in 1918. The mill race - the area of water behind the mill - today serves as a reservoir for the waterworks, and for supplying the Navigation Canal's water requirements in Langford Cut. By 1922 Springett was still foreman, but a company named Tucker & Gellion Ltd. held the lease. They had plans to convert Langford Mill into a roller mill and the conversion work was well under way when the company went bankrupt. Tucker & Gellion were succeeded (c. 1926) by J.C. Brian & L. Bradbury, who traded as The Langford Milling Co. with Charles William Chenery as manager, but their occupation was short-lived.

The late Ted Chalk recalled:

> I remember them – they didn't do anything. When I knew them it was Bradbury and Brian. They came and took the mill over after the Byrons had finished with it. Grandfather died in 1914 and a chap who worked with him, named Sexton, took over. He lodged with Tom Ward [*in Maldon Road*]. After a time the money didn't tally and he'd hooked off and they never see anymore of him.

The Mill and outbuildings in the 1930s

Another elderly man took over and ran it for a time – he lived in Mill Cottage, named Chenery, and he worked for the Byrons. Bradbury and Brian went bust. They didn't get on very well. Never made a start. Something went wrong so Bradbury and Brian packed it up and Tucker and Gellion took over. They were going to convert it into a roller mill. Well, they had practically everything installed, almost ready to start up and the waterworks started to interfere and they never got any further, and all that machinery had to come out. It was all practically new stuff...a lot of it was. That was the end of Tucker & Gellion.

The mill race under reconstruction in the 1930s

Negotiations must have already been underway at this time between the Byron family and the Southend Waterworks Company (SWC) to sell the property so that they could install an extraction pump as part of the major river works that were being constructed in the village at that time.

The Mill and House in the 1950s when the extensive buildings to the West of the Mill had gone

In *Some Essex Water Mills* Hervey Benham states that SWC removed the machinery in 1924 in order to install an extraction pump as part of the waterworks complex in Langford which he wrote, 'sprawls across the heart of the old Langford village obliterating Westcombe's quay.' Benham further claimed in his book that on the south side of the road the store sheds, granary and Wescomb's wharf were also demolished at this time. This is doubtful as images dating from 1928 (and living memory) confirm that at least the majority of these buildings were still standing at that time.

As a result of progress the waterworks modernisation excluded any further use of the Mill and for many years the building was used for storage.

The Mill Race Today

In 1989 rumours abounded that the Mill would soon be up for sale, prior to being converted into 'sheltered accommodation' or flats but, at the time of writing (2013), no such development has been proposed. In 1997 the Mill received a 'spring clean' and 'plastic' replacement windows and today is only occasionally used for storage. In early 2011 there were rumours around the village that the Board of the

Museum of Power (which occupies the site and buildings of the former Pumping Station just across the road) were in talks with the owners (Essex & Suffolk Water) to utilise the Mill for their own additional storage purposes, but nothing came of it.

As for the Langford Cut, the importance of this link to Wescomb and those villagers who worked at Langford Mill should not be underestimated. Over two centuries later, even as The Cut lies redundant, there is still a possibility that life might return to this little waterway. With the long-term planned expansion of the Museum of Power into a key leisure facility for all ages and existing plans to possibly link the miniature train from the museum to Beeleigh, perhaps some thought too can be given to utilising The Cut once again.

Currently there is a huge block of concrete (pictured above) about two-thirds of the way along the Cut which supports or houses a pipeline but could this problem be overcome? If so, then the future plans for the leisure park might include short waterway trips along The Cut up to Beeleigh, alight from the boat and then walk the short distance to the beauty spot of Beeleigh Weir. Perhaps longer trips could be arranged; to

Heybridge Basin or even to Chelmsford by water. The short journey to Beeleigh would enable visitors to witness the confluence of the Rivers Chelmer and Blackwater and walk along the banks of the canal – a fabulous experience on a warm summer's day – and to visit what remains of Beeleigh Mill. They might then return to the Museum of Power by train.

But whatever happens (or doesn't happen) to the Cut, Langford Mill is still one of the most iconic buildings in the village, and is known and loved by everyone.

The Mill in 2012

Mill House

At the time of the reconstruction of Langford Mill in 1776 Mill House was built on the site of a former seventeeth century building between the Mill and St. Giles' Church. A 'front range' was added to the property in the late eighteenth/early nineteenth century but since then the house and grounds have seen insignificant, mainly cosmetic, changes until recent years. However, there have been many changes of occupier and, after the turn of the twentieth century, a number of changes of use.

The earliest records discovered thus far begin in 1870 and from that date until about 1927 reflect the purpose of Mill House as the home of the millers that worked the mill. Adolphus and John Sampson Piggot (1870-1892) were succeeded by Edward and Susannah Baker (1892-1905), then the Hollingdale's (1906-1919) and, finally, John Gellion and Benjamin Tucker (1920 to circa 1923).

As previously mentioned, the massive fire in March 1879 had destroyed the weather-boarded mill. The main structure could not be saved but the skills of the firemen attending the blaze resulted in the Mill House escaping practically unscathed. With Langford Mill falling silent for the last time in the early 1920s, both the Mill and Mill House were purchased by the Southend Waterworks Company and the house converted into flats. Thereafter a number of the company's employees lived in the property.

Mill House in 1926

From around 1923/24 to the early 1960s senior members of the Southend Waterworks Company (and their families) occupied Mill House including the Resident Engineer, Wilfred Goulding. Goulding his wife Minnie and their maid Ellen Jones occupied the middle flat and they lived there from 1927 to about 1949 when Goulding passed away. The new Resident Engineer appointed in 1950 was Henry V. Cusworth and he and his wife Ruby lived in the property until the early 1960s.

Back in the early-to-mid 1920s the ground floor flat of Mill House was the home of the Waterworks' Chief Chemist Russell G. Pelly. He stayed there until the end of the 1940s. By 1957 John Slack had been appointed Chief Chemist and occupied Mill House with his wife June, later having their own home built in the village on a plot directly opposite the Mill.

The rear of Mill House from the mill race in 2011

But one of the most significant occupants of the ground floor flat, circa 1923/26 was Robert Walton. He was articled to Dr. John Thresh, the bacteriologist working for the Company at the Experimental Plant at Langford which preceded the construction of the pumping station. In later years Walton recalled, "I lived on the ground floor. Goulding had the middle floor. No electricity. I knew all the rats by name." Indeed, electricity was a service that did not arrive in Langford until the 1930s. Ironically, given his task relating to the extraction of samples from the river, whilst Walton lived at Mill House the property had no clean water supply.

But it was the work undertaken by Walton whilst resident in Mill House and his 'master' Dr. Thresh that would finally ear-mark Langford as the prime location for the Southend Waterworks Company's then 'hi-tech' pumping station in the centre of an erstwhile sleepy, agricultural village.

In the 1960s Mill House was sold into private hands and remains so to date. During the time that has elapsed the property has been a private residence, an old people's home, a hotel and a centre for asylum-seekers before reverting back to a hotel in 2004. At the time of writing, the current owner of the building, Richard Perry, offers bed and breakfast accommodation and café facilities.

The River and the River Bridge

Between the existing Mill and Mill House can still be seen what remains of the original course of the River Blackwater which passed under the mill wheel, under the road and then towards its confluence with the River Chelmer.

The waterway that flows under the main road bridge was originally called the 'Langford Stream' but over time it became wider as water poured through from the lock behind the Mill and it was renamed the River Blackwater. The original course of the Blackwater is nothing more now than a stream which runs into Wescomb's Cut which itself is no longer navigable except perhaps by canoe or kayak.

The responsibility for the maintenance and repair of bridges in years gone by was always seen to be that of the Lord of the Manor or the estate holder. Sixteenth century records show that 'The predecessor of Mr. Harvey, Lord of Langford, hath made it.' However, 'made it' more often than not only meant that he had mended it. The predecessors in title to Mr. Harvey were the Smyth family of Cressing Temple.

The first reference to Langford Bridge to appear in the Court Rolls relates to 'disrepair' in 1567 in which it was reported that Harvey owned the property on both sides of the bridge but that no one knew exactly who was actually liable for the bridge itself.

The bridge in the early 1900s

The same bridge from the ford

The current bridge, some 30-40 yards from the former waterworks entrance, was rebuilt out of necessity in 1924. By the early 1920s the bridge had become so unstable that any motor cars, and any locomotive driven agricultural vehicles had to divert through the ford on the north side of the structure. The picture on the left shows the ford and the old bridge in the early 1900s.

A meeting of the Essex County Council's Highways Committee on 20th May 1924 heard from the Council Surveyor that the existing timber bridge had been 'in a dangerous condition for many years' and was quite inadequate for the volume of traffic now using the road. The County Surveyor told the Committee that he had been in negotiations with Lord Byron, who owned the land adjoining the bridge and he had agreed to give the land necessary to widen the bridge on condition that the fees in connection with the deed of dedication were paid by Essex County Council. This was agreed by the Committee.

The old bridge looking towards Maldon from the Hatfield Peverel end.
The Granary is in the centre of the picture.

At the same meeting tenders for the work were received and that submitted by A. J. Arnold of Chelmsford for the rebuilding of bridge no. 226 in the sum of £6,001.18s.7d, being the lowest, was accepted. At its next meeting, on 1st

July 1924, the Highways Committee agreed that Mr. F. Rowbottom, who was at the time Clerk of the Works at the Stanford-le-Hope bridge at a salary of £5.5s.0d per week, also be given responsibility for the bridge at Langford. In recognition of this Rowbottom's salary was increased by fifteen shillings to £6 per week from 1st June 1924.

At the Committee meeting held on 5th January 1926 it was reported that the 'reconstruction' of the bridge (pictured above) had been completed at a total cost of £6,290; £288 over budget.

The reconstruction of the river bridge at Langford was timely indeed. At about the same time that the new bridge was completed, work commenced in earnest on the building of the Southend Waterworks Pumping Station only a few yards from the bridge. During the demolition of the old wooden bridge the villagers had cause for further celebrations over and above the provision of the 'New Bridge.'

The cross which had been stolen from the village church in July 1915 was found in the debris. The precious religious relic was then returned to St. Giles.' Over thirty years later this story, together with a pencil sketch of the metal plaque on the bridge bearing the seaxes of the Essex County Council, was sent to the *Essex Chronicle*'s 'Big Chief I-Spy' as a result of which eight-year-old 'Redskin' Patrick Chaplin was mentioned in the issue dated 10th March 1959 and awarded 25 'I-Spy' points and a genuine buff plastic wallet from the Big Chief himself (!) Today the ford can still be seen on the right-hand/north side as one drives over the bridge in the direction of Hatfield Peverel.

Restoration of the ford was identified by the Parish Council as their Millennium Project for Langford, and as a result they received a Government grant for this as part of the Millennium celebrations.

The picture above shows cattle in the ford at Langford walking from the Maldon end of the village, alongside the old bridge towards the fields beside the river. In the background can be seen a boy - Sid Russell - who worked for the waterworks from about 1938, having previously worked at

Wickham Hall, in Wickham Bishops. He had lived in Langford as a boy at No. 2 Church Cottages, and went to school in the village. The ford changed when the new bridge was built.

Shop and Post Office

There had been a shop or general store of some kind in Langford for many years until 1986. The earliest reference to a shopkeeper in the village traced thus far has been found in the 1845 *Pigot's* trade directory which shows William Emberson listed as a grocer. By 1851 Emberson appears to have expanded his business for by then he was described in *Pigot's* as 'carpenter and shopkeeper.' He was joined in the directory by Mrs. Elizabeth Halls, a shopkeeper; Mrs. Halls also being responsible for 'Letters received through Maldon,' this being the first evidence of a post office (of sorts) in the village - eleven years after the first postage stamp had been introduced.

In 1859 Emberson, who was also Parish Clerk for many years, seems to have given up the role of shopkeeper and concentrated on his trade as a carpenter. That same year Mrs. Hall was dealing with 'Letters received through Maldon and arrive at 8 a.m., dispatched at 5.15 p.m.' with Maldon being the 'nearest money order office.'

At the beginning of the new decade an 1870 directory shows Henry Hall as 'receiver' at the Langford post office/shop (now called 'The Old Post Office' and situated opposite where the bus shelter is today). From about 1874 until the early 1880s, first George and then Henry Beadle are listed as 'receivers.' By 1886 William Rudrum held the post but from 1890 until the turn of the twentieth century and beyond, Thomas Barber was listed as receiver, then later as 'sub postmaster.' Both lived in the Post Office building.

In 1906 Bertie Parmenter opened a shop in the village in the premises diagonally opposite the then existing post office.

239

The Post Office in the 1930s with May Harvey in the gateway

(The name Parmenter was to become synonymous with the village shop for eighty years.) By this time the post office was being run by Ernest Harvey, another surname that would be involved in village life for many decades. In 1917 Harvey was still listed as 'shopkeeper and post office' with Bert Parmenter as 'shopkeeper' and this would remain the case until the early 1930s.

In 1931 Bert's widow Emily married a local man, Charlie Freeman. A few months later the post office was closed when the Harvey's retired, and Emily was asked to take it on. She agreed, but it did not last long as Emily found the G.P.O.'s insistence that the post office section must be manned *at all times* impossible to comply with. The section was then closed for good; the nearest alternative for residents being the post office at Heybridge two miles away.

In 1953 Clifford Parmenter, who worked at the waterworks, took over the shop with his wife Winifred who had previously been in service at Langford Grove. (Cliff and Win had in fact first met in the shop.) Their daughter Angela recalled the day the family moved to the shop from their previous home in Hatfield Peverel. She said, "The entire family were in a state of shock when we found bucket toilets and only cold water!"

Langford (old) Post Office

With no pub in the village, the shop became the focus of daily village life and village gossip. Angela said "It was so much more than just a shop. In addition to being a valuable community facility and provider of supplies, mum's shop was also a left-luggage office. She also provided a reading service for gypsies (and writing replies)." In the summer vast numbers of short-trousered lads from the Boys' Brigade, who camped every year in the field behind the shop, would queue inside and outside 'Mrs. Parmenter's' to spend their pocket money. At certain times there were so many boys that she limited them to two at a time in the shop! Also, during the better weather, local boys and girls would cash in the 'money back' deposits of R. White and Corona bottles (3d per bottle) which they had rescued from the nearby rivers and elsewhere; every penny being spent on sweets, especially 'jamboree bags' and soft drinks.

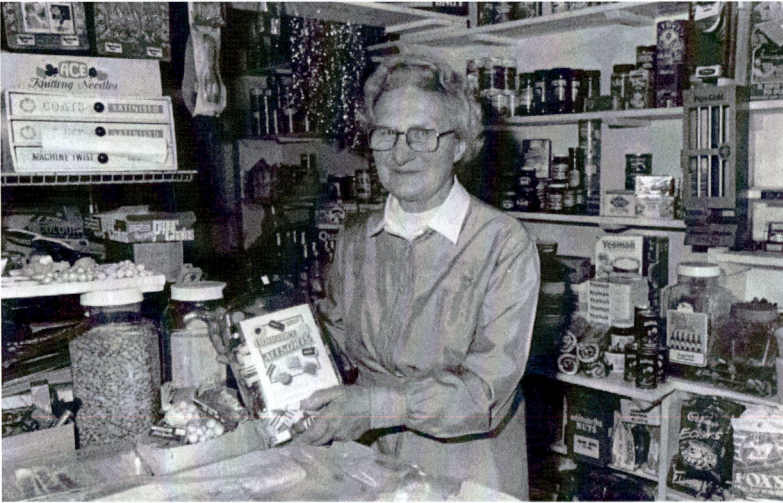
Win Parmenter on her retirement at 70 in 1986

In 1986 the shop closed. Mrs. Parmenter sold up and retired to *Magnolia View* the bungalow she had had built on a piece of ground next door. The shop building still stands in the centre of the village. At the time of writing it is in a ruinous state: a huge wart on the face of an otherwise beautiful Essex village. Despite the fact that it is a listed building, the Parish Council are powerless to enforce any restoration work to it, and it would appear that family issues are the reason for it being so neglected.

'The shop' in 2010

In 2009 a shop returned to Langford, uniquely housed in the vestry of St. Giles' Church. Opening two mornings during the week, on Saturday mornings and for two hours after church on Sundays, the shop, appropriately named 'Heavenly Supplies,' was the brainchild of Irene Allen, Churchwarden (and co-author of this book), pictured below with the (then) Bishop of Bradwell, Revd. Dr. Laurie Green.

Irene entered an Essex County Council-sponsored competition in their *Essex Matters* magazine, where the challenge was to suggest an innovative community project. The top prize was £10,000. Irene came up with the idea of a community shop based in the church. Her competition entry was submitted and a few weeks later her project was adjudged the winner. Through Irene's efforts, and those of a number of others within and without the village, the new shop was officially opened by Councillor Rodney Bass on Thursday 5th March 2009 with many villagers and TV cameras in attendance.

Manned by a small band of volunteers (without whom the venture simply could not survive), 'Heavenly Supplies' proves that the heart of the village still beats and that the sense of community is alive and very well indeed thank you in Langford. From March 2012 the shop began opening every day for two hours – 0900-1100 Monday to Friday and 1000-1200 at weekends. From March 2013 the hours were rationalised to open 1000-1200 every day.

So where's the shop?

Oh, there it is…..

The opening of 'Heavenly Supplies' generated much media interest, the shop (and Irene) being featured in local, provincial, national and international newspapers and on local and national television, including an interview on the *Newsnight* programme with church historian Richard Taylor. Suddenly Langford was the centre of attention again; the last time being when the Southend Waterworks Pumping Station was formally opened eighty years earlier. News of the venture spread through the ecclesiastical world, and other churches have contacted Irene to find out how they could emulate this success. It has enabled the church - which previously had to be kept locked when not in use - to be open every day so that those who wish to visit can come in and have a cup of tea and a chat, and enjoy the beauty of this unique building. This shop is a non-profit making venture existing purely to provide a service for the village.

The Workshop

A short distance from the church further up the road to Maldon on the right hand side there is now a bus shelter. Behind this used to stand Walter Harry Chalk's workshop, also known as the 'estate office' - long since demolished -

and the village pump, which was 'removed' by person or persons unknown one evening during the late 1960's. To access the loft space of this building 'Harry' (pictured left) had to close the front door of the building to enable him to climb the ladder (seen here forming part of the door). On many occasions impish

245

children would hide outside and wait for him to ascend the ladder when they would open the door again. This effectively meant he was stranded in the loft space and unable to climb down.

This building, like so many others in the village, fell into disrepair and was eventually demolished in 1965 and was used for the base of the bonfire on 5th November. However, the fire was accidentally lit an hour earlier than scheduled by Patrick Chaplin who, with Kelvin Brown, were skylarking about on an old sofa (also part of the bonfire) and they inadvertently set off some fireworks which lit the fire.

It is interesting to note that the village pump that had stood beside the building was either stolen or, as was rumoured at the time, removed by council workers.

The Pub

When visitors to Langford look around for a pub they do so in vain. The village has been 'dry' for over 140 years.

In the 1980s, scraps of available data assembled by one of the authors of this book for a very early guide to Langford were utilised by local pub historian, the late Ken Stubbings to fill a gap in his knowledge of places of refreshment in the Maldon District. This information was included in his book *"Here's Good Luck to the Pint Pot!" – A Brief History of Maldon's Inns, Alehouses and Breweries* published by Kelvin Brown Publications, in 1988. Ken wrote:

> Langford has never had a pub - so many people will tell you - but they are wrong! A house standing off the road near the driveway to Maldon Golf Club, the 'White Hart', was run by Edward Eavery in 1832. By 1845 the Goodey family - Charles and Elizabeth - had taken over. They reigned until 1874 when the Byron family took residence at Langford Hall. The Hon. Mrs. F. Byron of London, having taken over the old pub, stables and chaisehouse, complete with brewhouse and coal-house,

put Goodey into one of the three tenement houses called 'Turners' at Langford. Being strict Methodist her initial move in cleaning up the village had been to close the pub! Langford has never had another pub to this day. The house, now extended, is called 'Mill Cottage.'

Where Ken got the notion that the Hon. Mrs. Byron was 'a strict Methodist' is not clear, and as he sadly is no longer with us, we cannot ask him. However, as the present Lord Byron points out, her paternal ancestors (the Wescomb's) gained their wealth through brewing, this seems unlikely.

The date 1832 is significant as it is very close to the year of the introduction of the 1830 Beerhouse Act. This Act created a new type of drinking place which was outside the control of licensing justices – known as the beerhouse. Introduced 'to permit the general Sale of Beer and Cyder by retail in England' and to provide 'the better supplying the Public with Beer,' the Act of 1830 was also seen to be part of the strategy of the then Tory Government to revive its flagging support.

Another reason for its introduction was the Government's general wish to promote the consumption of wholesome beer (thus favouring the Tory-supporting drink interest) rather than spirits; the latter having lain waste large swathes of the under-classes. Other reasons included beer production benefitting the hop and barley producers (farmers and estate holders who were suffering the effects of a depression in agriculture) and the Act opening up the trade to promote competition and thus reviving the falling beer consumption and pleasing those in favour of free trade. The villagers of Langford were probably blasé to all other reasoning over and above the selling of beer from your own home being made legal (subject of course to the purchase of a licence) and it is likely that this is how the *White Hart*, as the pub was named, was first established.

Mill Cottage, which stands at the junction of Hatfield Road (the B1019) and what is known locally as 'the golf course road' was, in a previous life, the *White Hart* which consisted of the house, stables and a brewhouse. A painting by L. Burleigh Bruhl dated 1909 (thirty years after the pub closed for business) depicts a line of buildings as being of red brick construction with tiled roofs. The *White Hart* formed part of that building and served the population of the village and the employees of the nearby mill and doubtless slaked the thirst of the numerous agricultural workers taking a break from their labours during harvest time, and also served the occasional passing trade.

Burleigh Bruhl's painting of 1909 showing the 'White Hart' and the Granary building at the head of Mr. Wescomb's Cut

The earliest published reference to the pub (1832) is merely the extent of the information that the available directories record, but it is likely that an alehouse of some kind would have been found at the site much earlier. Indeed the name the *White Hart* might indicate a much older lineage.

The same buildings as in Bruhl's painting from the main road, from an ink sketch by H.M. Paterson in the 1920s

By 1845 Eavery was named in *Pigot's Directory* for that year as a 'Beer Retailer' but by then Charles Goodey (sometimes spelt without an 'e') was trading at the '*White Hart Inn*.' So Eavery had set up on his own elsewhere in the village; either that or *White's Directory* was incorrect. (Eavery is known to have later taken up the license of the *Flying Tinker* in Ulting, about 1½ miles west of the *White Hart*. The *Flying Tinker* closed in the 1950s.) The directories list Charles Goodey at the *White Hart* from 1845 to 1860, his wife Elizabeth Goodey from 1861-1865 and his son Stanford Charles Goodey from 1866 until the early 1870s. After 1873 there were no further entries for the *White Hart*.

Beerhouses were brought under magisterial control in 1869 but it appears that it mattered not to the population of Langford. Thus the village has been 'dry' for over 140 years. Subsequent research indicates that the earlier Stubbings/Chaplin theory about the Byrons has been challenged. Although no primary source material has (yet) been found to confirm the theory that when the Byrons came to Langford they shut the pub and sent Goodey to 'Turners,' one of the arguments against the theory is that the Byron family first came to the village in 1851, when Mary Jane

Wescomb (one of the daughters of Rev. William Wescomb) married the Hon. Frederick Byron and they moved in to Langford Grove (not Langford Hall). The 1851 date does not tally and with the Goodey's continuing in business into the 1870s, therefore the 'strict Methodist' theory seems to be expunged. Another rumour was that the pub was closed because of the unruliness of the Irish labourers employed on the railway; a branch line constructed to link the main line town of Witham to Maldon which lies on a hill overlooking the Blackwater estuary and at the time a key port. If this was so, then the navvies must have stayed around for quite some time as the railway was completed in 1848!

But the navvies did return...eventually.

Langford remained a sleepy rural village on the River Blackwater, with and without its pub, until in the mid-1920s until the Southend Waterworks Company obtained the Government's approval (and that of the Byron family) to extract and treat water from the River Blackwater. This involved the construction of a huge pumping station in the centre of the village and a water treatment plant near its western boundary about a mile away. The building work brought in hundreds of Irish navvies, all of whom worked long hours and all of whom were (presumably) in search of drink to wash the dust from their throats at the end of every tortuous day or at least on Saturday nights. But Langford had no pub... So the labourers had to travel by foot or cart or whatever to the nearest watering hole, the *Half Moon* in The Square, Heybridge, 1½ miles east of Langford (now an Indian restaurant). The *Anchor* (now [2013] also an Indian restaurant) was a few yards further on and the *Queen's Head* (now the *Heybridge Inn*) and the *Wave* (now a private house and workshop) around the corner in The Street and the *Maltsters Arms* in Hall Road.

Mill Cottage today (with 20th Century extension)

Stories of the rowdy labourers coming home on a Saturday night from an evening's imbibing abounded in the village for many years, and there are many stories of drunken brawls, and one or two of these are recounted in the next chapter.

Even today some say that on a quiet summer's night if you cup your hands to your ears and listen you can still hear the raucous singing or yelling of the boys coming home from Heybridge – either that or the sound of modern-day juggernauts thundering through the village.

There was a rumour a few years ago that the owner of Mill House, a few yards up the road from Mill Cottage, had applied for a licence that would extend alcoholic sales to non-residents, an action that would have brought the licensed trade back into the village for the first time since the nineteenth century. However, nothing further has been heard and thus Langford, for the foreseeable future, remains pub-free.

As traditional commerce fell victim to changing culture and lifestyle so new commercial ventures arrived in the village.

The former treatment plant at the west end of the village was demolished despite local opposition (as they had been informed that whatever use was made of the site, the buildings HAD to remain), and in time a technology centre called CML Microsystems Plc was established in what became called Oval Park, was built. In addition, outbuildings at Langford Hall were converted by the owner, Edward Watson, into office units and a small garage; he also keeps the traditional flag flying by farming and keeping rare breeds.

So now we turn to the coming of the railway.

CHAPTER SEVEN
THE COMING (AND GOING) OF THE RAILWAY

In 1845 an application was made to Parliament for an Act 'for making a Railway from Chelmsford to the Blackwater River, in the County of Essex, with several Branches and Side Railways thereto.' Those 'Side Railways' would eventually embrace the Maldon to Witham branch line which would include a station at Wickham Bishops and a halt at Langford. Following a private Act of Parliament, Royal Assent was given in June 1846 granting power to run a line from Maldon via Heybridge, Langford and Wickham Bishops to Witham.

The plans for the Maldon scheme for the new railway had already progressed well. Earlier in 1845 the promoters appointed Joseph Locke as engineer and James Beadall as surveyor. Initially they were a group of local businessmen led by Rev. Sir John Page Wood but, in September 1846, they sold their company to the Eastern Counties Railway for £6,300.

In March 1847 the contract was given to Thomas Jackson, an employer on railway work. Drawing labourers from all over the county was the first move that, by a circuitous route, eventually enabled this book to be written. One of those labourers, a platelayer from Earls Colne, was John Chaplin – the great-grandfather of one of the co-authors, of this book.

Progress on building the line was slow; heavy rain and bad weather delayed the project and the eventual completion date was not until mid-August 1848. It appears that goods trains to Braintree from Maldon were active even at this time, and records show that in one week in September 1848 they carried 300 tons of coal and 350 tons of 'other freight.' Initial hopes of a rail link between Maldon and Witham had been

253

fulfilled at last and all that remained was for the line to pass the inspection test.

On 30th September 1848 the Board of Trade Inspector - Captain George Wynne, R.E. - carried out the inspection and declared that 'it may be safely opened for the conveyance of passengers.' On the plans, the original line had two tracks and progressed from Witham through halts at Wickham Bishops and Langford and Ulting, to terminate at Maldon East Station. Two tracks were laid but one removed fairly quickly and thus the line was a single-track for the remainder of its existence.

Eastern Counties Railway passenger trains started to run on the branch line almost immediately and the first eager adventurers, comprising of, primarily, a number of merchants going to London markets, departed from Maldon East Station at 8 a.m. on Monday 2nd October 1848 to a great public send-off. The *Chelmsford Chronicle* dated 6th October 1848 emphasised the importance of the rail link 'connecting as it does, the inland town of Braintree with the port of Maldon, and giving its inhabitants the advantages which rapid transit invariably affords.' A second advantage of the new communicative link was that it resulted in a reduction of about five shillings per ton in the price of coals 'which hitherto have been carted from Maldon at an expense of 8s per ton.'

In a detailed description of the journey the *Chelmsford Chronicle* mentioned that at Langford 'a small temporary station' had been built, but this of course was the permanent halt. The reporter added, 'The scenery in this neighbourhood is very pretty, and the parish churches of Langford and Wickham [*Bishops*] form conspicuous objects in the landscape, whilst the woods at Langford Grove and the fruitful fields in the neighbourhood present a pleasing and varied picture of rural luxuriance.' All-in-all the *Chronicle* reporter and his fellow members of 'the pleasure party' were satisfied with the day's excursion. A few days later an excursion was run to Braintree 'for the working classes.' From that time, on average, the Maldon to Witham branch line was running five trains per day.

One of the reconstructed wooden trestle bridges that carried the line over the rivers from Langford to Wickham Bishops (photo taken in 2011)

Two long viaducts were needed to carry the railway over the River Blackwater, built by Joseph Locke with Thomas Jackson as the principal contractor. In 1854 the line was singled and both bridges were reduced in width. In the 1920s the northern one was reduced in length to 150 feet by extending the embankment on the northern side.

To reduce costs, the majority of the railway buildings were built from timber, rather than brick, although Maldon East Station was built to a far grander style. Sadly in 2008, just weeks before being considered for listed status, a brick built goods shed on the line was demolished. This proves how delays to such preservation can be disastrous.

The line was closed to passengers on 7th September 1964 and to freight on 18th April 1966, but the section from Witham to Braintree remains open as the Braintree Branch Line. Approximately half a mile of the branch from Witham station towards Maldon was used as a siding serving an industrial area for delivery of steel by railway, this section closed in the early 1980s after a rail strike and is now a cycle/walkway. The section of line into the old east station in Maldon has been used as the route for a new road into the Fullbridge area. The section of trackbed linking the two former railway stations in Maldon (Maldon East and Maldon West) has been used as the route of the Maldon bypass to the west of the town. Both viaducts have survived and were restored in 1995 by Essex County Council. They are listed as scheduled Ancient Monuments.

The station, or rather the 'halt,' at Langford was officially opened on 2nd October 1848 as Ulting Station! The station served both Langford and Ulting, although the village's boundary with the parish of Ulting is more than a mile and a half down the road in a westerly direction. (In 1923 the halt was more correctly renamed 'Langford and Ulting Station.' Later it was changed to 'Langford' and then, later still, back to 'Langford and Ulting.') The little halt at Langford was merely a platform with a canopy situated in the shadow of the railway bridge adjacent to the Maldon to Hatfield Peverel road. The arrival of the railway brought great benefits to the area and increased trade and the ability, for those who could afford it, to travel long distances with ease. However, such a relatively sleepy railway line was not without its occasional major problems. One in particular brought the villages of Langford and Wickham Bishops into the limelight.

On 18th June 1869, the *Chelmsford Chronicle* reported a "FEARFUL RAILWAY ACCIDENT AT WICKHAM. A MAN KILLED." Although the banner headline stated 'Wickham' the accident 'of a very serious character' happened just after the train had left Wickham Bishops on its way to Langford and then to Maldon East.

The *Chelmsford Chronicle* reported that, at approximately 8.30 p.m. on the previous Tuesday evening, the last down train to Maldon, consisting of tank engine no. 512, and five carriages, heavily laden with passengers, 'by some means ran off the line down an embankment between Wickham and Langford stations.' The fireman, named Day, was killed outright, and the driver 'very severely and dangerously wounded' whilst the lives of about fifty passengers 'were placed in the most imminent peril.'

The first alarm was raised at Maldon by Barnham, the guard of the train who 'rode in at full speed to summon the medical gentlemen of the town.' When Miller the driver was at last set free he was placed on a shutter and, with 'the Volunteers' keeping the crowds back, Mr. Gutteridge, the doctor, was able to properly attend to him. Afterwards, Miller was carried along the line to Langford, where an omnibus was waiting. He was placed inside the vehicle and conveyed home to Maldon. Day was confirmed dead at the scene.

An early inquest took place on the following day but no conclusive evidence was advanced showing the actual cause of the disaster and the inquiry was adjourned until 1st July.

An inquest into Day's death was held in a large barn at the Reigate House, a farm in Wickham Bishops owned by Joseph Smith. The inquest was presided over by Coroner William Codd Esq. The foreman of the inquest jury was local landholder Mr. John Wood of Langford Hall.

During the inquest into the accident that followed three theories were expounded. Firstly, 'excessive speed on the part of the driver; secondly, the 'sudden shutting off of the steam' and, thirdly, that it was caused by 'some defective state of the line.' The coroner dismissed the 'excessive speed' theory, being of the opinion that the train had only just left

Wickham Bishops station and was about to stop again at Langford. He added:

> [T]he distance between Wickham and Langford is very short and, moreover, there is an incline from Wickham towards Langford...[*and*] I have always observed that the train always passes slower along that part of the line. But even supposing it was going at the ordinary pace it is not likely the driver would go fast, for as soon as he got the train into full swing he would have to pull up again [*at Langford*].

The Coroner also dismissed the second theory as to possible cause. Mr. Codd said:

> If a train is to go off the line through a sudden shutting off of steam, a good many of us who travel stand in considerable jeopardy, and I can hardly believe that this accident is due solely to the shutting off of steam.

Thus the inquest focussed on the third probability, a defect to the railway line. After calling a number of witnesses and the jury visiting the site of the tragedy and after all the evidence had been heard, the building where the inquest was being held was cleared of everyone except the jury so they could consider their verdict. After approximately one hour of deliberations they returned the following verdict:

> We find, as regards William Day, a verdict of accidental death; that the accident was caused by the breaking of a defective chair [*a cast iron bracket screwed to the sleeper and used to support the rail*] at the point called 'the closer,' and that the chairs in use on the permanent way are too light for the engines in use; we recommend a more careful inspection on the line.

> The jury regret that the line was repaired immediately after the disaster and before it had been properly

inspected, and consider that this practice, though general, is highly reprehensible.

The jury had noted that the GER were able to move workmen on to the line to replace the track (and thus destroy vital evidence) before the Coroner, or anyone else, had had the opportunity of examining the site of the disaster. Should such an accident happen today, the line would have been immediately closed and the area cordoned off awaiting the visit of the Government inspectorate.

Two months after the disaster, the *Chelmsford Chronicle* reported, on 13th August, that the GER had promptly settled three claims made against them for slight injuries and surgeon's bills arising from the accident; 'Two persons have received fifty guineas each and one thirty guineas.' Two other passengers (unnamed) had not as yet made their claims.

For Ann Day, the widow of William Day, the fireman who was killed in the train crash, there was no social security or charitable organisation to help support her in her plight. However, all was not lost. In September, she wrote a letter to the editor of the *Chronicle* in which she acknowledged with sincere thanks the generosity of local people who had helped salve her misery and point to a brighter future than perhaps at the time of his death she could have imagined. She wrote:

> SIR, - With reference to the late accident on the Maldon railway by which the unfortunate man, William Day, the stoker, lost his life, leaving a widow and one child unprovided for, I beg, through your columns, to return my sincere thanks for the contributions which many kind friends have so liberally contributed to my aid, amounting to £14, to enable me to launch into a little business.

> I feel very thankful to all friends for their kindness. ANN DAY (Widow.)
> *Maldon, Sept.* 14th 1869

P.S. – The collection was made by Mr. Walter Ward, at the works of E.H. Bentall, Esq., M.P., Heybridge.

What exactly the 'little business' was is unknown but it is certain that, but for the generosity of her 'friends', Ann Day and her child would surely have been committed to the workhouse.

'Langford Station – The only Station in England having a Station Mistress'

The title of this section is taken from a postcard (pictured) post-marked 1910 of Langford Halt. At that time the lady with the designation of 'Station Mistress' was Mrs. Martha Chapman. Her name and that title appear in the 1901 census. Therefore, it was with some excitement that the authors, for a time at least, believed that the village could boast a 'first' as far as the ladies are concerned.

Langford Station.
The only Station in England having a Station Mistress.

However, further research revealed that the accolade of 'first in England' is erroneous. In her book *Railwaywomen, Exploitation, Betrayal and Triumph* (2005), Helena Wojtczak revealed that there were 'station mistresses' in England as far back as the 1870s. Wojtczak also demonstrated that among the first women employed on Britain's railways were those universally known as 'Station Mistresses.' These were the female equivalent of a clerk-in-charge (or porter-in-charge), an employee who sold tickets and performed administrative work. As the sole member of staff, the clerk-in-charge also performed the duty of crossing keeper (where applicable) and of porter, including duties such as weighing and handling parcels, attending to trains and passengers, lighting signal and station lamps at a small station or halt.

Thus the claim of 'The first Station Mistress in England' cannot be bestowed on Mrs. Chapman, but Helena Wojtczak has agreed that it is safe to say that Martha was one of only a handful of Station Mistresses in England, and that it might even have been the case that she was the only Station Mistress in the county of Essex. It is also interesting to note that, according to the 1911 Census, Fanny Chapman (Martha's daughter-in-law) is shown as the 'Official in Charge,' succeeding Martha at Langford station (Martha had died in 1910) which, as Wojtczak states, 'is interesting in itself.' Also in that Census, Fanny's husband, Frederick George Chapman, is shown as 'Signalman.'

Although the station, station house and enamel signs advertising 'Hudson's Soap' and 'Sutton's Seeds' can be seen on the postcard featured here, no photograph of the lady herself was included. Regrettably research (thus far) has failed to produce any image of Mrs. Chapman.

The red-bricked house at Langford which just happened to be in the vicinity of the station when the railway was constructed was established as the Station House. From the Maldon road customers would have descended wooden steps down the embankment and then passed the cottage gate *en route* to the platform.

Valerie Ellis, who lived in the station house (which had been renamed Railway Cottage) for more than thirty-five years during the second half of the twentieth century, had spotted the classic Grade II 1840s cottage, with its triangular garden, while driving over the railway bridge and later purchased the

261

property. Valerie featured in an article 'Railways Make Wonderful Homes' on the website www.railfan.net told a reporter, "The former residents sold train tickets from the window of what became my bathroom, put the flag out to stop the train..."

Langford resident Albert Chaplin who was born in 1920 and raised in Station Bridge Cottage across the road from Station House can only ever remember purchasing tickets on the train from the guard. Local Historian Dr. Paddy Lacey has commented "It seems likely that tickets were issued by the guard, at least, from the beginning of LNER days if not before," adding that "a similar procedure was in place at Wickham Bishops" although not, of course, with a station mistress.

In the same year as the aforementioned postcard was produced a serious illness befell Mrs. Chapman's husband Charles. The *Wickham Bishops & Langford Parish Magazine* (February 1906) stated:

> One serious case of illness in the parish was that at Langford Railway Station. Mr. Chapman, the husband of our station mistress was struck down suddenly, and slowly became weaker. Most unfortunately, Mr. Chapman became at the same time totally blind.

In July 1906 the local church magazine recorded Charles' death at the age of 81. He is commemorated by a kerbstone and Calvary cross in St. Giles' churchyard which bears the legend 'Charles Chapman of Langford Station.' In late 1909 Martha Chapman herself was taken ill. She died on 18th January 1910 aged 78 and was buried with her husband on 22nd January.

Little is recorded about other occupants of Station House. However, Dennis Bullard who worked as a porter at Maldon East station in 1961/62, recalled that the man who lived in Station House, Langford, at that time was a 'ganger' named

Hopwood. Bullard remarked that, 'the train would stop at Langford every morning and the guard would get out, go over to the house, and knock him up.' The guard's name was Bertie Parmenter and he lived at the railway houses in Spital Road, near to where the former Maldon West Station (long demolished) had stood.

Dennis also remembered that during those opening years of the 1960s Langford Halt was oil-lit. The servicing schedule consisted of station staff from Witham. They would trim the wicks of the lights, refill the oil, tidy up and then catch the next train back. Dennis recalled that the railway 'distance sign' near Langford Hall had to have its lamps changed periodically. A maintenance man would ride out from Maldon to Langford, then walk the track to the sign, replace the lamps, and then walk back to Maldon East.

Fire in the hole

Although there would be no other serious accidents occurring along the Langford stretch of railway line after 1869 there was one incident that caused consternation amongst the villagers. The August 1911 issue of the parish magazine noted with some gravity that 'A very serious fire occurred in the Ballast Hole near Langford Station, on Wednesday 19th July 1911.'

According to the report, 'Three little boys, who shall be nameless' set the Ballast Hole alight at about 12 o'clock and in a very short space of time the fire, fanned by a prevailing wind, saw the whole of the enclosure in flames. Many willing helpers appeared on the scene and after about an hour's hard work the fire was thought to have been subdued. However, at about 3 p.m., the fire broke out again 'with renewed vigour' and was not finally overcome until about 8.30 p.m. Even then it was smouldering 'in a most suspicious way;' but fortunately the wind abated around sunset.

The report continued:

At one time the village appeared to be in imminent danger as the fire was within a few yards of a group of buildings and houses, but fortunately the wind continued to blow from the same quarter and drove it in another direction. Also at one time several of the sleepers on the railway line were on fire. We would impress on all parents the danger of allowing their children to play with matches.

For over fifty years the perpetrators of the 'very serious fire' have remained unnamed in print, although the late Ted Chalk did reveal the names during an interview in 1977. Notes of a meeting with one of the authors that year show that the culprits were none other than Ted and his friends Stan Howlett and Charlie Chapman (son of the signalman at Maldon who lived in Station House) all three were aged between eleven and twelve years old.

According to Ted, the lads had been on a scrumping exercise and thought they would have 'a little bit of fun' and so lit a small fire in the Ballast Hole. Ted recalled that the fire set ferns alight and quickly went out of control. Land next to 'the hole' was rented by Ted's father at the time of the fire. It was set with oats, and the fire found its way through the hedge and to the oats which Ted said 'made things worse.' The fire also spread onto the railway sleepers and the fire engine had to be called. The three were caught and awaited their due punishment. The boys were subsequently banned from attending the Sunday school treat at Langford Grove, and in addition, Ted said: 'we had to write out a whole foolscap sheet of paper out of a book called *The Curfew Bell*, and that was sent up to Revd. Byron to look at.'

The end of steam

By the early 1950s steam locomotives (mainly F5's (a tank locomotive with a 2-4-2 wheel arrangement) and J15's (a tender locomotive with a 0-6-0 wheel arrangement)) were being phased out in the Eastern Region, and on the Maldon to

Witham branch line two-coach diesel sets replaced steam from 14th June 1958. One of these new breed of trains was the 'Railbus,' manufactured by the German company Waggon and Maschinenbau. Known as the '…fleetest thing on rails up to 65 m.p.h.', the Railbus could carry fifty-six passengers seated and forty standing and services began on 7th July, 1958. Denis Swindale, author of *Branch Lines to Maldon* felt that there was:

> a certain attractiveness about the buses as they trundled along from Witham to Maldon. Somehow their diminutive properties seemed to go well with the branch line scene and they radiated a personality of their own which seemed to be reflected by the staff and passengers.

Swindale's research also revealed that drivers on late schedules 'were not averse to allowing interested passengers access to the driving compartment *en route* and it was not unknown for unscheduled stops to be made for passengers who lived alongside the line.' He also discovered that on one occasion 'a honeymoon couple boarding the Railbus found it to be decorated with messages on the windows, tin cans tied to the rear and with detonators placed along the track to speed the happy couple noisily on their way.' One cannot envisage this ever happening in the present day.

Despite the apparent effectiveness of the Railbus, the diesels were not without problems. At the less important end there were difficulties with the carriage of parcels, prams, cycles and other bulky items of luggage. At the top end, as Swindale observed, the Railbuses 'could show a contrary streak at times' and that 'it was not unknown for passengers to assist on a chilly morning start by pushing a recalcitrant bus the length of the platform at Maldon East.'

The reason for this state of affairs was that the Railbus had small batteries, not really powerful enough to guarantee it starting on severely icy mornings. It was usually left out overnight unless there was a warning of inclement weather, when it was put into the loco shed, or rather half in as the back of the shed was always full of timber. It was, as Swindale stated, 'a case of left out and caught out.'

The penultimate 'Railbus' service at Langford Halt, 5th September, 1964.

One of the primary reasons for replacing the former steam locomotives was to save money, and this seemed to have been achieved when, at the end of the first operating year, costs were reduced by £66,000. However, those branches with Railbuses – the Maldon East to Witham included – were still losing around £40,000 per year.

Beeching's Axe falls
On 3rd October 1963 the Acting Traffic Manager of British Railways (Eastern Region) wrote to the Clerk of the County Council of Essex giving notice under Section 56(7) of the Transport Act 1962 to discontinue all railway passenger services between Witham and Maldon East from Monday 2nd March 1964 'and from the following stations' namely Wickham Bishops and Langford and Ulting.

266

On 23rd October 1963 the Council issued a formal Notice of Objection to the Secretary of the Transport Users Consultative Committee for the East Anglia Area based in Cambridge 'on the ground that it will cause hardship to users of the services concerned.' However, in a covering letter the Clerk informed the Secretary of the Consultative Committee that he was 'still making enquiries to ascertain whether the Council are able to give the Committee any evidence of hardship and the object of the enclosed notice is to ensure that the Council are able to give evidence to the Committee should they wish to do so.'

Already alerted to the possibility of closure of the branch line, a public meeting organised by the Maldon Trades Council was held on 24th June at the Moot Hall, Maldon. Approximately seventy-five people (out of a total population for the area affected of in excess of 10,000) attended and, as a result, the Maldon/Witham Campaign Committee was formed with Councillor W.S. 'Bill' Hutchinson elected as Chairman. Interestingly, the Maldon Rural District Council declined to lend their support to the campaign, a note of discussion between the County Council and K.S. Beavins, the Secretary of the Campaign Committee revealing that the MRDC 'were not interested.' A further blow to the branch line's future was suffered when the East Anglian Transport Users Consultative Committee stated that, in their view, the existing Eastern National bus services provided a reasonable and adequate alternative except to the railway at peak hours.

But how did the proposal of closure and the campaign to oppose it affect the residents of Langford? The evidence indicates little or not at all. Of the 100 names and organisations shown on the 'Key list of objectors' not one individual from the village appears – not one. The sole reference to Langford is recorded as 'Maldon Grammary [sic] School Parents Assoc., Langford Lee, Maldon.'

267

Therefore, on the 12th August 1964 the Chairman and Secretary of the Transport Users' Consultative Committee – East Anglian Area, formally notified the Clerk to the County Council of Essex that Ernest Marples, the Minister of Transport, had accepted their findings and given his consent to the closure. However, the closure was not to take place

> Unless and until the provision of the additional bus services…has been authorised by road service licences under the Road Traffic Acts 1960-62 and until all necessary arrangements have been made to ensure that these services are available to the public immediately upon the closure taking place.'

The Mayor of Maldon and Chairman of the Maldon/Witham Railway Campaign Committee, Councillor W.S. Hutchinson, described the closure as 'a disastrous and retrograde step.' He said "I consider that the Transport Users' Consultative Committee have not looked far enough ahead," adding that such a move would have an adverse effect upon the proposed increase in population of Maldon. Of the proposed additional bus services Councillor Hutchinson later said, "They have looked after the commuters, but not the general travelling public."

In addition to the existing number 38 bus route from Maldon to Chelmsford via Heybridge, Langford and Hatfield Peverel, and the number 335 service from Maldon to Braintree via Wickham Bishops, the Consultative Committee announced a new limited stop service (later to be designated service number 99) between Witham and Maldon which stopped at Heybridge, Langford and Ulting Halt and Wickham Bishops Halt. For the Maldon to Witham run, which was Monday to Friday only, buses would leave Maldon at approximately 6.50 a.m., 7.32 a.m., 8.17 a.m., 5.08 p.m., 5.48 p.m. and 6.30 p.m. For the return journey buses would leave Witham at approximately 7.13

a.m., 7.55 a.m., 8.40 a.m., 5.29 p.m., 6.11 p.m. and 6.53 p.m.

Despite acute staff shortages affecting additional bus services introduced elsewhere, Mr. R. Handley, Traffic Manager of Eastern National, was confident the new routes would work. Handley told the *Essex Weekly News*, "We are able to undertake these new services – and we anticipate no difficulty in maintaining them – because they will be operated from our Maldon depot, where we have no overall shortage of staff." He added, "There won't be a great volume of traffic on these services, but we shall run them under a subsidy from the Railways. It will still be cheaper for them than maintaining their own operations at a loss."

The Member of Parliament for Maldon, Mr. Brian Harrison, who had earlier expressed his support for the Beeching Plan, gave his support to the protest against closure but it was less than a cursory nod in the direction of his constituents, as at a public meeting in February 1964 Harrison told the 'fewer than 30 objectors present' that he thought the campaign against closure was started too late.

A Public Notice in the *Essex County Standard* dated 14th August 1964, confirmed the closure. So, despite less than strenuous opposition to the closure, the passenger train service between Witham and Maldon was withdrawn 'on and from Monday, 7th September, 1964.' The final passenger train was scheduled to pull into Maldon East station on Sunday 6th September at 9.05 p.m. The line was closed to freight three years later.

So it is clear that no-one in Langford vehemently (or otherwise) objected to the closure of the station. Photographer Keith Yuill, who lived a few hundred yards from the parish boundary in Holloway Road, Heybridge at the time, was the only 'near Langford' regular user of the rail services. However, on Sunday 6th September, when a passenger train left Witham station for Maldon East for the last time, 'Ban Beeching' banners, gas flares, dowsed station lights and pulled communication cords were some of the tokens of final protest. Dr. Beeching was sent an invitation to attend 'the funeral of the Maldon-Witham passenger rail service at East Maldon Station, Essex at 8.13 p.m., Sunday September 6th. R.S.V.P.' but no reply was received.

The last train left Witham station at 8.53 p.m. and was crammed with passengers all clutching their one-way tickets, despondently thinking that the current fourteen minutes on the train would soon be replaced by a forty minute journey on the bus. Mr. H. Ellis, the Witham ticket collector, who lived in Wickham Bishops, said that "For 117 years this line has been working. The Government spends £50,000,000 on rockets and then closes railway lines."

An *Essex Chronicle* reporter identified only as 'JM' noted:

> I stood with a group of despondent passengers and stared at the old train standing by the platform feeling the sentiment befitting the occasion when suddenly there was a loud yell followed by a lusty chorus of a newly-worded war song. Faces creased into grins as words expressing obvious disapproval of the line closure, rang across the station. Grins turned into hoots of laughter as there appeared a group of young demonstrators, dressed in sacks and toppers, carrying banners which read 'Ban Beeching not the Railway.' Throughout the journey the demonstrators kept spirits high with their antics but at the same time pressed their point home.

The boys, who all came from Maldon and thereabouts, included Keith Yuill. Unfortunately the words to the song have long disappeared from memory.

The Mayor of Maldon, Mr. 'Bill' Hutchinson, was also a passenger on the last trip. He had been the Chairman of the

Maldon/Witham Railway Campaign Committee which fought to keep the line open and which vowed to fight on to prevent any similar catastrophes. On the arrival at Maldon East Station about 200 people gathered on the platform to hear a speech from the Mayor, who stressed that the railway committee would carry on fighting and hoped it would receive plenty of support. Mr. Hutchinson said "This is a very sad day for Maldon. We have struggled hard since March 1963, and done all we could as a railway committee." The *Essex Chronicle* reporter noted that 'All eyes turned as the 'Crab and Winkle' hooted and slowly left the station. Traffic at the level crossing just outside the station waited for the train and drivers sounded their horns as it passed. Two hundred former Witham to Maldon rail travellers left the railway station in silence – many had to find another way to get back to Witham.' (It should be noted here that the nickname 'Crab and Winkle' did not actually apply to the Maldon to Witham line but to the Tiptree-Tollesbury line. The cub reporter for the *Chronicle* was in error.)

Swindale commented:

> As the diesel set moved off into the dusk, on its last passenger carrying trip to Witham, detonators banged under its wheels all along the route but at the main line station the promised reinforcements failed to appear, whilst the concern of the Witham station staff was centred on the running of main line trains to Liverpool Street.

He continued:

> The final return trip to Maldon was made in near darkness, the train slipping quietly along towards Maldon, past the darkening fields and lonely cottages, rumbling over the wooden viaducts, past the glow worm oil lamps of Wickham Bishops station and Langford Halt, where people dressed in sacking cavorted on the platform, past the Maldon home signal, over the level

crossing and into the pool of light surrounding the terminus. Slowing to a halt at the platform, the train brought 116 years of passenger service to a close.

As the *Maldon and Burnham Standard* commented, 'Maldon's rail service ended, oh so quietly.'

The closure of the line caused them great problems as they were not allowed to put bags of winkles on buses. Other regular users were greatly inconvenienced – women with prams had been able to put them in the guard's van on the train, but could not take them on the bus. Maldon commuters were also hit very hard by the closure as they had to arrange private transport to Witham in the early hours of the morning.

The Witham-Maldon branch now entered into a dreary period during which it was a freight-only line with trains three times a day, carrying mainly canned fruit and agricultural machinery, and although the track continued to be maintained, the signs of dereliction were beginning to appear. After the initial shock of the fall of 'Beeching's Axe,' the fact that the rails were still *in situ* and still in use had led to local hopes that all was still not yet lost as far as the resumption of passenger services was concerned – while there was track, there was hope. But of course, this was not to be. Langford Halt and its sister at Wickham Bishops took on the air of ghosts, and some 150 people in old Wickham Bishops village were, to quote the press 'cut off from the outside world' with no transport other than what they had themselves, and even the one tiny village shop closed.

In the end even the diminishing freight transport on the Witham to Maldon branch line ceased, and in early 1966 a statement was issued by Mr. P.R. Gillett, Public Relations Officer for British Rail (Eastern Region), to the effect that it was proposed to close Maldon East station (Goods) in April with a loss of twenty-six jobs. Maldon East would be closed as a public depot, and coals and parcels traffic would be transferred to Witham, giving an estimated saving of some £40,000 per year.

Various ideas for taking over the railway and running it as a going concern were bandied about over the next few months, but nothing happened, and even these were totally destroyed when in August and September 1967 the rails from beneath the two bridges carrying the Witham to Hatfield Peverel roads were removed.

Lifting the rails

Beneath the bridges strong concrete rafts were constructed with foot square timbers set in them at close intervals, to support the road above. Just enough room remained for the passage of a pedestrian or horseman, but certainly not for a train. The line now became the point just north of Langford and Ulting Halt. Maldon East station was cut off. Swindale noted:

The reopening campaign went on and a newspaper cartoon of the time showed passengers propelling themselves along the line in large roofed handcars bearing the inscription 'Maldon-Witham Do It Yourself

273

Railway. Keeps You Fit. Trains When You Like. No
Speed Limit.' Whilst this may have been faintly
amusing, it could not have presented the sort of image
desired by the promotors.

In the first week of 1968 the station house at Wickham
Bishops, together with three-quarters of an acre of land,
which included the garden and station yard, was offered
for sale by British Rail at a cost of £2,500 freehold. The
rails still lay between Witham and Maldon waiting for
something to happen, but nothing did apart from some
gaps appearing between Langford and Ulting Halt and
Maldon where farmers lifted the rails aside to gain easier
access to their fields on either side of the track. Swindale
observed that 'Now and then, a tiny Wickham trolley
spluttered its solitary way southwards out of Witham,
stopping every so often whilst its sole occupant collected
various small items of equipment from beside the track,
but then even these operations came to an end and the line
was completely dead.'

The station and yard at Wickham Bishops were duly sold
as a private residence, the tiny canopy/shelter at Langford
and Ulting Halt was removed leaving just a skeleton of the
framework and the platform intact. The house was sold.

In 1969 the track was at last removed. For ease of transport
much of it had been cut into two-foot lengths and scrap
metal thieves were particularly grateful for this as it eased
their transportation problems. After the closure proper, the
railway bridge at Langford (which had already been
supported underneath by wooden struts) was filled in with
earth to match the existing embankment. The road bridge
beyond Langford Hall had its parapets removed and
replaced by fencing. The third bridge, which used to exit
down a track opposite Langford Hall, was quickly
demolished, and the line filled in to extend the farmland.

The bridge over the Blackwater (before)

In May 1965 the 'bowstring span' of the viaduct across the River Blackwater on the Woodham Ferrers to Maldon Branch, was blown up. It had been suggested that the old viaduct might serve as part of a western by-pass around Maldon, but it had been deemed unsuitable as a road bridge and so was demolished. With the removal of the span, only the piers were left as a reminder of one of the best known landmarks in the area, and a lovely walk between the two Maldon stations came to an abrupt halt. Eventually the western by-pass was approved and, following the line from the Langford Curve to where the former Maldon West Station used to be, it became at that time the most expensive length of road, per mile, ever constructed.

So the story of the railway in Langford ended, and the track and halt became overgrown and derelict, but never quite forgotten.

Memories of the railway at Langford
Ken Pitt of Tillingham remembered that his mother used to take him to see his grandmother on the steam train. On a

Sunday afternoon the fare was 4d return for an adult. The guard-cum-ticket collector was a Langford man named Harry Parmenter. He remembered that his

2nd-SINGLE   SINGLE-2nd

Maldon East & Heybridge to
Maldon East &   Maldon East &
Heybridge   Heybridge
Langford & Ulting   Langford & Ulting
LANGFORD & ULTING
(E)   0/6   Fare   0/6   (E)
For conditions see over   For conditions see over

mother used to start from home after lunch with him (in his pram) and his elder brother. They lived then in the lower part of Maldon – Blackwater Terrace, now demolished – so they had to go across the Downs to the Shrimp Brand (Truman's Beer Storage) yard, across the old Fullbridge, down to Station Road and on to the train. Having alighted at Langford, they had to walk down to Langford Cross and up Maypole Road almost to the Shoulder of Mutton pub as his grandmother lived in the house before that. Clearly, although the train brought benefits, journeys were not always easy.

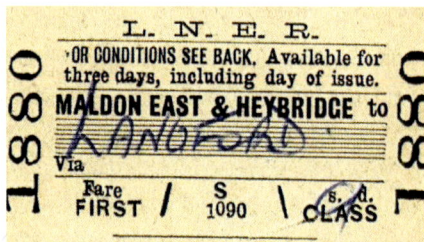

L. N. E. R.
OR CONDITIONS SEE BACK. Available for three days, including day of issue.
MALDON EAST & HEYBRIDGE to
LANGFORD
Via
Fare   S
FIRST / 1090 \ CLASS

Local reminiscences recall that the cost of travelling from Langford to Witham was 1d for children, and the time allowed for a journey from Langford to Maldon was three minutes. One villager recalled that you stopped the train by taking the green flag down; there used to be a fence along the platform with a hole in it, and the end of the flag was stuck in the hole so that the driver could see it. If you wanted the train to stop then you took the flag down. However, this method had its disadvantages, because if you were at Witham Station and you wanted to stop at Langford, there might not be anyone there to take the flag down. For night travel there was a light which was green on one side and red on the other. If you wanted the train to stop you'd turn the green light to face Witham (if the train was coming from Witham) and vice versa; a green light meant 'stop'!

Another anecdote, from the late Ted Chalk during an interview in 1977, was that a lot of fishermen used to come through to Langford on a Sunday to fish at Beeleigh or in the river. On one particular Sunday the train was rather long and the engine went beyond the platform, and someone in the carriage nearest to the engine stepped out, and there was no platform there.

In the publication *Maldon Past Times* in April 2005, local historian, Stephen P. Nunn, described an imaginary journey from Maldon to Langford based on 'ticket number 1885' from his collection of local memorabilia. It is an interesting foray into his imagination of the past.

Back in August 1980 Essex County Council was deliberating whether to buy the disused railway line, and there was talk of a six mile traffic-free link between Witham and Maldon which, according to the *Evening Gazette* would have been 'the answer to every rambler's prayer.' However, this came to nothing. The land was cleared for cyclists and runners following the Blackwater Rail Trail. Valerie Ellis, who lived in Station House, kept a few of the signs, and often showed enthusiasts old photographs and the remains of the platform.

There were again rumours that the branch line might be re-opened, but sadly, these were unfounded. With the changes that had been made this effectively meant that the line could not easily be re-established without a lot of upheaval (and expense).

In January 2000 hopes were again raised as a scheme was unveiled to create a continuous walk, cycle path and bridleway between Witham and Maldon via Langford utilising the route of the former branch line. The Blackwater Rail Trail project again tested the idea, and a £3,000 feasibility study was undertaken by Sustrans – the charity behind developing a national cycling network. Unfortunately, although the County Council had once owned the land, sections had been lost or bought, so there was no longer a continuous route and although unofficially it was possible to walk the route, it was not suitable for cycling or riding. The study noted that if the route were to become part of the national cycleway, the surfacing would need to be improved and the path would need to be widened for horses. However, the part of the old line from Wickham Bishops to Langford has now been bought by a private individual and walkers are redirected down a public footpath that by-passes his land.

A fitting memorial

In May 2005, one of the enamel station name plates that had hung on Langford and Ulting halt was presented to the Langford and Beeleigh Miniature Railway (LBMR), at the Museum of Power. Valerie Madle (formerly Ellis), the former owner of Station Cottage, donated the sign to mark the LBMR's first birthday. By doing so, Valerie also ensured that this valuable piece of local railway memorabilia would remain in the village for all time.

Today the LBMR, which circumnavigates the main site of the Museum of Power and is run for the public's enjoyment on event days and other special occasions, is thriving whilst the original halt less than half a mile away lies redundant, overgrown and dilapidated.

The railway may have gone, but it was the coming of the waterworks that set Langford apart from the numerous other picturesque Essex villages which today remain practically unchanged by time. Two large complexes (one in the centre of the village; the other at the western end about one mile away) were to change the face and nature of Langford forever.

CHAPTER EIGHT
AN 'OBSCURE VILLAGE' TRANSFORMED
The Coming of the Waterworks

Until the early 1920s the village of Langford had remained more or less entirely unaffected by progress or advancements in technology. True, the railway had arrived in 1848, but this was situated at the far eastern end of the village near the edge of the parish boundary and was a mere halt, nothing more. Trains were infrequent, and villagers who lived beyond St. Giles' Church would hardly have known it was there.

However, the same cannot be said about the coming of the Southend Waterworks Company (SWC) and Langford Waterworks - a massive hi-tech (for its day) structure built right in the centre of Langford which included a 150 feet tall hexagonal chimney, which was to become a prominent landmark for both residents (especially children finding their way home) and road travellers alike for nearly forty years.

The new Waterworks in 1929

279

Why should the idyllic village of Langford of less than 200 souls, with an agricultural heritage and not much else, be selected as the place into which to supplant a world-class, highly advanced waterworks? What made Langford special? Before we answer those questions it is important to outline the history of the SWC.

Southend Waterworks Company – A Brief History

The foundation stone of the Southend Waterworks Company was laid in 1865 as a private undertaking; the original works being provided for the supply of Cliff Town, Southend-on-Sea – a total of approximately 486 premises. The works consisted of a pumping station in Milton Road, Southend, and a reservoir in Cambridge Road. In 1871 the works were taken over by The Southend Waterworks Company and eight years later the company was incorporated as a Statutory Undertaking and the supply extended to some surrounding villages so that by 1900 the number of premises being supplied with water was 7,714.

The Company's area of operation in 1924 was 160 square miles, bounded on the south by the River Thames, the north by the River Crouch and extending west as far as the outskirts of Shenfield, near Brentwood. Bulk supplies on the northern fringe effectively increased the area supplied by the Company to 200 square miles. To begin with the increases in demand were met by sinking more wells and bore-holes so that eventually thirty-seven such sources existed within the area of operation. Extraction became increasingly difficult and expensive, so the Southend Waterworks Company turned its attention to the possibility of abstracting water from a number of Essex rivers. These included the river that flowed through Langford – the River Blackwater.

In the early 1920s, Dr. John Thresh M.D. D.Sc., at the time the world's leading authority on the chemistry and bacteriology of drinking water supplies, was appointed by the

Southend Waterworks Company to work at the new experimental plant which had been constructed at Langford. Dr. Thresh's brief was to act on that Company's behalf to help promote a bill through Parliament for the abstraction of water from the Rivers Blackwater, Chelmer, and Ter for purification and then pumping to Southend.

According to the HMSO publication *Water Supply from Underground Sources* by William Whitaker and John Thresh published in 1916, Langford was chiefly supplied with water from two public wells, both yielding 'doubtful water.' Cottages some distance away from these wells used ditch water which must have been even more doubtful in quality!

Langford was not the Company's first choice of site for their latest undertaking. In 1921 a proposed joint project with the South Essex Waterworks Company to extract water from the River Stour failed to gain Parliamentary approval due to strong opposition from local authorities in the Companies' area of supply. Langford was then selected as the next best alternative site with the Southend Waterworks Company going it alone. However, before the major expansion programme could be implemented (including the provision of a new steam-driven pumping station and water treatment plant), there was important research work to be undertaken and for this purpose an experimental plant had been constructed.

The Experimental Plant

In 1920 an experimental plant was constructed at the edge of the River Blackwater (near to where the Museum of Power visitor car park is situated today). Dr. John Clough Thresh was appointed by the SWC to work at the experimental plant; his brief being to discover a method of producing pure drinking water from the River Blackwater.

Articled to Dr. Thresh during the period 1920—1925 was Robert Walton, who first knew Langford in 1920 when he met Thresh for discussions regarding the operation of a possible model waterworks (later to be known as the 'experimental plant') which Walton employed to discover a method of producing pure drinking water from the River Blackwater. In a letter to one of the authors in 1985, Walton wrote that being articled to Dr. Thresh was "according to Thresh, reward beyond price." In other words, the salary Walton received was extremely low. However, Walton did have enough resources available to purchase a camera, and his donation of a small photograph album to the authors' archive enables a selection of these previously unpublished amateur 'snaps' to be reproduced here.

The final approved method of purification was formally adopted only after a long series of tests at the experimental plant conducted by Thresh, Walton and other associates in conjunction with the company's engineer. The Bill was lodged in Parliament on 24th May 1924 and received Royal Assent the following August, becoming known as The Southend Waterworks Act 1924. One condition of the Act was that a Resident Chemist and Bacteriologist be appointed for scientific management of the plant. Robert Walton was duly appointed from 21st June 1927 at a salary of £300 per annum (rising to £350 after five years) together with accommodation at the Mill House in the village, plus a three-speed Raleigh bicycle – generous terms indeed!

One might have imagined that after August 1927 (the time of the completion of the new waterworks complex), the small experimental plant had outlived its usefulness, but this was not the case; far from it. The then redundant experimental plant was used for storage, but was re-commissioned in 1929 when Langford caused an outbreak of 'taste' in Southend. Gilbert Houghton B.Sc. was appointed to find the cause.

Gilbert recalled, "The notion was that the trouble was algal growth, and I was soon sure that it wasn't.

The Experimental Plant c. 1925

Not until much later did we realise that it all arose from the activities of the Courtaulds' plant at Bocking, where they did a lot of bleaching, and the trouble was chlorophenols!" (Chlorophenols are a group of compounds that are used in a number of industries and products. Exposure to high levels can cause damage to the liver and immune system.)

The same building from another angle

In the 1930s, the experimental plant was once again used for storage.

283

At one time it housed a saw-bench and during the Second World War A.R.P. equipment was stored there. It also served for some time as a mess room for waterworks employees. Indeed the building itself stood for over 30 years in total before the majority of it was demolished in the early 1950s.

And another view....

Now long gone, the experimental plant stood where today trees, grass and the Museum of Power (MoP) visitors' car park forms a natural boundary between what used to be the cricket pitch (now an exhibition and display area) and the path and concrete bridge which leads over the river from the car park to the original pumping station building in which are housed the main MoP exhibits.

And from the end...

Visitors walking from the car park to the museum along the concrete path rarely think about the history of the building. But anyone who pauses on that bridge on their way to the museum and looks towards the road bridge will see the only remaining fragment of the experimental plant - the flow measurement weir.

The Flow Measurement weir

As for Robert Walton, whose 'snaps' have so helped to illuminate this aspect of the waterworks' past, he left Langford in December 1927 for what he euphemistically described as 'greener pastures' investigating the water supplies of Alexandria and Cairo where he remained for over thirty-five years, much of his work there being based on what he had learned and discovered in his seven years at Langford.

The Construction of the Waterworks

With the go-ahead given to build the steam pumping station and water treatment plant at Langford, on land previously owned by the Byron family, the anticipated completion date was 1928. Although the villagers had no say whatsoever concerning the 'invasion' of Langford by the waterworks (no strict planning laws in those days), in an interview in August 1977 the late Ted Chalk was of the view that any inquisitive residents were told everything would be concealed as much as possible. This was achieved by planting trees along the main road (which had until then been open ground), with the

285

result that most of the works was indeed concealed from view except, of course, the 150 feet tall chimney.

On 2nd April 1926, the *Chelmsford Chronicle* reported on the annual meeting of the Southend Waterworks Company, noting that Mr. Joseph Francis, O.B.E., Chairman, said:

> that he hoped that next year the directors would be able to report that the first section of the new works would be nearing completion. Anyone happening to go through the village of Langford, if he had not known it previously, would come to the conclusion that now, instead of being a calm, peaceful, pasture-land village, Langford was a hive of industry. The first, or Chelmer, section of the scheme was estimated to cost £638,000, and the second – the Blackwater section – £191,000, making a total of £829,000. The company still had to go to 34 different sources for water, and of course that cost money.

The workforce required to build this vast enterprise was extensive, and comprised mainly of Irish 'navvies,' and accommodation was built for them on the field to the west of Langford Stream. On the whole the workforce was disciplined and friendly, but on occasions this was not the case. The *Chelmsford Chronicle* of 24th September 1926 reported on a serious incident under the banner heading "Fight at Langford: Wounded at the Infirmary":

> As the result of a free fight about midnight on Saturday among some of the men employed on the Southend Water Works at Langford, two had to be taken to the Infirmary at Maldon after being attended to by Drs. Lee and Faulkner, who stitched up their rather severe wounds. Insp. Bilner received a telephone message that a serious disturbance was taking place, and at once proceeded to Langford with P.s. Spurling and three constables. They found a crowd of men fighting with bars of iron, bricks etc. and were able to put an end to it.

A hut that had been built for sleeping accommodation for the men had been practically demolished, and there was blood in all directions. There has been quite a lot of disturbance lately in this quiet little village.

Mercifully such episodes were few and far between, although merely a week later, on 1st October 1926 the *Chelmsford Chronicle* again reported violent behaviour among the navvies:

On Monday, at Maldon, before S.G. Tydeman and J.R. Ward, Esqrs., Michael Laffey, labourer, employed on the Southend waterworks at Langford, charged with unlawfully wounding David Frost, at the Mill, Langford, on Saturday, pleaded guilty. The charge was reduced to one of common assault.

The complainant stated that he was in the same employ, and on Saturday went to bed on the top floor of the Mill at 8.30 p.m. About 10.30 he was awakened by someone hitting him as he lay in bed. He could not tell who it was, but supposed it was the prisoner, who then pulled him off the bed on to the floor, got him by the throat, tried to strangle him, struck him again, and kicked him violently in the side. He shouted for help, and "the boss," Mr. Blayden, came and pulled prisoner off. Witness knew of no reason for prisoner's assault, and had not seen him before.

When the case came to court the prisoner was informed that this brutality and these brawls must cease; this kind of behaviour would not be tolerated. The prisoner was sentenced to two months' hard labour and the expense of conveying him to the police station (5/-), was ordered to be taken from the money found on him.

But it was not only the behaviour of the navvies that caused problems. The weather was poor for much of the building works, but the *Chelmsford Chronicle* of 4th November 1927 reported:

> Despite unfavourable weather, rapid progress has been made of late on the extensive new works of the Southend Waterworks Co., at Langford, and already Southend is being supplied with water from this source. One reservoir is in use, while another is nearing completion. When the two are in action, it will be possible to deal with 8,000,000 gallons of water a day. The second reservoir is expected to be ready by January, and it is anticipated that the whole works, including new intake works from the Blackwater, will be completed by the middle of next summer. At one time eight hundred men were engaged on this undertaking. The principal buildings are constructed, and the machinery, treatment appliances, etc., are installed...The pumping station with its imposing appearance; the huge reservoirs of reinforced concrete; and the treatment centre, with its filtering plant, are all exceedingly interesting. The premises are equipped with an electric generating plant, which also supplies eight cottages specially erected for waterworks staff. Other workmen are lodging in Langford Mill, which has been turned into flats. The water at present comes from the rivers Chelmer and Ter, and the elaborate system of purification prevents any possibility of contamination. "We have had many difficulties," said Mr. Green [*the resident engineer*], "but it now seems that we are getting to the end of them."

The new waterworks complex was actually completed in 1927 and taken into use fully on 29th August. A reporter for the *Essex Chronicle* at the time wrote that the arrival of the works had 'transformed the obscure Essex village into a place of considerable importance.'

Langford Waterworks were inaugurated on 18th September 1929 by H.M. Lieutenant of Essex, Brigadier-General R.B. Colvin, C.B. A large gathering was present at the inauguration and the Chairman of the Waterworks Directors, Mr. Joseph Francis, O.B.E. J.P. and of course Dr. J.C. Thresh 'MD, DSc, FIC etc.' who had been responsible for the experimental work at Langford, were congratulated on the successful issue of the five years' work.

The scheme had cost 'a million of money.' Care was taken to preserve the beauty of the riverside as far as possible, although the works and necessary housing for employees were, naturally, extensive.

In conjunction with the building of the pumping station, two large reservoirs were constructed, each having a capacity of 30 million gallons (136,380,000 litres) of water and covered some 10.5 acres of land (4.35 hectares). They were gravity fed from a water intake on the River Chelmer (at Rushes Lock) along a 33 inch diameter concrete pipeline for 2½ miles to the reservoir, and from the River Blackwater at Langford Mill. The raw water gravitated from the reservoirs to the pumping station then was raised by 'low lift' pumps to the purification works about a mile to the west. After treatment it gravitated back again, and was then pumped along a 28 inch cast iron pipe by 'highlift' pumps to Oakwood Service Reservoirs, fourteen miles from Langford, for distribution.

It was also realised at the time that sewage effluent from Chelmsford and Witham had to be piped below the extraction points. In essence this meant that the effluent from Chelmsford was piped through another 33 inch concrete main to below the Chelmer intake (Rushes Lock). In the case of Witham, the effluent from there was pumped through a 24 inch steel main to below the Langford Mill intake. (Later, when the Hanningfield No. 1 Pumping Station was constructed at Langford, the Chelmsford effluent had to be piped below the intake (which was at Langford) directly into the tidal River Chelmer. The new pumping station also pumped water into the Langford reservoirs.)

The Langford project was something completely new. Since the Great War, conditions generally had so altered with regard to both the increase in the constructional cost of sinking wells and of operating and maintaining the machinery at pumping stations, that these considerations led the Company to the conclusion that the future lay more economically, more securely, in the utilisation of rivers in conjunction with the existing underground water sources.

Building the reservoirs - 1926

The 1924 Act gave the Company authority to abstract water from the three rivers by separate intakes and to use such water for supply after purification.

The pumping station, apart from featuring its tall chimney, originally at the time of the official opening ceremony contained two steam-driven vertical triple-expansion rotative engines manufactured by the Lilleshall Company Ltd., of

Oakengates, Shropshire, each with a pumping capacity of between 4 and 4.4 million gallons of water per day. The Engine House was built large enough to house a third engine which was installed in 1931. When the steam pumping station was decommissioned on 31st October 1963 this third engine was 'retained for historical reasons' and now serves as the centre-piece in the exhibition hall of the Museum of Power and was returned to steam operation on 20th September 2011.

For those technically minded, the steam provided a pressure of 210lbs per square inch with the superheat of 150° Fahrenheit from the two boilers. Complete coal-handling gear was provided for feeding coal to the boilers via the chain grate stokers, the arrangement being designed to provide 'maximum convenience with a minimum of labour effort.' The Southend Waterworks Company was keen to point out that the works were 'electronically lighted,' power being provided for both the treatment plant and the pumping station by three 80 Kw steam-driven direct-coupled generators – a state-of-the-art affair. There was at that time no electricity supply in the village.

In addition to these main features the pumping station was equipped with a machine shop boasting 'Tools for practically all repair and maintenance work.' A recovery plant was also installed to convert into lime the waste chalk which resulted from the water purification process.

Housing accommodation, in the form of four pairs of semi-detached houses, was built in Ulting Lane in addition to four properties which had already been purchased by SWC. Langford Mill House was converted by the company into two flats to be occupied by the Resident Chemist and the Resident Engineer. The Ulting Lane residences were increased by a further eight properties in 1954 constructed by L. E. Claydon of Ulting.

Nos. 1-6 Ulting Lane under construction in 1927

And finished....

The works were designed by and carried out under the supervision of Messrs. T. & C. Hawksley and Mr. E.C. Bilham. They also carried out and supervised the building works. The contract for the chemical and filtration plant was awarded to the Paterson Engineering Company. The total cost of the works was estimated at approximately £1 million in 1928. In reality the actual capital cost of the project was £1,108,719, which included £88,470 for the 'estate,' purchase of land and houses, laying out of roads, replanting trees and general development of the site. Lord Byron had ensured that the Company could not just go ahead and build where and how they liked. Clause 43 (7) of the Act stated that:

All buildings to be erected by the Company on any lands acquired by them... shall be erected with due consideration to the amenities of the locality and of Langford Grove and all such buildings (other than temporary buildings during construction) shall be erected only in accordance with such elevations and general drawings as shall be approved by the owner's Surveyor...

Progress has meant that the 'excess lime process' of water purification has been long superseded, but it is interesting to look back and outline the process as described in the booklet published for the inauguration of the new works in September 1929:

The raw water is received at the treatment plant and measured in passing over a weir, which divides it into two variable portions in the approximate ratio of 1 to 6. The smaller portion is mixed with lime to produce sufficient lime water to give an excess of two grains of lime per gallon when mixed with the larger portion. The lime water is prepared by adding cream of lime in mixing tanks where it is continuously agitated, and it is then passed forward into a second set of tanks, where it is mixed with the bulk of the supply which has already been treated with alumina. The water undergoes agitation in these tanks for 20 minutes, the result being the formation of a very heavy precipitate which settles out rapidly in the primary settling tanks into which the water then flows, the supernatant water overflowing into a collecting channel. This partially clarified water enters three sets of contact tanks of long rectangular shape, each having a capacity of two million gallons. Leaving the contact tanks the water passes through the

293

carbonating chamber where Carbonic Acid Gas is forced through the water precipitating the excess lime and partially re-dissolving it. Final purification is effected by filtration through a battery of Paterson rapid quartz sand filters, 14 in number, each measuring 24 feet by 14 feet. These filters are cleansed by agitation with compressed air followed by a reverse flow of wash water to remove the collected matter loosened by the air scouring process.

The used wash water which has been softened and is not loaded with bacteria is collected in a reservoir, and after allowing 12 hours for sedimentation is returned to the mixing tanks, where it mixes with the water undergoing treatment.

Water samples were also sent to the laboratories of Dr. Thresh in London. In the March 1929 document *Description of River Works*, the Southend Waterworks Company announced that 'Examinations of the purified water…have shown uniformly excellent results since the works were brought into use on the 29th August 1927, and in no examination has the *B. Coli* [*Bacillus Coli*] been found in 100 c.c. of the treated water, whilst the total hardness has always been below the maximum limit of 15 parts per 100,000 as prescribed by the Southend Waterworks Act of 1924, the temporary hardness being almost completely removed.' ('*Bacillus coli*' was later reclassified in the newly created genus Escherichia and subsequently commonly abbreviated to '*E coli*'.)

When asked what effect the coming of the waterworks had on the community, one resident, the late Ted Chalk, said that there were a lot of Irish navvies about the village, especially when the reservoir was being built. He noted that 'great cranes were swinging about and five steam locomotives, like railway engines, ran on tracks and used to pull trucks around the site.' The navvies were always friendly, and would go down to Heybridge to the pub(s) and make a lot of noise coming back at night.

Lord Byron, ex-Rector of Langford, and owner of much of the land in the village, wrote to the Misses Baker, of Langford Lee, in September 1926:

> Langford seems to be going to the dogs! It is certainly far from a pleasure to visit it now. I only trust that after they have finished turning the place upside down it may settle down to some semblance of peace.

Jeanie Baker replied on 14th September:

> You are quite right about the Waterworks, they are awful, they work day and night and the noise is terrific, and the navvies are decidedly unpleasant. But in spite of all Langford remains very attractive to us.'

(This correspondence is now housed in the Essex Record Office in Chelmsford.)

The 'Black Gang' (the men who drove the engines) had their headquarters on the western side of the river bridge. Some lived in old army huts, others in the Mill. One villager, (the late Ron Harvey), recalled during an interview in August 2007 that "There were about 40-50 navvies who lived in the Mill, and sometimes they would sleep in the pipes they laid, using sacking as bedding. They used to drink in the *Half Moon* pub in Heybridge and were always rolling about the village, but they never interfered with anyone." Ron added that later P.c Oddy occupied an old cottage in Hall Road, presumably to ensure that the navvies behaved, but only lived there "for the duration of the building works."

There was no junction or branch line at the Langford and Ulting Halt in the mid-1920s or at Wickham Bishops station some distance away so nothing could be delivered to the river works site by rail.

The gang of workers building Langford Waterworks. (The man with the mark above his head is John Taylor, and he features in several other photographs in the series with the same identification mark)

Instead a number of standard gauge engines were utilised in the construction of the waterworks and they were brought to the village by road. Records show that in 1926 G. Shellabear & Son Limited had four standard gauge locomotives on a contract 'to build a reservoir at Maldon.' Of course the reference to Maldon is a misnomer – but only by about three miles. Maldon was, and of course still is, the nearest large town to Langford – and drawing nearer by the year! That reference to a 'reservoir' did, of course, refer to Langford.

Albert recalled one train in particular when he was a six year old which was "a lovely red loco." He also remembers "a little steam crane" (pictured on page 299) which used to unload goods from the trucks. As far as the authors are aware, only one photograph of an 0-4-0 (and the little steam crane) at Langford exists. It is included here but unfortunately the names of those standing on the engine are (currently) lost to history.

The 'Little red loco'

The standard gauge trains arrived at Maldon East Station on a goods train. Albert Chaplin said, "They simply couldn't get them off at Langford, and Wickham Bishops was only accessible by bending, winding country lanes." It would also have been too costly to construct a new branch line from Langford halt to the site about a quarter of a mile away. In addition, any such plan would probably have meant the demolition of private residences and certainly encroachment on farm land and there would have been an enormous outcry against that. So the engines were 'transported' to Langford along the main road. Two pieces of track were laid down on the road and the engine driven along to the end. The engine was then stopped to allow men to haul the first piece of track round to the front and then it was moved another length of track, and so on until the engine reached the site of the new waterworks three miles away. Albert said "Luckily there were no major corners on the road from Maldon East Station to Langford, but what there were, I think, were negotiated with the use of crowbars." He also estimated that "It must have been a good night's work," made easier by the fact that there would have been little or no traffic.

297

Construction begins

The main rail head at the river works site was on the other side of the river and so a small but strong timber bridge was constructed across to link the two parts of the site (the main pumping station and outbuildings and reservoir). By the time the works was brought into use on 29th August 1927 the four little locos and the temporary railway had been removed. Seven decades later the sound of trains on site would be heard again, with the opening of the Langford and Beeleigh (Miniature) Railway as part of the attractions at the Museum of Power.

In 2006, the river works railway became the focus of discussion between members of the Great Eastern Railway Society (GERS) in their magazine *Great Eastern News* (Spring 2006, Issue No. 126). The following appeared in that issue and was provided by Robin Waywell, a member of the Industrial Railway Society (IRS). Robin wrote:

> The loco in the photograph appears to be an 0-6-0ST built by Manning Wardle as one of their Class "L" locomotives. I have no record of a loco of this type being owned by Shellabear, not surprising as details of contractors locos are somewhat lacking. Certainly

298

Shellabear didn't acquire it from new as they are not listed in the makers' records as having been supplied with a new loco, therefore it's likely it was purchased second-hand or hired from a dealer or quite likely another contractor (not uncommon).

It should be noted that Shellabear had a plant yard at Park Royal in West London. This location was also the depot of another contractor Walter Scott & Middleton Ltd; this company known to have had a number of locos stored at Park Royal. Given the fact that two companies shared the same site it is quite likely that Shellabear bought or hired a loco from Walter Scott & Middleton for the Langford contract, but which one is anybody's guess."

The little steam crane and 'the workers'

Albert Chaplin recalls that the locomotives came from 'London docks.'

Following on from Robin's revelations it was not long before even more information was forthcoming. In this instance another member of the GERS who had visited the Museum of Power subsequently wrote a letter of enquiry to the Editor of the *Great Eastern News*. It was fellow member Gordon Wells who responded as follows:

> In the late 1950's I became friends with the now late Jack Shuttlewood who, at about the time the construction began at Langford Waterworks was driving a road locomotive for John Sadd of Maldon hauling round timber to their sawmill. He recounted to me many times how the engines were delivered to the site at Langford. They were delivered by rail to Maldon, once unloaded they were steamed along the public road to Langford. The method used was to lay the rails on their sides. They would probably have been 30 foot x 56 or 60lbs per yard much favoured by contractors.

Many years later in conversation with a farming contractor from Hatfield Peverel he also described the engines being moved as above. He also added that one of the engines had worked for the Port of London Authority (PLA),... sold sometime to G. Shellabear & Sons Ltd., the contractor for Langford Waterworks. Shellabear also used a large Ruston Steam Navvy on this contract. Sadly he could not remember make or names of the other engines employed.

Thanks to information gleaned from GERS members we are able to create a much more detailed picture of the waterworks 'railway.' In addition to the standard gauge engines there were also steam diggers. When they were building the waterworks chimney, the great landmark that identified the village to a whole generation, the late Ron Harvey recalled "They had a steam lift to take the bricks up, and steps were built inside. The iron cap on the top weighed three tons." This cap was to pose a particular problem when the chimney was demolished in 1964.

The Lime Recovery Plant

Constructed in the late 1920s and officially opened at the same time as the Pumping Station, the Treatment Plant and Lime Recovery Plant was situated about one mile away at the west end of the village. The complex comprised laboratories and offices, mixing, sedimentation and contact tanks, filter house and a lime recovery plant.

Construction of the treatment works begins (John Taylor again marked)

Very little was known about the construction of the lime recovery plant until early 2007. It was then that the authors made an exciting discovery; the existence of a whole series of in excess of fifty contemporary photographs of the construction of the plant. They were offered for sale and, thankfully, a generous benefactor from the village provided funds to ensure the photographs were secured, and now form part of the Allen Chaplin Collection.

The purpose of the Lime Recovery Plant was exactly as the title suggests - treating and recovering the lime so that it could be used again in the water treatment process. The company used quicklime in the treatment of water and as part of the process this was periodically discharged from the tanks and piped into Sludge Settling Tanks. The surplus water was then decanted off into a ditch and eventually into the River Blackwater less than half a mile away.

Having pumped the sludge into a smaller tank with a revolving agitator, the heavy sludge was then pumped to a tank where a revolving drum covered with gauze was rotating in it. Apparatus using air sucked the sludge on to the gauze, at the same time removing the water in it and forming a sludge 'cake' which adhered to the gauze. As the drum revolved the 'cake' was removed by a blade which then allowed the sludge to drop down into the kiln. This then began the operation of re-burning the lime.

The circular kiln was over thirty feet in length and tapered, supported on concrete plinths and steel rollers, driven by an electric motor connected to a cog-wheel fixed to the outside of the kiln. Inside there was a course of five bricks protecting

the steel outer casing. To enable the necessary high temperature to be generated - the decomposition of chalk can take place at any temperature in excess of 825 degrees C - fuel for the kiln was washed pea-coal which passed through a 'pulveriser' and was then blown into the kiln.

Work on the Lime Recovery Plant continues

The rollers supporting the kiln revolved in a tank of water to keep them cool. As the lime was re-burnt it dropped on to a conveyor, then on to elevators which took it to a hopper. When cooled it was transferred to the Lime Shed for reuse. Lime was re-burnt and reused approximately four times before a new supply was purchased. The men employed on the works took on maintenance duties when the plant was shut down, as it was only run periodically – approximately every ten or twelve weeks. In an early attempt at Health and Safety precautions, the vapour from the kiln passed through a

303

'Sirocco Scrubber' prior to being emitted into the atmosphere through a tall chimney. However, this precaution did not prevent white deposits from falling on to the Plant and its surrounds or onto washing hanging on the lines in the gardens of the nearby workers' houses in Ulting Lane.

The following photographs are all circa 1928/29. The first shows the kiln itself with less than safety-conscious flat-capped workmen sitting on and around it. The manufacturer of the kiln was Edgar Allen and Co. of Sheffield.

It is clear from the next photograph (of the Plant under construction) that the building was erected *around* the kiln.

The third photograph shows part of the inside of the Plant. The photo caption confirms that this view is of a 'British Rema No. 3 Ball mill and vacuum classifier arranged on a unit system firing a rotary lime burning kiln, the complete coal handling, pulverising and burning equipment designed, built and erected by the British Rema Manufacturing Co. Ltd.'

Finally, the fourth photograph shows the completed 20-ton storage bunker and bucket elevator of the Lime Recovery Plant, with platform and access ladders. Again, these were designed and built by British Rema Manufacturing Co. Ltd., as part of the complete pulverised fuel firing installation at the Langford plant.

With improvements in technology and methodology over six decades came the redundancy of the Treatment Plant and the Lime Recovery Plant.

In the 1980s the Plant was closed down and later, despite the insistence of Maldon District Council that the buildings had to be retained in any future development, all of them were demolished.

'Phenomenal' Flooding – January 1939

On 1st February 1939 the *Southend-on-Sea Observer* recorded the story of the 'phenomenal' flooding that caused chaos at the Langford waterworks, describing it as 'a story of heroic endeavour and Trojan determination' about how the works was kept running against the odds:

> The River Blackwater rose rapidly during the early hours of the morning of Thursday 26th January, and by 6.30 a.m. began to sweep – rather than seep – beneath the doors of the pumping room and down into the pump room basement. There the water level began to rise, eventually reaching a depth of 14 to 15 feet. At one time three inches of flood water lay on the actual floor of the pump room itself. The indoor staff already on duty did what they could, and when the outside staff, the gardeners and external maintenance men, arrived for work at 8 a.m. they immediately set about helping to stem the tide.

They worked with only the very shortest of breaks through to midnight by which time, with the aid of sandbags and other materials, the works was deemed 'fairly safe' from further flooding. Eventually, by three o'clock the following morning, the flood waters began to recede, enabling the workmen to clear the pump room by noon that same day. At ten o'clock on the evening of 27th January the pump room basement was finally pumped clear. In an interview with the *Essex Weekly News*, the Resident Engineer, Mr. W. Goulding, declared his pride in, and admiration for 'the wonderful work done by both the indoor and outdoor staffs.' Conditions in the pump room basement were particularly hazardous, and Goulding told the *News* reporter that whilst the men worked to pump out the pump room basement "We were sprayed by the giant fly-wheels as they churned their way through the water. Yet by sheer perseverance and loyalty the staff were able to keep the machinery going." Goulding added, "I want to pay a tribute to the loyal cooperation of the outdoor staff, who worked with a will, in sea boots and without, to prevent further water from entering the works."

Pumping out the Waterworks – January 1939

Keeping the machinery - the pumps - going was crucial. If the water had reached the boiler fires the workers would have been powerless and the pumping station would have been disabled. Although significant damage was occasioned to the electrical apparatus in the pump room basement, Goulding recorded how he and his staff "worked like Trojans, for we were all determined to drown rather than allow the floods to beat us. Together we won through but it was a great fight." Loyalty indeed! This then was a story of heroic endeavour and 'Trojan determination' by the staff of Langford Waterworks; staff who kept the pumping station functioning in spite of the rising flood waters that threatened not only the building but also the fresh water supply and, indeed, their own lives.

Going to work by boat!

Flooding has occurred occasionally since and has reached into the gardens of what is now the Museum of Power, but nothing has happened to match the flood of 1939.

A Strategic Target

During the Second World War, pumping stations and water reservoirs were strategic targets for enemy bombing, and so a number of air raid shelters were built in Langford for the local community and water workers. Significantly for the villagers the Luftwaffe and flying bombs managed, in the

308

main, to avoid Langford and the waterworks which is strange given that the waterworks lies in a river valley and that the towering waterworks chimney should have acted as a major landmark. Details of the few devices that fell on Langford during the war can be found in chapter nine.

Until 1945, 96% of the Southend Waterworks Company's water requirement was pumped from Langford. Large gravitational mains supplied Southend to the east and Canvey Island, Benfleet, Pitsea and Laindon to the west. Water required for the higher areas of Hockley, Rayleigh, Thundersley, Billericay and Ramsden Heath was supplied by booster stations.

Once the river works were completed in 1929, the existing bore holes and wells around the county were kept in reserve and were of significant value during the Second World War. The Company was justly proud of its facilities and encouraged visitors to come and see for themselves. The summer months were particularly recommended not just for reasons of the weather but because the work of the team of full-time gardeners could also be seen at its best. During the 1950s a film show was also available to entertain visitors. Entitled 'Jack Frost Strikes Again' the film dealt with the national water supply but included shots of some of the Company's installations. To date it has not been possible to trace a copy of this film.

All in a Day's Work
Of those who were around at the time of the opening of the river works few remain. The earliest memory of employment there was recorded in an interview with the late Ron Harvey who told the authors that he left school at fourteen and had a job in the office. He cycled around the plant taking messages on his bike for which he earned twelve shillings a week which included an allowance of two shillings a week for his bike. He later worked on the estate in the waterworks grounds as part of the maintenance team. More recent memories about

309

what it was like working for the waterworks company just after the Second World War were obtained in a subsequent interview with another ex-employee.

Albert Chaplin, 90 years of age at the time, was interviewed as part of the 'A Day in the Life…' series for *Power Up* the members' newsletter for the Museum of Power and so we are able to publish his memories here too. Albert was employed by the Southend Waterworks Company from 1946 until he retired in 1984.

Albert was born in Langford, and when he joined the Waterworks he was aged 26, freshly demobbed from the Army, married to Joyce and their first child, Michael, was on the way. He was employed by the company as a Driver. His war experience as a driver in the Royal Army Service Corps and his pre-war job as a delivery boy and man for Luckin Smith's grocers in Heybridge made him ideal for the post. Albert recalled that his first task at the waterworks was to take a Morris 10 cwt pick-up truck, and the works carpenter, to Bedford to pick up a CO_2 blower which had been undergoing repairs at Alldays & Onions.

Paid between £5 and £6 per week for a 44 hour week, Albert found that the job title was, to say the least, a very flexible one. He recalled, "Being a van driver was only part of it. Basically I did anything that I was asked to do. In those days we had a bricklayer and mate, a carpenter, painters, workshop and boiler fitters and outside gangs, including gardeners. They all had jobs to do and I was their transport."

At that time, the waterworks had three main elements; the Pumping Station (now the Museum of Power) and the Treatment Works and Lime Recovery Plant (a mile away on the western edge of the village) and whenever staff were needed on another part of the site, Albert was their man. He said, "Every part of the works needed fitters at some stage and the outside gangs were engaged all over the place, ditching, painting the various mains and intakes and

310

maintaining the riverbanks." But Albert did not just drive the gangs around. He recalled, "Although I was the driver, I did what the gang did. If the job was painting, then I did that. If we were working on the river bank then I was involved in that too. I really didn't know from one day to the next what I would be involved in." It sounds as though that was the 1940s equivalent of what today is known as 'multi-tasking.' "I suppose it was," said Albert, adding, "The job was really varied."

Occasionally – perhaps twice a year - Albert would be asked to cover for other colleagues on holiday. He recalled that the pumping station boilers and the lime recovery plant were run on coal which had to be carted from Maldon East railway station goods yard to Langford and that he and a colleague sometimes took on the job. He said, "The pumping station consumed about 120 tonnes of coal (doubles and singles) with washed pea coal being used at the lime recovery plant. It was our job to collect and bring the coal to the works. It was just another job to us but a very dirty one. However, we did receive overtime payment plus what they called a 'tonnage bonus,' so it was well worth doing."

As if this wasn't enough, Albert also occasionally helped out in the stores. "If there was little for me to do," he said, "I'd be assisting with the issuing of materials and small items of equipment. The painters, bricklayers, boiler fitters, workshop personnel and engine fitters all had to be supplied with their needs." Albert enjoyed that work so much that he eventually became a Storeman/Clerk at Langford.

"In those days," Albert added, "the list of jobs to do was endless and no week was the same, but for all that we were a contented bunch. And, yes, we had a lot of fun too but, as our outside Foreman 'Wink' Wilson used to say, we had to 'Do the job first.'"

The Waterworks did its bit to help servicemen after the war, as the *Essex Newsman* of 2nd November 1945 pointed out:

> Members of Forces on demobilisation leave (Class A) are invited to apply for four vacancies for Treatment Plant Attendants at the Langford Plant. Training will be given, and subject to satisfactory trial period the positions may be made permanent.

The Great Tide – 1953

Unlike the flood of 1939, in 1953 instead of people coming to the aid of the Langford pumping station, the Langford pumping station came to the aid of the people – the people, that is, of Canvey Island.

On 31st January 1953, Essex suffered its most severe flooding in living memory when the sea unleashed a furious onslaught upon the County's coastline with Canvey Island being by far the worst affected. Writing of the tragedy in her book *The Great Tide – The Story of the 1953 Flood Disaster in Essex* published in 1959, Hilda Grieve wrote:

> Loss of water supply from the local wells left only the mainland supply from Langford Waterworks through Benfleet. By installing a recording check meter it was found that a delivery to the island of some 12,000 gallons per hour was being maintained through Benfleet at a substantially constant rate over 24 hours. As under normal circumstances the average hourly consumption on Canvey Island was 8,100 gallons with a daily range of 2,600-15,000 this confirmed broken services pipes on the island, discharging fresh water into the salt and running to waste. With so much water about this discharge escaped notice until the low pressure on the mainland drew attention to it.

An emergency chlorination station was brought into action on the main supplying the island, and an emergency laboratory established 'on the spot' at the South Benfleet water pumping station. Until the wells on Canvey Island could be cleared and brought back into use the islands' entire fresh water supply came from Langford. Whether it was literally 'all hands to the pumps' is not clear, but what is clear is that without help from Langford waterworks, life would have been even more difficult for the stricken islanders.

Langford, like all other communities both large and small, wasted no time in raising funds for those who suffered from the effects of the Flood. On 20th February the *Essex Weekly News* reported that donations and a whist drive at the village hall had raised £40.00 for the flood victims. A collection at the waterworks itself and two collecting boxes had drawn in £19.3s and the whist drive competition and auction realised £11.13s. Mr. Hanner of Langford Hall Farm gave and auctioned two loads of logs.

The treatment plant's laboratory and an invasion of 'water worms'

Chelmsford born David Williams retired from the service of the water company on 26th April 1996 at which time he was Manager of the Langford Treatment Works. But David's association with Langford went back a long way, in fact to 3rd March 1958 when he began work at Langford as a Laboratory Assistant for the then Southend Waterworks Company, and from 1963 to 1966 he lived at Mill Cottage, Langford. What follows are some of David's memories of those early days in his career and how, in the early 1970s, he and his team rid the water supply of 'worms.'

When he first worked for the Southend Waterworks Company, David travelled to Langford by bus. There was no official bus stop outside the entrance to the Langford Treatment Plant but, as David recalled, "That did not matter. The driver slowed down as the bus approached the entrance thus enabling me to leap off without it stopping."

It was another short walk to the laboratory and within he would find 'Bunny' Rogers, another member of the laboratory staff, and Heather Morris the part-time Clerical Assistant. "Also," said David, "When I started at Langford there was another Chemist, Basil Kekwick. He trained me in chemical analysis but, after a few months, obtained a Chief Chemist post at Oxford." (Basil lived at 16 Ulting Lane.)

The main function of the laboratory staff at Langford was testing water samples. This key task was divided into two categories: the bacteriology and the chemistry. David explained, "The bacteriology methodology used was described as the 'multiple tube method' in which glass test tubes containing a sterile growth media, McConkey broth, and an inverted small tube, which had filled with media on sterilisation, and an aluminium cap. A known volume of water sample was added to five tubes and incubated at 37 degrees Centigrade.

If there were bacteria present the colour changed from red to yellow and gas collected in the small internal tube. Samples were then transferred from these tubes via a five millimetre loop of platinum wire that had been flame sterilised in a Bunsen burner, to a series of other tubes containing different media to confirm the type of bacteria present." David added, "Flaming the tops of the glass tubes which are held between your fingers, caused hard pads of skin to form which were heat resistant. You can see how evolution works. If several generations carried out these practices, eventually children would be born with the extra pads of skin!"

David added that the main indicator bacteria are known as coliform bacteria which are present in the most numbers in soil and untreated water. *E Coli* bacteria indicates a sewage pollution. "The first job of the day was to examine the bacteriological samples and record the results. If any were positive then action had to be taken." Next, daily samples were taken from both the treated water reservoir, situated

314

between the treatment plant and Ulting Lane, and the raw water entering the plant. The rivers were sampled on a weekly basis.

After lunch, samples were received from the Southend supply area. David said, "These would consist of samples from all boreholes in supply and underground treated water Reservoirs and Towers and newly laid mains awaiting approval." All were tested in the laboratory.

The Bacteriologist also analysed the recycled lime used for softening the water. Hydrated lime used for softening becomes chalk during the process; that chalk was burned in the Lime Kiln which formed part of the Treatment Works returning it to quicklime which was hydrated with water. After several cycles, the impurity level rose to make it impractical for use.

In the early 1970s the water supply was 'invaded' by 'worms' (actually the larval stage of the midge fly). These tiny invaders were to be found in the drinking water supply from Langford all the way down to Southend-on-Sea. Unless spotted in a glass of drinking water or in the bath many people were unaware of their presence. Although they were harmless the number of complaints increased and so something needed to be done. It was David Williams and his team who set about solving the problem.

Initially it was believed that the flies were laying their eggs on the tanks and filters of the water treatment plant. A fine screen mechanical micro-strainer was installed at a cost of approximately £120,000 but the 'worms' remained. Eventually after more tests and further detailed research it was found that a very low level of pyrethrin was effective and so, after a press campaign, treatment commenced for a ten-day period. The process was then repeated an additional number of times to ensure complete eradication. The problem has never manifested itself again. However, following international publication of two scientific papers describing

315

the outbreak (both of which gained David awards as author), similar occurrences were notified to the Waterworks from the Gold Fields of South Africa and the town of Lowell, Michigan, USA.

Goodbye to steam

In 1960, in order to maintain an efficient water supply, the Company decided to go ahead and replace the steam plant at Langford with three semi-automatic electrically operated pump sets.

When the river works was inaugurated on 18th September 1929 it had been designed to provide a daily supply of seven million gallons of water which were expected to meet 'the needs of the district' for many years to come. Essential to the efficient functioning of the works were the two (later three) Lilleshall steam-driven vertical triple-expansion rotative engines. Langford Pumping Station supplied millions of gallons of water per day for many years but in the late 1950s the company agreed plans to construct a new all-electric plant at Langford. By 1962 work was well underway and was completed in 1963.

The three Lilleshall engines which had served the company and their consumers faithfully for more than three decades officially fell silent on Wednesday 31st October 1963. Mr. F.A. Francis, J.P., Deputy Chairman of the Southend Waterworks Co. (SWC) can be seen shutting down 'Francis', named after his father Joseph Francis OBE., J.P., the Chairman of Directors at the time of the inauguration ceremony.

At that moment 35 years of history came to an end. The Chairman of the company, the Hon. Peter E. Brassey, DL., J.P., told a *Maldon and Burnham Standard* reporter, "It is a sad day when steam engines cease to turn. Steam engines have been with us long enough to become romantic and even beautiful," adding "One of these fine engines is to be retained for historical purposes." That engine was to be 'Marshall' named at the inauguration after the then Deputy Chairman of the Southend Waterworks Company, J. Maitland Marshall, J.P.

With the press of a button, the Chairman of the Essex County Council, Sir George Chaplin CBE., J.P., (pictured above, no relation to the co-author of this work) set in motion the new £260,000 electrical pumping station at Langford which was attached to the 'Hanningfield No. 1. Pumping Station' and steam was consigned to history.

In 1865 the Southend Waterworks Company had supplied a population of only 1,700 but by 1963 this had grown to in excess of 375,000 and the Langford works continued to play a major part. The new pumping station could handle a maximum daily capacity in excess of eight million gallons of treated water using the existing pipework that had been installed in the mid-1920s. In 1964 the decision was taken to scrap two of the huge engine and pump sets and the boilers. It would not be until April 2011 that the surviving Lilleshall triple-expansion engine, saved 'for historical purposes,' returned to steam, under the auspices of the Museum of Power, after 'resting' for nearly forty-five years.

The elegant 150 feet high chimney that had served as a local landmark (used by all Langford children as a beacon for home) was demolished on 23rd July 1964 with the aid of an eight-wheel Albion heavy recovery lorry which literally pulled the enormous structure over. At the same time the coaling plant was also demolished.

Albert Chaplin recalled the steeplejacks who periodically climbed the chimney, undertaking inspection checks and repair work. He said, "I used to pick up the ladders from the railway station in stacks. The men placed each section of ladder – five or six feet lengths – on the side of the chimney. They had connecting pieces like cocoa tins which they placed over the top of each leg of the ladder to lock each section into place." It was very primitive. They also drove pegs into the wall as they went up to secure each section of ladder to the wall. (The steeplejacks had to go up the outside of the chimney because the boilers were more or less always fired up and it certainly was not economical to close down the works for an inspection.)

Albert continued, "When the steeplejacks reached the top there was this big cast iron round piece on the top of the chimney that weighed several tons, but when the steeplejack went up his ladder he had to go... [*He indicated the sharpness of the angle at which the ladder had to be moved to enable the steeplejack to negotiate the overhang of the lip of the chimney top.*] ...like that and then once up there they used to get off the ladder and stand there - one hundred and

318

fifty feet high mind you - and walk round the chimney, kicking the soot in."

Apparently at that height there was little smoke. Even though the boilers consumed between 120-130 tons of coal every week if villagers saw smoke emitting from the chimney it was on very rare occasions. Somehow most of the smoke dissipated before it reached the top. Albert said, "The steeplejacks might have got a whiff of sulphur up there but little or no smoke."

Higher than he had ever been before (in Langford at least)

When writing a short article about the demolition of the waterworks chimney in an issue of *Power Up* the authors of this book were unaware that it would lead to the discovery of some unique photographs of the village belonging to an ex-waterworks employee.

Derek Sayer worked for the water company at Langford for many years and lived in one of the company houses in Ulting Lane, about half a mile distant from the pumping station. Whilst in discussion with one of the authors in 2005 Derek mentioned that he had some photographs that might be of interest which he had taken on the day the chimney was pulled over. "Of course" was the reply. "Great. What are they?"

What Derek then showed us took our breath away.

On 23rd July 1964 Derek, wearing no special protective gear whatsoever, climbed up *inside* the waterworks chimney, stood on the top and thus became the tallest ever resident of Langford; Derek's six feet odd plus the chimney's height of 150 feet. The only other people to have visited that point would have been steeplejacks and the men who built the chimney back in the late 1920s. Indeed his trip to the top using the internal route might have been unique as the

319

steeplejacks, as previously noted, usually climbed up the outside using interconnecting ladders.

But most importantly Derek was not doing this as some kind of mad dare. He had taken his camera with him. He emerged at the top and knelt precariously on the edge of the chimney, surveyed all around him and took a series of photographs. Now, forty years on, a selection of his unique photographs are included here.

The above photograph was taken looking towards the heart of the village with the Mill and Mill House clearly seen on the left. Unfortunately the unique church of St. Giles is hidden by trees. The cemetery and 'Langmere' can be seen on the right-hand side and at the bottom left of the picture can be seen the soot-encrusted top of the chimney.

For the second photo shown here Derek leaned over and pointed the camera down to take a picture of his colleagues far below. The speck in the centre of the picture is fellow waterworks employee Albert Parmenter. Also in shot is one of Derek's knees!

For the third photo Derek turned and looked across the River Blackwater towards the then new Langford 'Hanningfield Pumping Station.' The Langford Cricket Club's 'sacred turf,' the cricket square, can be made out in the centre of the picture and in the distance can be seen the Chelmer and Blackwater Navigation, known locally simply as 'the canal.' Also between the new pumping station and the canal can be seen the impression of the grass track course; grass track racing being held in that field during the early 1960s (see Chapter Ten).

Minutes after these historic photographs were taken the highest brick construction for many miles around was demolished. Fortunately, by that time Derek had climbed down and was positioned across the other side of the River Blackwater ready to take pictures of the chimney crashing to the ground.

(Our special thanks to Derek Sayer for allowing us to publish these unique photographs, the copyright of which remains with Derek.)

Now you see it. Now you don't – The Demolition of the Waterworks Chimney

For children living in Langford in the early 1960s, nothing much ever happened. They preferred it that way. They enjoyed making their own entertainment whether this was walking in the woods, climbing trees, playing kickabout in a field or going over to the canal in search of Corona bottles. But when something *really* important, something *really, really* important *did* happen - such as the demolition of the Langford waterworks chimney - they were at school.

Albert Chaplin recalled that, on the day of demolition, some of the brickwork at the base of the chimney was chipped away and filled with wood. This wood supported the chimney to make sure it did not fall before it was pulled over. That task was left to Hoyners. Albert added, "A hawser was run

from the Hoyners' lorry which was parked behind the cricket pavilion on the other side of the river. That was then run round the chimney a little way up and secured in place. The wooden chocks at the base of the chimney were removed so the chimney was just standing there with a huge great hole in it."

Just before 11 a.m. on 23rd July 1964 all traffic was stopped in Langford. This was in case the chimney accidentally fell in the other direction. Albert and many other works employees, villagers and other on-lookers stood watching and waiting. He said, "Then he [*the Hoyners lorry driver*] started the winch. For a few moments nothing seemed to be happening and then the chimney was pulled over and when that came down it just...well the top, the cast iron cap buried itself in the concrete. Terrific!"

In the excitement at seeing the chimney crash to the ground the winch was left running. Albert recalled seeing cabling snagging on the cast iron cap which was buried in the ground. "The winch kept running," he said, "and it began to pull the lorry towards the river. Several of us shouted to tell the driver to shut his winch off which he did with only moments to spare."

Once the dust had cleared it was evident that the chimney had fallen exactly as planned. It had been a most successful operation and Langford's landmark, which had stood proud over the village for nearly forty years, had been reduced to a pile of rubble in less than a minute.

The aftermath of the fall

The remaining buildings and the Lilleshall triple-expansion engine became Scheduled Ancient Monuments in 1986 (no. 220).

In the late 1960s the Southend Waterworks Company decided that it was time to expand again and construct a brand new complex on a site adjacent to the storage reservoirs. By 1970 the new works built within the trees adjacent to the reservoirs was completed (costing £1,500,000) and was officially opened on 30th June. Whilst building the new waterworks, workmen laying pipes found a large fine bronze palstave (a type of early bronze axe, commonly used in the mid Bronze Age in the north, west and south-west of Europe), a cast of which is now housed in Colchester Museum.

The Essex Water Orders Act 1970 came into effect from 1st April that year which amalgamated the South Essex Waterworks Company and the Southend Waterworks Company to form the Essex Water Company. On 1st April the following year the water undertakings of the Burnham Urban District Council, Chelmsford Borough Council, Chelmsford Rural District Council, Maldon Borough Council, Maldon Rural District Council and Witham Urban District Council all came under the Essex Water Company, which became one of the largest water undertakings in the country, supplying over 1.3 million people and associated industry with a daily average of approximately 400 Ml of pure water. The whole operation covered an area of 594 square miles.

The new Langford works had a treatment capacity of 55 Ml (twelve million gallons) per day (maximum), although the average was assessed to be 45 Ml (ten million gallons) per day, over 10% of the Company's total output. Before the establishment of the new works, water had had to be pumped to supply through an existing 710 mm diameter cast iron main. To facilitate the revised output part of the original main was duplicated by laying a main, 915 mm diameter of welded steel, alongside to help reduce the pumping head at Langford, so that more water could be pumped through the mains. In order to boost the water into the Southend area a new pumping station was constructed at Hullbridge, some ten miles away from Langford. However, this needed little manpower, being remotely controlled from Langford by radio link.

On 21st June 1988, the Boards of Lyonnaise des Eaux of France and the Essex Water Company announced that they had reached agreement on the details of the takeover of Essex Water by the French Company. Lyonnaise was established in 1880, fifteen years after the foundation stone was laid of the Southend Waterworks Company and by the late 1980s had become one of the largest service and technology groups in France.

Lyonnaise's operations were not limited to France, but were worldwide, with business activities which included not only water supply, water distribution and water purification, but also pollution control, industrial heating, energy distribution, cable television, leisure, health and funeral services. Before entering into water interests in England, Lyonnaise was already heavily involved in supplying water to approximately eighteen million people, of whom ten million were in France and the remainder in Spain, the United States of America, Canada, Morocco and the South Pacific. The press release at the time announced that:

> Lyonnaise seeks to develop its business internationally by establishing close relationships with companies operating in related fields of activity. Lyonnaise has taken significant shareholdings in such companies as a demonstration of its commitment and in order to participate in the benefits which Lyonnaise believes arise as a consequence of its involvement.

It is worth quoting further from the press release concerning the reasons for the French company's interest in the Essex Water Company:

> Lyonnaise and Essex believe that the future of the water supply industry worldwide lies in continuing improvements in related technology and in the quality of service provided. This can only be achieved alongside heavy long term research and investment programmes and enhanced operational efficiency.

> Essex, as a statutory water company, is limited in its business activities to the supply of water to consumers in its statutory area of supply. Both companies believe that there is scope for the development of water-related activities which, under the present statutes and orders forming the constitution of Essex, cannot be fully exploited by Essex. Accordingly Lyonnaise intends to develop the opportunities which will arise from the co-

operation and combined expertise of Essex and Lyonnaise in the water industry.

The terms of the offers by Lyonnaise were regarded as fair and reasonable by the Directors of the Essex Water Company and its financial advisers and it was unanimously recommended to stockholders to accept. The transition was painless.

In 2000 Essex & Suffolk Water (as the company was then known) under the Suez Group merged with the Northumbrian Water Group. In 2004 Northumbrian Water became a public limited company and was floated on the London Stock Market (a FTSE 250 company). On Friday 14th October 2011 the Northumbrian Water Group was delisted from the London Stock Exchange following a cash acquisition by UK Water (2011) Limited (a company indirectly wholly owned by a consortium comprising Cheung Kong Infrastructure Holdings Limited, Cheung Kong (Holdings) Limited and Li Ka Shing Foundation Limited.)

The remaining buildings associated with the river works opened in 1927 - the pump house, tool store, workshop and storehouse - stood abandoned until 1997. The gardens, where once weeds were unheard of, were unkempt and the weed held court whilst flowers struggled to reach the sunlight.

The 'Hanningfield No. 1' building was silent and for all intents and purposes the new block was silent too. In the 1920s the staff at the works totalled more than 100 men and women. By 1970 the workforce numbered 60. By the late 1980s only three men ran the complex; the activities of the works being controlled by the press of a few buttons.

In 1994 plans to transform Langford's redundant waterworks site previously occupied by the water treatment plant and lime kiln at the west end of the village into a hi-tech business park came to fruition. Planning approval for the creation of a high technology development on the site opened the door for the Witham-based CML Microsystems to move into a new, purpose-built factory where the old treatment works had once operated. CML Microsystems manufacture silicon chips for the communications industry. The design of the CML buildings ensured they merged extremely well into the villages' natural and sensitive landscape.

Thus a predominantly agricultural area met the challenges of the 21st century (just as it had done in embracing early 20th century progress) with the arrival of new businesses at the forefront of modern technology.

The Museum of Power

On 17th May 1994, the same year that the CML development was approved for the former water treatment works site, things began to move with regard to the future of the former pumping station and river works. On that day the Heritage and Countryside Sub-Committee of the Essex County Council considered a report by the County Planner referring to the 'Old Steam Engine Site, Langford,' and RESOLVED:

> That the views of the Library, Museum and Records Committee be sought and that officers explore the subject further with a progress report (to the Heritage and Countryside Sub-Committee) in September.

The proposal was to turn the buildings into a museum. The Museum of Power was formed in 1994 by a group of like-minded enthusiasts who held a number of small personal collections of power-related machines. The museum was originally based in Pitsea near Basildon but in early 1995 formal discussions were held with Essex & Suffolk Water to lease the former steam pumping station at Langford.

In 1996 the local press announced a 'Museum plan for pumping station,' revealing plans for the former pumping station to become the home of 'a unique power museum.' Negotiations between officers of the fledgling museum, Maldon District Council and Essex & Suffolk Water took place and in December 1996 museum organisers were given the go-ahead. A planning application to change the use of the building was granted and at the end of 1996 the last items owned by the water company were removed and the keys handed over.

Since then, the museum has gone from strength to strength as the number of volunteers increased and donations poured in. These included a 35 ton, 300 h.p. Mirrlees diesel engine from the Tendring Hundred Water Company, sectioned diesel engines from Paxman Diesel, an Ashworth & Parker vertical steam engine and several items from the Ford Motor Company. But at the heart of the Museum of Power was its main feature, the 1931 Lilleshall Pumping Engine No. 282 (known as 'Marshall') which had lain redundant and unloved since 1964.

Once 'Marshall' had been restored it was run successfully on compressed air whilst volunteers worked on its full restoration to steam. This was eventually achieved and 'Marshall' ran again for the first time in public for over forty-five years in April 2011. At the same time, the new Steam Pump Tearoom was completed and opened.

By preserving the building and developing the museum, Langford's important role in the industrial history of East Anglia is preserved.

CHAPTER NINE
A VILLAGE AT WAR

Throughout the ages Langford, as with every other village in Britain, gave of her young men (and women too in later years) to fight for their monarch and their country.

Although there had been many conflicts both in England and abroad up to the late nineteenth century, the earliest recorded enlistment by Langford residents appears in the *Wickham Bishops and Langford Parish Magazine* in the autumn of 1894. The October issue of the magazine reported that, in September, two young Langford men named Frederick Barford and Frederick Good(e)y had enlisted in the Norfolk Regiment.

Four years later, in September 1898, when the parish magazine recorded the 'wonderful victory' for Sir H. Kitchener over the Khalifa in the Sudan, who 'for 15 years' it said had committed unspeakable acts of cruelty, including, of course, the murder of General Gordon,' it carried the following stirring message for parishioners:

> All England (and indeed Europe) has been moved to admiration by the Langford people who will be proud to think that one of their fellow villagers has been through the glorious campaign. James Chapman, son of Charles and Mrs. Chapman, of Langford Station, has been present at the battles of Atbara and Omdurman. We are glad to be able to state that though in the Lincolnshire Regiment, which has been in the thick of the fights, Chapman's name has not appeared amongst the list of the wounded.

Fortunately, the following month, the editor of the magazine was able to bring good news to the readers: immediately after the battle of Omdurman James had managed to write a hasty letter in pencil to his mother, telling her that he was alive and well.

With the enlistment of these young men, the families left behind found life hard with little or no regular money coming in so the Church and village took up their case. The church offertory on Sunday 3rd December 1898 taken for the wives and families of the Essex Regiment amounted to £10, and Mrs. Wager, of the School House, took a collecting card round the village for the wives and families of soldiers who had been called for active service. Not everyone's generosity was recorded, unfortunately, as the list published in the parish magazine of those who had donated to this cause was incomplete, 'due partly to scarlet fever being in the parish, and partly for lack of time.'

Following the Egyptian Campaign into the Sudan, which had been supported by the British, James Chapman obtained a home post at Somerset House, London, but with the onset of the Second Boer War (1899-1902) he was called out to join the forces in South Africa. He left England again on 7th January 1900. At the same time Ernest and Albert 'Bertie' Goodey, of 'The Orchard' [*Orchard Cottages*], Langford, were called out to join the Essex Militia.

As happened in the majority of churches throughout England at the time, special services of Intercession were given for the troops in South Africa and at Langford the service was held in St. Giles' Church on Sunday 11th March 1900. Given the time of year and the poor condition of the roads, such services were very well attended. In his parish letter published in the parish magazine that same month, the Rector, Revd. & Hon. F.E. Charles Byron wrote, "We would draw especial attention to the fact that the turn for the better in our affairs in South Africa dates from that week of National Intercession."

In July 1900 news reached the parish that James Chapman had been taken prisoner 'after a most gallant defence,' near Pretoria. The whole village waited with baited breath for further news; but they had to wait nearly two years before James eventually returned home safe and sound in August 1902. James had previously been awarded the Egyptian and Sudan medals and now to those was added the South African medal. He had been a prisoner of the Boers for six weeks, during which time he was almost starved. It is unclear how and when James escaped from his captors but what was clear from reports was that he had seen some of the roughest living and marching and some of the hardest fighting, but through it all he returned home uninjured and in (surprisingly) excellent health.

For some weeks during the early part of 1901, prayers had been offered at St. Giles' for the safe-keeping of James Mott, the son of Mr. & Mrs. Mott of Park Cottages. The villagers' prayers were answered when James, who was serving with the Royal Artillery in Africa in the Second Boer War, returned safely to England in May 1901.

In October 1902 there appears to have been much excitement in the village when Herbert Goodey and Frederick Bell, of Maldon Road, joined the Essex Regiment and Albert Goodey of Orchard Cottages, returned from South Africa. But only a few short years later there were rumours of another conflict that threatened the peace of the world.

The Great War (1914-1918)

War was declared between Britain and Germany on 4th August 1914 and the tiny village of Langford braced itself. On 16th August 1914 the church collections amounted to £5.13s.0d which was sent to the funds for Sailors and Soldiers and the Secretary's receipt was posted on the church door. In September 1914, Revd. Byron wrote in the parish magazine:

Everywhere we see the notice 'Your King and Country call you.' The response has been great, but if we are to endure the blessing of peace for those who come after us, the call must be answered by very many more at whatever sacrifice to themselves. We are face to face with the gravest crisis perhaps our nation has ever had. Let us see to it we are one and all doing our duty as citizens.

Revd. Byron announced that those who had already joined the Army or Navy would be remembered in church every day and proudly printed their names in the magazine: Fred Bell, John Henry Colbear, Victor Gentry, Herbert Goody, Stanley Grout, Albert Howlett, George Howlett, Harry Howlett, Fred Jiggins, Albert Mysen, Bertie Parmenter and George Wiseman. True to his word, during that September there were daily services at 10 a.m. and an Intercession Service on Wednesdays and Fridays at 7.15 p.m.

Miss Amy Wynyard, of Langford Parsonage, promised the village children that she would make jam from all the blackberries they brought to her and would send it to wounded soldiers hospitalised in London. A grateful letter from Arthur G. Elliott, Assistant Secretary of the London Hospital was published in the parish magazine dated October 1914. It read:

> We have received the very useful gift of jam for the benefit of the wounded soldiers. It was indeed very kind of the children of Langford to have picked the blackberries for the making of the jam, and I would be glad if you will convey the thanks of the soldiers for their kindness in doing so.

In the same issue Revd. Byron praised members of Langford choir who had given 'an instance of exalted patriotism or self-sacrifice' by voluntarily foregoing the choir outing which had been 'their one earthly reward' by desiring that the money be given instead to 'alleviating the suffering which

333

this most terrible war has brought upon this country' the knowledge of it doubtless being 'of some comfort to them in these terrible times through which we are passing.'

In that same year, and at a time when the villagers needed to retain a familiar face as their spiritual and moral leader, Revd. Byron left Langford to take up his new post of Vicar of Thrumpton, in Nottinghamshire. His brother, the 9th Lord Byron, being now 57 and with no heir, Revd. Byron was also next in line to the title as the 10th Lord Byron, so it was right for him to move. However, realising that this was incredibly bad timing but unavoidable he told his flock in the November issue of the parish magazine:

> I am leaving you at an anxious time. There is war and the rumours of war, and they are brought very much before our eyes here in Langford. God save us, as He always has heretofore, from invasion. It would be a terrible thing for us Langford people should that ever come to pass. It would mean ruin, and the dreadful things which we read of daily in our papers. Pray all of you to God to save us. Pray to Him in your houses and in His House. By all these things God wishes to draw us to Him. Do not rouse His anger by refusing to learn.
>
> It is my last message to you. Learn what God is trying to teach you. It is your work for Him and for your country. Sincerely yours, F.C. Byron.

It was indeed a stirring 'last message' which must have left the village in awe of the man and in fear of the dark days to come. The helm was soon taken over by a new Rector, Revd. Charles Gough Littlehales, who immediately made his own mark on the village with the following message in the parish magazine dated December 1914:

> Before another number of the magazine is in our readers' hands the holy and happy season of Christmas will have come and gone. Though its joy and festivity

will be impaired by the thought of our brave soldiers spending their Christmas on the battlefield or in the trenches, and for very many the loss of those beloved heroes of the war, who lie in a soldier's grave, will be felt most keenly at such a time, yet there will be room for rejoicing, if only for the sake of the little ones upon whom war and its horrors sit so lightly.

We take this opportunity of wishing all our readers a happy Christmas, trusting that the true cause of happiness and rejoicing, the Birth of our Saviour Christ, and the commencement of His work on Easter for the salvation of all mankind, will not be obscured by war or bereavements, or festivities, or family gatherings.

The war was brought closer to home the following year when enemy aircraft dropped bombs in the vicinity. On the night of 22nd April 1915 the Maldon and Heybridge area was bombed, yet miraculously, no major damage or fatalities were reported. Though many Langford people were disturbed by the noise of the explosions in the distance, the war, for the moment at least, left Langford unscathed but the warning had been sounded that any place, large or small, on or near the River Blackwater was, as far as the enemy was concerned, a legitimate target.

By June 1915 the war that some predicted would be over by Christmas 1914 was proceeding at a ferocious pace. The cry of the moment was for 'Men and Munitions' and the men of Langford responded nobly to the clarion call and by the end of June, twenty-nine men (out of a total population of only 240) had joined the forces and were serving their King and Country. The parish magazine proudly published the names of those who had 'joined the colours,' and for whom public Intercession was to be made twice a week. They were:

Navy : Michael Barne and Harry Howlett

Army : Fred Bell, William Bonner, Edward Catchpole, Philip Chalk, Edward Colbear, John Colbear, Walter Everitt, Victor Gentry, Bertie Goodey, Herbert Goodey, Percy Grout, Stanley Grout, Albert Howlett, George Howlett, Fred Jiggins, George Jones, Frederick Joslin, Albert Mott, Albert Mysen, Henry Oliver, Bertie Parmenter, James Raisey, John Russell, William Sorrell, John Wakelin, Richard Wakelin and George Wiseman.

Already hailing the men as heroes, the parish magazine dated June 1915 added 'All honour to them and may they be kept safe in the hour of battle, from perils by sea and by land.' Regrettably not all of these heroes would return from the war.

At the same time as the list of heroes was being published, the parish magazine mentioned that 'The Boy Scouts from Langford are also doing good work at Tollesbury, in helping to watch the sea coast.' The Boy Scouts were indeed doing a wonderful job. Throughout the war all over the country the Scouts turned their hands to all manner of tasks and acquitted themselves well. They acted as messengers at railway stations, police stations, post offices and even the War Office itself. They formed first aid detachments and were hospital orderlies. They worked day and night and even came under fire in the north of England, where they were guarding telegraph wires and doing coastguard duty. Some apparently were also involved behind the front line in France, helping to move ammunition. Fortunately for them and their parents no Langford scout was ever sent that far afield but were clearly kept busy locally.

In the September 1914 issue of the parish magazine the editor (and doubtless the parishioners too) was full of praise for the Langford Scouts writing:

> That scouts are justifying their existence and the money expended on them is conclusively proved in this present crisis. There are many thousands now serving the government in work for which their training render

them competent, and thereby releasing men for active service in the Army and Navy. Our Scout Leonard Gibson [*of Holloway Road*] has already been sent for coast work and three other Scouts from the troop have volunteered and will be sent off as vacancies occur.

Two Langford scouts were later reported as 'working under the Coast Guard Officer at Bradwell' and an excellent report had been received of their work and usefulness. On Saturday 26th September the whole Langford troop went down to the coast and after examining the quarters in which Leonard Gibson and now Charles Chapman were placed, 'went out to sea, returning in the evening.' For the younger Scouts at least, the war must have seemed a great adventure.

Even those not immediately involved with the war were affected by it. In June 1915 at 'the great Festival of the Holy Spirit' [Pentecost] Revd. Littlehales had to leave St. Giles' very quickly after the morning service. His brother Richard lay in the Royal Victoria Military Hospital (also known simply as the 'Netley Hospital') in Hampshire where he was being treated for serious wounds. Heeding the urgent call to his brother's side, Revd. Littlehales' place at the evening service was taken by the Revd. F.T. Gardner, Rector of Goldhanger. Sadly the Rector's brother died of his wounds that night (13th June). (Richard Littlehales was eleven years younger than his brother and had joined the 4th Pioneer Battalion of the Coldstream Guards as a Private. He was a mechanic/fitter when he died aged 33.) Thereafter the Rector was certainly able to empathise with others in the village that were to lose family members in the Great War.

In May 1915, approximately six months after he had left the village and written his 'last message' to his parishoners, the Revd. Byron and his sister Margaret paid a visit to Langford. He stayed for a short while at Langford Grove and occupied the pulpit of Langford Church on the evening of 16th May, promising to preach at the morning service on Trinity Sunday.

In June an appeal from the Young Men's Christian Association (YMCA) was received by Revd. Littlehales in which they requested a contribution for the erection of recreation huts in various parts of the world where soldiers were engaged in military operations.

The YMCA established huts on the Western front that provided soldiers with food drink and free writing paper and envelopes. At one end of the hut was a platform that acted as a stage for musical concerts and a pulpit for religious services. At the other end of the hut was a counter where necessary items like chocolate and cigarettes were sold. The huts were popular with men on relief who could come to write letters, read books, relax and socialise.

The children of Langford School responded well to this appeal and twenty-five children contributed sums from a penny upwards. With the help of the teachers, the sum of 10/- (ten shillings) was collected and forwarded to the YMCA headquarters. In return each of the subscribers received a stamp presented by the YMCA as a memento of their effort for the cause.

The following is an extract from a letter forwarded to the Rector (Revd. Littlehales) from J. Palmer Howard in acknowledgement of the children's contribution to the soldiers' huts:

Lord Kinnaird has asked me to acknowledge the extremely kind gift of the boys and girls of your Sunday school towards the Huts we are erecting for the Soldiers. We are sure that the members of your council will value their donation very highly and we trust that your scholars will have the joy and satisfaction of knowing that the money is being devoted to a very good and patriotic cause.

The commemoration stamps were distributed, and a presentation scroll put up on the school wall. (To date examples of these stamps and the scroll have not been located.)

A TYPICAL HUT IN FLANDERS

By the spring of 1915 it had become clear that voluntary recruitment alone was not going to provide the numbers of men required. The Government passed the National Registration Act on 15th July 1915 as a step towards stimulating recruitment and to discover how many men between the ages of fifteen and sixty-five were engaged in each trade. Maldon Rural District Council took steps at once to implement this new Act by appointing volunteer Enumerators:

> for the purpose of distributing and collecting the Registration Forms, of assisting those who are in doubt or difficulty as to the proper method of filling up the forms, and answering the questions to which replies must be given, of helping to correct any errors, of distributing the Certificates of Registration, and of tabulating and indexing the forms when completed, so that the Return from the District was completed, accurate, and compiled with the least possible delay.

In addition the Council confidently appealed to the patriotism of women to volunteer their services as Enumerators, as they felt assured that though the ladies could not serve their Country in arms, they would 'gladly seize' the opportunity offered them to help the State to compile a National Register, which was the essential preliminary to National organisation. The ladies of Langford were only too happy to step forward and volunteer; the Baker sisters (Jeanie and Mary of Langford Meads) were prominent in that role.

But, inevitably, young men died. Public Intercessions at St. Giles' were being offered up twice a week for those who were loyally serving their King and Country in the Army and Navy, and until August that list had remained unaltered. However, news eventually came through that the village had lost one of its own.

George Arthur Howlett was born in Great Totham in 1893, and in 1901 was living with his parents, George and Ruth Howlett, at Howell's Farm, Heybridge, but in 1907, when George was fourteen years old, the family moved to Beavis Hall, Langford. George was twenty-one when war broke out, and he enlisted immediately at Shepherd's Bush, in Middlesex, enlisting into the 8th Essex Cyclist Corps (formerly 624, Essex Cycle Battalion) as Private No. 55. He was killed in action at Ypres on 9th August 1915 (aged 22) shot by a German sniper. As his name was placed on the 'Roll of Honour' the whole village (through the parish magazine) offered their sincerest sympathy to his parents who had lost 'a much cherished son.' George had a brother Henry who had also joined up at the outbreak of war. Fortunately for his family Henry ultimately came home safely.

At this time there was great general concern about British prisoners of war who were being held in various PoW camps in Germany.

8th Essex Cycle Regiment camped in Maldon

Even though they were not aware of any of their own having been incarcerated in such a camp, the people of Langford did what they could to raise funds for prisoners' creature comforts. The parish magazine dated December 1915 included the following description of a successful fund-raising event held at the school:

> Lack of space prevents a full account of the successful effort, organised on behalf of the British Prisoners in Germany, on Wednesday November 4th. An excellent tea was provided, materials for which were contributed by the kindness of the ladies of the Parish.
>
> About 65 participated, and at the conclusion an amusing Mock Auction was conducted of all supplies left over. At 7.15 the Entertainment commenced before an absolutely crowded room, and the repeated plaudits of the audience testified to the immense enjoyment afforded by the performers.
>
> Our thanks are due to all those who worked so energetically and heartily, and including performers both in and outside the parish, who lent without charge everything required, cups and saucers, spoons, lamps, etc., thus reducing expenses to absolutely nil.

By the summer of 1916, the war in France had reached stalemate, with both armies dug in and engaged in a war of attrition. Families throughout Britain lived in fear and dread of the knock on the door and the appearance of the telegram boy as an ever-growing list of casualties appeared in the newspapers. At home the war effort began to escalate.

Special Constables were appointed in Langford when a large force in the Maldon area was recruited, both to compensate for the loss of regular members of the police force who had joined the war effort, and to add an extra layer of public protection during the period of hostilities (and later in the General Strike of 1926). The parish magazine dated January 1916 reported that Special Constables had been enrolled and sworn in having volunteered 'to undertake the patrolling of the roads and other police duties within the boundaries of Langford Parish.' The magazine published a full list of the volunteers who were the Revd. C.G. Littlehales [Langford Hall] (Corporal), Mr. J. Crow [Cottage 'near the Mill'] (Lance-Corporal), and Messrs. W. Chalk [The Homestead], W. Dawson, I. Good [Hall Cottages], E. Harvey [The Post Office], E. Hedge [Hatfield Road], G. Howlett [Beavis Hall], G. May [Fords Farm], B. Parmenter [Maldon Road], A. Sheldrake [Maldon Road] and S. Unwin.

Drill took place every Monday evening in Langford Mill which had been kindly placed at the disposal of the force by Revd. the Hon. F.C. Byron. By the generosity of several subscribers, the force had been provided with 'capes, overalls and sou'westers and with a dark lantern;' the latter being a lantern with a sliding panel to conceal the light. The 'Specials' (who had become a familiar sight in the village) publicly thanked the subscribers for their kind donations which enabled this essential equipment to be purchased.

Those subscribers (and the amounts they donated) were named in the parish magazine as:

	£	s.	d
Mr. H.R. Hollingdale		5	0
Mr. G. Poole (per C.E. Harvey)		5	0
Miss A Wynyard		5	0
Messrs. Strutt & Parker		10	0
	£1	5	0

The New Year began and the war in Europe continued. So far Langford had escaped enemy bombing but soon the village was mourning the loss of a second Langford man, William Sorrell.

Despite detailed research no details of William's presence in the village has been traced. The closest match found is a William Sorrell, born in Steeple Bumpstead in 1887, the son of Thomas and Harriett Sorrell of that village. William joined the 9th Battalion, the Essex Regiment in Chelmsford as a Private (12226), and was killed in action on 15th October 1915 in Flanders aged 28. He is commemorated on the Loos Memorial in France (panels 85-87). Whether this is 'our' William is, at present, unclear.

The people of the village were also at this time mourning the deaths of two non-combatants. Both William Bingham Ashton Wynyard, Churchwarden and Miss Calver, the Church School Mistress died during this period. A column in the parish magazine read:

> The list of burials is a long one, longer than for many years, and while we sympathise with those who have lost their dear ones, we pray that the New Year may have brighter things in store. We all should be thankful for the sacrifices, the unselfishness, and the patriotism that have been so evident throughout our land, and we should pray fervently for a right and lasting Peace in God's good time.

Sadly 'God's good time' was not going to be any time soon, so more entertainments were arranged to raise funds for young men from the village who were now known to be prisoners of war. The proceeds of an 'Entertainment and Rummage Sale' was £4.8s.6d, (less 5s.3d expenses) and £7.10s.2d, (expenses nil). Of this, the sum of £5 was sent to the Church Army, which had undertaken to send 5/- parcels to the neediest prisoners. The sum of £2.10s.0d was handed to Miss Wynyard to defray the expense of buying and dispatching Christmas presents to 'Langford men in khaki.'

In view of the plight of the many prisoners held in captivity in Germany, a 'British Prisoners of War Fund' was set up in the village and, as always, the villagers responded magnificently. The response to an appeal for weekly subscriptions for a British Prisoner in Germany was 'splendid' resulting in a promised weekly income of 'about 7/- a week.' Mrs. Catchpole, Nellie Chalk, Ivy Harvey, Annie Colbear, Ivy Howlett, Ivy Dawson, Nellie Russell, Mabel May and Eva Cooper kindly undertook the collection of the 'weekly pennies.'

Sister Susie's sewing shirts for soldiers.
Such skill at sewing shirts our shy young
Sister Susie shows.
Some soldiers send epistles—
Say they'd sooner sleep on thistles
Than the saucy, soft, short shirts for
soldiers Sister Susie sews.

That amount of money was sufficient to send a weekly parcel of food to one man, to whom the parish had been asked to be 'Godmother.' It was finally decided to take over the 'entire charge' of a man from the 10th Essex Regiment, whose actual home was in Plaistow. This soldier was described as being in one of the worst prisoner of war camps and in urgent need of a regular supply of food, as the German allowance was not only insufficient but also 'coarse in quality.'

The lucky man (if indeed one could call him that) was Private 13762 Edward Sharp. Opportunities were afforded for anyone who was good enough to write him letters or send comforts in the way of 'woollies or under clothing, socks etc. or paper and games' and (again) the villagers responded well. In May 1916 a postcard was received in the village confirming that Private Sharp had received the first box of food in good condition. Further boxes had been despatched every Tuesday, the fourth being sent on 25th April and the villagers hoped that, in due course, 'Further acknowledgement will reach us.'

A few days later, Mrs. Littlehales, the Rector's wife, received a letter from Private Sharp's mother which was reproduced in its entirely in the June 1916 issue of the parish magazine. It read:

> Your welcome letter received. I am very pleased to hear you have all been so kind to my dear son Edward. He joined the army in September 1914, and he was 21 years old last January, and lived at home with his father and mother. He is single. I have another one, George, in the Army, also one in Egypt, fighting.
>
> I would have answered sooner, but waited to see if I got a letter from my boy, and thank God, I received one this morning. He tells me he is quite well and that he has received parcels from someone, but the address was all torn he could not see where they came from, but told me to thank all kind friends for him if I knew where they came from.
>
> Again thanking you and all your kind friends for your goodness to my son. I am, yours truly, E. Sharp,
> 37 Crofton Road, Plaistow, London E.

In September more news from 'our' Prisoner of War was received. Private Sharp had written again saying how much he appreciated the contents of the weekly parcels, which he said he had received 'every week without fail.' He expressly mentioned how acceptable the food was and also the cigarettes. Mrs. Littlehales appealed to the smokers of Langford to remember Private Sharp and to send her some packets of Woodbine or Gold Flake cigarettes for including in the weekly parcels. She also renewed her appeal for gifts of underclothing, shirts, or socks etc.

In addition to the usual weekly one, a Christmas parcel was sent to Private Sharp in November 1916. This included, among other things, tins of English beef and plum pudding, cake, some chocolates, a comforter and writing materials. Parishioners were again encouraged to write to him at No. 13762, 6 Komp, Kriegsgefangenen Lager, Merseburg, Sachsen, in the German state of Saxony-Anhalt. It is likely that many of the villagers who were raising funds were hoping that, at the end of the war, their adopted son Edward Sharp would come to visit them. However, they were to be disappointed.

Times were hard at home too and general conditions were becoming worse. In March 1917, several subscribers to the British Prisoners of War Fund expressed themselves unable to continue to support Private Sharp. The amount coming in weekly was insufficient to cover the amount which was due to be forwarded to the Central Association that sent Private Sharp's parcel to him each week. An appeal in the parish magazine read:

> We sincerely trust that our people who have hitherto responded so splendidly and till lately kept up their weekly donations, will not let the effort die away, as our prisoner is in as much need of his food today as ever he was – perhaps more so.

And once again the villagers responded when, as a result of that plea, a number of new subscribers were added to the list and grateful acknowledgement made of a 'special joint donation' of five shillings which was received from two regular subscribers. On 26th February 1918 a postcard was received from Private Sharp who had by then been transferred to Wittenberg Camp, in the same state of Saxony-Anhalt, gratefully acknowledging the receipt of one tin of milk, sausages, jam, a packet of sago, tea, sugar and soup powder.

In August 1918 the parish magazine noted that during the past month several postcards had been received from Edward Sharp, 'of Wittenberg Camp,' in which he stated that he was still receiving the parcels regularly, and tended his grateful thanks to the contributors in Langford for their continued kindness. Just over one year later the cost of war (even at a time after hostilities had ceased) was once again brought home to the people of Langford. Mrs. Sharp wrote a letter to the people of the village about her son Edward's death. He had died soon after his release from Germany. She wrote:

> I thank you very much for your sympathy and also parishioners and I can tell you I seem to miss my boys more every day. I did so long for my Teddy to come home, it is too sad for words. He used to write such cheerful letters, and was so full of hope. I do value his last photo; when I look at it I can see how ill he was.

> I have had a visit from a R.A.M.C. [*Royal Army Medical Corps*] man who was with him when he died, and he promised Teddy he would come and see us. He said what a fine fellow my boy was. He died at a Military Hospital in Holland, and was buried with military honours with four more British Tommies.

Despite the villagers' best efforts to support Private Sharp whilst he was in German PoW camps, their 'adopted son' had sadly not made it home. Despite the fact that he was not a

'Langford' boy – Private Sharp had been 'adopted' by the village as one of their own.

Fund-raising for various war-related causes continued in the village. In August 1916, the Rector received from Mrs Gowers, wife of the Coachman at Langford Grove, the sum of 15/- which was the result of a 'Penny Fund' started by her for the British Red Cross Society to be spent on the sick and wounded. The parish magazine noted:

> This sum has been collected in pennies from the various workmen engaged for several months on the work of repairing and redecorating the big house, and from the permanent servants on the estate. It only shows what can be done, and Mrs. Gowers is much to be commended on her splendid effort for this excellent object. The money was handed to Miss Jeanie Baker, who is the Local Secretary for the British Red Cross Society.

But it was not only the Red Cross Society that needed funds. Everywhere money was in short supply and the Government needed to both reduce borrowing and raise funds for the war effort. Consequently, the National Savings Movement was established in 1916 to encourage the British people to 'save and prosper.' Savings groups were formed in factories, shops, clubs, etc, across Britain and an appointed collector did the rounds each week to collect the savings and issue certificates.

Back in 1916 a 'National Mission of Repentance and Hope' was embarked upon. The day set apart for the Maldon Deanery was the 9th of each month, and three church services were arranged - Holy Communion 7.45 a.m., a short Intercession service at 12 o'clock, and a special evening service at 7.15 p.m. Members of Langford were also invited to make use of the church for private intercession at times other than those appointed for service - St. Giles' in those days being left open twenty-four hours a day. Revd.

Littlehales expressed his hope that this would be carefully noted and the day kept absolutely free from engagements.

With the end of war nowhere in sight, in the autumn of 1916 a group of ladies went round local parishes in a 'Pilgrimage of Prayer.' They held open air services and paid as many visits as time permitted. The parish magazine enthused:

> Langford people came up splendidly to welcome them, and joined in their prayer meetings. They were welcomed into the parish on the afternoon of Tuesday 26th September 1916, by over 20 parishioners, who accompanied them into Church for a short devotional service, which was conducted by the Rector. In the evening a well attended open air meeting was conducted by the Pilgrims, two impressive and instructive addresses being given by them. An afternoon meeting for Women only was held at Langford Hall to which about 30 came - a splendid gathering. Another evening meeting has been arranged to be held at Bevis Hall, on Wednesday. Miss Jeanie Baker is to be congratulated on her excellent arrangement for their entertainment, and those who have offered hospitality will feel amply repaid.

But the power of prayer alone did not seem to be working as in November more tragic news was received from the front. John Henry Colbear had been killed in action in France on 9th September 1916, aged only 19. The Colbear family had four sons serving in the Great War: Alfred, Thomas, Edward and John.

John was born in 1897, the youngest son of David and Mary Ann Colbear and the seventh of the nine children in the family. He was born in Heybridge, and was christened in St. Andrew's Church, on 31st October 1897. He spent his early life in that parish, living in Wood Lane (off Holloway Road) but the family moved to Langford sometime between 1902 and 1903 (when he is listed as living in Hatfield Road). The two youngest children were baptised in St. Giles' in July 1903.

When war broke out, John enlisted in Heybridge, joining the 2nd Battalion, the Royal Sussex Regiment as a Private (No. G/14596) and served with the British Expeditionary Force in France. He took leave during November 1915 to be a witness at his elder sister Dulcie May's wedding on 15th of that month in St. Giles' Church. Sadly he died less than a year later.

Not two months after John's death another villager died in the service of King and country.

Stanley Charles Harvey (pictured right) was killed on the Somme on 13th November 1916 aged twenty-one. Born in Heybridge in 1895, the son of Charles Ernest and Minnie Harvey (who later took over the Post Office in Langford), Stanley was the second of nine children (six boys and three girls). In May 1912 he was appointed the Patrol Leader in the newly organised troop of Langford Boy Scouts where Mr. Barne of Langford Place was Scout Master. Stanley enlisted at Chelmsford in 1914 into the 1st Battalion, the Cambridgeshire Regiment (formerly 25650, Bedfordshire Regiment). Everyone it seemed had a good word for Stanley Harvey and he was clearly highly regarded in the village. In addition he was described as 'a regular and useful member of the choir' and, of course, 'a dutiful son.'

The New Year brought the news that Driver T4 038194 Frederick Stephen Joslin of the Army Service Corps had been killed in action in France on 5th February 1917. Frederick was born in 1885, the son of Peter and Celia Sarah Joslin of Heybridge. In the 1901 census the family were living in Birch Cottage, Ulting - at that time part of Langford parish. Peter (then aged 60) worked as a horseman with his elder son Richard (aged 21). Frederick married 21 year old Emily Mills in St. Giles' Church on 1st February 1913 when he was 28 and working as an agricultural labourer - a job he had pursued since his early teens. A son, Richard Stephen, was born on 8th November 1913, followed by a second, Frederick Charles, on 7th December 1914.

Sadly Richard Stephen died aged 15 months, and was buried in the churchyard on 3rd March 1915. Frederick's youngest sister Edith Mary married William Joslin, a gardener from Little Waltham, on 5th July 1916. Frederick was not present at his sister's wedding and it is presumed that he was still serving at the Front, and news of his death devastated his family. He is buried in St. Giles' churchyard along the north side. His headstone is of the War Graves Commission and embossed with the R.A.S.C. regimental badge.

Tragedy struck the Joslin family yet again when, still reeling from the loss of her husband, and heavily pregnant with her third child, Emily's second son, Frederick Charles, died aged

351

only two and was buried twelve days after his father. The services for the burials were carried out by the Rector, Revd. Charles Gough Littlehales. Frederick's third son, Arthur George, was born on 20th April 1917. The child's father had been dead for two months.

In May, yet another name was added to the 'Roll of Honour.' On 4th May 1917, while returning to Egypt, Edward Colbear was drowned when the *SS Transylvania*, one of a number of liners employed to carry troop reinforcements to fight in the Salonika campaign, was struck in the port engine room by a torpedo from German submarine U63 and sank. A total of 414 soldiers and crew were lost. Another devoted and much-loved son had fallen victim to the enemy. He was also the second son David and Mary Colbear had lost to the war.

SS Transylvania

Another family in the village grieved when Frank Pedley was killed in action in France on 5th July 1917 aged twenty. He is buried in Langford churchyard (grave no. 023). Frank was the son of Francis and Alice Pedley, and was born in Leyton, in the Parish of Walthamstow, his mother having been born in Hatfield Peverel in 1873. Frank went to London to enlist in the Royal Horse Artillery (Royal Field Artillery). He was a gunner (No. L/30177) and was killed in Flanders fields. Sadly very little else is currently known about this Langford hero, although his parents are said to have been living at 102 The Causeway, Maldon, at the time of his death.

Throughout the hostilities all the fund-raising for war charities continued. Amy Wynyard, from Langford Rectory, wrote in the February 1917 parish magazine:

> I have been asked to tell the people of Langford about the Christmas parcels which I sent to the Sailors and Soldiers of Langford and Ulting, who are serving their King and Country with such self-sacrificing courage and heroism; and having been their 'Friend' for more than 16 years, I will do so. Thanks to the generosity and kind contributions of several Langford friends, I collected £4; so was able to send to each Sailor and Soldier 1 pair of socks, some cigarettes, and a picture postcard of Maldon. My thanks are also due to Mrs. Jones and the School children, who she kindly allowed to copy out some amusing verses, which were enclosed in each of the 57 Christmas parcels, and went to different parts of Europe. I have had many grateful letters of thanks.

Postcards, like the one shown on the right, were also enclosed with the parcels sent to those serving overseas.

But as we have seen before, Langford's generosity extended to more than its own children. A 'Sale of Needlework and Children's Entertainment' took place on Saturday 17th February 1917 being 'successful in every way.' In May 1917 villagers were informed that many more men were being taken prisoner and the village was urged to continue to contribute six

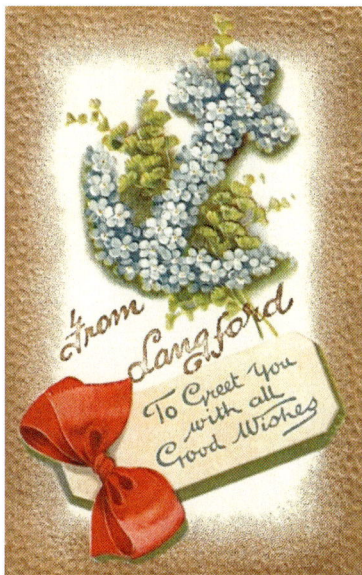

353

shillings per week which was considered a 'sufficient portion' but 'must be maintained without fail.' It seems that the people of Langford managed to continue to contribute at the required level even though collecting money under war conditions was proving increasingly difficult.

To try and raise more money, a flag day was held on 21st July 1917 in aid of the Essex Regiments comforts. This was 'excellently organised' by Mrs. Wilberforce, of Langford Grove, the result being 'highly successful and gratifying to those concerned.' The amount realised by the sale of flags was £1.17s.4d. The actual sales were effected by the Misses Wilberforce, and Miss Hilda Grout, of Stock Hall, whose appeals, according to the parish magazine, were 'irresistible.'

A highly successful entertainment was organised on Monday 11th February 1918 in Langford schoolroom to help reduce the deficit of the Prisoner of War fund. The programme included a duologue entitled 'Cheerful and Amicable' and patriotic and comic recitations; the audience appreciating the 'good music as well as the comic items.' Every performer did his (or her) bit 'very efficiently,' and the constant applause was 'well merited.' Every available seat in the room was occupied and many people had to be turned away. The 'satisfactory result' was the addition to the Prisoner Fund of £5.19s.9½d. The expenses amounting to two shillings and sixpence were defrayed by Mrs. Wilberforce.

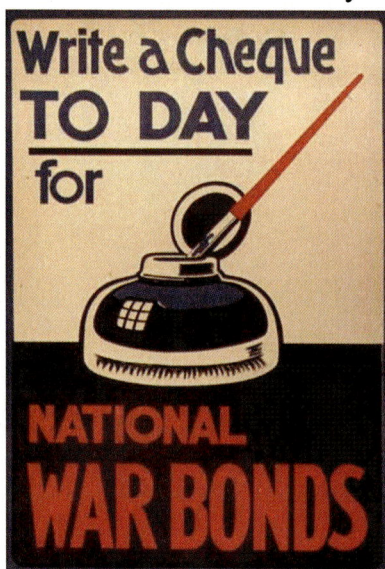

Another way of raising funds was to invest in National War Savings. A meeting was called in the schoolroom on 12th April 1917 at which Mr. Taylor of Maldon explained the aim and objectives of the scheme. The meeting was well attended, Mr. Taylor stating that the main object of the Association was to give the smallest investor a chance of subscribing to the War Loans. As a result of that meeting an Association was formed with the Committee comprising of officers, Revd. C. G. Littlehales, (Chairman) [of Langford Hall], H. R. Hollingdale, Esq., (Treasurer) [of Mill House], Miss J. D. L. Baker (Secretary) [of Langford Meads] and committee members Miss M. Baker [Langford Meads], Mrs. Grout [Stock Hall], Mrs. Jones [School House] and Miss Wynyard [Langford Old Rectory].

However, it was not only the adults who were 'doing their bit' for the war effort; the children of the village played their part too. Towards the end of 1917, as the result of a gift of money from the children of the school, a letter was received from Revd. Geo. Higgins, of St. Luke's Kilburn thanking them for 'such a nice sum of money' they had raised for 'our Soldiers and Sailors Christmas parcel.'

In accordance with the command of H.M. The King, 6th January 1918 was observed as a Day of National Prayer. Special Forms of Service were used and there was a good attendance at St. Giles' morning, afternoon and evening. The collection throughout the day for the British Red Cross Society totalled £3.8s.10d, including 5s 3½d which was the children's contribution. The parish magazine noted rather sarcastically, "We were pleased to notice several men present on that day, who seldom darken the doors of God's House." The objective was "to request God the giver of Victory that he would grant us Victory and Peace during the year."

Langford villagers seemed never to tire in their own war effort, and a very successful rummage sale was held in the schoolroom on Saturday 1st December 1918 raising funds for defraying the cost of Christmas parcels to all soldiers connected with Langford.

A 'saleable lot' of rummage was received and with buyers eager for bargains, it was not long before nearly everything was sold raising over £9 which was allocated: Soldiers' parcels (£5.5s.0d), Red Cross Depot (Witham) (£1.0s.0d) and Prisoners of War Fund (£2.18s.7d).

In 1918 yet another of the Langford boys, George Dorking, died, but his death was not at the hands of the enemy. George, the youngest son of Charles Cornelius and Sarah Ann Dorking, was born in Langford in 1900 and baptised privately on 11th February 1902. When war broke out the family was living in Ulting, and George enlisted in Chelmsford as soon as he was old enough into the 2/4th Battalion, Duke of Wellington's (West Riding Regiment) – formerly 38278, East Surrey Regiment as Private 54602. He died from a severe attack of pneumonia at Rugely Camp, Stafford, on 18th June 1918. He was just 17 years old. 'Peter', as he was affectionately known, had only been in khaki a few months, and his death came as a shock to everyone as it was so wholly unexpected. He was buried in Langford on 22nd June 1918 when the Revd. H.M. Laing, Vicar of Ulting (and Woodham Walter) carried out the ceremony. George's death meant that his parents had now lost two sons to the war. (George's brother Charles Victor of the 9th Battalion, the East Surrey Regiment, No. 25003, had been killed in France on 17th April 1917.) George's body rests in grave No. 019 (see picture above) along the north side of St. Giles' churchyard, whilst his brother Charles is buried in the Bulley-Grenay communal cemetery in France.

Another life lost was that of George Arthur Coates who died in 1919. Born in 1893, George was the only son of George Arthur Coates, house decorator. In 1908 the family was living at Langford Cross. George Jnr's funeral was conducted by the Rector, Revd. Littlehales but, unusually, the parish magazine in June 1919 merely reported that George had died on 19th May 1919 aged 26 and made no reference to his contribution to the war effort. Examination of the burial register revealed that George had not been killed in action, or succumbed to wounds sustained, but had died at the County Lunatic Asylum, Fulbourn, Cambridgeshire (originally the Cambridge District Asylum). The 1911 Census form does not record any problem with George (there is a column which

required the compiler to state whether someone was either 'Lunatic,' 'Imbecile,' or 'Feeble Minded') and as these were not completed we can only surmise that George was of sound mind in that year. Also, he was recorded as being a 'metal turner' and this would have required a degree of skill and mental capacity.

We have not yet managed to trace George's war record, but given the horrors that many endured, it is not unreasonable to believe that he was deeply affected by what he had experienced, and that this caused him to have a mental breakdown.

During the Great War many asylums and spas were brought into use to care for traumatised soldiers, and it is possible that George's death was the result of a condition that would become known as 'shell-shock.' The news of his condition and subsequent death must have been terribly hard for his parents who, having lost their only son to the war (although strictly speaking he had died after peace had been declared) probably did not receive the sympathy and support from the village they should have done, as those suffering from shell-shock were often perceived as malingerers. This might explain the lack of any detailed information about his death in the parish magazine.

Returning home, invalided out, mentally (and probably physically) injured with the incessant pounding of guns still resounding in his head, George would be moving ever closer to insanity. Whether he died of injuries, of complete mental breakdown or at the hands of possibly unsympathetic medical staff and indifferent care is likely never to be known. Today George's condition would have undoubtedly fallen into the category of Post-Traumatic Stress Disorder but back then his situation and condition would not have been properly understood by either those in power or the 'common man.' So his name is not commemorated on the war memorial that stands in St. Giles' churchyard, but his sacrifice *is* remembered and recorded in this book as one of the forgotten heroes of our village. (George is buried (see left) in grave No. 020 by the north boundary of the churchyard.)

But even in the last few days of the war, when everyone had hoped that there would be no more deaths, the sympathy of the entire parish went out to Mr. and Mrs. Walter Grout and family of Stock Hall Farm. At the beginning of October they received the sad news that their son Ernest Victor, who had emigrated to Canada on 7th September 1906, had died in hospital 'somewhere in France,' as a result of severe wounds received four weeks earlier.

358

The parish magazine of December 1918 recorded that 'Dick,' as he was more popularly known, joined the Canadian Field Artillery early in 1916, and 'saw a good deal of fighting.' The first news of his being hospitalised appeared to indicate that, though severely wounded, there was some hope of recovery. However, septic poisoning set in which caused a 'sudden collapse.' Dick died on 3rd October 1918. The parish magazine reported that 'His parents [*had*] lost a good son with a promising career before him as a farmer' and that he would be 'sadly missed from his homestead at Kamlooft, British Columbia, where he had gained the respect of all who knew him.'

But the war was now over and at last it was time to think about and celebrate peace. A meeting was held in the schoolroom on Monday 26th May 1919 to discuss and decide what part Langford should take in the Peace Celebrations of the country. The parish magazine reported that:

> After a good deal of discussion, it was finally decided, though not unanimously, to fix the second Bank Holiday – Tuesday August 6th, as the day for a Thanksgiving Service: A Tea for the whole parish and Presentation of Medals to the children. A committee was chosen comprising the following: Miss Baker, Mr. W. H. Chalk, Miss Ford, Mrs. Jones, Mr. Stanley Grout, Miss Wynyard, Mr. H. W. W. Wilberforce, and the Rector, with power to add to their number, in whose hands all the arrangements have been placed.

And so war, for the time being at least, seemed to have come to an end and thoughts then turned to how best to commemorate those who had fallen in the service of their King and Country. The parish magazine first mentioned the possibility of erecting a war memorial in the issue dated November 1918. Subsequently a meeting was held at the school on 21st November to receive proposals for the erection of a memorial (of some kind) and the debate was recorded in detail in the December 1918 edition:

> Various suggestions were made, among them a Lychgate at the main entrance to the churchyard, and a Stone Cross on the grass plot at the junction of the three roads by the Church. A further meeting is to be held to consider these and any other proposals which have been or shall be made, when it is hoped that at least one representative from every house in the parish will be present, as a matter so important and so solemn deserves the attention of the whole of our community. We know the debt we owe to the heroes of the village. They and their gallant comrades saved us from the unspeakable horrors which were inflicted upon the men, women and children of other lands who fell into the hands of the enemy. But for them, there might not have been a cottage left standing in Langford; no man could have reckoned on his life, no woman on her honour. Such a debt we can never pay, but at least let us see to it that the names and deeds of our preservers be kept in remembrance. Let us erect such a memorial to those dead ones that in time to come those who inhabit or pass through our borders may know that we were not ungrateful.

A second meeting in connection with the proposal was held in the schoolroom, on Tuesday 17th December 1918 and was reported in the January parish magazine albeit with an air of disappointment:

> Considering that every householder in the parish was personally invited to attend this meeting, the number present was far below that expected, only about fourteen houses being represented...The two schemes most in favour were (1) a Lychgate, (2) a Memorial Cross. A show of hands was called for and the meeting decided

360

in favour of a Memorial Cross. A Sub-Committee was then elected.

In February 1919 the Executive Committee of the Langford War Memorial finally decided upon the erection of an Ornamental Cross similar in design to that placed to the memory of the late Lord Kitchener in St. Botolph's Churchyard, Bishopsgate, London (just up from Liverpool Street Station.)

The work pressed ahead, and execution and erection of the War Memorial was placed in the hands of Messrs. G. Maile & Son of Euston Road, London. The site chosen was the extreme corner of the Churchyard at the angle of the Maldon and Witham (or Langford Hall) roads. The Rector contemplated 'the compilation of a small booklet with a biography of each fallen hero and complete list of subscribers and possibly a woodcut of the memorial itself.' If this was ever done, it has subsequently been lost.

Langford's War Memorial was erected on 21st June 1919. A Memorial and Dedication Service was taken by the Bishop of Colchester on Sunday 29th June. Holy Communion, at which the Lord Bishop was celebrant, was at 8 a.m. when each of the heroes, to whose memory the Cross was dedicated was commemorated by name.

Choral Matins followed at 11 a.m. at the conclusion of which, the Clergy, Choir and Congregation proceeded to the Churchyard corner, the site of the Memorial Cross, where Special Prayers for the departed were said by the Bishop. After this the Cross was unveiled by the Revd. Lord Byron, in his capacity as patron of the living and Rector of Thrumpton and former Rector of Langford, and when the dedicatory prayers had been concluded Hymn 225 (*The world is very evil*) was sung by all 'with great feeling.' The Bishop gave 'an impressive address' to the very large congregation pointing out 'the various facts of which the sight of the Memorial Cross should remind us;' these being 'the heroes and their self-sacrifice, the Love of Christ Himself and His great Sacrifice for sinners' and 'Our Duty of unselfishness, self-sacrifice, and devotion to the principles of Christianity.'

At Evensong the congregation was again a large one. At the conclusion a special commemoration was made of the Langford heroes and after Hymn 438 (*How Bright These Glorious Spirits Shine*) was sung, the sermon was preached by Revd. Lord Byron, who took for his text St John xxi, 19. ('He said this to indicate the kind of death by which he would glorify God. After this he said to him, "Follow me."') The service concluded with the Hymn 'Abide with Me' and the National Anthem. The parish magazine recorded that 'all parishioners were delighted to welcome Lord Byron among them again and it was a real pleasure to see him looking so well.'

On 6th July 1919, the day appointed by Proclamation of the King as a Day of Thanksgiving for the Restoration of Peace, was observed by the use of the Special Form of Service, which was commendably simple and suitable. The Rector preached in the morning emphasising the role of 'Brotherhood' which was deemed so necessary at a time of unrest and industrial strife to combat the spirit of selfishness which he told the congregation still, unhappily, prevailed. At the evening service he warned against 'the tyranny of labour' which was 'spoiling the efforts of Christian Socialism to improve the conditions of the working population of England.' Heavy stuff indeed, the thrust of which may well have been lost on many of those gathered in St. Giles.'

On 19th July, courtesy of Mr. and Mrs. Herbert Wilberforce, the whole Parish was entertained in the grounds of Langford Grove where 'a thoroughly enjoyable afternoon was spent' by all who were able to attend. An excellent tea was served to the children at 4.15, followed half-an-hour later by 'a sumptuous repast to the adults in the large Barn adjoining the stables.' At the conclusion of the meal, the Rector proposed the health of His Majesty the King, and the National Anthem was sung. The rest of the afternoon was occupied by a full programme of sports 'energetically carried through by the Committee, some of the events causing great amusement to the less energetic of the visitors.'

In December 1919, a dinner was held to celebrate and acknowledge the very real contribution made to the war effort by Langford's Special Constables. In recognition of their valuable services, rendered entirely without payment during the years of the war, they were entertained on the evening of 3rd December where they partook of 'an excellent dinner, the catering of which rested entirely in the capable hands of Mr. W.H. Chalk with the help of his wife and sister.' The chair was taken by Mr. Wilberforce, supported by Inspector A.E. May and the Rector, and sixteen constables were present.

After dinner the toasts of the King and the Langford Specials were given by the Chairman, who referred in glowing terms to the valuable services rendered by the men of the Langford Force. Inspector May also spoke highly of the 'regular and conscientious way' the duties had been performed throughout. The Rector added his testimony to the efficient way that all had filled their office. After the toasts, 'a number of songs were sung supplemented by amusing stories and recitations, and it was past 10 o'clock before the company dispersed.'

Since the first Service of Remembrance had been held it had always coincided with St. Peter's Day (29th June) but in June 1925 it was decided to change the date to the now officially recognised Remembrance Day, 11th November. On this occasion, immediately after the two minutes silence at 11 a.m., there was a short service in St. Giles' Church. It was also announced that Mrs. Ffinch would be organising the sale of poppies in Langford on Armistice Day, the proceeds of which would be sent to the Disabled Soldiers and Sailors association. The parish magazine stated 'We hope our people will respond generously on behalf of this good cause, which has been commended to the notice of all Britishers by His Grace the Archbishop of Canterbury.'

And, as usual, respond they did. The result of the sale of poppies for Lord Haig's fund for disabled soldiers and sailors must have been most gratifying to the two sellers, Miss Ivy Harvey (of the Post Office) and Miss Joyce Littlehales (daughter of the Rector, at Langford Hall) because, as the parish magazine noted: 'On their boxes being opened the amount collected was found to be £7.19.8.' adding a congratulatory 'Well done Langford' for good measure.

On Armistice Day 1937 the names on the Roll of Honour were read at the morning service by Revd. Ernest Augustus Butson Creed, who had taken over from Revd. Littlehales in 1931. In the evening a large congregation assembled. The lessons were read by the Churchwarden, Major Claude Tritton, and the service concluded with the National Anthem. The Scouts were also at the service. With the threat of another war in the offing, Air Raid Precautions (ARP) lectures were given in the school in December 1938 and January 1939 by a Mr. Wells. These rumblings of war soon lead to what was generally described as 'The European Crisis.'

Despite promises of never going to war with one another again, a second major world conflict seemed more and more inevitable, and Langford, along with the rest of Britain, started making preparations.

In keeping with the general 'Black Out,' the people of Langford took their part in a mock air raid on 10th August 1939. A 'bomb' was dropped near the River Blackwater bridge, causing 'casualties.' A.R.P. wardens and First Aid helpers were within reach to render necessary assistance and Special Constables were on duty. Afterwards, the Head Warden congratulated the village on the satisfactory way Langford had fulfilled its duties.

War was declared on 4th September 1939.

The Second World War (1939-1945)

The parish magazine dated October 1939 recorded:

> The news on the wireless tonight [*Wednesday 28th September 1939*] certainly seems brighter, but we must still, as the Archbishop of Canterbury says, go on praying for peace to Him who hears prayer, and for guidance of those controlling the destinies of the world. Special sermons were preached on Sunday and Intercessions made; and also on Tuesday and Friday at 12 noon. The Bishop's letter said "Today Christ is being crucified again. Brutality and injustice are stalking triumphant through Europe, trampling under foot every Christian virtue and destroying all Christian ideals. Evil is winning everywhere; goodness is defeated in every contest. So it was on Good Friday. But the world's Easter is coming, and goodness, we know, will be vindicated, and evil will be crushed, otherwise the devil is stronger than God. The highwaymen of Europe may carry on their brutal trade a little longer, but the end is bound to come, for this is God's world, and He hath said, 'Shall not I visit for these things?'

This 'new' war was a time of great worry and concern and so it was not surprising that the practice of saying Intercessions was re-introduced in St. Giles' on Wednesdays and Fridays at 12.30 p.m. The Bishop of Chelmsford, in his letter in the *Diocesan Chronicle* with reference to the war, wrote:

> I cannot honestly see what the Church could have done (which it has not done) to avert the war. The idea that the Church is an institution which comes to our rescue with a speedy and simple remedy when the nation has got itself into grave trouble is quite erroneous.
>
> The office of the Church is to teach people how to live together so that such trouble will never arise, and if through disobedience to that teaching misfortune and sorrow come, then the Church is there, not to disclose a 6½d remedy, but to proclaim that repentance is the only door to hope.

Perhaps that was just as well as there still remained between five and six years of conflict.

In September 1939 Mrs. Claude Tritton (wife of the Churchwarden) set up a working party at Langford Hall on Wednesday afternoons from 2.30-4.30 to make items for the hospitals. In the same month, Clifford Green (of Council Houses in Langford Road) and Albert Chaplin (of Railway Cottages), left Langford to serve their King and Country, the parish magazine confirming that 'They are both missed very much, especially by the Church they have served so faithfully from their earliest youth.'

Sunday 1st October 1939 was observed by order of the Archbishop as a day of national prayer, when special Intercessions were made for the King and all in authority; for all who were serving in the King's Forces, by sea, land or air; for those in anxiety; and for the sick, the wounded and the fallen. Remembrance Day was observed on Saturday 11th November, and on the following day a special service was held and an address given. The scouts were also in attendance under Assistant Scoutmaster F. Williams. Those on active service from Langford at this time were (in alphabetical order):

Bowyer-Bower, Thomas	Army Education Corps
Chaplin, Albert A.	Royal Army Serv. Corps
Chipperfield, Robert	Merchant Service
Church, Albert E.	Anti-Tank Regiment
Church, Arthur T.	Royal Army Serv. Corps
Crook, Jack	1st Border Regiment
Green, Clifford H.	Anti-Tank Regiment
Mansfield, Harold	Royal Navy
Moore, Robin J.	Royal Air Force

There had been a national feeling of 'wanting to do

something,' not least among ex-regular soldiers of the Great War. Even during the early stages of the war, the possibility of German paratroopers and Fifth Columnists landing in Britain's fields and byways was seen as a real threat, and this, of course, had been a reality in the invasion of Holland earlier in the war. Because of this perceived threat, a number of volunteer groups were formed to keep watch and patrol some of the more vulnerable areas of the country, and Langford was no exception. As a direct result of one of the darkest days of World War II (14th May 1940), when Germany had poured into France practically unchallenged, the War Minister, Anthony Eden, gave a (now) historic radio broadcast to the nation, urging all male civilians aged 17-65 who had (for whatever reason) not been drafted into the services, to form a new fighting force called the Local Defence Volunteers (LDV).

The immediate result of Anthony Eden's call to arms was a massive, and somewhat embarrassing, response, far above any means of training or arming the huge numbers of men suddenly available for part-time service. By the end of the following day some 250,000 men had volunteered from all walks of life. Weaponry was scarce, and the volunteers did what they could with home-made weapons, but this was unacceptable if the force was meant to fight a well-equipped foe. However, shortly thereafter Langford came under the Maldon Company (headed by Captain B.H. Bright, M.C.) of No. 2 Battalion, Essex LDV.

In addition to the LDV an order was issued in July, 1940 which laid down that no road block was to be without its pillbox. Langford is recorded to have had its own pillboxes but research has yet to discover exactly where. Brian Chalk (late of Langford) recalls that there was one just inside the gates to the waterworks' reservoir road opposite Bridge Cottages but this is yet to be formally verified. Certainly no physical evidence of it remains today. However, a number of air raid shelters were built in the village, two in the mounds behind the houses in Ulting Lane, one by the waterworks which now forms part of the garden of Mill Cottage), one within the grounds of the treatment plant and one behind the Old Post Office.

Only a month and a half after its creation, the LDV was renamed by Winston Churchill. The 'Local Defence Volunteers' had been considered too much of a title and it was felt that the 'Home Guard' better suited its role. Unfortunately the nickname for the LDV ('Look, Duck and Vanish') lingered on for some time - rather unfairly as the work done by the Home Guard was very important. It had a number of purposes: it made those in it feel as if they were doing something constructive in the war effort, and it was not simply for older men past conscription age. Those young enough to be conscripted but who did not pass the military's medicals could join the Home Guard. Men between seventeen and sixty-five years could join.

Improvisation was all important to the fledgling units, who went on patrol armed with such weapons as pick axes, broom handles, truncheons, pikes and even golf clubs! It was also reported that in at least one Home Guard unit, the guards took packets of pepper with them which would, if required, be thrown into the eyes of enemy invaders, thereby momentarily blinding or disabling them.

As previously mentioned, Maldon Company was commanded by Captain (later Lieut.-Col.) B.H. Bright, M.C. with sections at Dengie, Tillingham, Bradwell, Burnham, Southminster, St. Lawrence, Steeple, Althorne, Mayland and Latchingdon, Mundon, North Heybridge, Cold Norton, Purleigh, Woodham Mortimer, Langford (Waterworks) (a possible strategic target for enemy bombers) and Maldon. Battalion Headquarters were at West Bower Hall, Woodham Mortimer, at that time the residence of Colonel Sir Carne Rasch, Bt., A.D.C., the first Battalion Commander. He commanded the 2nd Battalion Essex Home Guard until he retired in July 1943.

The 'Maldon Section' of the Maldon Company covered Langford Waterworks, and the Heybridge sites of: Black Bridge, the Wave Bridge, Bentalls and Crittalls. When Major Bright was promoted to take over from Colonel Rasch, the battalion was divided into various 'Companies.' 'A' Company was charged with (i) holding the roads through Maldon and Heybridge, (ii) holding the Langford Waterworks, and (iii) counter-attacking with mobile platoons, if necessary, in the neighbourhood of Maldon and Heybridge.

The Maldon Battalion Headquarters was in Lodge Road, Maldon, the Company Headquarters were in Tenterfield Road Drill Hall, Maldon, and the Battle Headquarters were sited in the Civil Defence H.Q. in Silver Street, Maldon. It was the 2nd Essex Battalion Home Guard, No. 3 Platoon (Maldon Company) (above) that covered Langford.

The officer-in-charge was Lieut. E. W. Randall, M.M., (Chelmer House, Heybridge) with Sergeant W. Goulding (Mill House, Langford) as his second-in-command. Villager Ron Harvey recalled in 2007 that the Home Guard used to parade outside the Boiler House at the Waterworks (now the Museum of Power) and there was at one time a mark in the ground where a round was discharged by accident during an inspection. Later Mr. Goulding took over as Captain, and Mr. Jennings was the Sergeant Major. At that time the rifle range was up by the reservoir, and the fields between the waterworks and the river were ploughed up to grow vegetables. Ron said "We used to do firewatching in the Mill. A doodlebug came over one morning when the clouds were very low, and it couldn't be seen. The engine stopped, which meant it was coming down not far away."

Being a member of the Home Guard was far from an 'easy option.' The platoon met at the school every week for lectures and drill. All but a few of the members would work all day in their full-time jobs and then, later that evening, take up their Home Guard duties. The late Ron Harvey joined the LDV as he was declared unfit to join the forces and serve overseas. He had fallen from a ladder and sustained a fracture to his foot. Apparently someone had painted over a crack in one of the rungs, and when Ron stepped on it it had sheered through and he been thrown to the ground from quite a height.

Ron also told how he worked all day at the waterworks and then went on duty on the top floor of Langford Mill to watch for enemy aircraft during the night. He recalled that on several occasions, due to tiredness, he and his colleagues would fall asleep while on watch. He added that sometimes they had to ring the waterworks in the morning to find out if there had been any activity during the night as no one had managed to stay awake! On one occasion they were informed that they had slept through a 'bit of a battle' in the skies. Often they had to go and check the flood gates by bicycle to see if they were all right – not an easy job in more or less total darkness.

In the September 1940 issue of the parish magazine a list of additional Langford men (and one woman) who were by then also on active service was published. In alphabetical order they were:

Bonner, Edward	Military Police
Kewell, L.	Royal Army Med. Corps
Macklin, David	Training Corps
Pelly, Anthony R	Armoured Cars
Pelly, Michael B.	RAF Speed Boat Control
Piper, Reginald	16th Lancers
Smith, Percy R.	Royal Artillery
Smith, Robert V.	Royal Army Serv. Corps
Tritton, Capt. John	Royal Artillery
Williams, Frederick	Light Training Regiment
Wilson, Annie	Nurse

The magazine also included thanks to Albert Chaplin (pictured left) 'who comes forward willingly to help in the organ blowing when the organ blower is unable to come, through being on duty in these times.' By March 1941 others from the parish had joined up and gone to war namely Ralph Green, of The Council Houses, Gerald Groden, John Groden (both of 8 Ulting Lane) and Elijah Pratt of Black Cottages.

Services continued in St. Giles' church, despite air raid warnings but it was noted in the parish magazine that 'should warnings take place some 20 minutes before the hour of service, it is thought best to wait and have the service when the 'All Clear' has been given.' The Commander of the Local Defence Volunteers' [*shortly to be renamed The Home Guard*] detachment in Langford, Lieutenant Randall reported that the church bells would be rung in the event of enemy parachutists landing. However, the bells would *not* be rung for any report of parachutists at a distance greater than three miles. The bells of St. Giles' were under the charge of Sergeant Goulding of Mill House, as he lived right next door to the church.

During the war the waterworks employed 'telephone boys' who worked the same shift pattern as the engineers - 6-2, 2-10, 10-6. They were based in a kiosk at the corner of the pumping station (still in existence today). The late Ron Harvey said that their main job was to take air raid messages from the Telephone Exchange such as air raid warning red, or air raid message white. On the outside of the kiosk were two lights, one red and one white. If the message was air raid warning red, the red light was switched on, and they ran to the boiler room door and shouted 'Red!' With that the boiler room attendant sounded the siren which was a ship's hooter. Later the 'All Clear' came through which was air raid message white. The red light was switched off and the white one switched on. The boiler room attendant sounded the 'All Clear.' It must have been a fairly boring job for most of the time, but now and again there would have been great excitement.

While the Battle of Britain raged in 1940, many planes both friendly and hostile were lost over the skies of Essex. One such event happened on the afternoon of Saturday 24th August 1940 on the border between Langford and Heybridge behind Langford Park Cottages (now called 'Ravens'). As usual, eyewitness accounts varied. Ted Chalk said that he witnessed a 'dog fight' just after 2 p.m. He recalled that there were five, quite tall elms in his garden, and as the enemy planes came over they started firing and shrapnel came up his path. Much of the shrapnel hit the trees. Ted went outside to see what was going on, and noticed that the plane was low and it looked as if it was going into his house. It was only just over the tops of the willow trees when it swerved to the right, went behind Mill House and across towards the park. Ted said that he saw it become entangled with a pylon and "down it came."

The Heinkel came down near Maypole Road. One of the crew managed to parachute out, but the other four were killed on impact. One member of the crew was caught up in an elm tree, and Ted noted that he was "in a tidy state." He reported that when he got there, smoke 'black as soot' was spiralling skywards from the downed plane, and the road was full of people.

Ted noted that people from 'Hatfield' [Peverel] were on the scene in no time, but presumably there were also curious onlookers from Maldon and Heybridge, as well as those closer by in Langford. According to Ted there were no survivors, but a different story was told by Mr. Yuill who recalled that there were two, one of whom spat at him, so he was treated to a sharp kick in the nether regions for his pains and the words "Welcome to England." Another report of the crash came from Harry Yuill who had been in his mother's garden in Oak Road, Heybridge when the dog-fight occurred. He headed off as fast as he could towards the crash. "I suppose I got there within a quarter of an hour of it happening. It was a terrible mess. There were bits of bodies hanging up in trees, ammunition lying all over the road and wreckage was strewn everywhere." John Doubleday, who was born at the Old Rectory, recalled that his father Gordon often told him the story that wreckage from the crash landed in the Old Rectory garden. The picture (right) shows the aftermath of the crash in the garden of Langford Park Cottages, August 1940.

At 16.39 on 24th August 1940 a message was taken on form ARP/M4 from the Eastern Report Centre: 'Maypole Road blocked from Shoulder of Mutton to Langford Cross.' At 16.41 another message was sent 'Enemy plane down Maypole Road, Langford Cross. Time occurrence reported 15.58'

A reply from County Control, Chelmsford, asked: 'Please say why road is blocked stop Presume alternative routes available for services if necessary.' The response at 17.02 was 'Three or more unexploded bombs in potato field near plane on Langford Grove Road about six hundred yards from Langford Cross. Military have been informed.' Then again to County Control 'Referring yours 16.50, alternative routes are available. According to our information road presumed blocked by enemy plane.'

A further message at 17.12 stated: 'Reference to message 16.41 German plane in Gowers Garden, Langford Road, Langford Cross. Plane burned out; house slightly damaged; two Germans dead. Further report. Maypole Road blocked owing to unexploded bomb.' Eastern Report Centre reported again at 18.02. 'Re my message 16.36 Incident Officer reports [*May*]Pole Road, Langford Cross not blocked.'

A 'Situation Report Form' was filled out concerning the raid in Langford which was reported at 18.20 that evening. 'One burnt out enemy plane down Langford Grove Road about 600 yards from Langford Cross. Remains of two or more dead enemy airmen, one badly wounded baled out at Saltcote Hall and now in hospital. No road now blocked. Unknown quantity of bombs dealt with by Fire Brigade. Two houses slightly damaged, no unexploded bombs located. Military of opinion bombs exploded as plane fell. Ambulance stretcher party retain parity morale excellent. Total casualties 3-4, killed 2-3, admitted to hospital 1. One telephone wire down, overhead electric cable damaged.'

It was many years before the full facts about the crash emerged. Research undertaken in the 1980s by Stephen Nunn and Alen Wyatt, both members of the Maldon Archaeological Group, revealed that, on 24th August 1940 the Luftwaffe was engaged in a planned raid on the nearby fighter station of RAF North Weald. Heinkel bombers from unit III/KG54 took off from Lille-Nord, in France, and headed for the English coastline.

As they approached Essex the bombers were intercepted at 4 p.m. by Hurricanes from 151 Squadron and a desperate battle ensued. One particular Heinkel - HE111H-2, serial A1+BT - was picked off by RAF Pilot-Officer K. H. Blair. Following machine gun bursts from Blair's Hurricane, the Heinkel began to lose height. It was clearly in trouble and one of the five-man crew, a gunner - Gefreiter Hans Zaunigk - bailed out at a low altitude and drifted down on his parachute into a stubble field off Scraley Road, Heybridge, where he was promptly taken into custody.

Meanwhile the stricken aircraft continued on its final fateful journey and struck a tree near Howell's Farm, Maypole Road. Its full payload exploded on impact killing the remaining crew on board – Oberleutnant G. Hunn (pilot), Feldwebel W. Jahger (observer), Feldwebel G. Ultsch (radio operator) and another gunner, Oberfeldwebel J. Schmid.

The crash site (left) was a scene of absolute carnage with fragments of human remains and aircraft wreckage all around. The road was closed off from the Shoulder of Mutton public house to Langford Cross whilst the official services attempted to keep local souvenir hunters away from the main site – a potato field next to 'Ravens Cottages' – something they appear to have singularly failed to do.

Subsequent research by Stephen Nunn revealed that, four years later, on Friday 25th February 1944, a very different type of aircraft came to grief just a stone's throw away from the location of the Heinkel incident. An American P38-J Lightning of the 55th Fighter Group based at RAF Nuthampstead, Hertfordshire, piloted by Flying Officer 'Buzz' Buskirk, was flying back from supporting US bombers on a raid on Germany. At 3.49 p.m., the P38 force-landed near the park gates at Langford Grove and burned out. However, Flying Officer Buskirk was safe, and took charge of his plane.

Today, some seventy years later, there is little physical evidence on the ground of either of these two wartime aircraft crashes. However, at the time of writing (2013) both the

German, Hans Zaunigk, and the American, 'Buzz' Buskirk, had survived to tell their respective tales of the time that they unceremoniously visited the village.

But there were other, unwelcome 'visitors' from the sky as noted from reports now held at the Essex Record Office in Chelmsford. On the evening of 4th December 1940 a minor bombing report was received at the Regional Control Centre in Maldon. At 20.30 a high explosive (HE) bomb was dropped just north of Langford Grove, some fifty yards north of the Maypole (later the Shoulder of Mutton) Inn. Three minutes later two bombs fell on Heybridge. No damage or casualties were reported in either case except for broken windows and plaster dropping from ceilings due to the blast. A later message phoned through at 21.44 noted that eighteen HE bombs had been dropped in a line from Broad Street Green Road, Great Totham, to Langford Park, three of which had not exploded, and telephone wires were down at Langford.

As in The Great War (later re-titled 'The First World War') there were practical things that villagers could do to aid the war effort during the Second World War. There were paper and aluminium collections in the village - £5.3s.9d was realised from the collection of paper in the parish in January 1941, arranged by Mr. Pye [Langford Lee] - and wattle hurdles were made in the parish. The money raised was given to provide wool comforts for the troops. Church services also continued, despite air raid warnings, but Major Claude Tritton, as Churchwarden and Treasurer, noted in the minutes of the Vestry Meeting of 15th January that the balance sheet of the church showed a deficit of £8.1s.1d. which was due to the high cost of insuring the church against war damage.

After a fête at Langford Hall, Mrs. Tritton [Langford Hall] was able to send a cheque for £70 to Mr. Maillard, the man in charge of war workers at Milton Abbey. The abbey had been bought by the Ecclesiastical Commissioners in the late 1930s and for some time it was a healing centre and a place of respite during the Second World War. Mr. Maillard replied:

> I can only hope that all who have co-operated with you will feel some of the happiness which the Abbey provides for the London War Workers who come here as our guests. At supper tonight I shall tell them they are here as guests of Langford and your friends.

Seemingly a little late in the day, the villagers were called to a meeting on 8th September 1941 to discuss the formation of a Parish Invasion Committee. Major Tritton [Langford Hall], Chairman of the Parish Meeting, presided and explained that the formation of the committee was a 'precautionary measure' and emphasising the 'non-alarmist character' of the idea. By this time (the war had been fought for two years) it was unlikely that too many villagers would have interpreted the proposal in a non-alarmist way.

Major Tritton was elected Chairman and his Committee comprised Mr. W. Chalk (Organiser), Mrs. Ffinch [Langford Meads] (British Red Cross Representative), Mrs. Pelly & Mrs. Goulding [Mill House] (First Aid), Lieut. Goulding (Home Guard Commander, who seems to have been recently promoted to the post), Mr. Pye [Langford Lee] (Air Raid Warden) and Mr. B. Smith [Hall Cottages] (Special Constable).

The summary of responsibilities was followed by a lecture on 'Invasion Problems' given by an officer of the Somerset Light Infantry. The main lessons learned were 'readiness to shelter wounded, to advise refugees, to disbelieve all rumours, to take instructions only from known Police, Home Guard or Wardens, to give mutual help, to keep cool and stay put. During this period the Home Guard met at the school every week for lectures and drill and on the fourth Tuesday in the month at 7 p.m. there was a whist drive and every Home Guard was 'free to ask a friend.'

In November 1941, owing to the blackout, the 8 a.m. services of Holy Communion had to be moved to 8.45 a.m. until the days lengthened. There was a Church Parade on Sunday 21st December when officers and men attended the 11 a.m. service. The Rector noted "It was good to hear the men join in so heartily in the singing." The lessons were read by Major Tritton and Major Gwynne and the Sermon was preached by Revd. G.F. Hodges, Chaplain to the Forces.

On Armistice Day – 9th November 1941 – Intercessions were given for all those on active service and the names were read out of those both there and on the Roll of Honour. The Home Guard was in attendance with their Commander, Lieut. Goulding and his officers. A few minutes before the Service, the Home Guard proceeded to the War memorial where a wreath was placed by Corporal Kerridge and Corporal Finn on which were the words "We do not forget – Langford Home Guards." Another wreath was placed in memory of Captain Allan Tritton, Coldstream Guards, who had died in December 1914.

On New Year's Day 1942 the Langford detachment of the Home Guard entertained their own and other children of the village to tea and games. More than fifty children attended. Each child received a present and sweets on leaving. In the evening a social was held which was enjoyed by about eighty people. 'Progressive' games, (where players change partners for each new game) for which prizes were awarded were played and a humorous sketch presented by Volunteer Albert Carr, assisted by other Home Guard members was performed and musical games and refreshments enjoyed. The parish magazine commented that 'all went to make the evening a complete success. Well done Langford H.G.!'

Under the War Damage Act, and at the suggestion of the Archdeacon, insurance of certain contents of St. Giles' was arranged in the sum of £900. This comprised of the organ (including blowing apparatus and case) - £500; Bells (including ropes) - £100; Goods ('other than above') - £300. The fabric of the church, all fixtures, and the windows, were covered by the Government during the war and the premium was £13.10s. There was a deficit of £8.1s.1d due to this increased insurance against possible air raid damage, amounting to £19.2s.6d: a ladder in case of fire - £3 and microfilming the church register – 10/-.

Luxuries were particularly difficult to obtain during the war and these included Easter Eggs for the children in April 1941. However, in the afternoon of Easter Day 1942, the children brought their gifts for the 'Children's Saving Fund.' Easter cards were given to them and on this occasion three prizes for written descriptions of the stamps handed out to them for the seasons of the Church's year. The children's procession round the church was 'somewhat confused, but hopeful!' Though Easter eggs were unobtainable, a similar substitute was found for the children as they left the church. Exactly what this 'similar substitute' might have been was, unfortunately, not recorded.

Langford Waste Paper collections continued well and monies raised bought wool for the Central Hospital Supply Service. Efforts by the villagers in aid of the Merchant Navy Comforts Service were recognised in a letter received in the late summer of 1942 which was recorded in full in the September issue of the parish magazine. It read:

> To the Rector and Churchwardens of Langford, very many thanks. The gift of your congregation of £2.0.4 is officially and gratefully acknowledged. With so many demands upon your resources and the difficulty of maintaining church finances in war time we deeply value your gesture to the Merchant Services. Your donation is being passed to the King George's Fund for Sailors.

A garden party arranged by the Langford Home Guard was held in the Waterworks grounds on Saturday 22nd August

1942 by kind permission of the Managing Director. Races, competitions, music and bumper refreshments kept everyone entertained and happy from 3.30-7.30 p.m. A surprise feature was a large mystery box, filled with gifts for the children, given by kind friends. Prizes for the races and competitions were presented by Mrs. Heywood. A vote of thanks was given by Lieut. Goulding to all who helped to make the proceedings a success and the Rector, Revd. Creed, thanked the members of the Home Guard for their 'splendid effort.'

A children's party, held at the school on Thursday 3rd December 1942, was organised by the Langford Section of the Home Guard. The tea was given by friends in the parish and the Home Guard. There was an illuminated Christmas tree bearing many presents from which each child received something. Later in the evening a social was held for the adults.

On Tuesday 26th January 1943 a Ministry of Information film was shown in the school, depicting a variety of wartime activities such as munition workers, aircraft and food production etc. This was doubtless a propaganda film which would have encouraged the villagers.

The closing whist drive and social took place at the school on Thursday 25th March 1943. On this occasion it was organised by the ladies of the parish and 'the unanimous opinion of all present was that it was well done.' Thanks were passed to the Home Guard and especially to Mrs. Goulding, Mrs. Eastwood and Mrs. Jennings [of Hatfield Road]. Prizes were given by Mrs. Wells, and Mr. Basil Mugleston acted as Master of Ceremonies.

May 1943 brought good news for the village. The *Essex Newsman* of 1st May 1943 reported:

Mrs. D.M. Green, of Council Houses, Langford, has received a letter from her second son, Sergt. Clifford Harry Green, Royal Artillery, who was posted 'missing, believed killed' in North Africa just over a month ago. He is a Prisoner of War in Italian hands. Before joining the army in 1939, Sergt. Green, who is 24, was employed in the Hatfield Peverel Offices of Messrs. Strutt and Parker (Farms) Ltd.

This piece of good news spurred on further fund-raising activities in the village at this time, including a 'goodly collection of waste paper,' which enabled the Comforts Fund to buy wool. This was described in the parish magazine as 'an excellent result.' A 'Wings for Victory' Whist Drive was held in the school room on Wednesday 5th May 1943 to raise funds to cover the expenses of the main campaign. This raised the sum of £5.7s.6d. In June 1943, £273.7s.0d was collected in War Savings Certificates from the villagers. By the end of October 1943 Langford had raised £19.5s.9d from waste paper and £16.2s.1d from sundry collections, fetes etc. – an amazing amount for such a small village.

More home-focussed was the children's party held on Wednesday 29th December 1943 in the school which was organised by the Home Guard. But still there was the ever-present thought of others with 'Some of the good things left over [being] sent to St. Peter's Hospital, Maldon.' At the Langford Tennis Club AGM on 26th April 1944 it was decided that, in recognition of their service to the village, to extend free admission to the club to all serving in His Majesty's Forces 'who might be in Langford.' A National Day of Prayer was held on 3rd September 1944 attended by the Home Guard, the parish magazine reporting that 'Mr. Philip Chalk happened to be in Langford on this Sunday and well supported the choir.'

Intercession services continued to be held in St. Giles' on Friday afternoons during the war at 3 p.m. when the Litany was said and the names of those on Active Service in connection with Langford were mentioned. A statement made by Mr. Robert Douat, at a meeting of Members of Parliament, and reproduced in the parish magazine in March 1943 reinforced the quality of strength that bound British people together. He said:

> When the storm came to France she collapsed. When it came on us we stood firm. Who shall say how much we owe to our Sunday? The English Sunday is a gift handed down to us that we want to hand down to our children.

But there was still a war on with many months to go.

On Thursday 11th February 1943 a well-attended meeting was held in the school at 7 p.m. 'to consider how people should act in case of invasion.' This may have seemed like *déjà-vu* for some as a similar meeting had been called in September 1941 but clearly it was felt that the villagers needed reminding! As before the meeting was presided over by Major Tritton 'who gave an outline of the various duties that would devolve on each individual.' Commander Goulding of the Home Guard (another promotion?) also spoke not only about the responsibilities of the Home Guard in particular but also of the obligations that would fall upon everybody. This meeting seemed to focus more on morale than organisation and 'What to do if...' The parish magazine, under the sub-title 'Morale – How to play your part' published the advice received:

- 'Put into your task, whatever it may be all the courage and purpose of which you are capable. Keep your hearts proud and your resolve unshaken. Let us go forward to that task as one man, and with God's help we shall not fail.' – the King's message, Empire Day, 1940.

- The Army Council affirm their profound conviction of the value of Religious Inspiration as a source of moral strength in the present conflict.

- Everybody has his part to play in the moral re-armament of the world.

- To obey God is the highest form of national service for everybody everywhere.

Another meeting was held at the school on Wednesday 2nd March 1942 presided over by Major Tritton, to consider how and why each person should act in case of invasion. Major Tritton, having outlined a scheme, questions were invited for a clear understanding in case of emergency.

On the day of the official 'Stand Down' of the Home Guard on 1st November 1944, Colonel Bright addressed his 'Order of the Day.'

> We can claim with pride that our very existence has been among the most potent factors in deterring the enemy, even at his greatest strength, from attempting the invasion of England, and that our presence during these last summer months was sufficient to prevent even a single German from obstructing our own forces in their invasion of the Continent.

The final parade of the Battalion (including representatives from Langford) took place at Maldon on Sunday 12th November 1944.

When the Home Guard was disbanded in 1944, with more than one and a half million men having served in it countrywide, their enthusiasm and dedication had been legendary. Before taking the final salute of the Essex Home Guard at Chelmsford on Sunday 19th November, 1944, the Lord Lieutenant of the County, Colonel Sir Francis Whitmore, said:

> You have, by your sense of duty, by your loyalty and patriotism, contributed pages of tradition to the historical records of our nation…you took a prominent part in the defence of our country at the most critical

period of the war... In the name of our County of Essex, I thank you.

During the war Italian prisoners of war lived in a barn at Hall Farm, Langford – the German prisoners were living in Goldhanger Road, Heybridge – and they used to undertake work in the field opposite the Old Post Office. Village children used to lend the Italian prisoners books so that they could learn English properly (although some people felt that this was not quite the right thing to do). Many wounded British soldiers were billeted in Langford Grove.

Mrs. Janet Search (née Clanachan), who then lived at The Old Post Office, recounted travelling back with her mother, Ivy (née Harvey) on Moores' bus from a dancing class one summer evening during the war. The bus reached Langford Old Rectory (where the American soldiers were based), and as it turned the corner, a large American lorry smashed into the bus. Janet recounted that, as she and her mother were slightly hurt, they were taken into the American quarters where first aid was given (as well as nylon stockings for Janet's mother, and sweets and 'gum' for her). They were then taken home by jeep. Janet recalled that, at the time, her father was working away, and her mother was embarrassed when the next day two American soldiers were sent to see how they were. Janet's mother was convinced they would be the talk of the village!

Towards the end of the war the German rockets began to fall. Ted Chalk recalled that a German V1 Flying Bomb (a 'doodle-bug') landed in the lime ditch near the waterworks reservoir. He remembered that he was working at Claydons at Ulting at the time and it was raining. He said that people from the 'black huts' were pea-picking when the bomb fell and that "it put the wind up them." The force of the explosion blew the glass out of Ted's front door onto the lawn, and curtains were blown off their runners onto the floor. An ex-Heybridge resident remembered the same event at the

385

Pumping Station when a 'doodlebug' crashed and exploded on the banks of the raw water reservoir about 100 - 150 yards west of the building. At the time of the explosion, he was working at Hodge's Farm, which was 200 yards beyond the entrance road leading to the old Waterworks office building and its laboratories (now Oval Park).

Ted Chalk also recalled another 'doodle-bug' exploding just off Wickham Hall Lane: "I saw that go by my bedroom window that night. It was red hot. Captain Humphrys' house [Wharncliffe, in Langford Road] was damaged and his staircase collapsed at the bottom." In an interview with Captain Humphrys' daughter Patricia in 2006, she said that it wasn't a 'doodle-bug' that damaged the house, but a land mine that the Germans had dropped on their way back to Germany.

On Sunday afternoon, 26th November 1944, a short memorial service was held in Church after Evensong for John Woolmore, the elder son of Mr. & Mrs. Woolmore of Luards. John had enlisted into the Royal Artillery and the authorities initially stated that he was missing. Then after some few weeks his parents were notified that John had been killed in Normandy. The service consisted of special prayers and address and the concluding voluntary 'O Rest in the Lord' was played by the organist. The parish magazine reported that Mrs. Woolmore had been 'in charge of the little Post Office for several years and much respected', adding on behalf of the village, 'The family have our sincere sympathy.'

John Woolmore, who had lived in Railway Cottages, was one of four Langford residents who lost their lives in the Second World War.

The other three were Albert Fairs (whose father worked the land, probably for the Chalk family), William Groden (Royal Navy) who had lived with his parents in Ulting Lane and Robin Moore (Royal Air Force) who had come to live at the Children's Home at Langford Cross - the home run by Miss

386

Kathleen Hunt, the Choir Mistress. All four, along with all other Langfordians who served their country between 1939 and 1945, are commemorated in the 'Book of Remembrance' in St. Giles' Church.

The committee of the 'Welcome Home' fund organised a sale of work in the school on Saturday 2nd December 1944, when £100 was raised. A general meeting was held in the schoolroom on Friday 15th December. Major Tritton, President, was in the chair. The Secretary, Mrs. Goulding, read a report on the work accomplished by 'a very able committee.' It was agreed by all present to give each of 'the returning boys and girls gifts of money in Savings Certificates from the fund collected.'

When the general meeting was held a few days later, on 15th December 1944, those present agreed that the sum of £12 in savings certificates should be given to each Langford man and woman serving with His Majesty's Forces at the end of the war. It was further agreed that, when the necessary sum had been raised, a further meeting would be called 'to discuss whether any additional money shall be used to provide a memorial to the fallen.'

With the cessation of the war on 7th May 1945 a 'live committee' was set up to disperse the 'Welcome Home' funds to all Langford people who were serving with H.M. Forces. The condition was that only people who had lived in the parish 'for at least six months before the outbreak of war' qualified; thus discounting the troops then still currently billeted at Langford Grove. St. Giles' Church remained open all that day so that anybody might come and offer up their prayers and thanksgiving.

VE Day

VE (Victory in Europe) Day was observed on Tuesday 8th May 1945 when flags were flown from the church and school and the church bells were rung. The parish magazine stated:

We thank those who helped in these matters. It was good to hear our church bells 'ringing' out. We were glad to have the assistance of Mr. [Allen Stanley] Howlett [of Hall Cottages] who used to be the Church clerk and bell ringer for Langford.

The service in the evening was well attended when special prayers were offered and the hymns heartily joined in by the choir and congregation. A short address was given, the service commencing with the National Anthem. The lesson was read by Major C. Tritton. The special thanksgiving service was kept on the Sunday following.

The collections on this day were for the fund for the re-building of churches damaged by enemy action.

A VE party for the children of Langford was arranged for Wednesday 20th June. The parish magazine reported that:

The day was fine and sunny. Mr. Wakelin [of Langford Hall] kindly lent a field, for games and sports. The children, about 30 in number, joined in various games, organised by the committee, from 3 p.m. to 4.30 p.m. when they all adjourned to the Church Room, where tea was served by many helpers. The ice cream at the end was a great attraction. Tea was followed by a sing song, while waiting for Mr. Saunders, of Wickham Bishops, who thrilled everyone present by his clever conjuring tricks. At 6.30 p.m. children and adults returned to the field and prepared to enjoy sports arranged by the Youth Club. There were many keen contests and much amusement.

During the interval ices and drinks were again served, after which the rest of the events were contested. Mothers and fathers enjoyed it all as onlookers. We wish more had been able to come, and join in the fun. Major Tritton presented the small cash prizes. Thanks were given to all who helped in gifts of money and kind to make the party a real success. Money left over was divided equally among the children of school age and under.

In the August 1945 issue of the parish magazine, Revd. Butson Creed was wholesome in his praise for the volunteer services:

Now that our 'Home Guard' and 'Air Raid Wardens' have been disbanded, we feel that some grateful recognition should be made of their numerous and arduous duties so willingly and conscientiously carried out during the recent war in Europe. Speaking of our own parish, every parishioner must have felt grateful and proud to know that in the 'Home Guard' under Lieut. Goulding, a constant watch was being kept, day and night, so that any emergency that might arise, they would be there, ever alert and ready to challenge and defend their country.

And it was through the 'Home Guard' that enabled many of our soldiers to enlist for the army abroad. Passing to our 'Air Raid Wardens' under the superintendence of the Chief Warden, Major C. Tritton, he alone knows what it entailed to visit the various air raid centres over a large area, visits that were taken many a time at night, and most of us would have some idea what that meant in a black-out, and with dim headlights.

His Majesty the King has publicly recognised and thanked both the 'Home Guard' and 'Air Raid Wardens' for their invaluable services, and may we of Langford, too, offer our grateful thanks to Home Guard, Air Raid Wardens and Fire Watchers. And we can hardly close without also thanking God for sparing our little Church and parish from enemy air raids. They were very near round about us as we all realised, but failed in their object.

In the *Chelmsford Chronicle* dated 12th January 1945, notice was given under the War Charities Act 1940 to apply to Essex County Council for Registration of The Langford Victory Fund, the objects of which were:

> To provide a Fund, and the monies to be used as a Welcome Home, including a gift of Savings Certificates to each man and woman of the Forces in the Ecclesiastical Parish of Langford, and the administrative centre of which is situate at Mill House, Langford.

> Any objections to the proposed registration should be sent in writing to the above-named Council within 14 days from the date of this notice. Dated January 5th 1945.

VJ Day

Victory in Japan (VJ Day) (Wednesday 15th August 1945) was observed with a special service in the church at 7 p.m. There was 'a fair congregation,' and those present joined in heartily with the singing as also in the service generally, which commenced with the National Anthem.

At the close of the service an address was given. In the evening the parish was 'lighted up by a bonfire prepared by the young people who were determined not to be left out and gave enjoyment to many as they danced round it.'

Peace at Last?

The war was over at last but it had taken its toll on the village; such a small, some might say insignificant village. The September 1945 issue of the parish magazine noted:

> Now that the war is at an end, and peace, we hope, is dawning on the whole world, we would like to record with gratitude the names of those connected with our

parish who have been on Active Service for King and Country, 1939-1945:

Lt.-Col. John Tritton	Royal Artillery
Pilot Officer Michael Pelly	Royal Air Force
Capt. Anthony Pelley	Royal Army Corps
Fl/Sergt. Raymond Goulding	Royal Air Force
Telegraphist David Doubleday	Royal Navy
Pte. David Macklin	Queen's Royal Regt.
Pte. Edward Bonner	Pioneer Corps
Pte. D. Wyre	Royal Army Medical Corps
L.A.C. Elijah Pratt	Royal Air Force
Maj. Thomas Bowyer-Bower	Army Education Corps
L.A.C. Peter Skinner	Royal Air Force
Sgt. Francis Dempsey	Irish Guards
L.A.C. Reginald De'ath	Royal Air Force
L.A.C.W. Nellie Jones	Women's Auxiliary Air Force
Sgt. Violet Chipperfield	Women's Auxiliary Air Force
Sgt. John Hodge	Royal Air Force
Cpl. Frederick Smith	Royal Air Force
Dvr. Albert Chaplin	Royal Army Service Corps
L.A.C. George Henry Pratt	Royal Air Force
Sgt. Clifford Green	Royal Artillery
Cpl. Ralph Green	Royal Air Force
L.Seaman Harold Jennings	Royal Navy
Petty Officer William Groden	Royal Navy (Died)
Petty Officer John Groden	Royal Navy
Warrant Off. Gerald Groden	Royal Air Force
L.A.C.W. Eileen Groden	Women's Auxiliary Air Force
L.A.C.W. Margaret Groden	Women's Auxiliary Air Force
C.S.M. Gilbert Parker	Royal Engineers
C.P.O. Harold Mansfield	Royal Navy
Dvr. Gilbert Wilson	Royal Army Service Corps
Bandsman Jack Crook	Border Regiment
Reginald Piper	Tank Corps
Dvr. Ernest Howlett	Royal Engineer
L.A.C. Edwin Harrington	Royal Air Force
Sgt. Robin Moore	Royal Air Force (Died)
Radio Operator John Woolmore	Army (Died)
Pte. Albert Faires	Duke of Wellington's Regt. (Died)

It was certainly not an insignificant contribution.

The Battle of Britain Sunday was observed on 16th September 1945. The National Anthem was sung at the opening of morning service at St. Giles' Church, and the congregation united in the general thanksgiving prayer. An address was given in the evening, when the well-known words of Winston Churchill were quoted, "Never has so much been owed by so many to so few."

The annual tea for the children of Langford was held on Tuesday 1st January 1946 in the Schoolroom under the leadership of Mrs. Doubleday (of Langford Old Rectory) with the help of Mrs. R. Harvey, Mrs. Bewers, Mrs. S. Russell, Mrs. Jennings, Mrs. T. Chalk, Mrs. Chaplin, Mrs. Everitt, Mrs. Goulding, Mrs. Eastwood, Mrs. Bardwell, Miss Ford, and Mr. Ford. After tea, games were organised by sisters-in-law Mrs. Gladys Mansfield and Mrs. Joyce Chaplin, who were later assisted by Mrs. Goulding (of Mill House.) Mrs. Ron Harvey organised a social which followed, when games and dancing were enjoyed by a large company. At 9 p.m. 'a pleasant interlude' occurred, when Major Tritton presented to Pilot Officer Michael Pelly, Capt. Anthony Pelly, Flight Sergt. Raymond Goulding, Petty Officer John Groden, W/O Gerald Groden, RAF and Driver Albert Chaplin RASC, each a gift of £12 in savings certificates from the Langford Victory Fund. Pilot Officer Michael Pelly expressed the thanks of the recipients.

In addition, in February 1946, the parish magazine confirmed that gifts of £12 each in the form of National Savings Certificates had been distributed to Pte. Edward Bonner, Telegraphist David Doubleday, RN, Leading Aircraft-Woman Eileen Groden, Cpl. E.A. Harrington, Wireman Harold Jennings, RN, Sgt. Piper, Leading Aircraft-Woman Margaret Thurtle, Lt.-Col, J.H. Tritton and Driver Gilbert Wilson RASC. There was a small balance in hand and it was hoped to obtain permission to spend this on a book giving the names of all from our village who served during the war in H.M. Forces. This book would be kept in church, where it is to this day.

This thought was reinforced by an article in the April 1946 edition of the parish magazine which stated:

> A feeling has been expressed by many in the village that, as after the last war, 1914-1918, some memorial should be raised in honour of our Langford boys who have given their lives for us and our country and Empire in this last war. Perhaps there could be no more fitting memorial than to associate their names with their brothers-in-arms and fellow-villagers on the existing memorial. It is proposed that the following work might be done:
>
> 1. The memorial cleaned and the present names re-conditioned
>
> 2. On the west side under the years 1939-1945 add the new names
>
> 3. Make an approach from the road by pushing the palings back so as to enclose the memorial on three sides
>
> 4. If the nearby graves will allow, make a gravel path round the memorial.
>
> 5. No doubt we should require a good sum to carry this work through, but it should appeal to all sections of our community, and both small and large subscriptions would be welcome.

Not surprisingly, this memorial proposal was acceptable to most villagers, as the June 1946 edition of the magazine carried the following report:

It is proposed to add to those names already on the Memorial Cross in the old Churchyard the names of those residents of Langford who did not return from the last war.

In addition, a suggestion has been approved by the Archdeacon of Southend whereby the Memorial will be enclosed by a low hedge, and made accessible not only from the Churchyard but also from the road. This will entail a gate in the existing fence and stone steps leading up to what will be a small garden of Remembrance.

While it is hoped that most of the work will be done by voluntary labour, there will be some expenses which will be met by local subscriptions. It is confidently hoped that the small garden will be kept in good order · by the care and attention of the Village.

Two months later the magazine recorded that:

Mr. J.B. Slythe, of Witham, is prepared to carry out the necessary work of restoring the old and cutting the new lettering on the existing War Memorial in the Churchyard. While an exact estimate cannot yet be given, even with voluntary help over the work necessary for the proposed entrance to and surrounding of the Memorial, the cost will certainly not be less than £10. The fund as it stands at present is £6 odd. The donations already given and promised are very much appreciated by the Rector and Churchwardens.

The names of the fallen were added and Langford, and the rest of the country, entered a period of comparative peace. Since 1945 there have been, and continue to be, wars and conflicts across the globe in which, from time to time, sons and daughters of Langford have taken part and faithfully served their Queen and Country. Although there have been no further fatalities of villagers recorded since the Second

World War there have been those who returned from theatres of war whose lives were permanently changed as a result of their experiences, and we honour them for their contribution to our peace and stability.

The war memorial was rededicated on Sunday 19th September 1993 when new bronze plates bearing the names of the fallen were presented to Langford by the Western Front Association.

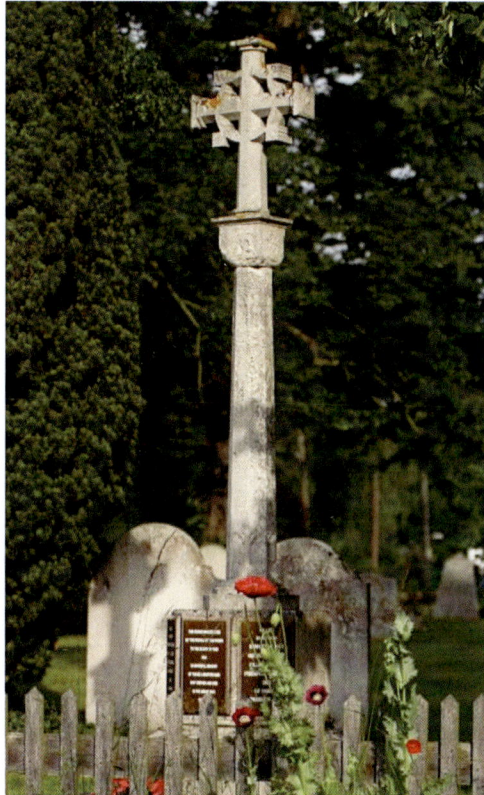

The War Memorial with the new plaques
put up by the Western Front Association

CHAPTER TEN
PLAY UP AND PLAY THE GAMES
SPORTS AND LEISURE

For a very small village, Langford once boasted an array of sporting activities, including cricket, football, hockey, fishing, tennis and even motor-cycle grass track racing. Records show that the most important and popular of these, and certainly the longest-running and (sometimes) the most successful, was the cricket team.

Langford Cricket Club

Cricket began as a game for rustics and schoolboys but only became established as an organised game in the eighteenth century when it was taken up by fashionable gentlemen, usually as a vehicle for gambling. As cricket became popularised, the 'fashionable gentlemen' of the village would form the Langford Cricket Club, and to begin with the game would be played on open fields rather than on properly drawn up cricket pitches.

The Langford team (unfortunately unnamed and undated)

It is impossible to say exactly when cricket became popular in Langford but it would certainly have been played in some primitive form long before the game was mentioned in the very first issue of *Wickham Bishops and Langford Parish Magazine* dated July 1894. Further reports of matches in this chapter will also come from that publication. The initial issue reported that:

> A cricket match was played on Saturday June 2nd at Langford which resulted in a victory for Langford; but it is only fair to add that the original time for drawing stumps was extended by consent of Wickham Bishops by half an hour so that the match might be played out otherwise the result would have been different – Wickham Bishops 1st innings 33, 2nd innings 20; Langford 1st innings 23, 2nd innings 32.

Clearly this was a very close, if not very high-scoring, match. Sadly no mention was made of exactly where this match was played, and it is known that the Cricket Club moved pitches several times during its existence.

Unfortunately for Langford, a match played in the village the following weekend against Great Totham resulted in a very severe defeat (Langford 35, Great Totham 106). Nearly three months later, in September 1894, Langford suffered two serious defeats at Woodham Mortimer and Wickham Bishops, the first deemed 'too severe to be recorded'! The parish magazine noted that the second might have proved more successful had the Langford team played as well in the first innings as they did in the second. The actual score is not recorded.

The first annual meeting of the Cricket Club recorded in the parish magazine was held in 1895. Lord Byron was re-elected President, so clearly had been in that role the previous year. Other committee posts included his brother, the Revd. and Hon. 'Chas' Byron and Fred Chalk, Captain and Sub-Captain respectively, Edward Baker, Treasurer, and G. Minett,

Secretary. The financial condition of the club was satisfactory and it was hoped the season might prove 'more victorious' to the Club than 1894. And so it proved.

The parish magazine faithfully reported on the regular cricket matches which subsequently took place and what follows are a few examples of the more interesting match reports and club-related issues which indicate the success (or otherwise) of the Langford team.

In 1896 a new cricket ground was provided for the team (possibly by Lord Byron), 'most pleasantly situated in Langford Park, by the West Lodge entrance surrounded on two sides by fine trees' which promised to become 'a very good ground.' The inaugural match was played on Whit Monday against Wickham Bishops. This resulted in a victory for the visitors by ten wickets! Incidentally, there is no building in the village known today as 'West Lodge' so it is assumed that this is a reference to the present 'Red Lodge' situated at the western end of Langford Park.

The match described was not a particularly good start for the home side on their new cricket ground but this collapse was soon forgotten as Langford triumphed over a Great Totham XI in an away match, played at Champion Lodge, Great Totham, in July, Langford scoring 38 runs and then bowling out Gt. Totham for only 19.

Unfortunately the much-lauded site in Langford Park that promised to become 'a very good ground' did not last long, for in the June 1897 the parish magazine it was announced that the new cricket ground situated behind Mr. A. Barker's shop, [*a space behind Church Cottages (which was where the shop was originally sited)*] had been most kindly lent by Mr. A. Lomas of Langford Hall. The reason for the move from the Park to this site is, as yet, unknown. However, things subsequently improved for the team at their new ground and by 1899 it was recorded that 'great progress' had been made compared to the very tentative beginnings back in July 1894.

398

In June 1899 one of the more bizarre Langford games took place. In a match against Boreham on Saturday 23rd May, the Boreham score at the end of the first innings was 52, while Langford's was a mere 27. The first innings was over by 4.30 p.m. when the curious discovery was made that the Boreham eleven (with the exception of three men) had 'silently vanished.' Consequently the game came to an abrupt and premature conclusion. Where the eight Boreham players had disappeared to is not revealed. Perhaps the team thought it was a 'one innings match,' assumed victory and went home. At a subsequent meeting of the Cricket Club Committee it was unanimously agreed that Langford scratch their return match against Boreham, and decline to play that team on any future occasion.

In a match against the Maldon 2nd XI, which Langford won emphatically, it was reported that 'the new ground played splendidly.' Sadly there is no indication thus far of where the 'new ground' was, except that it was on 'Mr. Wakelin's ground' most probably at Langford Hall, as at this time he had taken over from Alfred Lomas, and was the farmer there. Further matches were played against Danbury, Woodham Mortimer and Broad Street Green in August 1899 – in the latter game both Lord Byron and his brother Revd. Byron played. There cannot be many rural cricket sides who could boast a present and a future Lord amongst their team!

The November 1899's parish magazine confirmed that the cricket season which had ended in October was 'the most successful yet known,' and 'in great measure due to Mr. Wakelin's kindness' in letting the team use his land for the cricket ground.

In August 1901 four 'rather exciting' matches were played against Danbury. One played at Danbury on 10th August, after a most exciting game, ended in a tie. Scores Danbury 63, Langford 63. The 'man of the match' for Langford was the sub-Captain (also the Schoolteacher), William Chalk, who scored 36 runs. His nearest rival was the 13-year-old Richard Wakelin who scored six. The match played against Witham II at Langford on 17th August was won by the home side by 16 runs (Witham II 79, Langford 95). The top scorer in that match was again William Chalk with 37 runs, but close behind him was Henry Wynyard the younger (half) brother of William Wynyard of Langford Parsonage, with 17 runs.

In the away match against Woodham Mortimer on 24th August, an exciting finish resulted in a win for Langford by only two runs (Woodham Mortimer 69 to Langford's 71). The highest scorer on this occasion was Frederick Wakelin with 15 runs, William Chalk being out for a 'duck'!

However, in the last match of the 1901 season which was played at Heybridge on Saturday 7th September, Langford

imported some extra muscle in the shape of Captain Edward Wynyard (left) (elder brother of William), who was on leave from his teaching post at Sandhurst Military Academy.

Langford won the match by 69 runs to Heybridge's 61, with Edward scoring 31 and Henry Wynyard scoring 12. Their brother William, William Chalk and the Rector (Revd. Byron), were all out for a duck. (It is only fair to mention that Edward Wynyard had captained Hampshire at cricket, and also played for England, and had it not been for his Army career he would doubtless have gone on to a professional career in the game. He was also an excellent footballer and ice skater!)

On Saturday 23rd August 1902 Langford played at Woodham Mortimer a match which Woodham Mortimer won by 22 runs. Langford won the toss and went in first. (Langford 53, Woodham Mortimer 75). E. Woodcraft was the highest scorer with 20 runs, and H. Thorpe with 11. The parish magazine noted that sadly the inclusion of Revd. Gardner of Goldhanger (pictured above) in the side did not, this time, increase the score by much. Revd. Byron was last man in and ended the game not out for no runs. The next match between Langford and Hatfield Peverel on 9th August had to be abandoned on account of the Coronation Festivities at Hatfield Peverel.

Langford played Danbury on the Langford ground, on Saturday 6th September which resulted in a win for the visitors. The scores were Langford 46, Danbury 133, despite Langford again having Captain Edward Wynyard on their side. He could only manage 17 runs on this occasion. However, mention was made in the magazine that 'Messrs A. & R. Hoare were playing for Danbury' which seems to imply that Danbury had a decided advantage, although research to date has found nothing further about these two 'advantageous' players.

As the cricket season came to a close it became clear that all was not well with the cricket ground; concerns being expressed about 'attacks' on the Langford pitch. Although the 'attacks' were never defined in the records examined thus far, it might be assumed that these were acts of vandalism on the 'sacred turf.' A Cricket Club Committee meeting was held on 21st November 1903 to consider what was to be done to guard and protect the pitch as the latest plan had 'completely failed.' Tantalisingly we are not told what the 'latest plan' was and research to date has failed to show if the club was able to eventually combat and prevent further 'attacks.' Certainly there is no record of any matches having to be cancelled or abandoned due to the condition of the pitch.

On Saturday 25th June 1904 Langford played a home match against Danbury resulting in a win for the visitors who won the toss and put Langford in first (Langford 48, Danbury 62). Danbury had seven wickets down after scoring a mere 24 runs but Langford's subsequent defeat was 'due to the badness of the Langford fielding during the next two wickets,' the parish magazine noting, somewhat mysteriously 'one of the bats being missed nine times' although it did not elaborate on this.. Matches for the rest of the year were severely hampered by rain, and many were abandoned.

Only one match was played in July 1906, on Saturday 21st July, at Woodham Mortimer which resulted in a disastrous defeat for Langford by an innings and 30 runs. There were no leagues as such at this time. Although Langford had a cricket club it was not formally organised by the application of league rules and/or adherence to fixtures, the number of matches played per year or per month being totally dependent on invitations to neighbouring villages to play. So it is perhaps not surprising that only a few matches were played during any season.

The year 1910 was a disastrous season, and this continued into 1911. In the October 1911 issue of the parish magazine it was reported that the cricket news for August had been unfortunately omitted from the September issue owing to 'unforeseen circumstances.' The report continued, 'of the match against Wickham Bishops we need not further speak owing to that disaster having already been fully published by our neighbour.' In addition one match played on 9th September against Hatfield Peverel saw the Langford team skittled out for eleven runs whilst trying to reach the home side score of a mere 47 runs. The excuse was that Langford went in as the sun was setting, 'the light being so bad that play was impossible.'

The team's final match before the outbreak of the Great War was away to Hatfield Peverel which the home side won by 49 runs to 34. Significantly, this was to be the last game played for five years as, with the onset of the Great War the young men of the village went off to fight for King and country.

With the departure of Revd. Byron for Thrumpton in 1914, a new Rector, the Revd. Charles Gough Littlehales, took over. Revd. Littlehales was a great boost to the cricket team as he was not only a clergyman, but had been a first class wicketkeeper for Essex from 1896 to 1904. The picture on the left shows him (back row in the striped blazer) as part of the 1902 Essex team.

After the cessation of hostilities a meeting of the club was held on 8th April 1919 to consider ways and means of setting it up again but this was adjourned until 29th April. Permission to use the ground had been obtained, and the response to appeals for personal interest and support was considered 'encouraging.' Although we are not told where this new ground now was, villagers recall that there was a cricket pitch *and* tennis courts behind the shop in the field between the back of the shop and the Cut.

Home and away matches were arranged with Danbury, Goldhanger, Hatfield, The Warren and Little Baddow, but the season started badly for Langford which sustained three defeats. However, the parish magazine reported optimistically: 'in forthcoming matches we hope we may be able to record a series of victories, as the team is steadily improving and its members are very keen.' Indeed this keenness led to mixed fortune during ensuing seasons one of the more unusual matches being played on 25th May against H.M.S. Osea, who beat Langford by 70 runs to 30.

H.M.S. Osea had been the Coastal Motor Boat centre on Osea Island from 1918 until it was finally closed down on 19th April 1921. As the 'crew' were being stood down they had little to do at the end of their duty there, and so played Langford at cricket. The connection here had been through Revd. Gardner of Goldhanger, who had acted for a time as honorary chaplain to the base.

The parish magazine reporting on August 1923 noted that it was 'a dreadful month for Langford cricketers.' Three matches had been played against the British Legion, Hatfield Peverel and Sadds' Athletic all resulting in resounding defeats, the parish magazine recording, that 'the batting on all three occasions has been decidedly weak, but the bowling and fielding has been quite good' adding 'Our batsmen lack 'defence' and only painstaking practice can alter this and however we are still hopeful and by no means discouraged.'

Hardly a morale-boosting report for a clearly flagging team. The year continued very badly indeed with the final year's record showing that Langford had played 15, won 2, and lost 13.

Another Langford cricket team again unnamed and undated!

In July 1924 Langford recorded one of its heaviest ever defeats, at the hands of Sadds' when the opponents made over 200 for nine wickets. Langford was bowled out for 13 and 21.

After nearly 30 years in existence, an announcement was made in the parish magazine of March 1925 that 'the long-felt need of a small Pavilion will, we hope, be soon supplied.' This was to be made possible by the splendid offer of two of the vice-Presidents (Capt. M. Ffinch and Col. W.G. Lyddon) who had consented to bear a large share of the cost of material, on condition that the members take an active part in the construction of the building.

Despite the promise of this new and probably much needed and prestigious acquisition, the new season opened rather disastrously for the Langford team, as they experienced three defeats, chiefly owing to weak batting, (although in the match against Sadds the fielding also left much to be desired). In mitigation it was pointed out that 'owing to various causes, bad weather, work on the Pavilion, and overtime, there have been few opportunities for practice.'

The new pavilion was nearly finished, but progress had been necessarily slow, as it has only been possible to work on it during the last two hours of daylight, but it was reported that 'it will certainly prove a great boon to the players, and provide a much needed shelter in bad weather.'

Langford's cricketing performances continued to experience highs and lows, the results of the matches for 1926 showing that Langford had a better season than the previous year, but as in former years, their bowling was always better than their batting. It was felt that their failures in batting were due chiefly to 'lack of nerve,' for if the earlier batsmen failed, there were no determined batsmen following to atone for their failures.

The Annual General Meeting of the Cricket Club was held in the Schoolroom on 23rd November 1927 but was very poorly attended. Capt. Ffinch, who took the Chair, was supported by Col. W.G. Lyddon, Revd. C.G. Littlehales and two members. The Secretary reported that so little interest had been taken in the Club that it had been very difficult to carry on. In view of this fact and the small numbers present, it was decided to postpone the election of President, Vice-Presidents and Officers, and the meeting was adjourned to a later date.

The adjourned AGM of the Langford Cricket Club was held on Thursday 10th April, 1928, but was also very poorly attended. As so little interest was shown by 'old members,' and so many had left the district, it was decided to suspend the Club for the season. The Secretary was instructed to cancel the fixture list. The meeting elected Revd. Littlehales to be Hon. Sec and Treasurer, and to take charge of the Club property, 'until a fresh decision should be arrived at.'

The Club remained 'dormant' until May 1934 when a meeting was held at the Church Room to consider the formation of a new cricket club in the parish. After discussion it was agreed to take this forward. A committee was formed: the Rector was nominated President, Norman Chalk, Chairman and Harold Finn, Hon. Secretary.

By August the plans for a new team were making quite good progress, but funds were still needed to carry on; also someone who would help to coach the younger players. But in October 1934 it was announced that the Cricket Club was revived after a lapse of several years. The Hon. Sec. Harold Finn had worked very hard in connection with this and considering it was the first season of its new existence it had been quite successful.

By 1936 the Cricket Club balance sheet showed funds in hand. Matches had been organised with other teams and some good play had been witnessed at home and away. Langford had improved greatly, due mainly to the efforts of the Hon. Sec. Mr. Gilbert Parker, and the new Captain, Mr. Bonner. The club did well in 1937 with a successful season. Many of the matches had close and exciting finishes, and the standard of play had improved.

The Annual General Meeting of the cricket club was held in the School on Thursday, 17th March 1938. The Rector was again asked to be President. With the excellent balance in hand it was hoped that a new pavilion might be procured (although research hasn't yet revealed what happened to the old one), also a lawn mower, and the cricket pitch re-laid.

At a meeting held in the Schools on Wednesday evening, 20th April 1939 the balance sheet showed funds in hand of a healthy £23.7.11. A full fixture list was made for the coming season and, as always, there was a plea for fresh members. But once again, war intervened, and with the young men of the village being called up for action, the cricket club once again was suspended.

Little is known about the club between the outbreak of the Second World War and the 1950s, but it had a new lease of life in May 1955 when it was resurrected with the assistance of Blackwater Timbers Social Club. The Secretary of that club was involved at the outset and arranged for the new Club to have the use of the existing pavilion and ground situated at Langford Waterworks. Langford then became a members' Club, with individuals having responsibility for all aspects of its running both from the administrative and cricket point of view.

From the mid-1950s the club flourished in its fashion, taking on new and established adversaries. On 12th May 1961 in a match against Gt. Totham, Langford's star player, Gordon Goodwin, was hit by a bouncer. It looked very bad, and he had to have four stitches. Luckily, despite this accident, Langford won (57: 49).

In 1981 the club was admitted to the T Rippon Mid-Essex League and enjoyed considerable success over a number of years including winning Division 3 in 1983 and achieving the runners-up spot in Division 2 in 1990. The 1993 season saw the club's fortunes fall away somewhat, in line with the type of fluctuation frequently experienced by smaller clubs. However, Langford remained, as always, a friendly club and was open to new members with fresh ideas. The Club's colours were yellow and green and in 1993 the Captain was Rob Naybour and the Secretary was Andrew Craig – sadly neither of them actually Langford folk.

Towards the end of the 1990s the Langford Cricket Club was wound up for good.

The cricket ground is now used by the Museum of Power as a show ground.

Golf

On Tuesday 24th November 1891, a company of twenty local dignitaries sat at a large table in the King's Head Commercial

Hotel in Maldon High Street. Chairing this important meeting was 70-year old clergyman, the Revd. Edward Russell Horwood, MA, for over half a century the vicar of nearby All Saints Church. By his side was the unmistakable figure of Sir Claude Champion de Crespigny, JP, of Champion Lodge, Great Totham, described as "one of the pluckiest and hardest men of his time." Also present were Alfred Lomas, farmer of Langford Hall, Christopher William Parker, MA, JP, DL, of Faulkbourne Hall, Witham, and at least three local businessmen - Mr. Arthur Barritt, hay and straw merchant, Thomas Laurance Eve, corn merchant, and Thomas Elsey Bland, JP, wine and spirit merchant and manager of the Maldon Crystal Salt Company.

Although they were from very different walks of life, these influential men had a common interest, all of them had a passion for an up and coming pastime - the captivating game of Golf. As an organised pursuit, the sport was in its infancy and, although an association had been formed in the country as early as 1766, (the Royal Blackheath), the sun would set on Victorian Britain before Golf really teed off.

The golf links were situated so that the club house was just outside the Langford boundary, thereby enabling them to have a bar!

Football

Little is known about Langford's football team except that it was thriving in the early 1900s but was decimated by the Great War.

At a meeting held in the church room on Monday 8th September 1922 when about 18 prospective members were present, it was decided to form another football Club. The parish magazine noted that Officers were elected: Mr. C. Wager (Captain), Mr. G. Martin (Vice-Captain), Mr. G. Coe (Hon. Sec). Harold Harvey (Hon. Treasurer), Messrs. Arthur Everett, G. Challis and F. Gooch, Members of Committee. It was decided to solicit the interest and support of the leading residents in the parish. The subscription was fixed at 3s.6d, to be paid before the end of September. The Chairman was asked to write for permission to use the ground (although sadly it was not stated where this ground was), and it was decided to arrange friendly matches. In 1922 the team played two matches against Great Totham. The result of the first match (at Langford) was the defeat of the home team by 4-1. But they avenged this a fortnight later by a victory at Totham by 2-1. Not a bad start. The team played a very evenly contested match against Heybridge in December 1922, which was reported in the January 1923 parish magazine which noted that:

> The home side should have won, a penalty being awarded against Heybridge within 2 minutes of time, which however, their 'goalie' managed to save, a draw resulting.

In a creditable 3-1 victory over Hatfield Reserves the Langford team 'showed better combination' and deserved their success. Fred Gooch scored the three goals. On 20th January 1923, Langford played Tollesbury but were defeated 3-1. Tollesbury visited Langford on 10th February for the return match and after a very muddy contest were defeated by the home side 3-2. However, it was a different story on the following Saturday when Purleigh claimed a decisive victory by 6-2. The parish magazine noted 'We understand that owing to the absence of our regular 'goalie' the score of goals was heavier than it should have been.'

On 10th March Langford gained victory over a team from Heybridge. The parish magazine reported that 'some good football was seen', and the result was 4-1 with the Langford goals scored by C. Wager (3) and Boutwell (1). The parish magazine added: 'But for some good goalkeeping on the part of our 'goalie' the result might have been different.'

The season closed with a well-deserved victory over Purleigh by five goals to nil. The game was evenly contested up until half time with neither team scoring. On changing ends Langford's forwards attacked strongly in the second half and soon scored three goals, the last two coming within a few minutes of time. The 1923 season's results were as follows: Played 18; won 7; lost 9; drawn 2. Goals scored 31 against 49. The chief goal scorers were F. Gooch (12) and C. Wager (8). The team were congratulated on their performance during their first season.

At a special AGM in October 1923 Mr. H. Whybrow was elected as Captain, Vice Mr. C. Wager (resigned) and Mr. A. Bright to be Vice-Captain, vice Mr. Easter. Messrs. C. Gooch, L. Last and F. Chapman were elected to the Committee. The November parish magazine reported:

> The team are beginning to shape well and have already two victories to their credit – East Hanningfield and Little Baddow. They had to acknowledge defeat at the hands of Tollesbury (twice) – the second match was very evenly contested until Mr. A. Bright was carried off the field with a sprained ankle, of which their opponents took advantage to score the winning goals.

The Langford team claimed victories over Hatfield Reserves (3-2), Hatfield Wellington (2-0), Sadds' Athletic (4-3). However, with a weak team, they had to acknowledge defeat by Heybridge St. Andrews' and in the return match Sadds' Athletic had their revenge and beat Langford by five goals to two.

More victories followed in December: v. Little Baddow 4-3; v. Great Baddow 7-3 and v. Hatfield Reserves 6-2. The game against Tollesbury (a 2-2 draw) was very evenly contested throughout and the result showed how evenly matched the sides were. The season's record so far was: Played 14, won eight, lost four, drawn two.

Three more victories followed in January and only one defeat. The team proved their superiority over East Hanningfield (4-0), Seabrooks (5-3) and Heybridge St. Andrews' (4-1) but, though making an excellent fight with Danbury Rovers they failed to score, while their opponents scored twice. However, the parish magazine commented: 'Our team possess a splendid pair of backs and some fast and dashing forwards and a good goalie, and all have worked hard and thoroughly deserve their successes.'

In January/February 1925 Langford hit a purple patch in the Kelvedon and District League with six successive victories:

3rd January	Witham Reserves	6-2
10th January	E.C.C. Staff	3-1
24th January	Pattiswick	4-3
7th February	Pattiswick	2-1
14th February	Tolleshunt Major	7-1
21st February	Kelvedon Reserves	5-0

The parish magazine proudly reported 'This is a splendid record and the team have been playing so well together that they have thoroughly deserved their victories.' The chief scorers of goals were W. Easter and H. Whybrow, though others (Martin, Talbot, Fortey and Willis) had 'helped to swell the score of goals.' The magazine added that 'their chief strength lies in the capacity of the forward line to score goals, though at the same time the half-back and backs have put in a lot of hard and useful work [and] G. Gooch has always proved himself a safe goalie. We congratulate the team on their success.'

However, the team met its strongest opponents at the end of the season, for the following defeats were reported as due to 'superior play.'

28th February	Witham	Bridge	1-2
	Home		

7th March	Witham Warren O.B.	1-4
14th March	Chappel and Wakes Colne	1-10
28th March	Witham Bridge Home	1-6

There were three more matches to finish the season Chappel and Wakes Colne, E.C.C. Staff, and Witham Warren but the results of these are yet to be traced. Sadly, after this season, and despite some good performances during 1924/25 nothing more is heard about the Football Club and it is assumed that it was quietly wound down.

However, it is known that, much later, a football club known as Ulting Villa played their matches for a few seasons in the field behind the Estate Carpenter's shop – Walter Harry Chalk's shed, which stood near to where the bus shelter now stands.

Today the only football seen in Langford is that played by children.

Hockey Club

On Tuesday 8th December 1936 a 'military whist drive' was held in Mill House by Mr. & Mrs. Pelly and Mr. & Mrs. Goulding in aid of the newly formed Hockey Club. By 1938 the Hockey Club had a large membership and was flourishing, and another successful military whist drive was held at the same venue. Through the kindness of Mr. Wakelin, the club possessed an excellent ground, although it is not stated where that ground was. Sadly, nothing more is heard of the Hockey Club, and it is supposed that it, too, quietly broke up.

Tennis Club

A Tennis Club was formed in the village after the Great War; the first reference to this is in the parish magazine of November 1919 when:

> The Rector acknowledged, with many thanks, a donation from Mrs. Jones of 30/- for the Cricket Club, part of the proceeds of the concert which she organised on September 20th. The Tennis Club has benefited by a similar amount. Receipts amounted to £4.6.3 and expenses (Tax £1) £1.4.8½. The balance £3.1.6½ has been handed over as above reported.

A meeting of the Tennis Club was held at the Schools on Tuesday 5th April 1932.The accounts were passed showing a balance in hand of '£5 odd,' and arrangements were made for carrying on the club, which 'from all reports' promised well. Mr. Pelly was elected Chairman; Mrs. Doubleday, Hon. Sec and the Rector, President.

At a meeting of the Tennis Club Committee on Monday 30th April to consider the re-opening of the season, the Rector was again asked to be Chairman. Mrs. Goulding was elected Hon. Secretary in place of Mrs. Doubleday, who regretted being unable to continue the secretaryship. The closing of the season took place on Saturday 15th September 1934 when a general invitation to tea was made to all members of the Club, who met at Mill House, through the kindness of Mr. & Mrs. Pelly. The arrangement of the tea was undertaken by Mrs. Pelly and Mrs. Goulding and:

> [a]fter tea the Rector was asked to present some prizes of a unique character, the handicraft of Mr. Goulding, to the winners at the tennis matches. The season has been a very successful one, and the funds in hand, our Hon. Secretary Mrs. Goulding, states, are very satisfactory."

The Tennis Club met in the Church Room on Thursday 2nd April 1936, and the accounts and the balance sheet were considered. A good season was spent and several matches arranged. The parish magazine recorded:

> There is a substantial balance in hand and we look forward to another successful season. The court has had special attention paid to it and will be re-opened for play on April 13th. Mrs. Goulding has again been appointed Hon. Secretary to whom a hearty vote of thanks was passed at the meeting.

The tennis season for 1936 was marred by wet weather which interfered with some of the matches arranged. Eight matches were fixed, but of these only six were played. Langford lost two, drew two and won two. The other two matches were scratched. There were 29 members in the club in 1935 but the court was not at any time overcrowded, but it was well used and members enjoyed some good tennis. An inter-club tournament was arranged towards the end of the season but owing to weather conditions and members being away on holiday, it was found impossible to play the matches off, so the tournament was abandoned.

At the last committee meeting of the season, held on 5th October a suggestion was put forward that it would be a great advantage to get the Court turned round during the early autumn. Mr. Pelly and Mr. Goulding were asked to inquire into the matter, but it was not possible to get the work carried out. However, the groundsmen re-turfed the worn patches and the court was well rolled before being used. Mrs. Pelly very kindly, catered for tennis teas and lent her home [Mill House] - something greatly appreciated by the players.

The membership in 1936 was limited to twenty-five, but the court was never vacant throughout the season, and at the beginning of the season the club invested in a new net; this addition was much appreciated, also a 'somer' marking set was bought to assist in the marking out.

At the last committee meeting of the season it was decided to approach Mr. Wakelin on the subject of turning the court round and also if he would allow the club ground for another court. This he kindly consented to do; the extra ground was fenced and the bad patches re-turfed in readiness for next season. The club asked Mr. Wakelin to accept a yearly payment for the extra ground and he accepted a guinea.

The 1937 season was fairly successful. The Club played eleven matches, won six and lost five. A tournament was arranged but unfortunately it was impossible to complete it, owing to members going on holiday – a situation which happened all too frequently.

On 25th March 1937, the Rector (Revd. Creed) was elected President, Mrs. Pelly, Vice-President, Mr. B. Muggleton, Captain, Miss Joyce Goulding, Vice-Captain, Hon. Sec and Treasurer Mrs. Goulding and Miss Joyce Goulding and a committee of five. In 1938 the Annual meeting of the Tennis Club was held at Mill House on 17th March. The report of the past season was read by the Hon. Sec. and showed a satisfactory balance in hand. Through the kindness of Mr. Wakelin, the club looked forward to having two courts in use in the near future. Members met for supper at the Mill House on Tuesday 2nd August, and this was followed by a man-hunt and other games. The tennis club re-opened in May 1941 Mrs. H.G. Binder was their Hon. Sec.

The Annual Meeting of the Tennis Club met at Mill House Friday 16th April 1943. Mrs. Goulding was appointed the Secretary and Treasurer. On 26th April 1944 the AGM of the tennis club was held – Mrs. Goulding agreed to continue as Secretary and Treasurer, and free admission was extended to all serving in His majesty's Forces who were in Langford.
On 25th March 1937, the Rector (Revd. Creed) was elected President, Mrs. Pelly, Vice-President, Mr. B. Muggleton, Captain, Miss Joyce Goulding, Vice-Captain, Hon. Sec and Treasurer Mrs. Goulding and Miss Joyce Goulding and a

committee of five. In 1938 the Annual meeting of the Tennis Club was held at Mill House on 17th March. The report of the past season was read by the Hon. Sec. and showed a satisfactory balance in hand. Through the kindness of Mr. Wakelin, the club looked forward to having two courts in use in the near future. Members met for supper at the Mill House on Tuesday 2nd August, and this was followed by a man-hunt and other games. The tennis club re-opened in May 1941 Mrs. H.G. Binder was their Hon. Sec.

The club during 1938 enjoyed a very successful season in spite of a few bumps. Membership was still limited to twenty-five but actually there were only twenty-three members. The Club had nineteen fixtures of which four had to be cancelled. Results of matches were mainly in favour of Langford. A knock-out tournament was also held during the season.

Winners were: Ladies Singles – Miss E. Green; Men's Singles – Mr. M.B. Pelly; Ladies Doubles – Miss E. Green & Miss J. Goulding; Men's Doubles – Mr. H.G. Binder & Mr. J.V Binder; Mixed Doubles – Miss E. Green & Mr. M.B. Pelly. The prizes were presented by the Chairman at a supper held for all Club members.

The Secretary's Report for the 1939 Season noted that the Club was able to enjoy the use of the two courts, when the extra play was much appreciated. The membership was raised to 30, although actually there were 35 members. There were not many matches quite a number having to be scratched; of those played Langford won three, drew one and lost three. A knock-out tournament was again arranged, and it was nearly completed but the weather was unkind. A number of junior members joined during that season, who showed promise and were quite keen players.

The groundsmen kept the court in as good a condition as could be expected and their services were greatly appreciated.

The Annual Meeting of the Tennis Club met at Mill House Friday 16th April 1943. Mrs. Goulding was appointed the Secretary and Treasurer. On 26th April 1944 the AGM of the tennis club was held – Mrs. Goulding agreed to continue as Secretary and Treasurer, and free admission was extended to all serving in His majesty's Forces who were in Langford.

In the 1980s the rules of the Langford Tennis Club were:

1. No player shall be allowed on the courts unless wearing tennis shoes without heels.
2. No member to lay more than one short set when other members are waiting.
3. Members who bring guests are responsible for paying the visitors fee of 2/- per day.
4. Members must replace the balls and return the keys.
5. No cars are to be parked on the grass in front of the courts.
6. Hours of play:
    a. Full members:- Tuesday & Thursday evenings. Saturday from 1.0 p.m. Sunday from 1.0 p.m.
    b. Junior members:- Tuesday & Thursday up to 7.0 p.m. Saturday up to 1.0 p.m. Friday from 6.0 p.m. These times may be extended if the courts are not required by full members, and junior members may also be allowed to play with full members at the discretion of the Committee.
    c. Wednesdays will be reserved for members of the S.W.C. [Southend Water Company] only.

Officers for 1984 were: Chairman – Harry Pipe; Secretary – Jill Light; Treasurer – Lyn Rowe; Men's Captain – Hollis Cloughton; Vice-Captain – David Pipe; Ladies' Captain – Janet Macey.

The Golden Jubilee of the club was celebrated by an all-day American-style tournament at Langford. Almost all the club members competed for the Goulding Cup donated by Joyce Binder in memory of her parents who, with Joyce, were founder members of the club. The tournament was a great success and members thoroughly enjoyed playing and picnicking in the sunshine. The winners were Janet Macey and Tony Murray who beat June Cloughton and Norman Clarke in the final.

In the evening a celebration party was held at the Village Hall in North Fambridge. Members with families and friends enjoyed a ploughman's supper and dancing to Howard Carter's music. The Chairman of the club, Harry Pipe, was presented with a picture of Langford Church in recognition of his long standing association and service to the club. Mrs. Pipe was presented with golden chrysanthemums. Joyce Binder then presented the Goulding Trophy to the tournament winners and she also received some golden chrysanthemums. Thanks were given to Hollis Cloughton who organised the tournament, to Ron and Alice Clover for their hard work in organising the party, and to the ladies of the committee for preparing an excellent supper. Anyone interested in joining the club for the next season were asked to contact Jill Light.

Sadly, at the AGM of the Club held on 9th March 1988, it was decided to wind up its affairs due to lack of support, and the required three months' notice was given to Savills, agents for the Essex Water Company. As the Parish Council was taking over the land, the Club wrote to offer their equipment should the Council wish to re-open the courts.

For many years tennis courts were available for use by the club and residents of the village. These were situated at the rear of the cowshed (now the Langford and Ulting Village Hall). However, the courts fell into disrepair and the fences were removed and Mother Nature reclaimed the grassed area (now meadow) as her own.

Fishing

The Black Pool used to be a meander in the river from the sluice gates to the road bridge behind the village hall, and was a famous place for roach. The Black Pool meadow (between Bridge Cottage[s] and the river) was often alive with elvers. Bream, roach and pike were found in the river and this stretch of water was leased by Ilford Angling Club.

Grass Track

In early 1961 plans were announced that motorcycle grass track racing was coming to Langford courtesy of ESSA (Essex Sporting Sidecar Association) and a series of meetings took place on fields between the waterworks reservoirs and the River Chelmer in the early 1960s.

The dates tended to fit in nicely with the school holidays and so it wasn't surprising that a number of Langford lads, including the co-author of this book, his brother Michael Chaplin, cousin Peter Mansfield and Maurice and Ronald Heyhoe (boys from

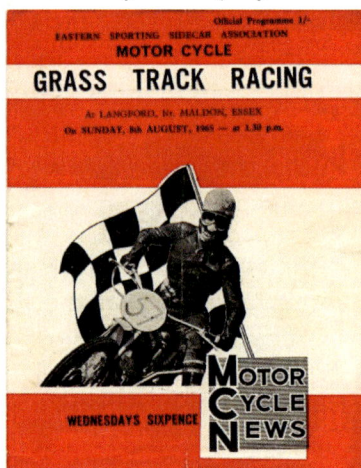

Ulting Lane) 'assisted' the organisers by painting posts, running errands and generally getting in the way. It was all worth it though as the boys were rewarded on the day by

420

being allowed to watch the action for free from a prime position with the Marshalls and officials within the centre of the race track itself.

Snooker, darts, cards and dominoes

Albert Chaplin at the Snooker table in 1992

After the school was closed in 1922 the premises were used for a number of community purposes including the Langford Men's Club. Here snooker, darts, cards and dominoes were regularly played by members and during the 1960s young people of the village were allowed to use the facilities, as long as they were supervised by an adult for the first hour or so on a Friday evening. As far as is known, the men were never organised into teams except for internal play.

Carpet Bowls

A meeting was held on 3rd October 1994 to discuss the formation of a Carpet Bowls club; those present were John and Joy Chalk, John Corbin, Cilla Driver, Agnes Blake and Albert Chaplin. It was suggested that the club meet on a

Monday evening for a two-hour session from 7.30p.m. – 9.30p.m. at a cost of £2 per person. The first bowls session was held the following week (Monday 10th October) with 16 people attending, and it has continued ever since. At first the club hired bowling mats, but later these were bought and are stored in the village hall for instant use. This pastime still thrives there on Monday evenings and Wednesday afternoons (for beginners) and occasionally 'friendlies' have been played 'home and away' with other clubs.

Summary

Like any other rural community, Langford has seen the development of organised games yet in addition to this is the wide variety of street games that the children of the village played; often their own casual versions of the sports and games that their fathers took so seriously.

Today Langford has no cricket club; the cricket square, for many years cordoned off with posts and ropes to protect it from the public, now forms an unidentifiable part of the events field of the Museum of Power. However, the cricket pavilion still stands, used for storage by the museum and forming a physical reminder that the field once (for many years) echoed to the sound of leather on willow.

Some of the early football grounds can no longer be identified as such and the most recent, the field used by Ulting Villa, remains an open field. The fencing around the last public tennis court was pulled down many years ago and the grass of that previously manicured court is now undistinguishable from any other area of grass.

Whilst we are certain that some Langfordians do play sport they have to play elsewhere as no facilities for outdoor sport have existed in the village for many years.

LANGFORD AT LEISURE

In this modern age it is hard to conceive that our ancestors (and in some cases our parents or even ourselves as children) did not spend their evenings 'glued to the box' as many do today. In an age far more social and inclusive than ours they created their own entertainment and we can glean a lot about the social mores by researching their activities. Although some of these entries may seem 'quaint' today, it is worth publishing them for their social history.

One of the first records of 'entertainment' is dated Tuesday, 27th November 1894 when a most successful entertainment was given in Langford School:

> The room itself was packed to its utmost capacity, the price for seats ranging from 2s to 3d. The stage was admirably arranged, the lighting being especially successful. The programme was divided into two parts, the former consisting of songs, the latter of a short comedy entitled 'Woman's Wrongs'. The performers in the first part were Miss L [Lily] Wynyard, Mrs. Willock, Miss Baker, Mr. [William] Wynyard, and Mr. Gowers. In the second part the characters were represented by Mr. and the Misses Wynyard, who all acted capitally, as one would expect, Mr. Wynyard being a member of a well-known Amateur Dramatic Company [*although sadly we are not told which one*]. The entertainment lasted about two and a half hours. The excellent piano was most kindly lent by Mrs. Lee Baker, [*of Mill House*] who thereby did much towards the success of the evening.

A variety entertainment took place in Langford School on Friday 21st December 1895 at 8 o'clock which:

> in spite of the dark foggy weather, was fairly well attended. Miss Ada Byron, Miss L. Wynyard, Miss Baker, the Revd. F.C. Byron, Mr. Wynyard and Messrs.

Chalk and Barber, contributed songs to the first part of the programme, accompanied by Mr. Gowers. The second part afforded great amusement by the clever acting of Mr. and Miss Wynyard in a short piece called 'A Love Suit' and which piece they kindly performed at Hatfield Peverel the following evening in the Schools, at an entertainment got up by Mrs. Toulmin.

This demonstrated a good rapport between the two villages. Another very successful concert was held in the Schoolroom in Langford on Saturday, 4th January 1896.

The concert opened with a recitation by the Rector, comprised songs by the Misses L. Wynyard and Clara Grout, Messrs. Wynyard and Woollard, and some lively selections by the Langford Amateur Bigotphone Band (kindly lent by Mr. Gowers of Maldon). Unfortunately the proceeds of the entertainment were almost entirely swallowed up by the expenses, but the 2/6 which was, alas, all that remained was handed over to the Cricket Club.

The parish magazine noted that a concert which had been arranged for Tuesday 2nd March 1897 had to be postponed:

owing to the arrival of a menagerie in Maldon, a counter attraction which would have proved fatal to the entertainment. A number of talented artistes had kindly promised their help, and these have had to be hastily informed of the change. Amongst the performers were several quite new to the Langford stage. We sincerely hope that none of the inhabitants of Langford will fall victims to the African lion or the Bengal tiger, and we advise all boys to be very careful how they approach the cages of the monkeys, lest they have their noses pulled.

A Magic Lantern entertainment was given by the Rev. A.L. Hunt in Langford Schoolroom on Tuesday 16th March 1897. The entertainment began at 7.30 p.m. and the room was crammed. The pictures consisted of Old and New Testament and other sacred subjects, 'Captain' Prince, of the Church Army, giving an explanation of each. The entertainment commenced and finished with prayers and hymns which were 'thrown upon the screen.' Such an evening may seem quaint these days, but it was very novel and 'hi tech' at the time.

Links with neighbouring villages were often successful. For example, the February 1899 parish magazine stated boldly:

When Wickham and Langford combine, what can one expect but a great success and this was the case not only musically but financially. Miss Katie Jones was an immense acquisition and sang charmingly, as did Miss Baker. Mr. Hayes opened the proceedings with a pianoforte solo, and Mr. William Chalk sang in his well-known excellent style. Mr. Bramston, Mr. W.B.A. Wynyard and Mr. H.B.W. Wynyard contributed to the humorous side of the concert, and the latter made an excellent chairman in the regrettable absence of the Rector. Miss Wynyard was first rate in her duologue, and Mr. Herbert Snell and Mr. Wynyard charmed the audience with their beauty and elegance in a song and dance, Mr. Snell in particular footing it with sylph-like not to say elephantine grace. The handbell-ringing of the Chalk family (father and sons) was also most delightful and altogether it was one of the most successful concerts we have had. The room was well filled, in spite of the inclement weather, and over £2 was cleared, part of which was expended in lamps for the school, the rest going to the cricket club.

Such events may seem tame and somewhat childish to us now, but show the talent of the villagers and their friends, and it would be wonderful to be able to step back in time to catch a glimpse of these evenings. For example

A capital concert took place in the schoolroom on Friday April 14th 1899. The programme contained pianoforte solo by Mr Hayes, songs by Miss Baker (who was encored for her excellent singing), Messrs. Jupp, Gowers, W.B.A. and H. Wynyard and William Chalk. Messrs. Gower and Chalk both sang admirably and obtained well deserved encores. Mr. Jupp was excessively funny in 'It is not for you, it's for a Friend,' and brought down the house in 'Galloping round the arena.' Mr. W.B.A. Wynyard proved as popular as ever and Mr. H. Wynyard fairly brought down the house. One of the greatest attractions of the evening was a most amusing Duologue, which is just now enjoying a great popularity, entitled 'A Backward Child,' given by the Misses Kaye, who came down to Langford for the purpose, and a Recitation by Miss Kaye of a martial character. There were two Part Songs (1) 'Tommy on the streets', with a chorus of ladies and gentlemen, and accompanied on the 'comb.' (2) 'Come listen to the band' by Mr. W.B.A. Wynyard, with chorus by Mr. Jupp, Captain Wynyard and Mr. H. Wynyard, to the accompaniment of the penny drum. In the song (which was revised by Captain and Mr. W.B.A. Wynyard) occurred the following topical verse which brought down the house:

> See how well we've all turned out tonight,
> That will make the cricket funds all right,
> All will wish us best of luck this year,
> For we've got to buy a roller,
> So as just to suit the bowler,
> And we must subscribe a bob,
> Instead of sixpence, now that's clear.
>
> Chorus

Oh! Come and see us play, that's always such a treat!
For with our brand new pitch,
No more we'll brook defeat.
Then come and have some tea,
Which you will find so sweet,
Always made so hot and strong by Mrs. Chalk and
Mrs. Smith,
I'm sure you'll find it very hard to beat

Sadly we don't have the music for this but it was too lovely not to include. There was also a violin solo by Mr. William Chalk and a reading by the Rector.

Success followed success as the parish magazine of February 1903 noted:

It is a trite remark that a Langford Concert is almost invariably first-rate, because they are too well known to need 'puffing'. But that held in the schoolroom on Friday 2nd January was quite one of the best that has ever been held, and was full of novelties. It was divided into two parts: the first part were: Mr. Hayes, pianoforte solo, Mr. W. Chalk, two songs, Miss L. Wynyard, two songs, Miss Mould, two songs, Miss Wakelin and Mrs. R. Wakelin, duologue 'Geese'. The Revd. & Hon. F. C. Byron imitations of birds and beasts, Mr. W.B.A. Wynyard, recitation 'The Haunted Conscience', and the Chalk Family with their celebrated performance on handbells.

The second part, 'Mrs. Jarley's Waxworks', the performers were Miss L. Wynyard, who made an admirable 'Mrs. Jarley' with her assistant 'John', Mr. R. Wakelin. 'You Dirty Boy', Miss G. Baker and Master Wakelin. 'The giggling girl', Miss M. Baker, 'The Chinese Giant', Mr. W.B.A. Wynyard. 'The Dwarf' Miss M. Baker and Miss Wakelin. 'Soothing Syrup' Miss E. Wakelin and Master Wakelin. 'The Spanish Dancer' Mrs. Gardener, and 'The Two-headed Nightingale', the

Hon. Alice Byron and Miss Wynyard. The acting was above praise. The audience was large, notwithstanding the counter attractions of a pantomime at Maldon, and most enthusiastic. £2.19s were taken. The proceeds (expenses deducted) were given to the Soldiers' and Sailors' Families' Association.

A most successful concert took place at Langford Mill - a place not usually thought of as a good venue - on Friday 21st February 1908, in aid of the Church heating apparatus.

The big room on the ground floor although not packed was very well filled and almost every seat was occupied. Owing to the shortness of the notice several items which ought to have been given were unable to be produced. On the other hand several ladies and gentlemen came forward and gave most invaluable help. The performers were: Mrs. Hugh Bawtree, violin solo, Miss Jones, songs; Miss Clara Grout, songs; Miss Leigh, songs; Mrs. Rayne, pianoforte solo; Mr. W. Chalk, songs; Mr. Rayne, songs; Mr. B. Wakelin, of Witham, used his magnificent gramophone, as Madame Patti, Madame Tetrazzini, Mr. Harry Lauder and others gave a series of most vocal performances. Two elderly persons, who described themselves as Langford ladies, also appeared on the stage and underwent the most terrible physical transformation in consequence of having (most foolishly) followed the advice of friends. The performance concluded with a short play, acted by Miss M. Grout and Miss Everitt, which completely brought down the house. The Concert did not terminate until close upon 10 o'clock. The concert produced the sum of £5:12:7. The greatest thanks are due to Mrs. Grout who not only lent her beautiful piano but worked at the organising of the performance and the sale of tickets in a masterly way. In addition to this Mrs. Grout has raised a considerable sum of money by a house to house visitation to which everybody in the parish has responded most liberally.

It would appear that most concerts of this time were in aid of local causes such as the Cricket Club as was given on Saturday 7th January 1911 in the School, 'the room being crowded to suffocation.'

> The programme was excellent, the performers being:- Miss Allen, violin soloist, accompanied by Miss Graves who also most kindly accompanied several others of the performers. Miss Bentall, Mrs Roulston, Mr. W.B.A. Wynyard, Mr. Roulston and Mr. William Chalk, a quartet without any accompaniment, being excellently rendered by Miss Fanny and Miss Emily Chalk, and Messrs. William and Walter Chalk. At the conclusion of the entertainment, a one act play was admirably acted by Miss F. Wakelin, the Misses French, Mr. Upson, Mr. R. Wakelin, and gave immense amusement to the crowded audience. Between £4 and £5 were taken.

On Saturday 21st January 1911,

> A social tea organised by Mrs. Wakelin and assisted by several ladies and gentlemen proved an enormous success, the room being crowded. The entrance price was 6d and this included tea. One of the features of the entertainment was a duet admirably rendered by Mrs and Miss Grout. The same ladies and gentlemen repeated the play on the evening of Saturday 7th, and besides this Mr. R. and Miss Wakelin gave their well-known rendering of the duologue 'Geese.'

Rummage and 'Aunt Sally'

Although perhaps not worthy of a note these days, the early part of the Twentieth Century provided an opportunity to obtain 'new' clothes by means of rummage sales. We would hardly think of them as social events today, but one held in the School room on Saturday 14th October 1911, held on behalf of the cricket club funds, bears mentioning:

> The stall holders were the Hon. Alice Byron, Mrs. Burns, Mrs. Hollingdale and Miss Sutton, Fancy Goods; Mrs. Wakelin, Millinery; the Misses Lee Baker, Hats; Mrs. Grout, Costumes; Mr. Wynyard, Men's Department; and the Rector, Boots and Shoes. The sale produced over £5.

But the social whirl was not limited to events within the village. On Thursday 9th July 1914 on the invitation of Mrs. Hollingdale (of Mill House), thirty nine women had a very enjoyable excursion to the Rodney in Little Baddow.

> A start was made at 2.30 and the Rodney was reached by the short way. Tea was provided and Swinging boats, Aunt Sally [*played by throwing batons at a wooden skittle known as a doll called 'Aunt Sally'*] and other games kept everyone going. The return journey was by way of Maldon and the party arrived home safely at 9 o'clock. The weather was all that could be desired, and everyone thoroughly enjoyed the outing.

Clearly they were blissfully unaware that war was only a few weeks away. There is also no mention of other entertainments during the war years, although it is inconceivable that all such events stopped, as many would have been held to raise money for the war effort. But the parish magazine began reporting village entertainments again in 1918:

> One of the charms of an entertainment given by children is the enjoyment conspicuously displayed by the young performers, and the enthusiasm evident to all. The performance given by the Langford School children, on April 19th 1918 was no exception to this, and many of the items were delightful. The Duologue 'A Niece by Marriage,' performed by the Misses Wilberforce, with which the programme opened, was most amusing and

deservedly applauded, and the Dialogue 'A Very Lame Dog,' with which the programme concluded, was full of fun. The following performers all did well: Nellie Chalk, May Harvey, Ivy Harvey, Emily Parmenter. Other items included song and chorus by troupes of boys and girls – 'Jingle Bells,' 'My Darling Clementine,' 'Polly Wolly Doodle,' 'Come Sing to Me.' Two recitations by boys, 'Prayers and Potatoes' and 'Rejected' had been well taught, the latter by Gilbert Parker and Albert Russell, the two youngest performers, was quite charming and had to be repeated. This effort for the Waifs and Strays Society was a great success. A collection made in the room amounted to £1.16.9½ which was highly satisfactory.

But these events were not altogether acceptable to the young men of the village, and so a meeting was held in the Reading Room in January 1919 with the object of 'discussing the formation of a Club or Institute to provide a place of recreation and amusement during the remainder of the dark evenings.'

There were seven present who showed great keenness in this project. A working committee was formed with which the Rector was asked to act as Joint Secretary and Treasurer. It was decided to open on Mondays, Wednesdays and Fridays, from 6.45-9 p.m., and anyone above the age of fourteen would be eligible to join, names being submitted to the Secretary and Committee for election. Members agreed to pay 3d a week to cover cost of firing and caretaking. They were trusting to the generosity of anyone interested in the project to supply them with paper and games, so the Rector made an appeal for the same. The Institute opened on Monday 27th January, and would 'carry on' till the first week in April when it would close down until October.

But it was concerts that brought people together in 1919, for example a full house testified better than anything else to the popularity of the entertainment given almost entirely by the school children and young people of the parish.

The infants figured largely in Part One and gained deserved applause for their song "My Dolly" and recitations given by Agnes Cottis (Mother's Helping Hand), Amy Warren (The Dolly's Lament), and Lucy Cooper (Grandma's Glasses), who seemed to enjoy themselves as well as amuse the audience. A sketch entitled "Black Brothers," by six boys (E, Gooch, E. Challis, F. Faircloth, S. Howlett, J. Cottis and G. Parker) was very funny and produced huge applause. The "Japanese Fan" by the girls had evidently been taught with great pains and was well received. G. Gooch and G. Challis spoke their lines clearly in the two recitations, "The Fisherman and the Porter" and "The Little Hero." A Pierrot Troupe contributed two well-known songs "Camp Town Races" and "When Johnny Comes Marching Home," and gained an encore. Miss Judith Wilberforce gave a pleasing rendering of "Plumstones" and "Humpty Dumpty," and was heartily clapped, and Miss Grout caused much amusement with her two songs "Take me Back to Bingville" and "Dennis." Special merit must be awarded to Miss Wilberforce for her excellent recitation "How a Slave saved St. Michaels," which was accorded the warmest reception by the audience; and also to the sketch given by members of the Girls' Club, viz: Ellen Chalk, May Harvey, Ivy Harvey, and Ivy Howlett, which kept the audience convulsed with laughter and provided a good finale to the Entertainment. The sum of £2.11.7 was taken at the door, the whole of which goes to the Society for providing homes for Waifs and Strays. Mrs. Jones and Miss Patten [*teachers at Langford School*] both put in a lot of work teaching the children their pieces and are to be congratulated on the result.

The Club (or Institute) which had duly closed during the summer months re-opened its doors on Monday 6th October, 1919, when the General Meeting was held. It was noted that there were eight members at present, and Magazines and Picture Papers were needed as were games and packs of cards.

Whist Drives were also extremely popular throughout the twentieth century in the village. One was held in the Church Room on Monday 27th February 1922 when £1.17.6 was raised for Church Room Funds. Another whist drive was arranged to raise funds for the purchase of a piano and other things which were required for the Church room.

In 1923 it was decided to start a social club during the winter months for old and young. The social club opened on Monday and Thursday from 7-9 p.m. There was a small charge for membership of 2d a night and about thirty members joined. It was noted that 'the chief need is a piano.' Shortly thereafter a piano, in very good condition was offered to the church room at a very low price. This was more in the nature of a gift to the village from Mr. & Mrs. H.W.W. Wilberforce, of Langford Grove, and they were heartily thanked for their generosity.

In April 1923 Mr. William Ingram gave a lecture on his personal travels 'Up the Nile':

> His audience were much interested (with the exception of a few restless boys) in the lecture which was illustrated by slides taken by the lecturer himself. The lantern was lent and worked by Mr. Last of Heybridge, and displayed to advantage some excellent and interesting views. A collection made after the lecture realised 7/4 all of which Mr. Ingram insisted should be handed over to the Social Club funds.

The club then closed its doors until the autumn when it was hoped it would be re-opened 'as great enthusiasm and interest has been shown during the past season.' It was also hoped that a 'Special Social Evening' would be arranged for Wednesday in Easter week when members and their friends would be welcomed. This evening was arranged for Wednesday 4th April 1923 to wind up the Spring Session.

> About 60 parishioners and friends took part and entered enthusiastically into all the games and dances. Miss Fanny Chalk was a host in herself in organising some splendid games, and songs were contributed by Mr. William Chalk, Mr. Philip Chalk and Miss Gladys Chalk, and perhaps the most popular item of all was that contributed by Mr. William Chalk, who played many well-known and popular airs on his hand bells. The music for the dancing was provided by Miss de Buriatte and Miss Littlehales. The refreshments were capably managed by Mrs. Parmenter, assisted by Mrs. Walter Chalk and Mrs. Ford, who, with Mrs. Littlehales and Mrs. A.E. May, also kindly contributed cakes, buns and sandwiches. The total receipts for this Spring Session amounted to £4.5.2 and expenses amounting to £2.15.0, leaving a balance in hand of £1.10.2 which has been paid in to the Church Room Fund.

A further concert in 1923 provided songs that would not be acceptable today, as they would be regarded as 'racist,' but our forebears had no such 'political correctness.'

> The concert on February 6th 1923 in aid of the Scout funds was well patronised by the villagers as the room was quite full when the curtain went up at 7.30 and the various items by the boys and their friends who helped with song and acting were deservedly applauded throughout the evening. Miss De Buriatte contributed a pianoforte solo and a song. Recitations were given by Scouts G. Parker and R. Bonner. The most youthful performers were Albert Russell and Vera Cook who showed unusual shyness in their amusing Duet 'Where

are you going to my pretty maid.' Scouts A. Joslin, G. Parker, W. Bonner and R. Bonner enjoyed their own fooling in the Nigger Songs as much as the audience. The remainder of the programme was filled by three short plays as follows:-'Brown Paper Parcels', in which the Misses Harvey acquitted themselves creditably and caused a good deal of amusement. 'The Scout Barbers' was a play in which two Scouts (E. Gunn and L. Last) undertook to take the place of the real barber (A. Joslin) who was suddenly taken ill. The pardonable mistakes perpetrated on the customers (Mr. Stout-Sydney Russell) and Scoutmaster R. Littlehales (disguised) created roars of laughter and must have been realistic, to have deceived a small member of the audience into thinking that her brother was being really hurt by the clumsy shaver. The 'Cheeky Domestic' (G. Parker) and the village youth (W. Bonner) both helped towards the success of the piece. The last play was 'Aunt Dorinda', in which the characters were as follows: Aunt Dorinda – Miss H. Ford, Niece Sylvia – Miss L. Seaborne. Maid – Miss I. Howlett, Miss Ford gained rounds of applause by her representation of the fussy and crotchety old maid. Miss Seaborne displayed the proper qualities of a dutiful niece, much worried by the exacting demands of her supposed Aunt (really her sister in disguise). Miss Howlett played the part of a sedate maid with success. The Scout funds benefited to the extent of £4.1.6 part of which will go towards Camp expenses in the summer. The piano was used for the first time since its purchase for the Church Room.

The Committee of the Langford Social Club arranged a 'long evening' on Thursday December 27th 1924

which resulted in a large attendance of young and old, who all joined heartily in the games and dances, and who seemed to thoroughly enjoy the songs and recitations contributed throughout the evening. We are indebted to the following for their valuable help in amusing those present: Miss Lewsey, Miss Gladys Chalk, Mrs. Walter Chalk, Mr. Philip Chalk, and Mr. William Chalk. Also to Mrs. W. Chalk, Mrs Harvey, Mrs. G. May, Mrs. Ford, Mrs. Littlehales, and Miss Ward, for providing and managing the refreshments.

But it was not only events in the school room that attracted villagers. An open-air fete was held in aid of the Church on Saturday 11th June 1926 in the grounds of Langford Hall. Lady Byron performed the opening ceremony, and Mrs. Curtis of Langford Grove, brought her pupils to do some Morris Dancing to entertain the visitors. The fete was also held the following year, and was again opened by Lady Byron, and proceeds were to go to new altar frontals. Lord Byron, who had been Rector of St. Giles from 1890 to 1914 said that the frontals had been in a poor condition when he was Rector, so it was an appropriate uses of funds.

The late 1920s were a time of liberation for women following the Great War, and a plethora of 'women's associations' sprang up. In December 1928 Miss Mary Baker asked that an announcement be made that the Annual Meeting of the Women's Conservative Association would be held in Langford Church Room on Thursday 3rd January at three o'clock, Mrs. Ruggles-Brise would speak and there would be a concert and tea afterwards, and that 'The Annual Subscription of 1/- is now due.' The 'Women's Unionist Association' also began in 1929.

The Annual Children's Party was held in the School room on Tuesday 30th December 1931. The entertainment started with a tea, continued with games and concluded at 6.30 p.m. each child leaving with a balloon, an orange and a bag of sweets. On the evening of the following day a social was held starting at 8 p.m.

The evening passed pleasantly with games, singing and dancing, and ended by singing in the New Year with

436

'Auld Lang Syne.' Attendance in both cases was good – 46 at the children's party and 56 at the social.

A Garden fete - opened by Lady Crittall - was held at Langford Lee courtesy of Miss Mary Baker on Wednesday 22nd July 1931. The total amount raised was £45 and Mr. Bruce Keeble was especially thanked for illuminating the grounds by electric light and also for the Wireless Gramophone! The following year a garden party was held at Langford Place on Saturday 18th June organised and hosted by Miss Packe and Miss Snell.

In 1933 the Children's Party took place at the School on Thursday 29th December, when the children:

> numbering about 60, spent a glorious time in games and amusements of all kinds, preceded by a substantial tea. Amongst the decorations was a wonderful Christmas Tree loaded with presents, from which each child had something presented by Father Christmas. The tree was kindly lent by the Managers of the Southend Waterworks Company, and was illuminated by various coloured electric bulbs. There were many kind helpers who willingly gave their services. The happy evening closed with 'God Save the King.'

The Children's Christmas Tea for 1934 took place in the Church Room on Friday 29th December. Seventy children received gifts from the Christmas tree and also sweets on leaving. Songs were sung by the children from the Langford Cross home. The parish magazine noted:

> Those who had the privilege of seeing the acting and of hearing the singing of the children of the Langford Cross Home on January 2nd will never forget it. The play was adapted from 'The Story of the Other Wise Man' by Henry Van Dyke, and the scenes were connected by a narrative, spoken with concentration and faultless diction.

The Children's Christmas Tea in 1935 was held on Saturday 29th December in the Church Room. This year, instead of a Christmas Tree, there was a 'Lucky Dip' and each child was lucky enough to catch something. Mr. Goulding was especially thanked as the children always looked forward to his games.

In 1941 a tea for the children of the parish was held in the schools on Friday 3rd January. Many children came as did some of the parents:

> and none of those present could have regretted coming. Kind people gave their share of rations, others contributed money, so that the children had a really sumptuous tea, apart from crackers and a small gift for each child. Miss Ford organised this.

A children's party held at the Schools on Thursday 3rd December 1942 was organised by the Langford Section of the Home Guard. The tea was given by friends in the parish and the Home Guard. The Christmas tree was illuminated and contained many presents from which each child received something. Later in the evening a social was held for the adults.

> A concert was given in the School room on Friday 5th March 1943 organised by Mrs. Doubleday, when songs were sung by Mrs. Ted Chalk, Mrs. Norman Chalk, Miss Nicholson, Mr. Goulding, Mr. Ingram and Martin Doubleday, and recitations given by Daphne Hales, Brian and John Chalk. Mr. Ingram's pianoforte solos were much appreciated. The second half consisted of a playlet entitled 'The Coming of Spring' with Vera Jennings as Mother Earth, Norah Groden as Fairy Moonshine, Pauline Robinson, Margaret Stubbings, Pat Groden, Daphne Hales and Rosemary Potter as flowers, and John Chalk and Martin Doubleday as goblins. Mrs. W. Goulding very ably presided and £2.17.6 less expenses was handed over to the local Red Cross funds.

Youth Club

A meeting was held on Thursday 1st March 1945 to consider the question of forming a Youth Centre in the parish. After much discussion it was decided to form such a centre. The chair was taken by Bert Morris, of Ulting Lane, and a committee was chosen: Chairman, Bert Morris; Secretary and Treasurer, Miss Gwendoline Harvey; Committee members, Allen Wilson, Rosemary Potter and Norah Groden. It was hoped the Youth Centre would run successfully, 'with the keen co-operation of the people of the parish.' In November the same year a meeting was held to elect a new committee for the Langford Youth Centre, and the following people were chosen: Secretary and Treasurer: Gwendoline Harvey, Committee members: Maurice Green, Terry Rushbrook, Bert Morris (Chairman), Rosemary Potter, Monica Simpson, and Vera Howlett.

A social was held by the Youth Club at the Schoolroom on 13th March 1946. Both the Ulting and Heybridge Youth Clubs were invited. Dancing and games were enjoyed by all present. Miss D. Hymas was the pianist. Refreshments of tea and cakes were handed round during the interval. A raffle of fifty cigarettes was won by a boy from one of the visiting clubs. The M.C. was Mr. A. Ford.

In addition the Church made several attempts to provide for the spiritual life of villagers, and set up clubs and organisations to serve this need.

Men's Club

A Men's Club was founded, and opened on Monday 1st October 1894. The Parish Magazine noted that it would 'be open for the winter months' and hoped it would be well patronised. However, it had to be closed in November 1896 due to the dropping off of many members who had either left the parish or migrated too far to be able to use it. It was finally closed in 1897.

However, a Meeting for Men was held in the school room on Sunday 19th March 1899 at 7.45 p.m. when the idea for the club was resurrected. After the Rector had read a few short prayers, Captain, the Hon. R. Moreton addressed the meeting, which was very well attended. It was remarked that it had been some years since the Men's club came to an end, but since then a considerable number of new inhabitants had come into the village, and it was therefore just possible that a Club room might be popular again. So a meeting was held for any who were interested in the scheme.

The club room did indeed open again on Wednesday 20th November 1901 and proved a great success. A General Meeting was held to elect officers and arrange other matters, but nothing more is recorded about this club, except a note in the parish magazine of November 1920 that "The Men's Institute reopened, but there were so many counter attractions in Heybridge and elsewhere that attendance was small." As is often the case with such institutions, it failed for lack of support.

Mothers' Meetings
Groups for women were also set up, and in 1895 the Hon. Miss Alice Byron, sister of the Rector, Rev. 'Chas' Byron, set up her 'Mothers' Meetings.' These, like the meetings for the men, were held during the winter months. These meetings started at the end of November, to be continued as usual throughout the winter months on every Thursday afternoon from 2.30-4.00. It certainly had an auspicious start, for on Friday 2nd August 1895, those who had attended the Mothers' Meeting during the winter months spent the afternoon at Langford Grove.

> The weather was beautiful and the party were able to have tea out in the garden, after which they walked about, some had a row on the ponds, others played croquet under the instructions of Mr. Byron. The party

broke up about 7.30 and all agreed they had had a very happy afternoon.

On Thursday 22nd July 1897, those who attended the Mothers' Meeting during the winter, were again entertained at the Grove. The parish magazine noted that they

> had tea out of doors under the shade of the trees, the day being beautifully fine and warm. After tea Miss Amy Wynyard most kindly offered her assistance in the canoe and took those who were good sailors a trip on the water in turn, and each voyage was accomplished in safety and much enjoyed. Later on she superintended a game of croquet, of which Mrs. Chalk and Mrs. Joslin were the winners.

The Mothers' Meetings closed for the season, on Thursday 19th April 1906 with a tea, which was well attended. 'The bread, which was baked by Mr. Brown of Wickham Bishops, with Langford Flour, was much praised.'

The annual Summer Meeting of the Mothers' Meeting was held on Thursday 26th July 1906, again at The Grove. The parish magazine noted:

> Those who were filled with the love of adventure and travel were taken for trips in the Canadian canoe. Tea was served in the garden and the party broke up about 7.15. The day was brilliantly fine.

This pattern continued until it was clear that Revd. Byron would inherit the title of Lord Byron from his brother. Miss Byron therefore spent quite a lot of time at Thrumpton Hall in 1913, but hoped to begin her Mothers' Meetings on Thursday 6th February when she returned from Nottingham. Her final Mothers' Meeting Tea was held at Langford Grove on Wednesday 16th July 1913.

After Revd. Byron left to take up his position as Vicar at Thrumpton in Nottinghamshire in 1914, Mrs. Littlehales, wife of the new Rector, took on the running of the Mothers' Meetings. She gave notice that she hoped to commence the Mothers' Meetings on the second Thursday in December, and would be glad to welcome all old members and any new ones who wished to join. The Vicarage was now housed in Langford Hall – the Rectory being inhabited by William Wynyard and his sister.

> The members of the Mothers' Meeting, which was held during the winter months, were entertained at Langford Hall by the Rector and Mrs. Littlehales, on Friday September 24th, 1915. Before tea, various out-door games were indulged in, and two trips were made in the boat up the little river, which were keenly enjoyed. The sky became suddenly overcast as tea was concluded on the lawn, and a heavy downpour of rain quickly drove everyone indoors. All took part heavily in the indoor games which were arranged in the front Hall and much laughter was the result. Mrs. and Miss Grout, Mrs. Ford and Miss Snell kindly assisted in amusing the guests.

Mrs Littlehales said the Mothers' Meetings would commence on Thursday 4th November 1915 at the Hall, and continue throughout the winter months.

Heybridge and Langford Women's Institute
In 1930, by the kind permission of Mr. & Mrs. Herbert Wilberforce,

> The Garden Fete organised by members of the Heybridge and Langford Women's Institute, was held in their beautiful grounds at Langford Grove, and was splendidly patronised by the neighbourhood. A magnificently fine day greatly helped towards the success of the undertaking. The tastes of all, both young and old, were catered for in the way of amusements, which comprised a great variety of games and competitions – vocal and instrumental items, Duologues

442

and short plays. We understand that between £40 and £50 was taken, only part of which is profit.

The Annual Summer Garden Party of the Heybridge and Langford Women's Institute was held in the Langford Hall garden, by the kind invitation of Mrs. Littlehales, on Wednesday 5th June 1931. The Committee was responsible for all the arrangements which were carried through very satisfactorily. The weather was not very kind, as a slight drizzle commenced as soon as people arrived, with the result that the one hundred visitors were compelled to take refuge indoors, and were 'packed closely like sardines,' when listening to Miss Judith Wilberforce. She gave a most attractive account of her experiences in connection with Dockland, and the great building scheme which is to do away with the slums and suggested ways and means of helping the same. They began their New Year's programme on Wednesday 6th January 1932 at 2.15 with a demonstration of cookery.

The annual flower show of the Heybridge and Langford WI was held in the Waring Room, Heybridge on Wednesday 6th July 1938, Mrs. E.E. Bentall presiding. Only one member from Langford exhibited at the flower show, and out of 105 members only five were from Langford. The WI held a demonstration on war-time cookery in the Waring Room on 5th February 1941 by Miss Hussey of Chelmsford Technical School. Members, under the organisation of Mrs. Wakelin and Miss Wyatt, formed a fruit-preservation centre in April 1941, and 365 eggs were collected from Langford for the Chelmsford Hospital, thanks to Mrs. Pye and Mrs. Hales. Congratulations were given to Mrs. Chaplin, of Langford, on winning the Silver Challenge Cup for the year, with seven first prizes, at the annual Flower Show.

Langford Girls' Club

The headmistress of Langford School, Mrs. Jones, started a club for girls above school age, whom she invited to her house. On 22nd October, 1919 Miss F. Ward

> very kindly commenced dressmaking with the members. Six girls out of 132 cut out and commenced to make a blouse. It is proposed to hold the meeting every Wednesday evening from 6.30 to 8.45, and to have a Social once a month, also a competition once a month (last Wednesday in month). The girls pay one penny a week. Two invitations have already been given for the Social Evenings, by Mrs. Littlehales, our President, and by Mrs. Grout of Stock Hall. Hon. Sec. R.M. Jones.

On New Year's Eve 1919 a Whist Drive was held in connection with the Girls' Club and an enjoyable evening was spent. The whole was ably carried out by Mrs. Jones. Later there were many other 'amusements' to keep the locals happy.

THE EAST ANGLIAN
TRACTION ENGINE CLUB
———
STEAM ENGINE RALLY

SATURDAY AND SUNDAY
SEPTEMBER 16TH & 17TH, 1967

STOCK HALL FARM,
ULTING, ESSEX
(by kind permission of W. Chalk, Esq.)
———
Programme . PRICE 2/6

On 16th and 17th September 1967, the East Anglian Traction Engine Club held a Steam Engine Rally at Stock Hall Farm, Ulting. The rally was held in the field next to the B1019 end of Ulting Lane, and villagers were delighted to ride on a genuine Carousel – something not seen for many years in the area.

Another rally was held in 1971 but this time in Langford Park.

444

This chapter has tried to demonstrate that for a period of over a century the people of the village of Langford have indulged in numerous experiences and enjoyed sports and indoor and often outdoor recreational activities and entertainments both for personal pleasure and, in the case of concerts and social indoor events, for good causes.

EAST ANGLIAN TRACTION ENGINE CLUB
AND
SOUTHEND ROUND TABLE 106

STEAM ENGINE RALLY

LANGFORD PARK, near Maldon
Saturday and Sunday
12th and 13th June 1971

SOUVENIR BROCHURE AND PROGRAMME 15p

Special events such as concerts continue to be provided today and, as in the past, they have to be organised and led by the same old faces - a small number of committed residents. However, the actual incidence of formal sporting events has, in recent years, been reduced to zero, an indication of the

445

changing culture of leisure and perhaps the lack of cohesion of spirit in the village that seemed to bond people together during the nineteenth and twentieth centuries.

CHAPTER ELEVEN
NOTABLE AND NOTORIOUS
LANGFORDIANS

Visitors to, or people travelling through, Langford for the first time may be forgiven for thinking that the village is a pretty but insignificant place. However, the foregoing chapters have shown that there was (and is) much more to Langford than was perhaps first thought.

To further emphasise the importance of the village this chapter will show that over the years some very illustrious people have been born in Langford, or lived among the tiny community. Lord Byron has already been extensively covered in the chapter relating to Langford Grove but is included here as are a number of other notables plus one or two Langfordians who were 'notable' for all the wrong reasons.

John William Strutt – 3rd Baron Rayleigh – Nobel Prize for Physics (1904)

In 1836, Colonel Joseph Holden Strutt of Terling Place was granted a peerage but as he did not wish to be ennobled, he asked that the title be conferred on his wife. This was agreed, but Lady Rayleigh then died the same year and the peerage passed to his eldest son, John James.

Colonel Strutt had declined personal honours throughout his life and perhaps did not wish to be raised to the peerage as then he would have had to resign as an M.P. The

447

title had been offered to him by George II for his many duties both in the army and to Parliament. He had not expected to outlive his wife, and the fact that his son inherited so early in life rankled with him, and he and his son did not appear to see eye to eye.

On 3rd February 1842 John James Strutt, then aged 46, married Clara Elizabeth La Touche Vicars, aged 17, at St. Georges, Hanover Square, London, officiated by the Revd. John Bramston of Great Baddow. According to *The Strutt Family of Terling* by Charles R. Strutt, immediately after the wedding:

> The bride and bridegroom went straight to Langford Grove, near Maldon, which they rented and made their home... The reason for its selection was that Colonel Strutt, though himself permanently residing at Bath, had laid it down that they must not live within eight miles of Terling. Why he did this is not clear, but it was a very characteristic action on his part.

There might well have been some jealousy on the part of the Colonel at his son inheriting the peerage so soon. Charles Strutt continues:

> Langford Grove was chosen by Lord Rayleigh as being large enough to house his wards and his own family; another advantage was it was a small parish, making correspondingly reduced demands on his charity which in those dark days of appallingly low agricultural wages was evidently an important consideration. The house was just within the eight mile limit, but the Colonel stretched a point and they were allowed to rent it. They paid £300 a year for the house, gardens and about thirty acres of land...they lived at Langford Grove for the next four years, he attending to County business and less regularly going up for debates in the House of Lords, she getting to know the neighbours in the intervals of child-bearing.

At 11.30 p.m. on 12th November 1842 John William Strutt was born at Langford Grove and was recorded as a 'seven months child.' In his early years John William suffered frailty and poor health. In addition, according to his sister Clara, John William very nearly met his death at the Grove when only about twenty months old:

> The nurse left the door open, and he got out and tried to walk downstairs. He rolled from step to step bumping his head on each one, but fortunately was saved from the final bump by a maid who was coming upstairs and caught him. His little head was black and blue afterwards. This was the first of many narrow escapes in his boyhood. Once at Southend he fell off a jetty into the water, a rough sea, having over-balanced himself in the excitement of throwing sticks into the water for a dog to fetch out. Col. Hearn who was talking to my mother on the beach, rushed into the water and pulled him out. I can remember thanks being returned in church by 'the parents of John William Strutt' for his preservation on that occasion.

John William attended Harrow School and began studying mathematics at Trinity College, University of Cambridge, in 1861. In 1865 he obtained his BA and in 1868 his MA, following which he was elected to a Fellowship of Trinity – a post he held until his marriage to Evelyn Balfour, daughter of James Maitland Balfour, in 1871. He and Evelyn had three sons.

When his father died in 1873 John William succeeded to the Barony, and took up residence in the family seat, Terling Place, near Witham, Essex. As Lord Rayleigh, he was elected Fellow of the Royal Society on 12th June 1873, and served as its President from 1905 to 1908.

He won several awards during his lifetime, including: the Smith's Prize (1864); the Royal Medal (1882); the Matteucci Medal (1894); the Copley Medal (1899); the Order of Merit

(1902); the Nobel Prize for Physics (1904, for his discovery of the gas Argon, the almost inert gaseous element presenting small quantities of air which was harnessed and turned into a major form of welding on which many engineering companies depend) and the Rumford Medal (1914 and 1920). He was also made a Member of the Royal Swedish Academy of Sciences in 1897. In addition craters on Mars and the Moon are named in his honour, as well as a type of surface wave known as a 'Rayleigh wave.'

He was a world-famous scientist who, at the height of his outstanding career, was named Cavendish Professor of Experimental Physics at Cambridge (1879-1884) and then Professor of Natural Philosophy at the Royal Institution (1887-1905). He was one of the very few members of the higher nobility who won fame as an outstanding scientist.

He also became interested in psychical research after reading about the investigations of his colleague, Sir William Crookes. He died on 30th June 1919 aged 76, a short time after delivering his presidential address to the Society for Psychical Research.

Rev. Frederick Ernest Charles Byron – Rector of St. Giles' Church, Langford 1891-1914 - the 10th Lord Byron

Born in London on 26th March 1861, the second son of the Hon. Frederick Byron, (second son of the seventh Lord Byron), he was an Anglican clergyman who, in due course, became the tenth Lord Byron. His father, the Hon. Frederick Byron who was 'as handsome as the poet' was called to and practised at the Bar. His main interest in life was hunting and it was as a result of a fall in the hunting field that he died at the early age of thirty. His

450

mother was the Hon. Mary Jane Byron (née Wescomb), one of the three heiresses of their bachelor uncle Mr. John Emerton Wescomb, on whose death in 1838 the Thrumpton estate had passed to her elder sister Lucy, and the Langford estate had passed to her. It was Mary Jane who restored St. Giles' Church.

Frederick (or 'Charlie' as he was known to many), gained his BA at Exeter College, Oxford, in 1887, was made deacon in 1888 and was ordained in 1889, and was curate of Royston in Hertfordshire from 1888 to 1890. He was instituted Rector of Langford on 22nd November 1890 by Revd. Alfred Snell, Rural Dean and Rector of Wickham Bishops, and was given the Rectory, thereby following his grandfather, Revd. William Wescomb, who was Rector of St. Giles from 1813 to 1832. Churchwardens at this event were Silas P. Greenslade and John Moore, and Alice Byron was also present. Frederick was Rector of St. Giles from 1891 to 1914.

According to Miranda Seymour, Charlie was 'a shy bachelor, capricious, old-fashioned…unlike his Grandfather's cousin, the poet, of whom he stoutly disapproved, this Lord Byron possessed a character of flawless respectability.'

Throughout his life he suffered from intense bouts of influenza and sciatica, which often meant that he was unable to preside over church services.

On the death of his mother in 1909, Charlie succeeded to the Langford estate, and on the death of his Aunt Lucy, the widow of the 8th Lord Byron, in 1912, he inherited the Thrumpton estate – his elder brother having been excluded from his Aunt's will due to his financial difficulties.

Charlie was much loved and respected by his parishioners who were also his tenants and was long remembered by some of them.

In 1914 Charlie moved from Langford to take up his long ministry as Vicar of Thrumpton, and in 1941 assumed also the responsibilities of Rector of Barton-in-Fabis. He resigned both appointments in 1942. On the death of his brother on 30th March 1917, he assumed the title of 10th Lord Byron, and took up residence in Thrumpton Hall.

He married late in life, (aged 60) Lady Anna Ismay Ethel FitzRoy, daughter of Revd. Lord Charles Edward FitzRoy, and Lady Charles FitzRoy, of Hawstead Lodge, Bury St. Edmunds, on 31st January 1921 in Bury St. Edmunds at 2p.m. The bride was the sister of the 10th Duke of Grafton. The marriage took place at the Cathedral Church of St. James, Bury St. Edmunds. Canon R.F. Wilson (Vicar of the Cathedral Church) officiated, assisted by the Revd. Leslie Mercer (Rector of Hawstead). A detailed description of the wedding was given in *The Times* dated 1st February 1921.

There was no issue of the marriage. Charlie died on 6th June 1949 at Thrumpton Hall aged 88. His memorial service was held in St. Giles', Langford on Thursday 9th June, 1949; the Revd. B.A. Whitford, now Rector of the United Benefice of Heybridge with Langford, officiated, assisted by the Revd. H.M. Lang. He was succeeded in the peerage by a great-grandson of the 7th Lord Byron, his first cousin once removed, Mr. Rupert Frederick George Byron, who lived in Australia.

On his death, his widow, Lady Anna Byron, returned to Langford and on her death in 1966 the property passed to the 11th Lord Byron – Rupert Frederick George Byron.

Michael Barne – One of Captain Scott's officers, and last survivor of the 1901-1904 Discovery Expedition to Antarctica

Michael Barne, known informally as 'Mick', lived at Langford Place from 1911 to 1919, and was the last survivor of Captain Scott's 1901 expedition to Antarctica.

Born on 15th October 1877 at Sotterley Park, Suffolk, he was the son of Frederick Barne and his wife Lady Constance Adelaide Seymour daughter of Francis Seymour, 5th Marquess of Hertford. His father was Member of Parliament for East Suffolk. He was educated at Stubbington School in preparation for the Navy, which he joined as a Midshipman in 1893. In 1898, on *HMS Majestic*, Barne met the Torpedo Lieutenant, Robert Falcon Scott. A year later he volunteered to serve as Third Mate on the *Discovery* at one shilling (5p) per month plus £200 per annum expedition money. Scott said, "I had thought him, as he proved to be, especially fitted for a voyage where there were elements of danger and difficulty."

Michael Barne, the in-house cartoonist and caricaturist, and Second Lieutenant to the Polar Expedition, took a very active part in Scott's 1901-1904 expedition, carrying out a number of magnetic surveys. The 'Barne Glacier' was named after him, as was 'Cape Barne,' and 'Barne Inlet.' Scott rated his ability to calm possible tensions very highly, and he was awarded the Polar Medal for his contribution to the expedition. He was very badly frostbitten on that expedition and this precluded him from the last, fateful journey.

On one occasion a sledge party was hit by a blizzard so Barne went to look for them and brought them to safety. On a later foray with Scott and Shackleton another blizzard hit. Scott woke to find himself outside the tent. He noted:

> [It] was straining so madly that something had to be done at once to prevent its flying away altogether. With freezing fingers we gripped the skirting and gradually pulled it inwards and half sitting on it, half grasping it, endeavoured to hold it against the wild efforts of the storm. A later inspection of hands showed that all had been pretty badly frost bitten. But the worst was poor Barne, whose fingers have never recovered from the accident of last year, when he so nearly lost them. To have hung on to the tent through all those hours must have been positive agony to him, yet he never uttered a word of complaint.

In 1911 Barne lived at Langford Place, with his wife and two servants, and was very active in the formation of a troop of Boy Scouts. The news of Scott's death in 1912 came as a severe blow to him. Had Barne not been so severely frostbitten in the first venture he would have been on that fateful expedition as second in command.

In 1914 Barne went on a three-month voyage to Spitzbergen in the Arctic Circle, for which he was well equipped following his former voyage to the South Pole with Capt. Scott. Whether this was for a specific purpose or simply another 'voyage of discovery' is not clear.

During the 1914-1918 war Barne was appointed Commander in *HMS Majestic* which was sunk in the Dardanelles in 1915, and while in this ship he was awarded the Royal Humane Society's medal for trying to rescue a seaman who had been washed overboard. He later served as captain of *Monitor 27* (one of a fleet of shallow-drafted coastal bombardment vessels) in the Dover Patrol. Barne was mentioned in despatches four times and awarded the Distinguished Service Order (DSO) on 16th August 1915 when 'Acting Commander Michael Barne, R.N. was commended for Service in Action.' He finally retired in 1919 with the rank of Captain, and shortly thereafter he moved to Norfolk.

Between the wars, Barne lived in Birch, near Colchester and is said to have had a sledge and other mementos in his house and garden. He came out of retirement in WWII to command the anti-submarine patrol ship *HMS Radiant* in the Channel. However, he was invalided out and retired once more. Nothing daunted, in 1944 he joined the small craft that supplied ships with stores for D-Day. He died aged 83 in 1961 at Depwade in Norfolk.

Barne really was a very brave man who overcame adversity wherever it appeared and who was ready to answer the call whenever it came.

Herbert William Wrangham Wilberforce – Wimbledon Doubles Champion 1887

Herbert Wilberforce was born on 1st January 1864 in Munich, Germany, the second son of Edward (1834-1914) and Fannie Flash (Wilberforce) (1831-1895), and was christened at the British Chaplaincy, Muenchen Stadt, Oberbayern, Bayern on 29th March that year.

Wilberforce was educated at London International College, University College, London and Downing College Cambridge (B.A.) (Exhibitioner and Scholar). The 1881 census shows him living at Elmhirst, Heston, London. He was a Law Exhibitioner, at London University with a 1st Class Law Tripos, 1885; BA and LLB. He represented Cambridge at lawn tennis against Oxford 1883-1886 and was the winner of the University Singles and Doubles, and the Northern Lawn Tennis Champion in 1883. In 1887 he and Patrick Bowes-Lyon (Uncle of H.M. Queen Elizabeth the Queen Mother) won the doubles championship at Wimbledon. The following year he became a Barrister-at Law.

On 5th November 1892 he married Florence (born 1863, died 30th October, 1937), daughter of Charles James Monk, M.A. of Bedwell Park, Hatfield, Herts. MP, DL, JP. Charles Monk was Liberal Unionist MP for Gloucester and his wife Julia Ralli, was the daughter of P.S. Ralli, Consul-General of Greece, and they had two daughters, Irene Florence and Judith Monica.

He lived in Langford Grove from 1916 to April 1923 when the family moved to London. The parish magazine noted:

> For nearly eight years they lived in the village and proved themselves in every way to be keenly interested in all parish doings, and the friends of all. For seven years Mr. Wilberforce ably filled the office of Churchwarden and by his personal example and wise counsels was of the greatest assistance in all church matters. Mrs. Wilberforce too, and her two daughters were active in all good works and devoted much time and energy to the social welfare of the village. Their familiar figures will be greatly missed in future, and we certainly feel that they, as a family, will be hard to replace, and it is with the greatest reluctance that we wish them all goodbye.

Wilberforce was Chairman of the All England Lawn Tennis and Croquet Club from 1921 to 1936; Parish Churchwarden at St. Giles' Church from 1916 to 1921 and was made a Knight Bachelor in the New Year's Honours List in 1931.

He died in 1941.

Rev. Charles Gough Littlehales – Rector of St. Giles' Church, Langford 1914-1930 - First Class Cricketer for Essex

Born on 20th May 1871 at Bulphan, Essex, Charles Gough Littlehales was christened on 29th June that year in St. Mary the Virgin Church, Bulphan, by his father, Walter Gough Littlehales, who was Rector of the church.

Littlehales was curate at Goldhanger with Little Totham from 1896 to 1900, and before taking up his post in Langford he had been Rector of Blidworth, Nottinghamshire. He was not only Rector of St. Giles' Church, Langford from 1914 to 1930, but also a First Class Wicketkeeper for Essex from 1896 to 1904. An article in the *Essex Review* (Vol. 13, 1904) entitled 'Cricket in Essex: A Resume of the past season' by Robert Cook included the statement that 'The Rev. C.G. Littlehales, [*had*] made a promising appearance at the end of the season…comes from Mistley – and he is well worth a place in the eleven…' He was a right-handed batsman.

He married Anna Snell – daughter of the Vicar of Wickham Bishops Church – on 24th April 1900, and the service was conducted by his father, Walter Littlehales. He took over from Revd. Byron at St. Giles' Church, Langford, and was instituted as Vicar on 30th October 1914. The parish magazine gave an account of the event:

A large congregation of Langford parishioners attended the Institution and Induction of their New Rector, on Saturday October 30th. The Bishop of Barking, commissary to the Bishop of Chelmsford, performed the institution. After the singing of the hymn 'O Lord how joyful 'tis to see,' the Rector-designate was presented to the Bishop by his predecessor in office, the Rev. The Hon. F.E.C. Byron, who is also patron of the living. The usual oaths were taken and prayers offered, the Bishop read the letters of Institution and pronounced the Benediction. The Office of Induction followed; the newly instituted priest being conducted to the Church Door and to the various parts of the building by the patron, the Churchwardens (Messrs. W.B.A. Wynyard and W. Chalk) and the Rev. F.T. Gardner, Rector of Goldhanger, who held the Bishop's mandate to induct. Before the address by the Bishop of Barking the "Veni Creator" was sung. His Lordship referred in terms of high appreciation to the work done by the retiring Rector during his 22 years labour at Langford, and appealed to the parishioners to accord his successor their sympathy, help and loyal co-operation in his work among them. The service concluded with the hymn "O thou who makest souls to shine", and the Blessing. The new Rector read himself in on Sunday, Nov. 1st, and addressed a large congregation in the evening.

In January 1916 he was enrolled and sworn in as a Special Constable (Corporal), having volunteered to undertake the patrolling of the roads and other police duties within the boundaries of Langford Parish during the war.

In July 1930 Littlehales left Langford and moved to the Vicarage of St. Andrew, Allensmore, Hereford where he stayed until at least 1941. He died on 28th August 1945, and his funeral took place at St. Bartholomew's Church, Wickham Bishops on Friday 31st August. He had only just retired from duty as a clergyman and passed away after a short illness.

He was much respected and loved by those who knew him, and his funeral was well attended. It was conducted by the Rector of St. Bartholomew's Wickham Bishops, Revd. A.J. Lloyd, and the Revd. Canon Luard, Reader of Birch, and he was buried in the churchyard there. It was reported in *The Times,* of Wednesday 29th August 1945 that 'No mourning' was requested, which shows what kind of a man he was.

Isaac Walter and Sophia Grout – Stock Hall – 21 children

Isaac Walter Grout was born in Great Totham in 1841, the son of James Grout (wheelwright) and his wife Margaret. On 6th October 1869, aged 28, he married Sophia Ann Lucking (aged 18) in St. Andrew's Church, Hatfield Peverel. Their union lasted fifty-seven years and produced twenty-one children!

At the 1871 census, Isaac and Sophia lived in Totham Plains, where he was a Licensed Victualler. In the 1881 census the family had moved to Plains Farm, Great Totham, and Isaac was now a farmer. In the 1891 census they were living at Stock Hall, Langford where they would remain until their deaths in 1926.

Three of the twenty-one Grout children died early and in the same year. Alfred James cut himself in a barn, and his Aunt put cobweb on the wound to try to heal it but he died of lock-jaw aged only four. He was buried on 26th March 1887 in St. Giles' Churchyard. His brother, Albert Edward, drowned in a pond whilst playing. He was a mere two years old and was buried on 6th November 1887. Both were buried by the Rector of St. Giles', Revd. Charles Leigh.

Another child, Victor, emigrated to Canada on 7th September 1906, aged 18, where he intended to settle and start a new life. However, when war broke he joined the Canadian Field Artillery early in 1916 (Service No. 303659), and saw a good deal of fighting.

Violet Grout (later to marry Tom Cullen of The Elms, Ulting – the farm next to her father's) recalled in an article in the *Essex Chronicle*, of Friday 28th April 1995:

> We never went short of food because living on the farm meant we had fresh vegetables, eggs and meat. There was rabbit, chicken and duck, so we had plenty of variety, and consequently, a very healthy family. It was a wonderful life despite not having pocket money and having a limited amount of sweets.

Violet also recalled that although her mother was helped with housework and cooking by her children, a washer-woman had to be hired to cope with the weekly drudgery of a never-ending mountain of linen and clothing:

> Mother was a strong woman, but even she needed help. The washer-woman would boil the clothes in the copper in our scullery, and wring them out in the Mangle room....The boys mostly became butchers, while the girls were drapers, cashiers or housekeepers.

Isaac and Sophia were buried, together, in the churchyard at St. Giles' on 9th August 1926, by Revd. Charles Gough Littlehales.

Walter not only had twenty-one children of his own, but also provided for his late brother's seven children and ran his farm in Totham.

Although Stock Hall was officially in Ulting Parish, Langford's St. Giles' Church was much nearer for the family and they were regular worshippers there. Walter and Sophia's son Victor is remembered on the War Memorial.

Notorious Langfordians

Although Langford has produced or housed some of the best people, it has also been home to some of the worst...

You would imagine that Langford, a rural idyll, would be a place of tranquillity and peace. However, over the years Langford has had its own problems, including a few that we would perhaps sooner forget!

'A Perfect Terror' sent to Prison
Francis Cranmer, a strongly built young fellow of 19, of Langford, was charged with breaking out of the casual ward of Maldon Workhouse on the 2nd January 1897. In court, John Hole, the labour master at the workhouse stated that the defendant was 'a perfect terror in the house', and always behaving in a most disorderly manner.

Cranmer said he had escaped because he was 'put in the tramps' ward' and he did not consider himself a tramp. Mr. Timperley, the master, said the prisoner was simply making a lodging-house of his workhouse. He told the court that all Cranmer wanted to do was 'spend each night there, do no work, and go out every morning'.

At this point Police Inspector Gibbons told the court of the prisoner's background. He reported that Cranmer had been previously convicted of assault, and on one occasion was sentenced to fourteen days imprisonment and five years in a reformatory, but he was discharged from the reformatory after a few days in consequence of a murderous attack on the superintendent. On another occasion, when feigning to be in a fit, after assaulting some relatives, Cranmer had to be secured with ropes and he was then almost too much for the constable. The Mayor then sentenced the prisoner to twenty-one days' hard labour for breaking out of the ward.

In September 1906 Cranmer was back in court. Having been discharged from Chelmsford Prison after undergoing four months' imprisonment for assault, he was charged with using threatening language towards his brother, Fred Cranmer. Fred told the court that Francis had come into his yard on the previous Sunday and then came into the house where he swore and cursed at his brother after which the complainant asked Francis to leave. Francis then interrupted his brother's statement by saying "You hit me on the side of the head" whereas Fred countered that his brother threw two large stones and then seized a hoe and threatened to knock his brains out. The outcome of this altercation that lasted for some time was that the Chairman told Francis Cranmer, "You will have to find to sureties in £5 and be bound over yourself in £10 to keep the peace for six months. If you fail to find sureties you must go to prison for that period without hard labour." The prisoner being unable to find said sureties was taken to Chelmsford Prison.

Child adopted for love dies from violence. Foster mother remanded
The somewhat mysterious circumstances surrounding the death of Clara May Crowfoot aged two years and five months, the daughter of Lucy May Crowfoot, of Frimley, Ipswich, a school teacher at Somerleyton, Lowestoft, were investigated by Dr. J.F. Macdonald, coroner, and a jury at

Langford. At the time of her death the child was living with Mrs. Wood, wife of a coal carter, of Black Cottages, Langford. Superintendent C.A. Harwood, of Chelmsford, watched the proceedings on behalf of the police.

The mother, Miss Crowfoot, stated that as the result of an advertisement in a paper offering a good home for a baby, and giving an address at Langford, she wrote and received a favourable reply from Mrs. Wood, who agreed to take the child. Miss Crowfoot took the child there on 5th February 1921. Afterwards she forwarded sums of five shillings from time to time. In court Miss Crowfoot said it did not strike her as peculiar that Mrs. Wood should keep the child for practically nothing. Mrs. Wood had told her that she wanted a companion for her own baby. Miss Crowfoot told the court that she had not seen the child since she left her with Mrs. Wood at which time she was perfectly healthy, and there were no marks visible on the body.

Dr. W.H. Lee, of Maldon, said that on being requested to visit Mrs. Wood's house to attend to a child on Saturday, he found her nursing the deceased, who seemed to be gravely ill. Mrs. Wood appeared to be in doubt as to what to do with the child, and was endeavouring to open her mouth with a teaspoon. The doctor saw that the child was very ill, and informed Mrs. Wood, drawing her attention to the bruised condition of the little one's forehead.

Mrs. Wood told the doctor that a few days previously the child had fallen in an adjoining room, but seemed no worse for the accident. Both cheeks were bruised, and there were also bruises on the body, and blisters below each knee. Just below the left knee there was a wound where the top of a blister had been knocked off. There were sores on each buttock. The child died within a few hours, and Dr. Lee, who refused to give a death certificate, notified the police of the matter the following day. A post mortem examination showed that there were extensive bruises on the head, forehead, cheeks, arms and thighs. One wound looked as if it had been inflicted by a sharp instrument. It was declared that the death of the child was due to shock, as the result of external violence.

In reply to a juror, the doctor said that he thought the smaller bruises on the arms, legs and face were produced from blows by a hand and that the bruises on the forehead must have been done by 'something harder.' He did not think the bruises on the head were the result of the child falling on the floor as they were 'very severe,' and would have required 'considerable violence.' The doctor added that the blisters might have been caused 'by the child being held too close to the fire.' The court heard that the house was beautifully clean, and the condition of Mrs. Wood's own child was all that could be desired. At this stage the Coroner adjourned the inquest for one week.

When the inquest resumed Miss Lucy May Crowfoot gave further evidence, and a neighbour and her husband at Langford spoke of hearing screams and sounds of beating. Superintendent C.A. Harwood (Chelmsford) watched the proceedings on behalf of the police.

Ada May Phillippo, Langford, wife of Edgar W. Phillippo, living next door to Mrs. Wood since the latter came to Langford from Heybridge more than two years previously said that at that time Mr. Wood was in the Army and Mrs. Wood lived with her own little girl, aged seven years. Mr. Wood came home from the Army in September or October, 1919. The deceased child was brought to Mrs. Wood on 5th February. She was then about a year and eight months old, and was 'a nice, rosy child, not able to walk very well.' The Coroner then asked Mrs. Phillippo "How was she treated by Mr. & Mrs. Wood?" to which she replied "I think she was treated all right when she first came." The Coroner then asked, "And how long did that good treatment continue?" and

Mrs. Phillippo replied, "About three or four months. I don't think I noticed bruises on her until June."

Mrs. Phillippo then gave further evidence of the child next door being ill-treated. She heard 'Mrs. Wood hitting the child' and subsequently 'heard screams.' The witness when asked if she had spoken to Mrs. Wood about this replied, "Not to Mrs. Wood, but to other people in the village. One was the parish nurse who came to my sister when she was staying with me."

After hearing further damning evidence from her neighbour and others, including Mr. Walter Ernest Read, Spital Road, Maldon, Infant Life Protection Officer for the district, and further reports from Dr. Lee the Coroner announced that Mrs. Wood would be committed for trial at the next Assize on the jury's verdict of manslaughter, and he accordingly issued a warrant for her arrest.

AFTERWORD

This book is the result of the two of us working together on and sharing our enthusiasm for, and love of, the history of the village of Langford.

We hope that you have enjoyed learning about Langford and that our research has perhaps in some small way aroused your curiosity in local history in general or in Langford in particular. We hope you agree that there is much, much more to the village of Langford than initially meets the eye.

Having said that, and even though *A Great Oddity: The Story of the Village of Langford* has now been published our research has not ceased. How could it? Once the local history research bug bites…

So we are still looking for more research material. This could take the form of images or photographs of the village or any personal memories of Langford (perhaps you are a former resident). If you can help us in our quest to expand even further our knowledge of life in the village please contact us.

If you have any information, memories or photographs, please telephone 01621 856040 (Patrick) (e-mail patrick.chaplin@btinternet.com) or 01621 855447 (e-mail irenea@lepra.org.uk) (Irene). We look forward to hearing from you.

Sincerely,

Irene Allen   **Dr. Patrick Chaplin**
Churchwarden – St. Giles'
Local Historical Recorder for Langford

APPENDIX 1

List of School Teachers

Year	Name	Average Attendance
1874	Miss Eliza Gimson Jones	n/k
1878	Miss Eliza Gimson Jones	n/k
1882	Miss Eliza Hobby	30
1886	Mrs. Sara Rebecca Paggi	30
1890	Miss Louisa Pounds	33
1894	Miss Louisa Pounds	31
1895	Miss Louisa Pounds	31
1899	Mr. William Chalk	31
1902	Mr. William Chalk	31
1903	Miss Alice H. Calver	31

School now described as a 'Public Elementary School'

1906	Miss Alice H. Calver	31
1908	Miss Alice H. Calver	34
1910	Miss Alice H. Calver	34

From 1912 the school is shown as a Church of England School under the control of the Maldon District Education Sub-Committee

1912	Miss Alice H. Calver	36
1916	Mrs. Rose Margaret Jones	n/k
1917	Mrs. Rose Margaret Jones	49
1918	Mrs. Rose Margaret Jones	40
1921	Mrs. Rose Margaret Jones	20

APPENDIX 2

Cart Horses

- Smiler, grey mare, 25½gs. Mr. G. Hare, Boreham
- Smart, ditto, 16½gs. Mr. Mead
- Boxer, bay gelding, 30gs. Mr. H.W. Sadd, Maldon

Harness Horses

- Gilbert, chestnut gelding (ex. Horsfall's Darling), 36gs. Mr. T. Lott, Heybridge
- King of England, bay gelding (s. Sultan, d. Kate) 30gs. Mr. Walkington, Ireland
- King of Wessex, bay gelding (s. Wm Rufus, d. Cowslip) 26gs. Mr. H.W. Sadd
- King Harold, bay gelding (s. Sultan, d. Horsfall's Helen), 24gs. Mr. Wood
- Chilblain, br. gelding (s. Chilblain, d. Bonny 2nd), 45gs, Mr. J.B. Pash, Chelmsford
- King of Langford, br. gelding (s. Sultan, d. Horsfall's Darling) 26gs. Mr. Walkington
- King Boniface, bay gelding (s. Sultan, d. Bonny 2nd), 20gs. Prof. Almoud, Chelmsford
- King Canute, bay gelding (s. Sultan, d. Caprice), 31gs. Mr. A Poole, Chelmsford.
- Duke, bay gelding (s. Sultan, d. Grand Duchess) 37gs. Mr. C.H. Berners, Wolverton
- King Arthur, bay gelding (s. Sultan, d. Ellen Terry), 43gs. Mr. Berners
- Dowager Duchess, bay mare (ditto), 58gs, Mr. H.W.M. Davis, Suffolk
- Bay yearling filly (s. Hedon Squire, d. Queen of the East), 43gs. Sir W. Gilbey, Risenham
- Ditto, (s. Hedon Squire, d. Queen of Beauty), 36gs. Sir W. Gilbey

Cleveland Bays

- King Frederick the Great, bay stallion (s. Sultan, d. Nellie Farren), foaled 1895, 17 h.h. considered by many judges to be the best Cleveland stallion of his age in the kingdom. As a foal (with his dam) he won two first and a special premium given by the Hunters' Improvement Society: and as a yearling was first in his class and reserved for the championship at the York show, certified sound, 525gs. Mr. Davis, Sutherland
- Bonny 2nd, brood mare (s. Sportsman, d. Bonny) 20gs. Mr. Finch
- Pride of the Village, ditto (s. Prince George, d. Daughter of Lucks All) 55gs. Mr. Davis
- Horsfell's Darling, brood mare (s. Fidius Dius, d. Star of the East), won 3 first prizes and 5 seconds, 61gs. Mr. Walkington
- Bay colt foal (s. Hedon Squire, d. Horsfall's Darling), 26gs. Mr. Davis
- Horsfall's Helen (s. Fidius Dius, d. Mavourneen) 15gs. Mr. J. Webb, Lincolnshire
- Nellie Farren (s. Prince George, d. Daughter of King William 2nd). The pick of the stud as a brood mare; she dropped her first foal at three years old, and has had one each year since, all being good ones. She has won 5 first prizes and a silver cup; 450gs. Mr. Davis.
- King Edward, colt foal (s. Cleveland's Pride, d. Nellie Farren) 45gs. Mr. Davis.
- Queen of Beauty, bay mare (s. Sultan, d. Nellie Farren), v h c at Doncaster and Manchester Royal Shows and at the great Yorkshire show, 180gs. Mr. Davis
- King of Essex, bay colt foal (s. Cleveland's Pride, d. Queen of Beauty), 35gs. Mr. Davis.

- Queen Victoria, yearling (s. Sultan, d. Nellie Farren), 100gs. Mr. Finch, Canterbury
- Queen of Langford, brood mare, (s. Forunatus, d. Bonny 2nd), 65gs. Mr. Davis
- King Fred, colt foal (s. King Frederick the Great, d. Queen of Langford), 15gs. Mr. G. Scoby, Helmsley
- Queen of the East (s. Sultan, d. Horsfall's Darling), 42gs. Sir W. Gilbey
- King of the East, colt foal (s. King Frederick the Great, d. Queen of the East), 15gs. Mr. W. Horsfall, Northallerton
- Queen Helena (s. Sultan, d. Horsfall's Helen), 14gs. Mr. Blaxall
- Queen Hilda (s. Sultan, d. Horsfall's Darling), 47gs. Mr. Berners
- Queen Empress, two-year-old filly (s. Sultan, d. Pride of the Village) 60gs. Mr. Davis
- Queen Dearest (s. Sultan, d. Horsfall's Darling) 90gs. Mr. Finch

Shorthorn dairy cows fetched from £6 to £17 15s. Three Suffolk ram lambs were offered, and one obtained £3 7. 6d and the other two £3 each. Some registered Suffolk ewes made from 25s to 53s. Among the swine one in-pig sow realised £5, and a sow and 12 pigs £9 10s.

470

SELECT BIBLIOGRAPHY

Books

Benham, Hervey. *'Some Essex Water Mills'* (Colchester: Essex County Newspapers, 1976)

Booker, John. *'Essex and the Industrial Revolution'*, (Chelmsford: Essex Record Office, 1974)

Briggs, Nancy, *John Johnson 1732-1814 Georgian Architect & County Surveyor of Essex,* 1991, Essex Record Office

Brown, A. F. J. *Essex at Work 1700-1815* (Chelmsford: Essex County Council, 1969) Essex Record Office Publications, No. 49

Brown, A. F. J. *Essex People 1750-1900 from their diaries, memoirs and letters* (Chelmsford: Essex County Council, 1972)

Came, Peter, *Maldon and Heybridge in old picture postcards* (Zaltbommel, The Netherlands: European Library, 1989 and 1994)

Cromwell, Thomas. *Excursions in the County of Essex* (London: Printed for Longman et al, 1818-1819)

Morris, John (ed.) Domesday Book 32 Essex (Chichester: Phillimore, 1983)

Doubleday H. A. (ed.) *Victorian History of Counties of England – Essex* (London: Archibald Constable & Co. Ltd, Vol. 1 (1903), Vol. II (1907) and Vol. III (1963))

Edwards, A. C. *A History of Essex*, (London: Darwen Finlayson Ltd, 1958 and Sixth Edition 2000)

Fitch, E.A. *Maldon and the River Blackwater* (Maldon: H. C. & E. Gowers, 1894 and 1905)

Fowler, Simon, *Workhouses: the places, the people, life behind closed doors*, (Kew: National Archives 2007)

Grieve, Hilda. *The Great Tide – The Story of the 1953 Flood Disaster in Essex* (Chelmsford: County Council of Essex, 1959)

King, Henry William. *Ecclesiae Essexienses* (description of Churches), Essex Record Office Ref: T/P 196/4

Marriage, John. *The Chelmer & Blackwater Navigation* (Stroud: Tempus Publishing Ltd, 2002)

Moncrieff, A. R. H., (With illustrations by L. Burleigh Bruhl) *Essex* (London: A & C Black, c.1910)

Morant, Philip. *The History of Antiquities of Essex* (2 volumes) (London: Printed for T. Osbourne *et al*, 1768)

Nunn, Stephen P. and Wyatt, Alen L. *Heinkels over Heybridge* (Maldon: Published by authors, 1987)

Pevsner, Nikolaus *The Buildings of England* (London: Penguin Books, second edition revised by Enid Radcliffe 1965)

Scarfe, Norman. *Essex – A Shell Guide* (London: Faber and Faber Ltd, 1968)

Seymour, Miranda. *Thrumpton Hall – A Memoir of Life in My Father's House* (New York: HarperCollins, 2007)

Strutt, Charles R., *The Strutt Family of Terling* (London: Printed by Mitchell, Hughes and Clarke, privately published, 1939)

Strutt, Robert John Strutt, *John William Strutt, third Baron Rayleigh by his son Robert John Strutt, fourth Baron Rayleigh*, (London: Arnold, 1924)

Stubbings, Ken. *"Here's Good Luck to the Pint Pot!" – A Brief History of Maldon's Inns, Alehouses and Breweries* (Maldon: Kelvin Brown Publications, 1988)

Swindale, Dennis L. *Branch Lines to Maldon* (Maldon: Windover Publications, 1978 (Reprinted 1983))

Wojtczak, Helena. *Railwaywomen. Exploitation, Betrayal and Triumph in the Workplace* (Hastings: Hastings Press, 2005.)

Worley, G. *Essex: A Dictionary of the County – Mainly Ecclesiological* (London: G. Bell & Sons Ltd., 1915)

Wright, Thomas. *The History and Topography of the County of Essex [History of Essex Vol. 2]*, 1836. Originally published in London by Geo. Virtue, 1831.)

Young, Arthur. *General View of Agriculture in Essex.* (London: Board of Agriculture, 1807, Volume II)

Directories
Kelly's Directories – Various
White's Directory of Essex 1848

Newspapers, Magazines and Journals
Chelmsford Chronicle, 28th March 1879 (Essex Records Office T/P 147/1), 18th June 1869
Essex Chronicle, Friday September 11th, 1964, Friday April 28th 1995
Essex Review Vol. 13, 1904, p.243, Vol. 38, 1929, pp. 204-205, Essex Review Vol. 58 1949, p. 164
Essex Weekly News 20th February 1953
Evening Gazette, January 18, 2000
Gentleman's Magazine, Vol. XXVIII (July-December inclusive 1847) (London: John Bowyer Nichols & Son p.331.
Great Eastern News, Spring 2006, Issue No. 126
Maldon and Burnham Standard, 4 March 1999, August 23, 2000 ('Years Gone By')
Maldon Past Times in April 2005
Heybridge & Langford Parish Magazine - February 1953
Southend-on-Sea Observer – 1st February 1939
The Times Tuesday 1st February 1921, Wednesday August 29th 1945
Wickham Bishops and Langford Parish Magazine, July 1894 - August 1946

Thesis
Came, Peter. *A History of the Chelmer & Blackwater Navigation Company 1793-1914*, University of Sussex, 1971

Other documents
Conveyance from the Guardians and others of the Maldon Union (Langford Parish) to the Hon. Mrs. M.J. Byron dated 1878 (ERO D/DBw T25)
Cuttle collections of newspaper cuttings 12th August 1898 and November 1906 – Essex Record Office Ref: T/P 181/7/12

Elementary Education School Management Committee
Reports 1903-1925

Essex Archaeological Transactions No. 9, vol. 10

Essex County Medical Officer of Health Reports 1891-1895
and 1913-1914

Hall, Sarah (Will of), 1680 (ERO D/ABW 70/3)

Langford Church' from Transactions of the Essex
Archaeological Society Vol. X. (New series) pp. 12-13

Langford School Log Book (ERO E/ML 13/1 1875-1902)

Record of Insurance Policies (1881-1887) (ERO D/F21/23)

School Log Book, ERO E/ML 13/1 1875-1902

School Managers Minute Book 1906-1920 Essex Record
Office Ref: D/P 356/28/1 and D/P 356/28/2

Southend Waterworks Company *Inauguration of the River
Works at Langford by The Lord Lieutenant of the County
(Brigadier-General R. B. Colvin, C.B.) on 18th September
1929* (Printed by Harrison and Sons Ltd., London, 1929)

Southend Waterworks Company *Southend Waterworks
Company 1865-1966* (April 1966)

Summary of the Reports of the District Medical Officers of
Health in the Administrative County of Essex for the year
1891, 1894-97 1899. (Essex Records Office Ref: TS 505/13),
1901 (Essex Records Office Ref: TS 505/14) and 1900-1919
- Essex Record Office TS 505/13

Wakelin, Richard. *The History of the Wakelins of Essex*,
Unpublished manuscript in authors' possession, 1994

HMSO publication *Water Supply from Underground Sources*
by Whitaker and Thresh published in 1916

Interviews
Ted Chalk – Interview with PC - 4th August 1977
Ron Harvey – Interview with IA and PC – 13th August 2007

Websites
Agency for Toxic Substances & Disease Registry (ATSDR)
(for information re. chlorophenols – Waterworks chapter)
www.atsdr.cdc.gov

474

British Cathedrals and Historic Churches Foundation (for glossary of Terms) – www.britishchurches.org
Byron family – www.thepeerage.com
Disused stations www.subbrit.org.uk
Museum of Power, Langford www.museumofpower.org.uk
SubUnlocking Essex's Past
    http://unlockingessex.essexcc.gov.uk

Index

Calver, Miss Alice Harriet   115, 116, 122, 124, 125, 126, 127, 128, 129, 132, 343, 467
Campion, Emily   113
Capra, Alice   2
Chalk, Brian   368
Chalk, Ellen   432
Chalk, Emily   113, 118, 120, 429
Chalk, Fanny   106, 113, 434
Chalk, Frederick   74, 397
Chalk, Gladys   434, 436
Chalk, John   46, 421, 438
Chalk, Joy   421
Chalk, Laura A   114
Chalk, Lucy Rose   41, 174, 392
Chalk, Michael   46
Chalk, Nellie   344, 431
Chalk, Norman   407
Chalk, Norman (Mrs)   438
Chalk, Philip   336, 382, 434, 436
Chalk, Walter Edward (Ted)   41, 174, 225, 227, 264, 277, 285, 294, 373, 374, 378, 385, 386,438
Chalk, Walter Harry   78, 114, 115, 117, 120, 124, 209, 210, 245, 342, 359, 363, 413, 429, 438
Chalk, William   31, 106, 109, 110, 111, 115, 138, 224, 225, 226, 399, 400, 425, 426, 427, 428, 429, 434, 436, 467
Challis, E   432
Challis, G   409, 432
Challis, Sydney   132, 133
Challis, William   79, 143
Chancellor, Frederick   85, 86, 187, 222, 223
Chandler, William   130
Chaplin, Albert   262, 297, 299, 310, 318, 322, 366, 367, 372, 391, 421
Chaplin, Sir George   317
Chaplin, John   253
Chaplin, Joyce   392
Chaplin, Michael   420

480

Tayler, Revd. Frederick Thomas   85, 86, 87, 88, 89, 95, 96, 97, 99, 100, 101, 103
Tayler, Mrs.   89
Tennis Club   143, 382, 414, 416, 417, 418
Thresh, Dr. John C.   54, 57, 58, 60, 61, 62, 65, 122, 233, 234, 280, 281, 282, 289, 294
Thrumpton   5, 6, 21, 27, 124, 153, 198, 334, 362, 403, 441, 451, 452
Tiptree Heath   9, 10, 65
Tramps   63, 64, 461
Tritton, Captain Allan   379
Tritton, Major Claude   46, 197, 198, 199, 364, 377, 378, 379, 383, 384, 387, 388, 389, 392
Tritton, Captain [Lt. Col] John   371, 391, 392
Tritton, Joseph Herbert   197
Tritton, Lucy Jane   197
Tritton, Mrs.   46, 366, 377
Typhoid fever   57, 63, 65, 66
Wager, Mrs.   331
Wager, C   409, 410, 411
Wakelin, Mr. B   428
Wakelin, Edith   427
Wakelin, Fanny   196, 429, 430, 443
Wakelin, Florence   429
Wakelin, Frederick   77, 114, 115, 194, 195, 196, 388, 399, 400, 413, 416, 417
Wakelin, John   336
Wakelin, Natalie Violet Mary   40, 46
Wakelin, Richard   336, 400, 427, 429
Wakelin, William Frederick   40, 210
Ward, Willie   76
Wallis, Henry   81
Walton, Robert   233, 234, 281, 282, 285
Wescomb, Jane   20, 26, 33, 85, 87, 150, 152, 153
Wescomb, John Emerton   5, 451
Wescomb, John William   26, 27
Wescomb, Lucy   26